The Indians of the Western Great Lakes
1615-1760

FRENCH POSTS OF THE
17TH AND 18TH CENTURIES

SCALE
0   100
MILES

Lake Superior

CHAQUAMEGON BAY
KEWEENAW
KEWEENAW BAY

MENOMINEE RIVER

SAULT STE MARIE

ST IGNACE
UNTIL 1703 MACKINAC IS. MANITOULIN IS

MICHILIMACKINAC
1715-1760
L'ARBRE CROCHE

WASHINGTON IS

HURON VILLAGES
1615-1648

TRAVERSE BAY

Lake Huron

POST OF GREEN BAY

BLACK RIVER

FOX RIVER

Lake Michigan

WISCONSIN RIVER

MUSKEGON RIVER

GRAND RIVER

SAGINAW BAY

DULUTH'S
FORT
ST JOSEPH

FORT PONTCHARTRAIN
OF DETROIT

FORT
ST JOSEPH

ST JOSEPH RIVER

Lake Erie

CHICAGO

DESPLAINES R

MISSISSIPPI RIVER

ILLINOIS RIVER

FORT ST LOUIS

KANKAKEE RIVER

FORT WAYNE

MAUMEE RIVER

SANDUSKY

WABASH RIVER

RIVER

OUIATENON

PIQUA

MIAMI RIVER

WHITE RIVER

VINCENNES

OHIO RIVER

MAP I

The Indians

OF THE

Western Great Lakes

1615-1760

by

W. Vernon Kinietz

Ann Arbor Paperbacks
The University of Michigan Press

First edition as an Ann Arbor Paperback 1965
All rights reserved
ISBN 0-472-06107-0 (paperback)
ISBN 0-472-09107-7 (clothbound)
First published by The University of Michigan Press 1940
Published in the United States of America by
The University of Michigan Press and simultaneously
in Rexdale, Canada, by John Wiley & Sons Canada, Limited
Manufactured in the United States of America

1983   1982   1981   7   6   5   4

PREFACE

A SURVEY of documents relating to the Indians of Michigan and the Great Lakes region during the contact period was made in 1935-36 in the archives of Ottawa, Montreal, Quebec, Chicago, Detroit, Ann Arbor, and Washington, D.C. Several hundred volumes of manuscripts, transcripts, and photostats of manuscripts were examined in the various archives. The present study is the outgrowth of that survey. To the manuscript material gathered has been added the published material of the same period. It was the purpose of this project to compile synthetic ethnographies of various tribes from the historic background so assembled.

In pursuing this objective it was necessary to set beginning and closing dates. The beginning date was determined by the first explorers, whose first contact with a Michigan tribe, between the Ottawa and Champlain, was on the eastern or northern shore of Georgian Bay in 1615. Aside from the Huron, who did not come to Michigan until after 1650, the number of contacts between Michigan tribes and Europeans was negligible until after 1660. The period of Indian-white contact west of Lake Huron may then be said to begin about 1660. The selection of a closing date had to be made rather arbitrarily, but it was felt that there were ample reasons for choosing 1760, the date of the capitulation of Canada by the French. For seven years before the fall of Canada the struggle with the British kept the French so occupied that the records of the times are practically devoid of comments of ethnographic significance. Hence the contact period as determined here was of less than a hundred years in duration. In this period the political control of this region remained in the hands of the French, and most of the accounts of the various tribes were written by Frenchmen. The question of language and the consequent translation was another reason for limiting the period to the French regime. The French were not especially interested in settling upon the land and so disturbed the Indians very little in their villages. The missionaries' efforts and the urgent demands for furs by the traders had a great influence upon the religion and the material culture of the Indians, but the presence of the whites was not actively resented until after the French lost control of the region.

After the determination of chronological limits it was necessary to decide upon the tribes to be included in the survey and study. In the beginning all references to the tribes which frequented Michigan were noted. It was found that tribes such as the Sioux, Cree, Kickapoo, Fox, and Sauk were never more than visitors during historic times. The list of tribes to be considered as residents in Michigan during this period narrowed down to the Huron, Ottawa, Potawatomi, Chippewa, Miami, and Menominee. Comparison of the records of the contact period with fairly recent ethnographic work disclosed that practically every early reference to the Menominee had been included in the monographs of Hoffman, Jenks, and Skinner.[1] Consequently, the material on this tribe is not repeated here. Another intentional hiatus is the mythology of the Huron. This subject has been ably covered by Barbeau,[2] who gave all historic references in an appendix; it is unnecessary to repeat them here, since Barbeau's work is generally available.

In presenting the recorded ethnography of the contact period, direct quotation has been used wherever it was practicable. Frequently, the material might have been paraphrased without detracting from the meaning of the author, but often a certain charm and atmosphere conveyed by the

[1] Walter J. Hoffman, *The Menomini Indians, Fourteenth Ann. Rept., Bur. Amer. Ethnol.* (1896); Albert E. Jenks, *The Wild Rice Gatherers of the Upper Lakes, Nineteenth Ann. Rept., Bur. Amer. Ethnol.*, Pt. 2 (1900); Alanson B. Skinner, "Social Life and Ceremonial Bundles of the Menomini Indians," *Anthrop. Papers Amer. Mus. Nat. Hist.*, Vol. 13, Pt. 1 (1913); *idem*, "Associations and Ceremonies of the Menomini Indians," *ibid.*, Pt. 2 (1913).

[2] C. Marius Barbeau, *Huron and Wyandot Mythology, Canada Dept. of Mines, Geol. Sur., Memoir* 80, *Anthrop. Ser.*, 11 (1915).

words of the eyewitness are lost by extracting the gist of a passage.

The authors of the accounts of the contact period may be divided into three groups: missionaries, traders, and administrative officers. As a general rule members of each of these groups shared viewpoints contrasting with those of the other two. The group to which an author belonged was considered in evaluating his statements. When it was possible the account of an author was also weighed in the light of his other writings. Evaluations are not always reported directly, but are reflected in the selection of the material cited.

One of the inevitable shortcomings of a study of this sort is its limitation to the subjects discussed by the early ·missionaries, traders, and officers. No one has a keener realization of this limitation than the investigator who has looked in vain for information on some particular item. Deficiencies of the material of the contact period have not been supplied from later sources and only rarely have the deficiencies of the records of any tribe been filled from the records of other tribes, even though cognate.

The objective of collecting and organizing all the pertinent data discoverable for the selected tribes and period was not thrown aside for the purpose of filling in a pattern of what an ethnography should cover. On the contrary, one of the aims of this project has been to indicate those points on which the documents of the period yielded no information. Negative results of this nature are not as satisfying to the investigator as positive ones, but they may be one of the most important products of a diligently pursued inquiry.

The Bibliography is composed only of those works which are cited in the text. There were many more publications and manuscripts examined than were used. The value of the material determined its selection or rejection. By inference those works not cited were tried and found wanting in one respect or another: the information was without tribal designations; the remarks were obviously made without any direct knowledge of the Indians; the information was so sketchy as to be worthless by itself; or extensive borrowing from other works was evident. As an instance of the last there is *The Four Kings of Canada*, published anonymously in 1710. This is a plausible account of various Indian customs and ceremonies, but in whole paragraphs it agrees word for word with the 1698 English edition of Hennepin's *A New Discovery*. There were also examined innumerable stories of captivities among the Indians which contained few or no remarks of ethnographic significance.

Readers acquainted with the general history of the Great Lakes region may be surprised by the infrequent use of the accounts of many well-known writers such as Lahontan, Hennepin, Charlevoix, and Lafitau. Some of these writers, for example Charlevoix and Lafitau, borrowed most of their material from earlier accounts, usually without any acknowledgments, and were eyewitnesses of very little that they related. Consequently, all of their material is suspect, whether or not the original account can be identified, and must be used only with the utmost caution. Another fault common to many of the writers of the period was the neglect of applying tribal designations to the tribes of which they were writing. A number of these general accounts could not be used at all. Others, such as Perrot's, have been used sparingly, and only when their applicability is fairly certain from external as well as internal evidence. Critical notes after the entries in the Bibliography indicate the investigator's opinion of the value of the works.

The investigator accepts the responsibility for any errors there may be in the translation of the works of Cadillac, Lafitau, Le Beau, Raudot, and Sagard, and of the excerpts from the documents in the Paris archives. Otherwise, acceptable published translations have been used in preference to the original French. Examples of these are the *Jesuit Relations*, Champlain's *Voyages*, and Perrot's *Memoir*. C. M. Burton had a complete translation of Margry's *Découvertes* made in the expectation of publication. This translation has been utilized.

The pursuance of this study and the publication of its results have been made possible by grants from the Horace H. Rackham School of Graduate Studies. The progress of this study has been aided immeasurably by the advice and whole-hearted co-operation of the following individuals, to whom the investigator offers most grateful acknowledgments: James F. Kenney and Gustav Lanctot, Dominion Archives, Ottawa; Raoul Bonin, St. Sulpice Library, Montreal; Aegidius Fauteux, Municipal Library, Montreal; Father Arthur Melançon, Archives of St. Mary's College, Montreal; Z. C. Massicotte, Palais de Justice, Montreal; Msgr. Camille Roy, Seminaire de Quebec, Quebec; Pierre-George Roy, Musée, Quebec; Miss Grace G. Griffin, Library of Congress, Washington, D.C.; and particularly Miss Elizabeth Steere, William L. Clements Library, Ann Arbor.

CONTENTS

HURON

THE Huron was one of the first tribes of the interior with which contact was made by the French. Cartier found a village of Huron–Iroquois affiliation on the island of Montreal in 1535. The next European in this region was Champlain. In 1603 he found the village site at Montreal deserted. The Montagnais and other Algonquian tribes were scattered along the St. Lawrence River. These tribes were on peaceful terms with the Huron, who apparently visited them annually for purposes of trade and to join them in war against the Iroquois. In 1608 Champlain and two of his men joined these allies on an expedition into the Iroquois country. At its conclusion he entrusted a French lad to the Huron chiefs to return with them to their country that he might learn their customs, language, and territory. Seven years later Champlain visited the Huron country between Lake Simcoe and Georgian Bay. His account is the first we have from an eye-witness of the situation of their villages. To the west and southwest of the country of the Huron proper lay that of the Tionontati, Tobacco Huron, or Tobacco Nation. Still farther south of the Huron proper and mostly westward from the Niagara River were the villages of the Neutrals.

The Tionontati and the Neutrals both belonged to the Huron–Iroquois linguistic stock. The Tionontati received their name from the large amount of tobacco that they grew. At the time of first white contact they had entered into an alliance with the Huron, although there is some evidence that this peaceful state was rather recent in origin. The Neutrals, occupying the region between the Huron and the Iroquois, received their name from the French on account of their policy with regard to their neighbors. These three groups occupied essentially the same regions until the raids of the Iroquois, from 1648 to 1651, razed their villages, reduced the population by massacre and the taking of captives, and put the remainder to flight. Remnants of all three groups were united in seeking a refuge. It is the movements of these refugees that will be followed. The villages of the Huron proper were first to be attacked. In 1649 some Huron sought safety with the Tionontati, others among the Neutrals, and another group on St. Joseph Island. After the attacks on the Tionontati and the subsequent destruction of the Neutral villages, the survivors who escaped captivity fled by way of Mackinac Island to the northwest shore of Lake Michigan. Hereinafter these combined groups of refugees will be called Huron. A rendezvous with various Algonquian tribes was reported in 1653 to be taking place three days' journey south of Sault Ste Marie.[1] A year or so later the Huron and Ottawa had their village on an island, according to Peter Radisson[2] and Nicolas Perrot.[3] This was probably Washington Island at the mouth of Green Bay, formerly known as Huron Island. On the approach of a party of Iroquois they retreated to the mainland and built a fort near the Potawatomi village of Mechingan, where, according to Perrot,[4] they successfully withstood a siege for two years. They then retreated farther inland and in 1658 were reported by Druillettes to be six days' journey southwest of Lake Superior, where they were visited by Radisson and Groseilliers.[5] Difficulties with the Sioux, upon whose territory they were encroaching, required another move. Chaquamegon on the southern shore of Lake Superior was their next abode. They lived there near the Ottawa until 1670. The Ottawa then removed their residence to Manitoulin Island and the Huron to Mackinac (St. Ignace).[6]

[1] Paul Ragueneau, *Journal of the Jesuits, J.R.*, 38 : 181. See the Bibliography for full citations.

[2] *Voyages*, pp. 147-48.

[3] *Memoir, ITUM.*, 1 : 151.

[4] *Ibid.*

[5] Gabriel Druillettes, *Relation* . . . . *1659-60, J.R.*, 45 : 235.

[6] Claude Dablon, *Relation* . . . . *1670-71, J.R.*, 55 : 171.

Cadillac persuaded the Huron to settle near the fort which he built at Detroit in 1701. He reported in 1703 that only about twenty-five remained at Mackinac.[7] They maintained a village at Detroit throughout the rest of the contact period. A division took place about 1738, and a group under the leadership of Orontony, or Nicholas, moved to the vicinity of Sandusky Bay.[8] In 1744 at least part of this group returned to the neighborhood of Detroit and settled on *les grands terres*.[9] Within a short time this group again moved southward and shifted from one place to another. Originally, the Huron village at Detroit was situated on the west side of the river, but some time before 1733 it was shifted to the other side.[10]

In the earliest accounts of the Huron they were estimated to number from 30,000 to 40,000 persons.[11] This was not counting the Tionontati and the Neutrals, who together were thought to be equally numerous. In 1640 and 1641 the three groups were estimated to have been reduced by war, plague, and famine to a total of about 24,000 people.[12]

After being driven from their Ontario villages, no estimate placed their number higher than fifteen hundred. The *Relation* of 1649 recounted that three hundred families had gathered on St. Joseph Island.[13] If there were an average of five persons in a family, the total number of individuals at that time would have been fifteen hundred. Approximately half of these retreated to Quebec with the returning missionaries. Thereafter, the number of Huron about the Great Lakes was very small. Reports in 1653, 1736, 1741, and 1749

---

[7] "Report of Detroit in 1703," *Cadillac Papers, MPH.*, 33: 162.

[8] "Noyelle Goes to Sandusky to Meet the Indians," *Cadillac Papers, MPH.*, 34: 163.

[9] François Beauharnois, "Tranquility in the Upper Country . . . . ," *The French Regime in Wisconsin—II, WHC.*, 17: 440.

[10] Jean de Bonnecamps, *Account of the Voyages on the Beautiful River Made in 1749, J.R.*, 69: 199.

[11] Samuel de Champlain, *Voyages*, 3: 122; Gabriel Sagard, *Le Grand voyage*, p. 116; Jean de Brébeuf, *Relation . . . . 1636, J.R.*, 10: 313.

[12] *Relation . . . . 1640, J.R.*, 18: 127; *Relation . . . . 1641, J.R.*, 21: 191.

[13] *J.R.*, 34: 223.

set their number at eight hundred.[14] Accounts of the years between 1653 and 1736 usually gave a lower total, somewhere between four hundred and six hundred.[15] All of these figures are only estimates and should be accepted as such. Some of the lower figures may have been estimated when part of the band was absent at war, or on a hunting or trading expedition. Even without considering such a possibility, the estimates are remarkably uniform and hence the more credible.

CHARACTERISTICS

The Huron men were well proportioned, well shaped, strong, and robust; the women were also well proportioned, and a good number of them were pleasing in figure, complexion, and features, and there were some powerful women of extraordinary stature.[16] The description of them by Sagard is more detailed: bronzed complexion, which he attributed to their nudity, the heat of the sun, and the oils, greases, and paints which they applied to their bodies; white teeth; black hair, with the exception of a few who had chestnut, and only on the head; well formed and proportioned; no big bellies; and neither too fat nor too thin.[17] Bressani stated that the Huron were not naturally bronzed, but became so with age.[18] Du Peron found them robust and much taller than were the French;[19] to Lalemant the Neutrals appeared taller, stronger, and better proportioned than the rest of the Huron.[20] The testimony of Dallion, Sagard, and Bressani is unanimous that

[14] Ragueneau, *Journal of the Jesuits, J.R.*, 38: 181; Pierre J. Celeron, "Census of Indian Tribes: 1736," *WHC.*, 17: 251; AC., C 11 A, 76: 316 vo.; "Histoire de l'Amérique Septentrionale," BA., MSS fr. 3817: 257.

[15] Jacques Marquette, *Relation . . . . 1670, J.R.*, 54: 169-71; Jean Enjalran, *Relation . . . . 1679, J.R.*, 61: 103-5; AC., C 11 A, 13; Jacques Sabrevois, *Memoir, WHC.*, 16: 370; Pierre Noyan, "Memorandum," *MPH.*, 34: 76.

[16] Champlain, *Voyages*, 3: 135-36.

[17] *Le Grand voyage*, pp. 179-82.

[18] Francesco-Giuseppe Bressani, *Breve relatione, J.R.*, 38: 257.

[19] "Letter from François du Peron," *J.R.*, 15: 155.

[20] Jérôme Lalemant, *Relation . . . . 1641, J.R.*, 21: 199.

the Huron had no hunchbacked, dwarfed, one-eyed, or otherwise crippled or deformed members.[21]

Sagard termed the Huron the nobility of the various Indian nations in Canada, for he found them to have rather good sense and understanding and not to be so coarse and clumsy as imagined in France; also they were of a rather cheerful and contented humor, although at all times a little taciturn; and they were greatly given to vengeance and deceit, but showed gentleness and mercy in victory to women and children. They feared dishonor and reproach, scorned to haggle in trade, were incited to do well by honor, were praiseworthy for their liberality and hospitality, promised much but did little, and thought it no crime to steal from strangers.[22] Visiting the Huron in 1615, eight years before Sagard did, Champlain said: "They are charitable enough to one another in respect to victuals, but otherwise very avaricious. They give nothing for nothing."[23] Then, he added the ambiguous remark that "all these people are of a very cheerful disposition although many among them are of a sad and saturnine humour."[24]

A Jesuit missionary, Brébeuf, thought the Huron were lascivious, although they were less so than were many Christians in two leading points: "You will see no kissing nor immodest caressing; and in marriage a man will remain two or three years apart from his wife, while she is nursing." Then he stated that they were "gluttons, even to disgorging; it is true, that does not happen often, but only in some superstitious feasts—these, however, they do not attend willingly. Besides, they endure hunger much better than we,—so well that after having fasted two or three entire days you will see them still paddling, carrying loads, singing, laughing, banter-

---

[21] Joseph Dallion *in* Christien Le Clercq, *First Establishment of the Faith in New France*, 1: 266; Sagard, *Le Grand voyage*, pp. 179-82; Bressani, *Breve relatione*, J.R., 38: 257.

[22] *Le Grand voyage*, pp. 184-87.

[23] *Voyages*, 3: 52-53.

[24] *Ibid.*, p. 135.

ing, as if they had dined well." Further faults were laziness, lying, thieving, and persistent begging.[25] In commendation, he said they were not as vindictive as were other nations. He greatly admired the love and unity which existed among them and which were carefully cultivated by their marriages, their helping of each other in sickness, the exchange of presents, their feasts and frequent visits, and their patience in the face of poverty, famine, and sickness.[26] The peace and friendship which they maintained among themselves he found most praiseworthy, and their gentleness and affability were almost incredible for savages. They were not easily annoyed, and they concealed wrongs done to them, seldom making a public display of anger and vengeance. For the most part they were fairly intelligent—almost none were incapable of conversing or reasoning well. There was some propriety, courtesy, and civility observed among them, although there was no handkissing, compliments, and lip service that meant nothing; but they rendered certain duties to one another, and certain customs were preserved in their visits, dances, and feasts, through a sense of propriety that would be offended by the failure to observe them. In conclusion, Brébeuf gave the following examples of customs observed among the Huron:

When they meet, the only salutation they give is to call the other by name, or say, "my friend, my comrade,"—"my uncle," if it is an old man. If a Savage finds himself in your Cabin when you are eating, and if you present to him your dish, having scarcely touched anything, he will content himself with tasting it, and will hand it back to you. But, if you give him a dish for himself, he will not put his hand to it until he has shared it with his companions; and they content themselves usually with taking a spoonful of it. These are little things, of course; but they show nevertheless that these Peoples are not quite so rude and unpolished as one might suppose.[27]

[25] *Relation* . . . . *1635*, J.R., 8: 125-27.
[26] *Ibid.*, pp. 127-31.
[27] *Relation* . . . . *1636*, J.R., 10: 213-16.

Du Peron wrote to his brother in 1639 that "the nature of the Savage is patient, liberal, hospitable; but importunate, visionary, childish, thievish, lying, deceitful, licentious, proud, lazy."[28] He also reported that "they nearly all show more intelligence in their business, speeches, courtesies, intercourse, tricks, and subtleties, than do the shrewdest citizens and merchants in France."[29]

Lalemant, another Jesuit missionary, was enthusiastic over the virtues to be found among the Huron and, even more then Brébeuf, seems to have judged their actions and capacities in the light of their own culture. He hoped that these characteristics would make them amenable to conversion to Christianity, as is evident in the letter he wrote to the Father Provincial on May 15, 1645:

I can say in truth that, as regards Intelligence, they are in no wise inferior to Europeans and to those who dwell in France. I would never have believed that, without instruction, nature could have supplied a most ready and vigorous eloquence, which I have admired in many Hurons; or more clear-sightedness in affairs, or a more discreet management in things to which they are accustomed. Why, then, should they be incapable of having a knowledge of a true God?

In truth, their customs are barbarous in a thousand matters; but after all, in those practices which among them are regarded as evil acts and are condemned by the public, we find without comparison much less disorder than there is in France, though here the mere shame of having committed the crime is the offender's punishment. What, therefore, would their innocence be if the Faith reigned among them?[30]

In his *Breve relatione*, Bressani gave substantially the same favorable characterization of them, but especially admired four things: their senses of sight, hearing, and smell; their fortitude; their sense of orientation; and their memory.

[28] *J.R.*, 15: 155.

[29] *Ibid.*, p. 157.

[30] "Letter to the Father Provincial," *J.R.*, 28: 63.

Nearly a century later Charlevoix described the Indians of Canada in almost the same words, but without naming any tribe—undoubtedly an uncredited quotation from Bressani. Bressani, on his part also, made extensive use of the *Relations* written before his own, which was published in 1653.[31]

For twenty years after the destruction of their Ontario villages by the Iroquois, there was little contact between the Huron who stayed in the West and the French. With an increasing number of fur traders about the Great Lakes, the importance of the Huron to the support of that trade was realized, particularly in two respects. The first was their loyalty to the French, and the second was their agricultural skill and practice, which went a long way toward supplying the trading posts with needed corn, reduced the necessity of bringing flour over the long haul from Montreal for the subsistence of the traders, and thus increased the quantity of merchandise that could be brought up for trade. Occasionally, however, when they were perturbed by incursions of the Iroquois and by the lack of desire or strength on the part of the French to curb these enemies, the Huron entered into negotiations with the Iroquois themselves, being concerned above all with their own safety. Whenever such action was taken, or when the Huron attempted to break up relations between the French and the Iroquois in which the Huron thought the French were sacrificing the well-being of themselves and their upper lakes allies, the contemporary French opinion of them was apt to be unfavorable. An example of this is provided by the comment of Cadillac, written some time before 1699:

[The Huron] was formerly the most powerful, the strongest and also the most numerous tribe, but the Iroquois destroyed them and drove them from their lands, so that they are now reduced to a very small number; and it is well for us that it is so. For they are cunning men, intriguing, evil-disposed and capable of great designs, but, fortunately, their arm is not long enough to ex-

[31] *J.R.*, 38: 257-63, 267.

ecute them; nevertheless, since they cannot play the part of lions, they act like foxes, and use every possible means to stir up strife between us and our allies.[32]

After founding Fort Pontchartrain at Detroit in 1701 Cadillac made every effort to induce the Huron to settle there, and succeeded, which action seems to nullify his previously expressed opinion. On his visit to Detroit in 1718 Sabrevois characterized the Huron as an exceedingly industrious nation who hardly ever danced, being constantly at work in the fields. He added that they were very clever, intelligent, the bravest of all the nations, and the most loyal to the French.[33]

DRESS AND ORNAMENT

The first description of the manner of dress of the Huron is the most detailed in the documents. It was written by Champlain in 1615:

As to their clothing they have several kinds and styles, and varieties of wild beasts' skins, both of those they catch and others they exchange for their Indian corn, meal, wampum and fish nets, with the Algonquins, Piserenis (Nipissings), and other tribes who are hunters and have no fixed abodes. All their clothes are of the same make, without variety of new designs. They dress and prepare the skins very well, making their breeches of a moderately large deer-skin, and of another their leggings which reach as high as the waist, with many folds; their moccasins are made of the skins of deer, bear and beaver, of which they use great numbers. Further they have a robe of the same fur, shaped like a cloak, which they wear in the Irish or Egyptian fashion, and sleeves which are tied behind by a cord. That is how they are dressed during the winter. . . . When they go into the fields they gird their robe about their body, but when in their village they leave off their sleeves and do not gird themselves. The Milan trimmings to adorn their clothing are made of glue and of the scrapings of the said skins, with which they make bands in many ways, as they fancy, in places

[32] Antoine de la Mothe Cadillac, MS "Relation on the Indians."
[33] *Memoir*, *WHC.*, 16: 368.

putting bands of red or brown paint amidst those of the glue which are always pale, and do not lose their markings however dirty they may get. Among these tribes are some more skilful than others in preparing skins and clever in inventing patterns to put upon their clothes. Above all others our Montagnais and Algonquins are those that take most trouble with it; for they put on their robes strips of porcupine-quill which they dye a very beautiful scarlet colour; they value these strips very highly and take them off to make them serve for other robes when they wish to make a change. They also use them to beautify the face and have a better appearance when they wish to deck themselves out.

Most of them paint their faces black and red, mixing the paint with oil made from the seed of the sunflower or else with bear fat or that of other animals, and they also dye their hair, which some wear long, others short, others on one side only. As to the women and girls, they wear it always in the same manner; they are clad like the men except that they always gird up their robes, which hang down to the knee. In this they differ from the men; they are not ashamed to show their body, that is, from the waist up and from mid-thigh down, always keeping the rest covered, and they are laden with quantities of wampum, both necklaces and chains, which they allow to hang in front of their robes and attached to their belts, and also with bracelets and ear-rings. They have their hair well combed, dyed and oiled, and thus they go to dances with a tuft of their hair behind tied up with eel-skin which they arrange to serve as a band, or sometimes they fasten to it plates a foot square covered with the same wampum, which hang behind. In this manner gaily dressed and adorned, they like to show themselves at dances, where their fathers and mothers send them, forgetting no device that they can apply to bedeck and bedizen their daughters; and I can assure you that at dances I have attended, I have seen girls that had more than twelve pounds of wampum on them, without counting the other trifles with which they are loaded and decked out.[34]

Champlain is not clear as to whether the Huron made use

[34] *Voyages*, 3: 133-35.

of porcupine quills for ornaments, but Sagard said they made belts and other ornaments of them which were very exactly woven and tinted crimson.[35]

François du Peron in a letter to his brother in 1639 gave a very pithy description of the Huron men:

Their only covering is a beaver skin which they wear upon their shoulders in the form of a mantle; shoes and leggings in winter, a tobacco pouch behind the back, a pipe in the hand; around their necks and arms bead necklaces and bracelets of porcelain; they also suspend these from their ears, and around their locks of hair. They grease their hair and their faces; they also streak their faces with black and red paint.[36]

Bressani in his *Breve relatione* corroborated the report of Champlain that the Huron women were covered at least from the waist to the knee and that in winter (all?) the Huron wore sleeves and leggings.[37] The Neutrals shocked Dallion and Lalemant, for many of them did not even wear breech clouts, although the women were, like the Huron women, covered at least from the waist as far as the knees.[38] According to Raudot, even in 1710 the Huron were remarkable for their modesty, for he wrote that they "are always covered and take great care to hide that which modesty forbids them to show."[39]

In confirmation of the statement of Champlain that the Huron women always wore their hair in the same way, well combed, oiled, and arranged in a single tress hanging down the back and tied with eelskins, are the reports of Sagard, Bressani, and Raudot.[40] There was no one method of fixing the

[35] *Le Grand voyage*, p. 192.

[36] *J.R.*, 15: 155.

[37] *J.R.*, 38: 245-47.

[38] Dallion, *in* Le Clercq, *First Establishment of the Faith in New France*, 1: 271; Lalemant, *Relation . . . . 1641, J.R.*, 21: 197.

[39] Antoine Raudot, "Memoir," Letter 72. See Appendix for Letters 23-41 and 45-72.

[40] Sagard, *Le Grand voyage*, p. 189; Bressani, *J.R.*, 38: 249; Raudot, "Memoir," Letter 72.

hair followed by the men. According to Sagard, "they wear two great moustaches above their ears, and some wear only one, which they plait and twist rather often with feathers and other trifles, the rest of the hair is cut short, or even in boxes, clerical crowns, and in all other ways that please them."[41]

As for the young men, Sagard wrote: "They oil their hair, stick feathers in it and others make little ruffs of the down of feathers to go around the neck: some have head bands of snakeskins the tails of which hang down behind, the length of two French yards."[42]

In his *Breve relatione* Bressani stated that the Huron men wore their hair in various ways: some shaved half the head; others all of it, leaving only some tufts here and there; the most common way was to allow the hair to grow very long; others roached theirs, that is to say, left it straight in the middle or on the forehead. It was this last manner of wearing the hair, according to Bressani, that caused the first Frenchmen to call this tribe "Huron," from the straight locks on the middle of their heads, which reminded them of the bristles of the wild boar, called *hure* in French.[43]

In the latter part of the seventeenth century Cadillac also wrote that the Huron kept their hair very short except for a tuft on the top of the head; he added that the Indians told him that the reason was to give their enemies less to take hold of.[44]

The Huron women did not paint or tattoo themselves, according to most observers, although Sagard said he saw a few who were tattooed. Their ornamentation was confined to oiling their hair and to embellishments that might be called their jewelry, such as porcelain beads and chaplets. These were described by Sagard as follows:

Their porcelains are strung various ways, some in necklaces

[41] *Ibid.*, p. 190.
[42] *Ibid.*, p. 192.
[43] *J.R.*, 38: 249.
[44] MS "Relation on the Indians."

three or four fingers wide, made like a horse's girth with all its
threads covered up and inserted [in the pieces of shell]. The
circumference of these necklaces is about three and a half feet
or more, and the women put many of them on their necks, according to their means and wealth. Then they have others
threaded like our rosaries, attached and hung from their ears,
and some chains of beads as big as nuts of the same porcelain
which they fasten to both hips and these are arranged in front
in a slant over the thighs or the breech clouts they wear. And
I have seen other women who also wore bracelets on their arms
and great plates in front over the stomach, with others behind
circular in shape and like a card for carding wool hanging from
their tresses of hair. Some of them have also belts and other
ornaments, made of porcupine quills tinted crimson red and
very exactly woven. Then feathers and paintings are never lacking, and each one is devoted to them.[45]

The ornamentation of the men included porcelain beads
and necklaces, althought not to the same extent that they were
used by the women and girls. Sagard had seen a man whose
nose had been pierced in the middle, and which had a rather
large blue stone hanging from it; but it is likely that this
referred to a member of an Algonquian tribe, rather than to a
Huron. The methods of decoration peculiar to the men were
painting and tattooing. Not only the face but the entire body
was painted in various styles and colors: black, green, red, and
violet, according to Sagard.[46] Bressani merely reported black,
red, and various colors; but he said that the black was commonly taken from the bottom of pots, and the other colors
were of various earths or were derived from certain roots
which yielded a very fine scarlet. As to the styles of painting,
he said that some appeared artistically bearded, others seemed
to wear spectacles, some had the whole face striped with
various colors, others only half, but all were shining with
the oil or grease which they mixed in their colors. He noted
that they painted their bodies so well that at first sight some

[45] *Le Grand voyage*, pp. 191-92.
[46] *Ibid.*, p. 192.

persons supposed certain Huron to be clothed who were entirely naked—their clothes consisting only of paint. The reasons they gave for painting themselves seemed not at all barbarous to Bressani:

This painting serves them in winter as a mask against the cold and the ice; in war, it prevents their countenances from betraying them by revealing inward fear, makes them more terrible to the enemy, and conceals extremes of youth or age, which might inspire strength and courage in the adversary. It serves as adornment at the public feasts and assemblies. They also paint the prisoners destined to the flames, as victims consecrated to the god of war, and adorn them as the ancients adorned theirs. They do the same also to their dead, for the same reasons for which we adorn ours.[47]

Tattooing was described by Sagard as an alternative to painting:

Others, principally those of the Tobacco Nation, have the body and face engraved in sections, with figures of snakes, lizards, squirrels, and other animals; almost all have the body thus figured, which renders them frightful and hideous to those who are not accustomed to it: it is pricked and made in the same way that are made and graven in the surface of the flesh the crosses which those who return from Jerusalem have on their arms, and it is forever; but they get it done at different times, because the prickings cause them great pains, and they often fall sick from them, as far as having a fever and losing their appetite, and for all that they do not desist, but continue until all is finished and as they desire it, without evincing any impatience or vexation in the excess of pain.[48]

Bressani gave a few more details of the methods and instruments used in tattooing, which he called permanent painting:

But those who paint themselves permanently do so with extreme pain,—using, for this purpose, needles, sharp awls, or

[47] *Breve relatione*, J.R., 38: 253.
[48] *Le Grand voyage*, pp. 192-93.

piercing thorns, with which they perforate, or have others perforate, the skin. Thus they form on the face, the neck, the breast,
or some other part of the body, some animal or monster,—for
instance, an Eagle, a Serpent, a Dragon, or any other figure
which they prefer; and then, tracing over the fresh and bloody
design some powdered charcoal, or other black coloring matter,
which becomes mixed with the blood and penetrates within these
perforations, they imprint indelibly upon the living skin the de-
signed figures. And this in some nations is so common that in
the one which we called the Tobacco, and in that which—on
account of enjoying peace with the Hurons and with the Hiro-
quois—was called Neutral, I know not whether a single individual was found, who was not painted in this manner, on some
part of the body. And indeed, when the painting covers a great
part of the body, it is dangerous, especially in cold weather;
and—either through some sort of convulsion, or for some other
reason—it has caused the death of more than one, making him a
martyr to vanity and a fantastic caprice, in the fulfillment of
which they commonly give no sign of pain, although they experience it most acutely.[49]

In the *Relation* of 1641 Lalemant wrote that the Neutrals
were commonly covered from the head to the feet with many
different designs of charcoal pricked into the flesh, upon
which they had previously traced their lines.[50] Sabrevois
reported the Huron to be still practicing tattooing in 1718.[51]

ECONOMIC LIFE

The Huron villages were occupied throughout the entire
year. They were moved at intervals of ten to twenty years, if
no emergency arose, such as an attack by their enemies. They
moved when the soil failed to bear good crops and when there
was a lack of suitable firewood.

The women were occupied with the care of the fields and
the house, stripping and spinning hemp, and making the

[49] *Breve relatione, J.R.,* 38: 251-53.
[50] *J.R.,* 21: 197.
[51] *Memoir, WHC.,* 16: 373-74.

baskets, mats, and pottery. The men made the cabins, canoes, nets, and weapons and attended to the fishing, hunting, trading, and fighting. In the hunting and fishing expeditions the women and children did not accompany the men.[52]

Agriculture

Of the cultivation of corn Sagard wrote:

Their custom is, that each household lives on what it fishes, hunts, and sows, having as much land as is necessary for it: for all the forests, prairies, and uncleared lands are common property, and it is permitted to each one to clear and sow as much as he wishes, as he can, or as is necessary for him; and the land thus cleared remains to the person as many years as he continues to cultivate and use it, and being entirely abandoned by the master, is used after that by whoever wishes to use it himself, and not otherwise. They clear it with great trouble, lacking the proper tools. They cut down the trees at the height of two or three feet from the ground, then they strip off all the branches, which they burn at the foot of these trees to make them die, and with the passage of time they remove the roots; then the women clear the land between the trees and dig a place or round hole at intervals of a pace, in which they sow nine or ten grains of maize that they have first selected, sorted, and soaked several days in water; they continue this until they have enough for two or three years' provisions, either for fear of having a bad year or for trade with other nations for peltries or things of which they have need; every year they sow their corn in the same places, which they till with their little wooden shovels, made in the form of an ear, which have a handle at the end; the rest of the ground is not worked, only cleaned of weeds; they take so much care to keep all clean that the fields appear to be roads; and that was the reason why going alone sometimes from one village to another I usually lost my way in these cornfields, more than in the prairies and forests.

The corn being sowed, in the manner that we sow beans, only one stalk or cane grows from one grain, and the cane bears two

[52] Champlain, *Voyages*, 3: 136-37; Sagard, *Le Grand voyage*, pp. 122, 130-32.

or three ears; each ear yields a hundred, two hundred, sometimes four hundred grains, and there are some which yield more. The stalk grows to the height of a man and more, and is very thick (it does not grow so well and so tall, nor the ear so large, and the grain is not as good in Canada nor in France as there). The grain ripens in four months, and in certain places in three. After that they gather it and tie it by the turned-down leaves; they do it up in packets, which they hang all along the length of their cabins, arranged from top to bottom on poles set up in the form of a rack descending to the front edge of the bench; all is so exactly arranged that it seems as if there were tapestries hung the length of the cabins. The grain being well dried and fit to pound, the women and girls shell, clean, and put it in their large vats or casks for this purpose and place them on their porches or in corners of their cabins.[53]

This account of agriculture is the most complete that is known for the contact period.

Besides corn, the Huron cultivated beans, squashes, sunflowers, and tobacco (see cultivated products in Table I). Bressani stated in 1653 that the Huron did not have beans until after the arrival of the French.[54] In view of the testimony of Champlain and Sagard that the Huron were cultivating beans when they went among them in 1615 and 1623, respectively, I believe Bressani to have been in error. The peas reported by Sagard in his *Histoire* are not in the same list in which beans are mentioned, and the latter may have been intended, as no other writer reported them being cultivated by the Huron until several years later. Likewise, none of the early references to pumpkins coincide with mention of squashes, and it is likely that the authors used one name in

[53] *Le Grand voyage*, pp. 133-35. One thing requires a little amplification. Throughout the account, except immediately after the words "the women," the pronouns used are in the masculine plural. The wording of the text in both the original French and in translation indicates that the clearing of the land was done by the men, and probably the pronoun *"ils"* where it followed the mention of women, referred to the latter and was used either in error or in the generic sense.

[54] *Breve relatione, J.R.,* 38: 245.

TABLE I

FOOD OF THE HURON

AUTHORITY	DATE	CULTIVATED PRODUCTS	UNCULTIVATED PRODUCTS	FISH	LAND ANIMALS
Champlain	1615	Corn; red beans; squash; sunflowers	Blueberries; raspberries	Fish	Deer; bear; dog
Sagard	1623	Corn; squash; beans; peas	Strawberries; plums; blueberries; currants; raspberries; pears; blackberries; grapes; onions; maple syrup; acorns; *sondhatates* and *orasquanta*—roots	Fish—several kinds	Deer; beaver; muskrat; turtles
Brébeuf	1636	Corn; squash (pumpkins)	Strawberries; raspberries; blackberries	Fish	Game
Le Mercier	1637		Strawberries		
Lalemant	1639	Corn; beans	Wild fruits	Fish	Game
Du Peron	1639	Corn; beans; squash		Carp	
Lalemant	1641	Corn; beans; squash	Small fruits and wild apples	Fish	
	1644	Pumpkins	Acorns; roots		Beaver Wild cattle
Ragueneau	1648	Corn	Acorns; a bitter root "otsa"; garlic	Fish	
Chaumonot	1649	Corn	Acorns; boiled bark; rock tripe; punk	Fish	
Ragueneau	1650			Fish	
Bressani	1653	Corn; pumpkins; beans (after arrival of French)	Hazelnuts; haws; wild plums; blackberries; strawberries; walnuts; cherries (?); grapes (?); garlic; chives; roots; acorns; cranberries (?)		
Boucher	1664	Corn; pumpkins; beans; sunflowers; tobacco		Fish	Beaver
Hennepin	1679	Corn		Whitefish and others	
Joutel	1687	Corn; pumpkins; beans; watermelons			
Lahontan	1688	Corn; peas; beans; citruls; melons		Fish	Elk; stag; buffalo
Cadillac	ca. 1695	Corn; watermelons; peas; beans; pumpkins			Beaver; deer; bear
La Potherie	1702	Corn			
Sabrevois	1718	Corn; peas; beans			

one place and the other elsewhere to designate the same product. Later, after these plants and also watermelons had been introduced by the French, they were grown by the Indians.

The cultivation of pumpkins (i.e., squashes) was reported by Sagard:

They also sow many native pumpkins and raise them with great ease by this invention: The Huron women in season go to the neighboring forests to gather a quantity of rotten wood powder around old stumps; then having prepared a large bark box they make a layer in it of this powder on which they sow the pumpkin seed; afterward, they cover it with another layer of the same dust and again sow seeds, up to two, three, and four times, as much as they wish, in such a way nevertheless that there still remains four to five good fingers of empty space in the box, in order to leave room for the shoots of the seeds. Afterward, they cover the box with a large bark and put it on two poles suspended in the smoke of the fire, which heats gradually the powder and then the seeds so much that they sprout in a very few days; being well grown and ready for planting they take them by bunches with their powder, separate them, and then plant them in the places prepared, from whence they afterwards gather the fruit in season.[55]

In the mission villages on the island of Orleans and at Lorette the Huron men apparently soon joined the women in their agricultural pursuits. Of the former place in 1656 Perrot wrote that they "at the usual hour went out, both men and women, to work on their lands; for among that people, who are naturally industrious, the men assist the women in their work, contrary to the custom of the savages."[56]

The only other exception to the general consensus that the women had charge of agriculture is the statement by Pierre Boucher that it was the men who cultivated the fields of tobacco.[57] There is no contradiction in this, for no other author does more than mention the cultivation of tobacco.

[55] *Histoire*, pp. 283-84.
[56] *Memoir, ITUM.*, 1: 192-93.
[57] *Histoire véritable*, p. 101.

Hunting

In Ontario hunting seems to have played a minor role in the activities of the Huron; not because of their lack of skill in the art, but rather because of the scarcity of game. This condition was undoubtedly caused by the density of their population; they eventually killed off or drove out the game. The Neutral Nation was as numerous as was the Huron proper, but it spread over a much larger territory. There was an abundance of deer in this country, the hunting of which was described by Champlain:

They went into the woods near a little grove of firs where they made a triangular enclosure, closed on two sides, open on one. This enclosure was made of great wooden stakes eight or nine feet in height, joined close together, and the length of each side was nearly fifteen hundred paces. At the extremity of this triangle there is a little enclosure, getting narrower the farther it goes, and partly covered with branches, with only one opening five feet wide, about the width of an average gate, by which the deer were to enter. They did so well that in less than ten days their enclosure was ready. . . . When everything was completed, they set out half an hour before daybreak to go into the woods about half a league from their enclosure, keeping about eighty paces apart, each having two sticks which they strike together, walking slowly in that formation until they reach their enclosure. The deer, hearing this noise, flee before them until they reach the enclosure into which the savages force them to enter. Then the latter gradually coming together towards the opening of their triangle, the deer steal along the said palisades until they reach the extremity, whither the savages pursue them hotly with bow and arrow in hand, ready to shoot. And when the savages reach the extremity of their said triangle, they begin to shout and to imitate the cry of wolves, whereof there are many that devour deer. The deer, hearing this terrifying noise, are forced to enter the retreat by the small opening, whither they are very hotly pursued with arrows, and when they have entered, they are easily caught in this retreat, which is so well enclosed and barricaded that they can never get out of it. I assure you one takes a peculiar pleasure in this mode of hunting, which took place every second day, and they did so well that in the thirty-eight days that we were there, they captured one hundred and twenty deer, with which they made good cheer, keeping the fat for the winter and using it as we do butter, and a little of the meat which they carry home for their feasts. They have other devices for catching deer, such as traps wherewith they cause the death of many.[58]

Another means of hunting large numbers of deer and bear, which Champlain saw practiced on his expedition with the Huron against the Iroquois in 1615, was by forming a long line through the woods from one bend of a river to another and beating toward the river, shouting and making a great noise, so that the animals were driven into the river. Those which tried to break through the line were killed with arrows, and those that took to the water were pursued by the hunters in canoes and easily killed with "sword blades fastened to the end of a stick like a half-pike." This mode of hunting was also practiced on islands on which there was considerable game.[59]

Dallion described the deer hunting of the Neutrals as being substantially the same as that observed by Champlain:

The country of this Neutral nation is incomparably larger, more beautiful, and better than any other of all these countries. There is an incredible number of stags (which they do not take one by one, as is done on this side, but, making three enclosures in a spacious place, they run them all ahead, so that they enclose them in this place, where they take them, and have this maxim for all kinds of animals, whether they need them or not, that they must kill all they find, for fear, as they say, that if they do not take them the beasts would go and tell the others how they had been hunted, and that then, in time of want, they would not find any more).[60]

Another superstition in connection with this mode of hunt-

[58] *Voyages*, 3: 83-85.

[59] *Ibid.*, pp. 60-61.

[60] Dallion, *in* Le Clercq, *First Establishment of the Faith in New France*, 1: 269.

ing was said by Champlain to be that none of the meat taken
in this way was roasted, nor was any of the fat allowed to
fall into the fire, nor were any of the bones thrown into it, for
fear that no more deer could be taken.[61]

The hunting of individual animals is described by Sagard:

When they are hungry they consult the Oracle, and afterward they go bow in hand and quiver on the back to the place
where the *Oki* indicated to them or to other places where they
believe they will not waste their time. They have dogs who
follow them, and notwithstanding that they do not yelp, nevertheless they know well how to discover the shelter of the beast
that they search, which being found they pursue it courageously
and never abandon it until they have thrown it down and mortally
wounded it. The hunters open its stomach, give the entrails to the
dogs, feast, and carry off the rest. If the beast too closely pressed
meets a river, sea, or lake, it dashes freely in, but our agile and
ready Indians are immediately after it with their canoes, if there
are any there, and then give it the death blow.[62]

The Neutrals hunted deer in winter on snowshoes and
were rather successful.[63] Although the fields of ripe grain
attracted large numbers of cranes, geese, and crows, they
were seldom able to kill any of them with arrows, although
they sometimes succeeded in taking them with nets. The
crows were not eaten.[64] Snares were also used to take rabbits, called *Queutonmalisia* by the Huron, but with scant
success according to Sagard, because the small cords were
easily broken or cut by the rabbits.[65]

Beaver were sought by the Huron in both summer and
winter for food and for pelts. Sagard described the hunting in
both seasons:

Beaver hunting is usually done in winter, principally because the beaver stays in its dwellings, and its fur is heavy in

[61] *Voyages*, 3: 92.
[62] *Le Grand voyage*, pp. 128-29.
[63] *Ibid.*, p. 312.
[64] *Ibid.*, pp. 302-3.
[65] *Ibid.*, pp. 306-7.

that season, and is worth very little in summer. When the Indians wish to take beaver they first block all the passages by which it can escape, pierce the ice of the frozen lake at the place of its house, and then one of them puts his arm in the hole, awaiting its coming, while another goes over the ice knocking on it with a stick to frighten it and make it return to its home; it is necessary to be skillful to take it by the neck, for if one seized it elsewhere it could bite and would make a bad wound. The Indians also take beavers in summer by stretching nets from stakes driven in the water, in which when they leave their houses, they are killed; they are eaten fresh or smoked, at the desire of the Indians. The flesh or fish, as one wishes to call it, seems to me very good, particularly the tail, which the Indians esteem as a very excellent food, as, in fact, it is, and the paws also.[66]

Muskrats and turtles were also taken by the Huron for food, according to Sagard, although he reported no details as to the procedure followed.[67]

Accounts written at the beginning of the eighteenth century relate that the Huron men were hunting winter and summer. La Potherie, for instance, wrote in 1702 that the young men went only thirty to forty leagues to hunt in summer; whereas they went a hundred or more leagues for the winter hunt, departing in autumn and not returning until spring.[68]

According to Lahontan the Ottawa and Huron hunted beaver in the valley of the Saginaw River every other year.[69] In this the Huron were following the practice of the Ottawa, who had for a long time placed considerable importance upon hunting.

Evidence as to the relative unimportance of hunting in the life of the Huron in the first half of the seventeenth century is supplied by the statements of missionaries to the effect that the usual food of the Huron was corn or sagamité,

[66] *Ibid.*, pp. 321-22.
[67] *Ibid.*, pp. 322-24.
[68] *History, ITUM.*, 1: 281-83.
[69] Louis Armand Lahontan, *Voyages*, 1: 319.

in which they put meat, when they had it.[70] Our earliest authority on the life of the Huron, Champlain, remarked that their clothing was "wild beasts' skins, both of those they catch and others they exchange for their Indian corn, meal, wampum, and fish nets, with the Algonquins, Piserenis, and other tribes who are hunters."[71]

Fishing

From Table I, it may be seen that fishing was a more important enterprise to the Hurons than was hunting. Fish were caught both in summer and in winter. In some places, according to Champlain, they were taken in large numbers by closing straits between lakes with small weirs, leaving only small openings where nets were placed.[72] Of the winter fishing, he wrote:

They make several round holes in the ice and that through which they are to draw the seine is some five feet long and three feet wide. Then they begin to set their net by this opening; they fasten it to a wooden pole six or seven feet long, and place it under the ice, and pass this pole from hole to hole, where one or two men put their hands through and take hold of the pole to which one end of the net is tied, until they come back to the opening five or six feet wide. Then they let the net drop to the bottom by means of certain small stones fastened to the end of it. After it has been to the bottom they draw it up again by main force by its two ends, and thus they bring up the fish that are caught in it. That in brief is the method they use for fishing in winter.[73]

Sagard[74] stated that only a twine was attached to the pole which was passed from hole to hole under the ice. The twine was as long as the nets that were to be spread. Drawing on the twine set the net and, when the net was pulled up to

[70] See Table I.
[71] *Voyages*, 3: 131.
[72] *Ibid.*, pp. 56-57.
[73] *Ibid.*, pp. 166-68.
[74] *Histoire*, p. 259.

remove the catch of fish, it was a simple matter to reset the net, as the twine was left attached, and drawing it back through the last hole again stretched the net.

The summer and autumn fishing and all the attendant ceremonies were described in great detail by Sagard:

Being desirous of witnessing the absurd ceremonies and practices they carry on when they catch the great fish called *Assihendo* [whitefish], which is a fish as big as the largest cod, but much better, I set out from *Quieunonascaran* with the chief *Auoindaon* in the month of October, and we embarked in a small canoe, five together, on the Fresh-water Sea, and directed our course toward the north. After a long sail out into the sea we stopped and landed on an island suitable for fishing and put up our lodge near several households already established there with the same object of fishing. On the evening of our arrival we had a feast with two large fish, which had been given us by a friend of our Indian as we were passing the island where he was fishing; for it is their custom that friends visiting one another in the fishing season should give mutual presents of a few fish. When our lodge was erected in the Algonquin fashion each of us chose his place in it, the four chief men in the four corners, and the others after them, arranged side by side, rather crowded together. At first they had given me a corner, but in the month of November, when it begins to be rather cold, I placed myself more in the middle, in order to be able to share in the heat of the two fires that we kept up, and yielded my corner to another. Every evening they carried the nets about half a league or a league out into the lake, and in the morning at daybreak they went to draw them in, and always brought back many fine big fish such as *Assihendo*, trout, sturgeon, and others. They gutted them, cutting them open as one does cod, and then spread them out on racks made with poles set up for the purpose in order to dry them in the sun. But if the weather is unfavorable and rain prevents and counteracts the drying of meat or fish they smoke it on hurdles or poles, and then pack it all into casks, for fear of dogs and mice, and this serves them for feasts and for a relish to their soup, especially in winter.

Sometimes they put aside the biggest and fattest *Assihendos*, and set them to boil away in great kettles in order to get the oil from them, which they skim off from the top of the boiling mass with a spoon and put into bottles like our calabashes. This oil is as sweet and nice as fresh butter, moreover it comes from a very good fish unfamiliar to the Canadians and even less known over here [in France]. When the fishing is good and there are a number of lodges it is a perpetual round of feasts and banquets, given in common and in requital to one another, and they make merry together very gladly and without licentiousness. The feasts they give in the villages and towns are sometimes good, but those they give during fishing and hunting are the best of all.

They take special care not to throw any fishbone into the fire, and when I threw them in they scolded me well and took them out quickly, saying that I did wrong and that I should be responsible for their failure to catch any more, because there were spirits of a sort, or the spirits of the fish themselves whose bones were burnt, which would warn the other fish not to allow themselves to be caught, since their bones also would be burnt. . . .

One day, as I was about to burn in the fire the skin of a squirrel, which a savage had given me, they would not allow it and sent me to burn it outside, because of the nets then in the lodge, saying that otherwise the nets would tell the fish. I said to them that the nets could see nothing; they replied that they could, and also that they could hear and eat. "Then give them some of your sagamité," I said. One of them replied to me: "It is the fish that feed them, not we." Once I was reproving the children in the lodge for some nasty and improper language they were using; next morning it happened that they caught very few fish, and they put it down to the reprimand which had been reported to the fish by the nets.

One evening, as we were talking about the animals of the country, I wished to make them understand that we had in France hares and leverets, which they call *Quieuronmalisia*, and showed them the shape of them with my fingers, the bright fire casting their shadow against the wall of the lodge. It happened by chance that next morning they caught far more fish than usual, and they believed that these shadow pictures had been the cause, so simple are they, and they begged me, further-more, to be so good as to make them every evening in the same way and to teach them how; this I would not do that I might not be responsible for this superstition, and to give no counten-ance to their folly.

In each of the fishing lodges there is usually a preacher of fish whose practice it is to preach a sermon to the fish. If these are clever fellows they are much sought after, because the Indians believe that the exhortations of a clever man have great power to attract the fish into their nets. The one we had considered himself one of the best, and it was a spectacle to see him gesticu-late when he preached, using both tongue and hands, which he did every evening after supper, after having imposed silence and made each one take his place, like himself, lying flat on his back with his abdomen upward. His subject was that the Huron never burned fish-bones; they, he went on with matchless senti-mentalities, exhorted the fish, conjured them, begged and en-treated them to come, to allow themselves to be caught, to take courage, to fear nothing, since it was to be of service to some of their friends, who respected them and did not burn their bones. He also made a special one for my benefit, by order of the chief, who said to me afterwards, "Well, my nephew, is that not fine?" "Yes, my uncle," I replied, "according to you; but you and all the rest of the Hurons have very little judgment to think that fish hear and understand your sermons and your talk."

In order to get good fishing they also sometimes burn tobacco, uttering certain words which I did not understand. With the same object they also throw some into the water for certain spirits, which they suppose have authority there, or rather for the soul of the water (for they believe everything material and destitute of life has a soul which comprehends), and they pray to it in their customary way to be of good courage and to allow them to catch plenty of fish.

We found hooks made of a bit of wood, with a bone attached serving the purpose of a bar, tied very neatly with the hempen cord they make, in the stomachs of many fishes. Since the line was too weak to drag such big fish alongside, they lost their labor as well as the hooks they had cast into the sea. For indeed in this Fresh-water Sea there are sturgeon, *Assihendos,* trout, and pike, of such monstrous size that nowhere else are they to be found bigger, and it is the same with many other species of fish that are unknown to us here. And there should be no doubt felt about this, since that great lake or Fresh-water Sea of the Huron is estimated to be three or four hundred leagues in length from east to west and about fifty in breadth, and contains countless islands, on which the Indians encamp when they go to fish or go on a journey to the other tribes bordering on this sea. We took soundings near our town, fairly close to land in a cul-de-sac, and found forty-eight fathoms of water; but it is not of equal depth everywhere, being more in some places and much less in others.

When the wind blew strong our savages did not take their nets to the water, because at that time the waves were very high and swollen; and when the wind was moderate they were still so tossed about that it was enough to make me admire and greatly praise God that these poor people did not perish, but got away in their little canoes out of the midst of such raging waves and billows, upon which I looked down from the top of a rock that I ascended for the purpose.[75]

Some weeks after the catch of the big fish, the savages go to catch the *Einchataon*, which is a fish rather like the red mullet here, about a foot and a half long or a little less. This fish is used to give a taste to their sagamité during the winter, and for this reason they make much of it, as well as of the big fish; and, in order that it may make their soup smell better, they do not remove the viscera, and keep the fish hanging in bunches on the poles of their lodges. But I can assure you that in Lent, when the weather begins to be warm, it stank and had such a frightfully bad smell that our gorge rose at it, while to them it was musk and civet.

At another season they catch with the seine net a certain kind of fish that seems to be a species of our herring, but smaller, which they eat fresh and smoked. And as they are very skillful, like our cod-fishers, in knowing one or two days before, the time when each kind of fish comes, they never fail to go for this little fish, which they call *Auhaitsiq*, and to catch a large quantity with their seines. The catching of this fish is done communally, then they divide the catch in large bowls, and in this we had

[75] Sagard, *Le Grand voyage*, pp. 252-60.

our share as fellow townsmen and residents. They fish for and
catch many other kinds of fish besides, but as these were unknown to us, and none resembling them are found in our rivers,
I make no mention of them.[76]

Sagard did not give any information about the nets used
by the Huron at the time of his visit, other than to say that
they were made of hemp. In 1687 Henri Joutel found the
Huron at Mackinac using substantially the same methods as
those recounted by Sagard, and also gave more data about
the nets:

Their usual food consists of fish and Indian corn. They are
very skillful at fishing, and the fishing is very good in these
parts. There are fish of various kinds which they catch with nets,
made with a very good mesh; and, although they only make
them of ordinary sewing thread, they will nevertheless stop
fish weighing over ten pounds. They go as far as a league out
into the lake to spread their nets, and to enable them to find
them again they leave marks, namely, certain pieces of cedar
wood which they call *aquantiquants*, which serve the same purpose as buoys or anchors. They have nets as long as two hundred fathoms, and about two feet deep. At the lower part of
these nets they fasten stones, to make them go to the bottom;
and on the upper part they put pieces of cedar wood which the
French people who were then at this place called floats. Such
nets are spread in the water, like snares among crops, the fish
being caught as they pass, like partridges and quails in snares.
The nets are sometimes spread in a depth of more than thirty
fathoms, and when bad weather comes, they are in danger of
being lost. As these lakes, although they are very large, are
frozen over at certain times, they have to make holes in the ice
to get the nets in, and they spread them under the ice, which
gives them more trouble.[77]

Preservation of Food

As was mentioned in connection with agriculture, ears of
corn were preserved by pulling back the husks and by hanging

---

[76] *Ibid.*, pp. 316-18.
[77] *Journal, in* Pierre Margry, *Découvertes*, 3: 503.

the ears in the cabins until dry, when they were placed in
large bark casks. Fish taken during the different seasons
were preserved for winter use by smoking or drying in the
sun. The extraction of oil from large fish and its treatment
are discussed in the quotation on fishing from Sagard. Small
fruits, such as strawberries and blueberries, were dried.[78]
There is no mention of any steps being taken to preserve
squashes, although Brébeuf said that they sometimes were kept
four or five months.[79]

Preparation of Food

The principal article in the diet of the Huron was corn.
Courses in a meal among them were unusual. Aside from the
feasts during hunting or fishing there was usually only one
dish, which was of corn, into which the available fresh or
dried meat or fish was put. This was called sagamité. Even
the fruits were added to this dish, in lieu of meat or to
furnish a change. Although the diet of the Indians did not
meet with the approval of many of their visitors, Brébeuf
found that the change of provisions from France was not
very great, that the only grain of the country was a sufficient
nourishment, when one became somewhat accustomed to it,
and that the Indians prepared it in more than twenty ways
and yet employed only fire and water, since the best sauce
for it was its own.[80]

Brébeuf did not itemize these twenty ways, but several
examples of the food of the Huron are described in the
following excerpts from Champlain and Sagard, respectively:

Their principal food and usual sustenance is Indian corn and
red beans, which they prepare in several ways. They pound them
in wooden mortars and reduce them to flour from which they
take the hull by means of certain fans made of tree-bark, and
of this flour they make bread with beans which they first boil,
as they do Indian corn for soup, because it is easier to beat up,

---

[78] François le Mercier, *J.R.*, 13: 231.
[79] *Relation . . . . 1636, J.R.*, 10: 103.
[80] *Ibid.*

and they mix it all together. Sometimes they put in blueberries or dried raspberries; at other times they put pieces of
deer-fat, but not often because it is very scarce with them. Afterwards, steeping the whole in warm water, they make loaves
of it, shaped like cakes or tarts, which they bake in the ashes, and
when cooked, wash them; and very often they make others out
of them, wrapping them in leaves of Indian corn fastened together, and put them into boiling water. But this is not their
ordinary kind, for they make another which they call Migan,
that is, they take pounded Indian corn without removing the
bran, of which they put two or three handfuls into an earthen
pot full of water, boil it, stirring it from time to time lest it
burn or stick to the pot, then put into the same pot a little fish,
fresh or dried, according to the season, to give a taste to the said
Migan, which is the name they give it. They make it very
often, although it is a bad-smelling dish, principally in winter,
because they do not know how to prepare it properly or do not
wish to take the trouble. They make two sorts, and prepare it
very well when they like, and when there is fish, the said Migan
does not smell bad but only with venison. When it is all cooked
they take out the fish, and crush it very fine, not caring whether
they take out the bones, scales or entrails as we do, but putting
it all together into the said pot, which usually gives it its bad
taste. Then when it has been made in that fashion they deal out
a portion to each person. This Migan is very thin and not of
much substance as may well be supposed. As for drink it is not
needed, the said Migan being thin enough in itself. They have
another kind of Migan, to wit, they roast young corn before
it is ripe, preserve it and cook it whole with fish, or meat when
they have any. Another way is to take very dry Indian corn
and roast it in ashes; then they pound it and reduce it to meal,
like the other mentioned above; this they keep for journeys
they undertake in one direction or another, and this Migan
made in this manner is the best to my taste. And to prepare
it they cook a quantity of fish and meat which they cut
into pieces, then put it into large kettles filled with water,
letting it boil well. After this they skim with a spoon the fat
which comes from the meat and fish, then add this roasted meal,
stirring it constantly until the said Migan is cooked and becomes

thick like soup. They give and serve out a portion to each person,
with a spoonful of the fat. This they are in the habit of doing
at banquets, and not as an ordinary thing, in fact very seldom.
Now the said young corn roasted, like that described above, is
highly esteemed among them. They also eat beans which they
boil with the bulk of the roasted meal, adding to it a little fat
and fish. Dogs are in demand at their banquets which they often
give each other, especially during the winter when they are at
leisure. If they go deer-hunting or fishing they keep what they
get for these banquets, having nothing left in their cabins but
thin Migan for ordinary use which is like the bran-mash given
to pigs. They have another way of eating Indian corn, to prepare which they take it in the ear and put it in water under the
mud, leaving it two or three months in that state, until they
judge that it is putrid; then they take it out and boil it with
meat or fish and then eat it. They also roast it, and it is better
that way than boiled, but I assure you that nothing smells so
bad as this corn when it comes out of the water all covered with
mud; yet the women and children take it and suck it like sugar-
cane, there being nothing they like better, as they plainly show.
Their usual custom is to have only two meals a day. For ourselves we fasted the whole of Lent, more especially to stir them
by an example, but it was time wasted. They also fatten bears,
which they keep for two or three years, for their usual feasts. . . .
Nevertheless with all their wretchedness I consider them happy,
since they have no other ambition than to live and support
themselves, and they are more secure than those who wander
through the forests like brute beasts. They also eat much squash,
which they boil and roast in the ashes.[81]

In order to eat it in the form of bread, they first boil the
grain a little in water, then wipe it and dry it a little. Afterward, they crush it, knead it with lukewarm water, and cook
it under hot ashes, wrapped in leaves of corn, and without the
leaves wash it after it is cooked; if they have some beans they
cook them in a little pot and mix them in the dough without
crushing them—or strawberries, blueberries, raspberries, wild

[81] Champlain, *Voyages*, 3: 125-31.

mulberries, or other small fruits dry or green, in order to give it taste and make it better, for it is very flat of itself, if one does not mix in some of these small relishes. This bread and all other kinds of biscuit that we use are called *Andataroni*, except the bread which they call by a particular name, *Coinkia*, made and arranged as two balls joined together, wrapped in corn leaves, and then boiled and cooked in water and not under the ashes. They make bread of still another kind: for this they gather a quantity of ears of corn before they are at all dry and ripe, then the women, girls, and children detach the grains with their teeth and spit them, after a while, into large bowls that they keep near them; they finish pounding it in the large mortar. As this paste is very flabby it is absolutely necessary to wrap it in leaves to cook it under the ashes in the usual way; this chewed bread is the most esteemed among them, but for me I ate it only by necessity and against my will, because the corn has been half chewed, crushed, and kneaded with the teeth of the women, girls, and small children.

The corn bread and the sagamité which is made of it is of very good substance, and I was surprised that it nourished as well as it did. In spite of drinking only water in that country, and not eating this bread very often, and meat still more rarely, using almost nothing but sagamité with very little fish, one keeps well and in good condition, provided that one has enough of it. One never lacks in the country save only on long voyages, where one often suffers from great want.

They prepare their corn in various ways in order to eat it; for as we are inquisitive after various sauces to please our appetite, they also are careful to make their ragout in various ways, in order to enjoy it better, and the way which seems to me the most agreeable is *Neintahouy*, after that, *Eschionque*. *Neintahouy* is made in this manner: The women roast a number of ears of corn before they are quite ripe, keeping them propped up against a stick resting on two stones before the fire; they turn one side and then the other until they are sufficiently roasted, or, in order to get them done the quicker, thrust them into a heap of sand, which has first been well heated by a good fire on top of it, and take them out again; they then strip off the grains and spread these out on bark to dry still further in the sun. After it is dry enough they store it in a cask along with a third or a quarter as much of their beans, called *Ogaressa,* mixing them up with it. When they wish to eat it they boil it whole in their pot or kettle, which they call *Anoo,* with a little meat or fish, fresh or dried, if they have any. To make *Eschionque* they roast on the ashes of their hearth mixed with sand a quantity of dried corn, like peas; then they pound this maize very fine, and next, with a little fan of tree bark, they take away the fine flour, and this is *Eschionque.* This meal is eaten dry as well as cooked in a pot or else steeped in warm or cold water. When they wish to have it cooked they put it in the broth into which they have first minced and boiled some meat or fish, together with a quantity of squash, if they like, or they put enough of it into quite clear broth to make the sagamité sufficiently thick. They keep stirring it with a spatula, called by them *Estoqua,* for fear of it sticking together in lumps; immediately after it has boiled a little they pour it into the bowls with a little oil or melted fat, if they have any, on top of it. This sagamité is good and very satisfying. The hull of this flour meal, which they call *Acointa,* that is peas (for they give the same name to our peas), they boil separately in water with fish, if they have any, and then they eat it. They do the same with corn that is not crushed, but it is very hard to cook.

The ordinary sagamité, which they call *Ottet,* is raw maize made into meal, without separating either the flour or the bran; this they boil rather thin, with a little meat or fish, if they have any, and mix in it at times some squashes cut in pieces, if it is in season, and rather often nothing at all. For fear the meal will stick to the bottom of the pot they stir it often with the spatula, then eat it. This is the soup, the meat, and the daily food, and there is nothing more to expect for the repast; even when they have a little meat or fish to distribute among them (which rarely happens, except at the time of hunting or fishing) it is divided and eaten first, before the soup or sagamité.

Leindohy, or stinking corn, is a large quantity of corn, not yet dry and dead, in order to be more apt to spoil, that the women put in some pond or stinking water for the space of two or three months; at the end of this time they take it out, and it serves to make feasts of great importance; it is cooked like the

Neintahouy, and they also eat it baked under the hot ashes, licking their fingers at handling these stinking ears, just as if they were sugar cane, although the taste and smell of it is very foul, and it stinks more than do the sewers; this corn thus rotted is not my meat, however much they esteem it, nor do I handle it willingly with my fingers or hand, for the bad odor that it imparts and leaves for several days. Accordingly, they did not offer it to me after they had recognized the distaste I had for it. They also make regularly a food of acorns, which they boil in several waters to draw the bitterness from them, and I found them rather good; they eat also sometimes a certain bark of raw wood, similar to the willow, of which I ate in imitation of the Indians; but as for the grasses, they do not eat them at all, neither cooked nor raw, except certain roots that they call *Sondhratatte* and others similar.[82]

In many places, regions, islands, and countries, along the rivers and in the woods, there is a great quantity of blueberries, which the Hurons call *Ohentaqué,* and other small fruits, which they call by the general name *Hahique,* which the Indians dry for winter, as we dry prunes in the sun, for preserves for invalids, to give flavor to their sagamité, and also to put in their small loaves that they cook under the ashes. We ate a quantity of them on the road, as also strawberries, which they call *Tichionte,* with certain reddish berries as large as large peas which I found very good; but I have never seen similar ones in Canada nor in France, any more than several other kinds of small fruits and berries unknown here of which we ate as delicious dishes when we could find them. There are some red ones which appear almost like coral, that grow almost on the ground in little bunches with two or three leaves, resembling the laurel, which gives them charm; they seem like very fine bouquets and would serve for such if there were any here. There are those other berries, twice as big, as I have sometimes said, of blackish color, which grow on stems a cubit high. There are also some trees which look like the white pine, which bear little hard fruits, as large as filberts, but hardly good to eat. There are also red berries, named *Toca,* resembling our *cornioles;* but they

---

[82] Sagard, *Le Grand voyage,* pp. 135-41.

have neither stones nor kernels; the Hurons eat them raw and also put them in their rolls. . . .

As for the plums, named *Tonestes*, which are found in the country of our Hurons, they resemble our violet or red damsons, except they are not so good by far. The color deceives, and they are sour and acrid to taste, if they have not felt the frost; that is why the Indian women, after having carefully gathered them, bury them several weeks in the ground to soften them, then take them out, dry them, and eat them. But I believe that if these plums were grafted, they would lose this acridity and roughness, which renders them disagreeable to the taste before the frost.

There are pears, certain small fruits a little larger than peas, of a blackish color and soft, very good to eat by the spoonful like blueberries, which grow on small trees, which have leaves similar to the wild pear trees here, but their fruit is entirely different. Of the raspberries, blackberries, currants, and other similar fruits that we know, there are enough in places, likewise vines and grapes, of which very good wine could be made in the country of the Hurons, if they had the invention of cultivating and dressing them; but lacking greater knowledge, they are satisfied to eat the grapes and the fruit.

The roots that we call Canadians, or apples of Canada, which they call *Orasquanita*, are rather rare in the country; they eat them raw as well as cooked, likewise another sort of root, resembling parsnips, which they call *Sondhratates*, which are in truth far better; but they very seldom gave us any, and then only when they had received some present from us, or when we visited them in their cabins.[83]

The mortar in which the women crushed corn Sagard described thus:

[It is] made of a big tree trunk of maple or other hard wood, cut to measurements, two feet high, hollowed out little by little with charcoals or burning tinder which they keep on it until it is sufficiently wide and deep; they have sticks six to seven feet long and the thickness of an arm, which as pestles serve better than if they were shorter, as I have thus experimented, for it

[83] *Ibid.*, pp. 326-30.

was rather often that we had to pound our own corn in order
to live, and to treat our Frenchmen who came to see us at feasts
for the holy Mass and, seldom, to confess, except a few.[84]

The Indians continued to use their wooden mortars and
pestles long after the French came among them with substitutes for such articles of native manufacture. The French
also used the Indians' method of pounding corn, until grist
mills were built. As early as 1635 Brébeuf wrote that he
and his brother missionaries did not use the mill that they
brought with them from France because they had learned
by experience that their corn was better when pounded in a
wooden mortar than it was when ground in the mill. He
thought that the mill made the flour too fine.[85]

In times of famine, such as the Huron experienced in
1644 and 1649, they had recourse to acorns and roots, which
they did not ordinarily eat.[86] When these failed, they turned
for sustenance to tree bark, mosses, and "a sort of punk
which, being first rotted in water, becomes absorbent, and
swells out like a sponge," an edible lichen (*Umbilicaria dil-
lenii*) usually called *tripe de roche* by the French.[87]

There has been much discussion concerning aboriginal
use of maple sugar and maple syrup. I have no desire to
prolong the argument here, but simply state the facts relating to the Huron as they appear in the early documents.
The testimony of the Jesuit missionaries is that the Montagnais dwelling to the east of the Huron used the sap of
maple trees as food in time of famine.[88] The Ottawa on
Manitoulin Island were collecting maple sap in 1672.[89]
Neither of these tribes was reported to be reducing the sap
to syrup or to sugar. No record is to be found of the collection of the sap by the Huron while they were living in On-

[84] *Histoire*, p. 275.
[85] *Relation . . . . 1635, J.R.*, 8: 111.
[86] Lalemant, *Relation . . . . 1644, J.R.*, 27: 65.
[87] Ragueneau, *Relation . . . . 1650, J.R.*, 35: 175-77.
[88] Paul le Jeune, *Relation . . . . 1634, J.R.*, 6: 273.
[89] Henri Nouvel, *Relation . . . . 1671-72, J.R.*, 56: 101.

tario. Many remarks by the missionaries on the use of sugar or sweetmeats for gaining entry to Huron cabins indicate that sugar was not common. Many sick children were baptized through the ruse of giving the child sugar water. Examples of such baptisms were frequently reported[90] until opposition of the shamans arose. This was related by Le Jeune: "Within a short time Sacondouane had taken it into his head to forbid to the sick the 'French snow,'—thus they call sugar—and has persuaded some that it is a species of poison."[91]

Toward the end of the contact period the Huron were reported to be making maple sugar. An account of the procedure of the Huron in Ohio in 1756 is as follows:

In this month (February) we began to make sugar. As some of the elm bark strips at this season, the squaws after finding a tree that will do cut it down, and with a crooked stick broad and sharp at the end, took the bark off the tree, and of this bark, made vessels in a curious manner, that would hold about two gallons each: they made above one hundred of these kind of vessels. On the sugar-tree they cut a notch, sloping down, and at the end of the notch, stuck in a tomahawk; in the place where they stuck the tomahawk, they drove a long chip, in order to carry the water out from the tree, and under this they set their vessel, to receive it. As sugar trees were plenty and large here, they seldom or never notched a tree that was not two or three feet over. They also make bark vessels for carrying the water, that would hold about four gallons each. They had two brass kettles, that held about fifteen gallons each, and other smaller kettles in which they boiled the water. But as they could not at all times boil away the water as fast as it was collected, they made vessels of bark, that would hold about one hundred gallons each, for retaining the water; and tho' the sugar trees did not run every day, they had always a sufficient quantity of water to keep them boiling during the whole sugar season.[92]

[90] Le Jeune, *Relation* . . . . *1637, J.R.,* 14: 31, 41, 43, 69.

[91] *Ibid.,* p. 51.

[92] *An Account of the Remarkable Occurrences in the Life and Travels of James Smith,* pp. 36-37.

The same group of Indians were forced to use a different method the next year:

We had no large kettles with us this year, and they made the frost, in some measure, supply the place of fire, in making sugar. Their large bark vessels, for holding the stock-water, they made broad and shallow; and as the weather is very cold here, it frequently freezes at night in sugar time; and the ice they break and cast out of the vessels. I asked them if they were not throwing away the sugar? they said no; it was water they were casting away, sugar did not freeze, and there was scarcely any in the ice. . . . I observed that after several times freezing, the water that remained in the vessel, changed its colour and became brown and very sweet.[93]

SHELTER

The first account of the Huron houses was written by Champlain in 1615:

Their lodges are fashioned like bowers or arbours, covered with tree-bark, twenty-five to thirty fathoms long, more or less, and six wide, leaving in the middle a passage from ten to twelve feet wide which runs from one end to the other. On both sides is a sort of platform, four feet in height, on which they sleep in summer to escape the annoyance of fleas of which they have many, and in winter they lie beneath on mats near the fire in order to be warmer than on top of the platform. They gather a supply of dry wood and fill their cabins with it, to burn in winter, and at the end of these cabins is a space where they keep their Indian corn, which they put in great casks, made of tree-bark, in the middle of their lodge. Pieces of wood are suspended on which they put their clothes, provisions and other things for fear of mice which are in great numbers. In one such cabin there will be twelve fires, which make twenty-four households, and there is smoke in good earnest, causing many to have eye troubles, to which they are subject, even towards the end of their lives losing their sight; for there is no window nor opening except in the roof of their cabins by which the smoke can es-

[93] *Ibid.*, p. 69.

cape. . . . This is the shape of their dwellings, which are separated from one another about three to four yards for fear of fire which they greatly dread.[94]

Sagard gave a description very similar to that by Champlain, in fact it was identical in all of the dimensions noted, in the location of platforms, in their uses, and in the general layout of the cabin, which was called *Ganonchia* by the Huron. The latter part of his account includes other material:

At each end there is a porch, and these porches serve them principally for holding their vats and tuns of bark, in which they store the corn, after it is very dry and shelled. In the middle of their lodging there are two thick poles suspended, called *Ouaronta*, where they hang their pot hanger and put their clothes, provisions, and other things away from mice and to keep them dry. As for the fish of which they make provision for winter, after it is smoked they store it in bark vats called *Acha*, except *Leinchataon*, a fish that they do not cut open, which they hang at the top of their cabins with small cords, because closed in a vat it would smell too badly and would get rotten at once.

For fear of fire, to which they are subject, they often put whatever they have that is most precious into vats and bury them in deep holes dug in their cabins and then cover them with the same earth; this gives protection not only from fire but also from the hands of thieves, for they have no other chest nor closet in all their household but these little casks.[95]

The length of the cabins as given by Brébeuf in 1635 varied from two to forty *brasses*, although the width was usually about four *brasses*. A *brasse* was the equivalent of five old French feet or 5.318 English feet. He added nothing else to the information given by Champlain and Sagard, except that the cabins were covered with the bark of ash, elm, fir, spruce, or cedar, the last of which was the best and the most used, although it was very inflammable and often caused a

[94] *Voyages*, 3: 122-25.
[95] *Le Grand voyage*, pp. 120-21.

conflagration destroying entire villages; that the usual height of the cabins was twenty-four feet; and that the Huron called the benches at the sides of the cabins *Endicha*.[96]

Brébeuf said that each village had a least one cabin that was purposely made larger than the others as a place for holding feasts and entertaining visitors.[97] Two such large cabins seem to be indicated in the following description by Le Mercier of the torturing of a captive:

It was in the cabin of one Atsan, who is the great war Captain; therefore it is called "Otinontsikiaj ondaon," meaning, "the house of cut-off heads." It is there all the Councils of war are held; as to the house where the affairs of the country, and those which relate only to the observance of order, are transacted, it is called, "Endionrra ondaon," "the house of the Council." We took, then, a place where we could be near the victim, and say an encouraging word to him when the opportunity occurred. Towards 8 o'clock in the evening eleven fires were lighted along the cabin, about one brass distant from each other. The people gathered immediately, the old men taking places above, upon a sort of platform, which extends on both sides the entire length of the cabins.[98]

According to Du Peron, the ordinary cabin had five fire-places, at each of which there were two families.[99] The doors of the cabin were closed with rush mats.[100]

As to the construction of the cabins, there is only the description by Cadillac of the dwellings of the Ottawa and Huron at Mackinac, written toward the end of the seventeenth century:

They drive poles as thick as one's leg and very long into the ground, and join them to one another by making them curve and bend over at the top, and then by fastening them together with whitewood bark, which they use in the same way as we do

[96] Brébeuf, *Relation* . . . . *1635, J.R.*, 8: 107-9.

[97] *Relation* . . . . *1636, J.R.*, 10: 181.

[98] *Relation* . . . . *1637, J.R.*, 13: 59-61.

[99] "Letter from François du Peron," *J.R.*, 15: 153.

[100] Sagard, *Le Grand voyage*, p. 131.

our thread and cordage. They then entwine with these large poles, crosspieces as thick as one's arm, and cover them from top to bottom with the bark of fir trees or cedars, which they fasten to the poles and the cross branches; they leave an opening about two feet wide at the ridge, which runs from one end to the other. It is certain that their huts are weatherproof, and no rain whatever gets into them; they are generally 100 to 130 feet long by 24 feet wide and 20 feet high. There is an upper floor on both sides, and each family has its little apartment. There is also a door at each end. Their streets are regular like those of our villages.[101]

The furniture of the Huron cabins was very scanty. Brébeuf wrote: "They sleep beside the fire, but still they and we have only the earth for bedstead; for mattress and pillows, some bark or boughs covered with a rush mat."[102]

The fires were kept small and bright, using little wood. That the problem of providing firewood was an important one is indicated by the donation of it to brides on their marriage. Sagard said that it was almost a continuous occupation with the Huron women to provide a proper supply, for they used only very good wood. Dead trees were preferred; but lacking them, they cut down trees whose branches were dry. The trunks of the trees were not used until dry and rotten, when they could be easily broken. These preferences entailed long trips to obtain wood and, eventually, a change in the location of the village, but they were necessary in order to provide the cabin with a fire which threw off a minimum of smoke.[103]

For light, aside from that of the fires, torches made of little horn-shaped rolls of birchbark were used.[104]

The drought which afflicted the Hurons in 1636 was said by a shaman to be caused by the red color of the cross which Brébeuf had erected outside his cabin. The shaman told

---

[101] MS "Relation on the Indians."

[102] Relation . . . . 1635, J.R., 8: 109.

[103] Le Grand voyage, pp. 119-20.

[104] Ibid., p. 101; Lalemant, Relation . . . . 1641, J.R., 21: 247.

the elders of the village that it would have to come down, and when they relayed the information to the missionary he replied: "And then what does the thunder fear? This red color of the Cross? Take away then, yourselves, all those red figures and paintings that are on your cabins."[105] Brébeuf did not explain these paintings on the outside of the cabins, but they were undoubtedly totemic designations, indicating the clan affiliations of the occupants.

The border villages in particular, according to Sagard, were protected by walled enclosures:

Strong wooden palisades in three rows, interlaced into one another and lined inside with great and thick barks to the height of eight or nine feet; underneath, there are large trees placed lengthwise in strong short forks of tree trunks. On top of these palisades there are galleries or watch towers which they call *Ondaqua*, that they fill with stones in war time, to fling on the enemy, and with water to extinguish the fire that could be set to their palisades; our Hurons mount there by a ladder rather poorly worked and difficult to climb and defend their ramparts with a great deal of courage and skill.[106]

He also stated that the Huron picked sites easy to defend on which to build their villages, sites near a good stream, on a slightly raised place, and surrounded by a natural moat if possible. The gates into the enclosure were closed by bars and were so arranged that one had to pass them sidewise. The enclosure was circular, and the cabins were placed compactly in the center, in order to leave an empty space between them and the walls for the convenience of the warriors in defending the village.[107]

The height of the walls, as given by observers, varied, probably because of the location and natural protection or the distance from the enemy. Champlain said thirty-five feet was the height of the palisade around the village of Carha-

[105] *J.R.*, 10: 47.
[106] *Le Grand voyage*, pp. 115-16.
[107] *Ibid.*, pp. 116-17.

gouha;[108] Ragueneau placed the height of the stockade at fifteen to sixteen feet on a site naturally strongly fortified.[109]

In describing the fortifications of the Huron and Ottawa villages at Mackinac about 1695, Cadillac spoke as if both tribes made them in the same manner:

Their forts are made of stakes. Those in the first row, on the outside, are as thick as a man's thigh and about thirty feet high; the second row, inside, is quite a foot from the first, which is bent over on to it, and is to support and prop it up, the third row is four feet from the second, and consists of stakes three and one-half feet in diameter standing fifteen or sixteen feet out of the ground. Now, in that row they leave no space at all between the stakes; on the contrary, they set them as close together as they can, making loopholes at intervals. As to the first two rows, there is a space of about six inches between the stakes, and thus the first and second rows do not prevent them from seeing the enemy; but there are no curtains nor bastions, and the fort is, strictly speaking, only an enclosure.[110]

The Huron fort at Detroit, in 1718, according to Sabrevois, was an enclosure with a double row of palisades, with gates and bastions.[111] The gates and bastions were unquestionably the result of European influence, as all previous accounts definitely denied their existence.

The cabins built for temporary use by the Huron were described by Claude le Beau:

This cabin was soon made, as well as those we built afterwards. The shape rather resembled the sheds or shops of our foreign merchants, which are open in front. To build this kind of cabin, the savages simply set up some stakes with sticks across, on which they put tree bark, stripped off in the following fashion. First, they make notches in the trees as high as they can reach with their axes. Then they make a perpendicular slit, that is to say, from these notches to the foot of the tree, and at

---

[108] *Voyages*, 3:48.
[109] *J.R.*, 34:123-25.
[110] MS "Relation on the Indians."
[111] *Memoir, WHC.*, 16:368.

one end push in a stick in the form of a spatula, with which they raised the bark without damaging it; afterward, they build their cabins with it, to shelter them from the inclemency of the weather. They always turn the back of the cabin to the wind, because the front is entirely open, and they put their feet to the fire, which is made opposite—it would be an annoyance otherwise. I speak only of the cabins they make when they are traveling or on a hunting trip.[112]

Trade

The Huron engaged in trade within the several divisions of the tribe, such as the Huron proper with the Tobacco Nation and the Neutrals, and with the neighboring Algonquian tribes with whom they were at peace. The articles traded were corn, wampum, and fish nets, for which they received meat and the skins of deer and beaver.[113] This was in 1615, before the trade of furs to the French had become very well established. Annual trading trips to Quebec and Three Rivers were customary. In 1634 the Huron were reported carrying corn and tobacco to those places to trade with the Montagnais for moose skins.[114]

Writing after the disruption of the Huron, Boucher in 1663 said that the Huron traded with other Indian tribes to a great extent and almost all over the country.[115] Even in the eighteenth century they maintained their position as traders of corn.[116]

Originally, there were rules governing the conduct of trade, the number and identity of those who could engage in it at any one time, and so forth. Of these laws Brébeuf wrote:

Besides having some kind of Laws maintained among themselves, there is also a certain order established as regards foreign Nations. And first, concerning commerce: several families have

---

[112] *Avantures*, 1: 155-56.
[113] Champlain, *Voyages*, 3: 131.
[114] Le Jeune, *Relation* . . . . *1634, J.R.*, 6: 273.
[115] *Histoire véritable*, p. 101.
[116] Raudot, "Memoir," Letter 72.

their own private trades, and he is considered Master of one line of trade who was the first to discover it. The children share the rights of their parents in this respect, as do those who bear the same name; no one goes into it without permission, which is given only in consideration of presents; he associates with him as many or as few as he wishes. If he has a good supply of merchandise, it is to his advantage to divide it with few companions, for thus he secures all that he desires, in the Country; it is in this that most of their riches consist. But if any one should be bold enough to engage in a trade without permission from him who is Master, he may do a good business in secret and concealment; but, if he is surprised by the way, he will not be better treated than a thief—he will only carry back his body to his house, or else he must be well accompanied. If he returns with his baggage safe, there will be some complaint about it, but no further prosecution.[117]

These rules about the monopoly of trade applied to nations as well as to individuals. Lalemant reported in 1640 that the Arendaronon, who were one of the four nations comprising the Huron proper, being the most easterly situated, had met the French first and so possessed the sole right to trade with them. They did not choose to enjoy this trade alone, but shared it with the other nations, retaining for themselves more especially the character of allies of the French.[118]

Manufactures

Large casks for the storage of corn were made of bark, as was stated in the descriptions of their shelter and of their preservation of food. Brébeuf reported a Huron having two of them, each of which held one hundred to one hundred and twenty bushels of corn.[119] According to Sagard, the women also made baskets of rushes for this purpose, and bowls of bark for drinking and eating and to use as dippers.[120]

[117] *Relation* .... *1636*, J.R., 10: 223-25.
[118] *Relation* .... *1640*, J.R., 20: 19.
[119] *Relation* .... *1635*, J.R., 8: 95.
[120] *Le Grand voyage*, p. 132.

Boucher said that wooden dishes and spoons were made by the men.[121] The latter also stated that the women made earthen vessels and a number of small articles adapted to their uses, which he did not describe because they were unknown in France.[122] The only description of the pottery of the Huron and of its manufacture was written by Sagard and is not as detailed as one would like:

But as for our Huron and other peoples and sedentary nations, they had (as they still have) the usage and the skill of making earthen pots, that they bake on their hearth; these are very good and never break in the fire, even though there is no water in them; but yet they cannot withstand humidity or cold water for long without softening and breaking at the least blow that is given them, otherwise they last a very long time. The Indian women make them, taking suitable earth, which they clean and knead very well, mixing in it a little sandstone, then the mass being reduced to a ball, they make a hole in it with the fist, which they enlarge continuously while beating it inside with a little wooden paddle, as much and as long as is necessary to complete them; these pots are made without feet and without handles and are entirely round like a ball, except the mouth which projects out a little.[123]

Mats to sit or lie upon and also to cover the doorways were made of rushes,[124] and, as was mentioned above, baskets were made of the same material. Other textile work included scarfs, collars, and bracelets, which both the men and women wore. These were made by the latter. The nets and snares were made from nettles or Indian hemp. The manufacture of them is briefly covered by Sagard:

[121] *Histoire véritable*, p. 101. Sagard also indicated that the men made bowls of knots of wood, using beaver incisors to polish them. *Le Grand voyage*, p. 322.

[122] Boucher, *Histoire véritable*, p. 101.

[123] *Le Grand voyage*, pp. 142-43.

[124] *Ibid.*, p. 132. In his *Histoire*, Sagard revised his information a bit. He wrote: "At the end of fall they make mats of reeds and of corn leaves (husks), with which they cover the doors of their cabins to protect themselves from the cold, and others are used to sit on, all very neatly made." He stated further that the Ottawa colored their mats, implying that those of the Huron were plain. *Histoire*, p. 276.

In marshy and humid places there grows a plant named *Anonhasquara,* which makes very good hemp; the Indian women gather and pluck it in season and prepare it as we do ours, without my being able to learn who gave them the invention of it other than necessity, mother of inventions. After it is prepared they spin it on their thighs, as I have said; then the men make snares and fishing nets of it. They use it also for various other things, but not to make cloth, for they have not the use nor the knowledge of that.[125]

Boucher wrote that the Huron and Iroquois used this hemp to make sacks, nets, necklaces, and armor;[126] but there is no other mention of such armor among the Huron.

Skins were dressed by the women. The principal ones used were those of deer, beaver, and moose. Besides the clothing and moccasins that were made of skins, there were undoubtedly many little articles of the same material. One such was the tobacco pouch, which Sagard said was decorated with porcupine quills colored red, black, white, and blue; he added that these colors were much more vivid than any used by the French.[127]

Weapons of war and hunting were, of course, made by the men. Of the bow and how it might differ from that of other tribes there is no information. The bow string was made of the intestines or tendons of animals. The arrows were said to be very long and straight, tipped with stone or bone, and after the arrival of the French, with iron. The point was fastened on with fish glue, and doubtless the same glue was used to fasten the wing or tail feathers of the eagle to the stem.[128] Knives and the points of short spears were made of stone.[129] War clubs were carved out of wood. Large shields, which almost wholly covered their bodies, were made of cedar, and smaller ones were made of boiled leather.[130]

[125] *Le Grand voyage,* p. 332.
[126] *Histoire véritable,* pp. 34-35.
[127] *Le Grand voyage,* p. 132.
[128] *Ibid.,* pp. 125-26.
[129] Champlain, *Voyages,* 3: 61.
[130] Sagard, *Histoire,* pp. 259-60.

The only musical instrument described in the documents relating to the Hurons is the rattle, called *astaouen* in Huron. This term was applied, according to Joseph Lafitau,[131] to the rattle, whether it was made of a gourd or the shell of a turtle. The latter type was made by drying a turtle and emptying the shell without damaging the head, the tail, the legs, and the skin which joined the two shells. Some beads or pebbles were then placed inside, and a stick was pushed through the shell into the skin of the neck to serve as a handle. In 1639 Lalemant reported that there was something in the semblance of a turtle to which the Huron attributed their origin, but that he did not know what it was.[132] This was a reference to the myth of a turtle supporting the world on its back.

Transportation

For transportation of baggage and firewood the Huron depended upon their own backs when the loads were carried on land in summer, the load being fastened with a band over the forehead. Such goods were transported in winter on sledges (*arocha*)[133] made of long planks of white cedar.

Snowshoes were used by both men and women, but were made by the men. Sagard reported that they were laced with intestines and were two or three times as big as the tennis rackets of the French.[134] Snowshoes and birchbark canoes appealed to Bressani's imagination as solving the problems of journeying and navigation so well that he said that Europeans could not have devised better ways and hence the Huron were hardly barbarians, save in name.[135]

Birchbark canoes were the only vehicles which the Huron used upon the rivers and lakes. In the manufacture and use of these canoes, they differed from their kindred, the Iroquois, who made canoes principally of elm bark. Whether or not the

---

[131] *Moeurs des sauvages ameriquains*, pp. 215-16.
[132] *J.R.*, 17: 157.
[133] Sagard, *Le Grand voyage*, p. 117.
[134] *Ibid.*, pp. 104, 126.
[135] *Breve relatione*, *J.R.*, 38: 257.

birchbark canoe was a feature borrowed from their Algonquin neighbors, it is impossible to tell; but at any rate such borrowing, if it occurred, took place before the first white contact, for the Huron had these canoes in the time of Champlain and Sagard:

Their canoes are eight to nine paces in length, about a pace and a half in width at the middle, and diminish toward the two ends, as a weaver's shuttle; those are the largest that they make; they have others smaller, which they use according to the occasion and the difficulty of the voyages they have to make. They turn over very easily if one does not know how to handle them well, being made of birchbark, re-enforced inside with little circles of white cedar, very exactly arranged; they are so light that one man carries one of them easily on his head, or on his shoulders. Each can carry the weight of a "pipe," and more or less, according to its size. Also one can usually make each day, in a hurry, twenty-five to thirty leagues in the said canoes, providing there are no falls to pass and that one sails with the wind and the current, for they go with so great swiftness and lightness that I was astonished, and I do not think, when they are conducted by good rowers, that the post could go faster.[136]

Claude le Beau traveled with two Huron men, probably from Lorette, through the rivers of eastern Canada in 1738 and wrote the only other description of canoes that can be definitely attributed to the Huron:

The canoes are made of birchbark and can pass as the masterpiece of the art of savages. Nothing is prettier or more admirable than these fragile machines with which, however, they carry immense loads whose weight does not prevent great speed. They are of different sizes of two, four, and up to ten places, distinguished by the crosspieces. Each place must accommodate easily two paddlers, except the ends, which can only accommodate one. The bottom of the canoe is only of one or two pieces of bark to which they sew others with the root that they gum inside and out, so that they appear to be of one piece. As the bark of which the bottom is made is scarcely thicker than

---

[136] *Le Grand voyage*, pp. 129-30.

an ecu, they re-enforce it inside by laths of very thin cedar, which are placed lengthwise of the canoe, and by small floor timbers of the same wood and of the thickness of one or two ecus, placed close together the way of the curve of the canoes from one end to the other. In addition, the edges of the sides, in which these floor timbers are set and fastened and where the crosspieces which serve to strengthen the entire work are attached, are thickened by hoops, much as would be those of our casks. There is neither stern nor prow. The two ends are identical, for they attach no rudder, and, in case it is a question of returning over the same way, he who is last at one end can become first by only turning around without changing places. The paddles are very light, although made of a maple wood which is rather hard. They are scarcely four feet long; the blade takes up one and one-half feet and is five or six inches wide.[137]

He added that, having to navigate the St. Lawrence and other rivers with rapids, the Ottawa and other nations of the upper country made their canoes so that the sides and ends were much higher than were those of the tribes of the eastern part of Canada, such as the Abenaki, who used canoes only on small streams where overhanging branches of bordering trees would break the canoes if they were not very flat.[138] Le Beau also wrote of a board two and one-half feet long by ten inches wide which one of his Huron companions attached to the middle of one of the crosspieces to aid him in carrying the canoe on a portage. With his back against this board and his hands on one of the crosspieces in front of it, he could tip the canoe either up or down in ascending or descending a slope, and he could also find his way better through the woods.[139] There is no other mention of this method of carrying the canoe on a portage being used by the Huron or any other tribe.

In speaking of the Huron, Ottawa, Potawatomi, and Missasauga, Sabrevois in 1718 wrote that all of these nations

[137] *Avantures*, 1: 94-96.
[138] *Ibid.*, pp. 98-99.
[139] *Ibid.*, p. 152.

made a great many bark canoes, which was a very profitable enterprise for them. The canoes were made in the summer. The men cut and shaped the bark and made the gunwales, crosspieces, and ribs, after which the women sewed the pieces of bark with roots and gummed them.[140] The texts of Sagard, Bressani, and Boucher would indicate that the men performed all the work in the manufacture of canoes.

Many of the later accounts mention the use of sails of very thin bark, which were erected to aid in the navigation of canoes when traveling with the wind. There is no definite evidence that such sails were used by the Huron, and since most of their voyages were upon rivers, it is not likely that they could have been used to much advantage.

Fire Making

As with many other features, the most complete account of fire making is to be found in Sagard:

The invention that they have for starting fire, which is practiced by all the savage people, is the following: they take two sticks, of willow, bass, or other kind of dry light wood and cut one about the length of a cubit or a little less and about the thickness of a finger; there is a little hole with a small notch beside it on the edge of its side, hollowed out by a knife point or beaver tooth, in order that the powder converted into fire, in falling from the hole, will fall down on some tinder or something suitable for catching fire. They put the point of another stick of the same wood, the size of a little finger or a little smaller, into the hole thus started, and being on the ground with one knee on the end of the wide stick they turn the other between their hands so quickly and so long that the two woods being well heated the powder that comes out because of this continuous movement is converted into fire, from which they light one end of their dry cord, which keeps the fire as the match of an arquebuse; afterward with a little thin dry wood they build the fire to heat the kettle. However, it must be noted that all woods are not fit to make fire, but particular ones which the

[140] Sabrevois, *Memoir*, *WHC.*, 16: 370.

Indians know how to select. When they had trouble getting fire, they chopped up a little charcoal or a little dry powdered wood that they took from some stump. If they did not have a wide stick, as I said, they took two round ones, tied together at the two ends, and being down on one knee to hold them, they put between them the point of another stick of this wood, made in the fashion of a weaver's shuttle and turned it by the other end between their hands, as I have said.[141]

SOCIAL LIFE

Political Organization

Of all the visitors among the Huron in the first part of the contact period, probably no one became so well acquainted with the political system as did Brébeuf. Of the duties, responsibilities, and compensation of the chiefs at the head of the social order, and how they conducted their councils, he wrote the following account:

As regards the authority of commanding, here is what I have observed. All the affairs of the Huron are included under two heads: the first are, as it were, affairs of State—whatever may concern either citizens or strangers, the public or the individual of the Village; as, for example, feasts, dances, games, crosse matches, and funeral ceremonies. The second are affairs of war. Now there are as many sorts of Captains as of affairs. In the large Villages there will be sometimes several Captains, both of administration and war, who divide among them the families of the Village as into so many Captaincies. Occasionally, too, there are even Captains to whom these matters of government are referred on account of their intellectual superiority, popularity, wealth, or other qualities which render them influential in the Country. There are none who, by virtue of their election, are of higher rank than others. Those hold the first rank who have acquired it by intellectual pre-eminence, eloquence, free expenditure, courage, and wise conduct. Consequently, the affairs of the Village are referred principally to that one of the Chiefs who has these qualifications; and the same is true with regard to the affairs of the whole Country, in which

[141] *Le Grand voyage*, pp. 69-70.

the men of greatest ability are the leading Captains, and usually
there is one only who bears the burden of all; it is in his name
Treaties of Peace are made with foreign Peoples; the Country
even bears his name—and now, for example, when one speaks of
Anenkhiondic in the Councils of Foreigners, the Nation of the
Bear is meant. Formerly only worthy men were Captains, and
so they were called *Enondecha,* the same name by which they
call the Country, Nation, district—as if a good chief and the
Country were one and the same thing. But today they do not
pay so much attention to the selection of their Captains; and so
they no longer give them that name, although they still call
them *atiwarontas, atiwanens, ondakhienhai,* "big stones, the
elders, the stay-at-homes." However, those still hold, as I have
said, the first rank as well in the special affairs of the Villages
as in those of the whole Country, who are most highly esteemed
and intellectually pre-eminent. Their relatives are like so many
Lieutenants and Councilors.

They reach this degree of honor, partly through succession,
partly through election; their children do not usually succeed
them, but properly their nephews and grandsons. And the latter
do not even come to the succession of these petty Royalties, like
the Dauphins of France, or children to the inheritance of their
fathers; but only in so far as they have suitable qualifications,
and accept the position, and are accepted by the whole Country.
Some are found who refuse these honors—sometimes because
they have not aptitude in speaking, or sufficient discretion or
patience, sometimes because they like a quiet life; for these
positions are servitudes more than anything else. A Captain must
always make it a point to be, as it were, in the field; if a Council is held five or six leagues away for the affairs of the Country,
Winter or Summer, whatever the weather, he must go. If there
is an Assembly in the Village, it is in the Captain's Cabin; if
there is anything to be made public, he must do it; and then the
small authority he usually has over his subjects is not a powerful
attraction to make him accept this position. These Captains do
not govern their subjects by means of command and absolute
power; they have no force at hand to compel them to their duty.
Their government is only civil; they represent only what is to
be done for the good of the village, or of the whole Country.

That settled, he who will takes action. There are, however, some who know well how to secure obedience, especially when they have the affection of their subjects. Some, too, are kept back from these positions by the memory of their ancestors who have badly served their Country. But, if they are received therein, it is by dint of presents which the Old Men accept in their Assembly and put into the Public coffers. Every year, about Spring, these resurrections of Captains take place, if some special cases do not delay or hasten the matter.[142]

The usual wages of these Gentlemen are assigned according to the strength of their arms, to their zeal and good management. If they clear the ground better than the others, hunt better, fish better—in short, if they are successful in trading, they are also richer than the others; but if not, they are the most necessitous, as experience has shown in some instances.

The incidental advantages are, in the first place, the best portions of the feasts, to which they are sure to be invited. 2. When any one makes a present, they get the best part of it. 3. When some one, be he Citizen or Stranger, wishes to obtain something from the Country, the custom is to grease the palms of the principal Captains, at whose beck and call all the rest move. I am quite sure of what I have just said. The regret that some private individuals have for such irregularities, and the envy of the other Captains who have not been called upon to share the booty, discourage the practice more than they like; they decry one another, and the mere suspicion of these secret presents stirs up sometimes great debates and divisions—not so much through desire of the public good as from regret at not having a share in them; and this jealousy hinders good measures.[143]

I shall speak of the general Councils or Assemblies, the special ones being ordered in almost the same way, although with less display.

These general Assemblies are, as it were, the States-General of the Country, and consequently they take place only so often as necessity requires. The place of these is usually the Village of the principal Captain of the whole Country. The Council Chamber is sometimes the Cabin of this Captain, adorned with

[142] Brébeuf, *Relation* . . . . *1636*, J.R., 10: 229-35.
[143] *Ibid.*, p. 253.

mats, or strewn with Fir branches, with several fires, according to the season of the year. Formerly, each one brought his fagot to put on the fire; this is now no longer the custom, the women of the Cabin take this responsibility; they make the fires, but do not warm themselves thereat, going outside to give place to Messieurs the Councilors. Sometimes the assembly takes place in the midst of the Village, if it is in Summer; and sometimes also in the obscurity of the forest, apart, when affairs demand secrecy. The time is oftener night than day, whole nights often being passed in Council.

The Head of the Council is the Captain who calls it. Matters are decided by a plurality of votes, in which the authority of the Captains draws over many to their views; in fact, the usual way of coming to a decision is to say to the Old Men, Do you give advice; you are the Masters. . . .

In the first place, the Captain, having already consulted in private with the other Captains and Old Men of his Village, and having concluded that the affair warrants a public assembly, sends invitations to the Council, to as many persons of each Village as he desires. The Messengers are young men who volunteer or sometimes an Old Man, in order that the summons may be more efficacious, inasmuch as they do not always put faith in young people. These Messengers address their errand to the principal Captain of the Village, or, in his absence, to the one who is nearest him in authority, stating the day on which they are to assemble. These summons are entreaties, not commands, and accordingly some excuse themselves entirely, others delay setting out; whence it happens that these assemblies are sometimes tedious, for they do not like to set out in bad weather, and certainly they have enough difficulty in sometimes coming ten or twelve leagues on foot, and this in Winter and over the snow.

All having arrived, they take their seats each in his own quarter of the Cabin, those of the same Village or of the same Nation near one another, in order to consult together. If by chance some one is absent, the question is raised whether, notwithstanding this, the assembly would be legitimate; and sometimes, from the absence of one or two persons, the whole gathering is dissolved, and adjourns until another time. But if all are gathered, or if, notwithstanding, they think it their duty to go on, the Council is opened. It is not always the Leaders of the Council who do this; difficulty in speaking, unwillingness, or even their dignity dispenses them from it.

After salutations, thanks for the trouble taken in coming, thanksgiving rendered, I know not to whom, that every one has arrived without accident, that no one has been surprised by enemies, nor has fallen into any stream or River, nor has been injured—in brief, that every one has arrived happily, all are exhorted to deliberate maturely. Then the affair to be discussed is brought forward, and Messieurs the Councilors are asked to give their advice.

At this point the Deputies of each Village, or those of one Nation, consult in a low tone as to what they will reply. Then, when they have consulted well together, they give their opinions in order, and decide according to the plurality of opinions, in which course there are some things worthy of remark. The first is in the manner of speaking, which, on account of its unlikeness (to common speech), has a different name and is called *acwentonch*; it is common to all Savages; they raise and quaver the voice, like the tones of a Preacher in olden times, but slowly, decidedly, distinctly, even repeating the same reason several times. The second remarkable thing is that the persons giving their opinions go summarily over the proposition and all the considerations brought forward, before giving their advice. . . . 3. After some one has given his opinion the Head of the Council repeats, or causes to be repeated, what he has said; consequently, matters must be clearly understood, so often are they repeated. 4. Each one ends his advice in these terms, *Condayauendi Ierhayde cha nonhwicwahachen:* that is to say, "That is my thought on the subject under Discussion"; then the whole Assembly responds with a very strong respiration drawn from the pit of the stomach, *Haau.* I have noticed that when any one has spoken to their liking, this *Haau* is given forth with much more effort.

The fifth remarkable thing is their great prudence and moderation of speech; I would not dare to say they always use this self-restraint, for I know that sometimes they sting each other—but yet you always remark a singular gentleness and discretion. I have scarcely ever been present at their Councils; but, every time I have been invited, I have come out from them astonished at this feature.

One day I saw a debate for precedence between two war Captains; An Old Man who espoused the side of one, said that he was on the edge of the grave, and that perhaps on the morrow his body would be placed in the Cemetery; but yet he would say frankly what he believed to be justice, not for any interest he had in the matter, but from a love of truth: which he did with ardor, though seasoned with discretion. Then another Old Man, beginning to speak, replied to him and said, very properly: "Do not speak now of those things, this is not the time for them; see the enemy, who is going to attack us; the question is one of arming ourselves and fortifying with one mind our palisades, and not of disputing about rank." I was particularly astonished at the wise conduct of the Council, at which I was present, which seemed to be steeped in a condescending humor and fine words, notwithstanding the importance of the questions discussed.

This Council was one of the most important that the Huron have: to wit, concerning their feast of the Dead: they have nothing more sacred. The question was a delicate one, for the matter discussed was whether the whole Country should put their dead in the same grave, according to their custom; and yet there were some discontented Villages, who wished to remain apart, not without the regret of the whole Country. Yet the thing passed over with all the gentleness and peace imaginable; at every turn the Masters of the Feast, who had assembled the Council, exhorted to gentleness, saying that it was a Council of peace. They call these Councils, *Endionraondaone,* as if one should say, "A Council even and easy, like the level and reaped fields." Whatever the speakers say, the Leaders of the Council always say only this, "That is very well." The mutinous persons excused their division, saying that no evil could arise therefrom to the Country; that in the past there had been similar divisions, which had not ruined it. The others softened matters, saying that if one of their friends went astray from the true road, they must not immediately abandon him; that brothers sometimes had quarrels with each other. In short, it was a matter for great astonishment to see in these embittered hearts such moderation of words. So much for their Councils.[144]

Sagard said that the Huron country was divided into several provinces—on what basis he did not report—and that there was one chief in command over each province. He gave the names of three provinces and their chiefs as: *Enarhonon*, under command of Atironto; *Atigagnongueha*, under Entauaque; and *Atingyahointan*, under Auoindaon.[145] These were the Rock, Cord, and Bear people in that order. Later writers added a fourth important tribe of the Huron proper, the *Tohontaenrat* or Deer people. Each of these head chiefs considered himself master of his province and allowed no one to pass through without obtaining his permission, which was usually won without difficulty by giving him some present.[146]

The Bear and Cord people were the two most important groups, having received the others into their country. According to Lalemant they spoke of the different sites of their ancestors for more than two hundred years back and termed each other "brother" and "sister."[147] In 1638 Brébeuf reported that the Bear Nation comprised fourteen villages, large and small, and the Rock and Cord people each numbered four very populous villages.[148]

Sagard's account of the chiefs and their place in the government does not differ materially from that of Brébeuf. Sagard stated that the great chief of the province was called *Garihoùa andionxra*, to distinguish him from the ordinary chiefs of war, whom they called *Garihoùa doutaguéta*. Apparently, the great chief was ordinarily superior in authority to all other chiefs, of whom there were many, both civil and military, scattered among all the villages in varied numbers,

[144] *Ibid.*, pp. 251-63.
[145] *Le Grand voyage*, p. 115.
[146] *Ibid.*, p. 127.
[147] *Relation* .... *1639*, J.R., 16: 227-29.
[148] *Relation* .... *1638*, J.R., 15: 39.

according to the population. The great chief had an assistant or lieutenant, who made the announcements of meetings or news. The great chief called the councils, although this might be done at the request of some of the lesser chiefs or of other individuals. A council was attended by the great chief, the minor chiefs, and the elders of the village or the province, depending on the scope of the object for which it was called. The women and girls never attended, and the young men of twenty-five or thirty years only if it were a general council, in which event they were informed by a particular cry. These general assemblies were held annually and were attended by representatives of all the parts of the nation. Feasts and dances were numerous, and presents were interchanged. The general object seems to have been to acquaint themselves with what was transpiring in the different parts of the country, to renew friendships, and to advise among themselves what should be done for their mutual preservation from their common enemy.[149]

The fear of their enemy, the Iroquois, was also manifest in the special councils held every year to determine the number of men who could absent themselves for purposes of trade or war, without leaving the village stripped of warriors for its defense. Others in excess of such number were not forcibly prevented from leaving, but were condemned and regarded as foolish and imprudent.[150]

The Tionontati or Tobacco Huron and the Neutrals seem to have had substantially the same system as that described by Sagard and Brébeuf, although Dallion reported that Souharissen, who was the chief among the Neutrals in 1627, was an exception. This man, he said, had more credit and authority than any other chief had ever had in all these nations; he was chief not only of his village, but of all his nation, which was composed of twenty-eight towns, cities, and villages, like those in the Huron country, and also of several

[149] *Le Grand voyage*, pp. 196-200.
[150] *Ibid.*, pp. 126-27.

little hamlets of seven or eight cabins, built in sundry places convenient for fishing, hunting, or agriculture. Further, it was unexampled in the other nations to have so absolute a chief; he had acquired this honor and power by his courage and by having been at war repeatedly with seventeen enemy nations, from all of which he had taken prisoners or heads.[151] Thus, even under the democratic form of government of the Indians, the accumulation of all the power exercised by a chief was dependent upon the reputed merit of the individual. If he were strong enough it was possible for him, at least among the Neutrals, to become the leader of the entire nation.

The general name of the Rock, Cord, Bear, and Deer peoples, in their own language, was Wendat.[152] This applied to these four tribes and possibly also to the Huron known as the Tobacco Nation, although it is usually very difficult to tell just what the term Huron covered at any one time. In later times the Tobacco Huron became known as the Wendat or Wyandot, which they claimed as their name, although they said that they were not Huron and laid no claim to that name.

Many of the early writers mentioned the inheritance of the possessions and position of a chief by his sister's son rather than by his own. These writers attributed this system of inheritance to the known infidelity of the women and to the fact that a man could be sure that his sister's son was related to him, whereas he could not be certain that his wife's children were related to him by blood.[153] Actually, this line of inheritance indicates the existence of clans and exogamy. Membership in a clan was inherited from the mother, and a man's children belonged to his wife's clan rather than to his own, whereas he and his sister's children belonged to the same

[151] Dallion *in* Le Clercq, *First Establishment of the Faith in New France*, 1: 265-66.

[152] Lalemant, *Relation* .... *1639*, J.R., 16: 227.

[153] Le Jeune, *Relation* .... *1634*, J.R., 6: 255.

clan. Obviously, the chieftainship of a clan could not be passed on to a son who belonged to another clan.

Data regarding the clans of the Huron proper are very scarce. Designations such as the Bear nation and the Deer people may have referred to clans, but it is difficult at this time to tell, since these divisions were wiped out, along with the political independence of the Huron, in 1648. Concerning conditions among the Tobacco Nation or the Tobacco Huron, the situation is not much better. Ragueneau wrote in 1648 that this tribe was "divided in two different Nations which occupy the whole of that country—one called the Nation of the Wolves, . . . the other . . . the Nation of the Deer."[154] In 1679 the Huron at Mackinac, according to Enjalran, were divided into three different "nations."[155] The term "nation" was frequently misused by the writers of the contact period, and here one cannot tell whether Enjalran was referring to three clans or to the three divisions of the Huron of which this village was composed, the Huron proper, the Neutrals, and the Tionontati or Tobacco Nation. The last of these was the most numerous of the three, and often the whole village was called that name rather than Huron. Pachot reported in 1719 that the Huron were divided into three families: the roebuck, the turtle, and the wolf; the first family, he said, was that of the roebuck, the other two treating each other as cousins and calling the family of the roebuck their brother. The chief of the family of the roebuck was called *astarensay*, and it was in his name that all business was transacted. The village had the porcupine as its mark.[156]

The totems of the Huron at Detroit in 1736 were given as the turtle, the bear, and the plover.[157]

In later years the common usage was to call the bands by the name of the chief, but still the tripartite division of the Huron remnant is discernible, as in the following excerpt:

[154] *Relation . . . . 1648*, J.R., 33: 143.

[155] *J.R.*, 61: 115.

[156] "Le Scioux," AC., C 11 A, 122.

[157] Celeron, "Census of Indian Tribes: 1736," *WHC.*, 17: 251.

Other Hurons of Sàstaredzy and Taychatin's tribe came, also, to speak to M. de Longueuil, and have, in like manner, assured him that they had no share in the misconduct of Nicholas' people, meanwhile, asking pardon, they endeavor to exculpate themselves, and propose settling near Detroit. [Marginal note] *Sastaradzy,* the Principal chief of the Huron Nation; *Taychatin,* another chief, were not present at the attack.[158]

References to the eminent position of a chief named Sastaretsi are numerous in the documents of the contact period. They refer to various individuals, as each successor to the position assumed the name also. Besides variations in the spelling of Sastaretsi, this chief was also known as Kondiaronk, the Rat, and Adario. The last designation appears to have been applied mostly to the man who was chief in the last quarter of the seventeenth century.

Justice

The earliest authority on the Huron, Champlain, said that he did not find any laws among them, nor anything approaching laws; that they had no correction, punishment, or censure of evil-doers, except by way of revenge, which rendering of evil for evil through passion made wars and quarrels very frequent.[159] Later visitors to the Huron, who lived among them for a longer period, came to have a better understanding of their criminal code. Brébeuf, for instance, said that if laws are like the governing wheel regulating communities, they were not without laws, in view of the perfect understanding that existed among them.[160] At least two crimes, theft and murder, were recognized as deserving of punishment.

Theft.—A person who was robbed, according to Sagard, had recourse to an Oki or magician to learn through his power the location of the lost article. The Oki went to the cabin of the victim of the theft, where he ordered feasts to

---

[158] *Journal of Occurrences in Canada, 1746-1747, NYCD.,* 10: 115.
[159] *Voyages,* 3: 142-43.
[160] *Relation . . . . 1636, J.R.,* 10: 215.

be made; at these he practiced his various rites to discover the thief, with success if the thief were present in the cabin.[161] Sagard mentioned no penalty that was inflicted on the guilty party.

Bressani thought theft one of the most common vices of the Huron. Individuals stole anything, whether of utility to them or not, when they were able to accomplish it without being discovered, and even prided themselves on their skill. However, he recorded that a rigorous penalty was inflicted on a proven thief—the victim was free to despoil him. This might be carried out to such an extent that a man who had stolen some small thing, such as an ax, lost all of his goods that the offended party could lay hands on, both on the person of the thief and in his cabin. The Huron established two rules, continued Bressani, for the purpose of avoiding contests in case of theft. First, an article lost or dropped, which the owner has left, if only by three paces, might be taken without it being considered a theft—which was judged to be such only when an object was taken from a cabin; second, the person from whom something had been stolen, on recognizing it in the hands or on the person of another, must not seize it, but must ask who gave it to him. If the person made no answer, he was considered guilty; but if he said that it was sold or given to him by some one else, he must name that individual, who in turn was questioned, and if he named another, the same questions were asked that person, and so on until the guilty party was found.[162]

At least some individuals considered a convicted thief a dishonor to the family. Brébeuf reported in 1635 that a girl thief was killed by her own brother, for which action there was no inquiry or penalty.[163]

Murder.—Punishment for the crime of taking a life was visited not on the murderer, but on the tribe to which he

[161] *Le Grand voyage*, pp. 187-88.
[162] *Breve relatione*, J.R., 38: 267-71.
[163] *Relation . . . . 1635*, J.R., 8: 123.

belonged. This seemed very strange and conducive to law-lessness to the visiting Europeans, but most of them ad-mitted that this system engendered more restraint than did punishment by death in Europe. There was another feature that set the code of the Huron apart from that of Europe. Since the crime was punished rather than the criminal, satis-faction had to be rendered for every crime, even if the criminal were not identified. Therein lay the reason for the infre-quency of murder. The individual who committed the crime might escape detection, but he would be certain that his family, village, or tribe would suffer as the result of his action.

Satisfaction for a murder was made by presents. These might number as many as sixty, according to Brébeuf, each at least of the value of a beaver robe. Each present was accom-panied by a speech, and, consequently, the proceedings at-tending their presentation might consume several days. The presents, wrote Brébeuf, were of two kinds:

Some, like the first nine, which they call *andaonhaan*, are put into the hands of the relatives to make peace, and to take away from their hearts all bitterness and desire for vengeance that they might have against the person of the murderer. The others are put on a pole, which is raised above the head of the murderer, and are called *Andaerraehaan*, that is to say, "what is hung upon a pole." Now, each of these presents has its particu-lar name. Here are those of the first nine, which are the most im-portant, and sometimes each of them consists of a thousand Porcelain beads. The Captain, speaking, and raising his voice at the name of the guilty person, and holding in his hand the first present as if the hatchet were still in the death wound, *condayee onsahachtoutawas*, "There," says he, "is something by which he withdraws the hatchet from the wound, and makes it fall from the hands of him who would wish to avenge this injury." At the second present, *condayee oscotaweanon*, "There is something with which he wipes away the blood from the wound in his head." By these two presents he signifies his regret for having killed him, and that he would be quite ready to restore him to life, if it were possible. Yet, as if the blow has rebounded on their Native Land, and as if it had received the greater wounds, he adds the third present, saying *condayee onsahondechari*, "This is to restore the Country"; *condayee onsahondwaronti, etotonhwentsiai*, "This is to put a stone upon the opening and the division in the ground that was made by this murder." . . . They claim by this present to reunite all hearts and wills, and even entire Villages, which have become estranged. For it is not here as it is in France and elsewhere, where the public and a whole city do not generally espouse the quarrel of an individual. Here you cannot insult any one of them without the whole Country resenting it, and taking up the quarrel against you, and even against an entire Village. Hence arise wars; and it is a more than sufficient reason for taking arms against some Village if it refuses to make satisfaction by the presents ordained for him who may have killed one of your friends. The fifth is made to smooth the roads and to clear away the brushwood; *condayee onsa hannonkiai*, that is to say, in order that one may go henceforth in perfect security over the roads, and from Village to Village. The four others are addressed immediately to the relatives, to console them in their affliction and to wipe away their tears, *condayee onsa hoheronti*, "Behold," he says, "here is something for him to smoke," speaking of his father or his mother, or of the one who would avenge his death. They believe that there is nothing so suitable as Tobacco to appease the passions; that is why they never attend a council without a pipe or calumet in their mouths. The smoke, they say, gives them intelligence, and enables them to see clearly through the most intricate matters. Also, following this present, they make another to restore completely the mind of the offended person, *condayee onsa hondaionroenkhra*. The eighth is to give a drink to the mother of the deceased, and to heal her as being seriously sick on account of the death of her son, *condayee onsa aweannoncwa d'ocweton*. Finally, the ninth is, as it were, to place and stretch a mat for her, on which she may rest herself and sleep during the time of her mourning, *condayee onsa hohiendaen*. These are the principal presents,—the others are, as it were, an increase of consolation, and represent all the things that the dead man would use during life. One will be called his robe, another his belt, another his Canoe, another his paddle, his net, his bow, his arrows, and so on. After this, the relatives of the deceased regard themselves as perfectly satisfied.[164]

Brébeuf went on to say that formerly instances of murder were not so easily settled and that the guilty party was punished by being compelled to lie down and stay under a scaffold upon which the body of his victim was stretched, where the putrid exudations of the corpse would drip upon him and into his dish, which he was not allowed to move out of the way. The murderer had to remain in this position as long as the relatives of his victim pleased, and even then he had to make them an expensive present, called *akhiatsendista*, to obtain release. He also stated that if the family of the murdered person should avenge the crime on the person of the murderer or one of his family, the latter would not be compelled to render satisfaction for the first murder, but the former would be obliged to give satisfaction for this crime.[165]

The account of satisfaction rendered to the French missionaries for the murder of one of their domestics, as reported by Bressani, outlines a slightly different ritual. First, he said, the offended party or family presented the principal men of the family or tribe of the offender with a bundle of little sticks, a bit longer and thicker than matches, which indicated the number of presents that were required for satisfaction. These were divided among the chiefs involved, and each of them undertook to raise his quota of presents. When the total was gathered the chiefs presented themselves and made a present at the door, that it might be opened to them; a second, that they might enter; a third, after entrance, called "drying of tears," in order that they should no longer be regarded with clouded eyes; a fourth, called a medicinal potion for restoring the voice of the offended; a fifth, to appease the mind agitated by thoughts of grief; and a sixth, to soothe a heart justly provoked. Then there were nine gifts

[164] Brébeuf, *Relation* . . . . *1636*, J.R., 10: 215-21.
[165] *Ibid.*, pp. 221-23.

to erect a sepulcher to the deceased—each of which had its own name; four were for the four columns to support the sepulcher, four for the four stretchers to form the coffin of the dead, and one to serve him as a pillow. Afterward, in the case of the murdered Frenchman, captains of eight Huron nations each brought a present for the eight principal bones of the human body. The recipients of these gifts were then required to make a large present, in order to re-establish and strengthen the country.

The following morning fifty gifts were hung on a scaffolding erected in the center of the village. These represented the principal satisfaction. The number varied with the status of the individual murdered. For a Huron slain by another Huron, thirty was the customary number of presents required; for a woman, forty were asked—more than the number for a man, because women, unlike men, were not able to defend themselves, and also because it was they who peopled the country; for an alien a larger number of gifts was required, since if the offended party was not entirely satisfied, reprisals might ensue, trade be disrupted, and war follow. Presents were given to clothe the body as it was in life, another present to withdraw the hatchet from the wound, and as many presents as the body had received blows to heal the wounds. Three more gifts were made: the first, to close the earth, which had opened itself; the second, to make it solid, and when this was accepted the whole assembly began to dance in token of gladness; and a third, to prevent with a great stone the chasm from ever opening again. Presents were made to the missionaries to persuade them to maintain their various services in the Huron country. The Jesuits made several presents to the Huron to have them give audience to the words of the missionaries. Bressani closed by saying that when presents were not forthcoming at the second or third offense against a nation war was declared.[166]

Magicians or "sorcerers," as the French called them, meaning those who used poison and charms to cause deaths, were

[166] *Breve relatione*, J.R., 38: 281-87.

punished severely when caught in the act. Any one catching them was authorized by the consent of the whole country to cleave their skulls, without fear of being called to account or of being obliged to give satisfaction for his deed.[167]

Le Mercier recorded an instance of a man who believed that a woman had bewitched him. The woman was summoned and told of her sentence and asked to name the one who was to give her the death blow. She was dragged outside the cabin, and her face and part of her body burned with pieces of lighted bark. Her godfather split her head. The next day her body was burned and reduced to ashes in the middle of the village.[168]

Hospitality

Before the Huron were subjected to much contact with the French, they practiced a hospitality that amazed the French observers. All strangers that were not enemies, as well as other members of their own nation, were at all times welcome to partake of the shelter of the cabin and the food available. An invitation was not necessary to lodge in any cabin, and one could stay as long as one wished without having to make any other recompense than to say *"ho, ho, ho, outoécti"* ("many thanks") at departure. According to Brébeuf in 1635, no other tribe known to the French at that time was as hospitable as were the Huron.[169]

This hospitable treatment was reciprocal between all friendly nations, according to Sagard, and although the Huron helped passers-by, they extended help to the other members of their own nation to such an extent that there were no beggars among them. In the custom of a Huron smoking a pipe and then presenting it lighted to the guest, he found a similarity to the European custom of drinking toasts to a person to show friendship.[170]

[167] Brébeuf, *Relation* . . . . *1636*, J.R., 10: 223.
[168] *Relation* . . . . *1637*, J.R., 14: 37-39.
[169] *Relation* . . . . *1635*, J.R., 8: 93-95, 127, 129.
[170] *Le Grand voyage*, pp. 110-12.

Ragueneau wrote in 1650 that Huron hospitality was
even extended to whole villages and to nations of seven or
eight hundred persons who were fleeing from the arms of
their enemies. These were welcomed, lodged in different
households, and even given a share in lands already sown,
in order that they might be able to live, although in a foreign
country, as in their own land.[171]

Games

In common with most of the tribes of the Great Lakes region, the Huron possessed three games which were played
frequently: the game of straws, the dish game, and lacrosse.
Sagard reported that they had several other kinds of games,
but did not say what they were.[172] From the same source it is
learned that the game of straws (*aescra*) was played with three
or four hundred little white rushes, all about a foot long.[173]
Both this game and lacrosse are mentioned by Du Peron and
others, but nothing is told about them except that lacrosse was
played as a remedy for a sick person, as a benefit for the whole
country, and also in memory of some deceased lacrosse
player.[174] Of course, these games were played for their own
sake between members of the same village and between
villages. Wagers were placed by both sides on all of the occasions on which the games were played.

The dish game received most attention from the writers
of the contact period; Sagard, Brébeuf, Lalemant, and
Charlevoix gave it considerable space. It was played with five
or six fruit stones or small flat pellets, painted black on one
side and white or yellow on the other. The men and boys
sat in a circle to participate in the game and placed the "dice"
in a bowl, which they raised a little off the ground and
brought down again, hitting it sharply against the ground.

[171] *Relation . . . . 1650, J.R.*, 35: 207-9.

[172] *Le Grand voyage*, p. 123.

[173] *Ibid.*

[174] "Letter from François du Peron," *J.R.*, 15: 179; Brébeuf, *Relation . . . .
1636, J.R.*, 10: 185-87.

The player who was throwing the "dice" continually repeated "tet, tet, tet," believing that this influenced the play in his favor. The women, too, played with the dice, but without the bowl; they took the fruit stones in their hands and, throwing them up in the air, let them fall on a hide or a skin spread on the ground. The men and boys, according to Sagard, sometimes amused themselves by playing this game with the women and girls.

"Dice" or the dish game was also played by entire villages, one often challenging another. The wagers lost on this game appalled Sagard, but the spirit with which the losses were taken surprised him. He said that he had often seen the Indians return to their villages entirely naked, having lost all their possessions, but singing gaily. Sagard did not state what constituted the game, nor did he report that the game was played for any purpose other than entertainment, such as for a remedy, for the deceased, or the like.[175]

Brébeuf and Lalemant gave accounts of the game as it was played for the recovery of some one who was sick. These reports are more detailed than is the narrative of Sagard. They mentioned only the one purpose of play. The game might be prescribed by the physician, but it was supposed to be particularly effective if the sick man dreamed of it. However initiated, the chiefs were informed, and they assembled the council, which fixed the time for the meeting and chose the village to be invited to play. Each side chose a player to represent it. He was selected from a group of candidates who, having previously fasted and abstained from their wives for some time, assembled at night and ascertained who had the best hand with the "dice." They also exhibited all of their charms at this time and exhorted the "dice." Then, after a feast, they slept, according to Brébeuf, to learn in their dreams the result of the game; but, according to Lalemant, not only to have a favorable dream, but also to dream of charms that would bring them good luck. These were gath-

[175] *Le Grand voyage*, pp. 122-24.

ered and carried to the place of the play, along with other charms that were reputed to bring good fortune in the game. Even old men, whose presence was regarded as efficacious in augmenting the strength of the player, were carried with their charms to the game.

There seem to have been some sleight-of-hand performances connected with this game, from the account of Brébeuf. He wrote that at the assembly the night before the game, the one chosen to hold the dish took the stones, put them promiscuously into a dish, and covered it to prevent any one putting his hand into it. After they all sang a song the dish was uncovered, and the plum stones were found to be all white or all black. Brébeuf asked an Indian if the opposing side did likewise and was informed that it did. The man told him that the person chosen to handle the dish was someone who had dreamed that he would win or who had a charm; moreover, those who had a charm did not conceal it, but carried it everywhere; and also that in making the trial shake some of the plum stones disappeared and were found some time after in the dish with the others.

The spectators disposed themselves for the game along the sides of the chosen cabin, the sick man for whose benefit the play was made was brought in, with the chosen player walking behind him with his head and face wrapped in his garment. The two players, with their assistants holding the charms, were placed in the middle of the cabin and, after bets were made by whoever wished to do so, the game began. Brébeuf and Lalemant agree that there were six plum stones, black on one side and white on the other, shaken in a wooden bowl. Brébeuf said that the game consisted of throwing all black or all white. To aid the player in accomplishing this, each spectator on his side prayed, as Lalemant put it, "or muttered I know not what words, with gestures, and eager motions of the hands, eyes, and the whole face—all to attract to himself good luck, and to exhort their Demons to take courage and not let themselves be tormented." At the same time others were deputed to utter execrations, and to make precisely contrary gestures—with the purpose of driving ill luck back to the other side and of imparting fear to the demon of the opponents.

Brébeuf reported that when the player on the opposite side held the dish the spectators cried at the top of their voices *achinc, achinc, achinc* ("three, three, three") or perhaps *ioio, ioio, ioio,* which apparently referred to the same number, one calling for the player to throw three white dice and the other for three black. Neither Brébeuf or Lalemant mentioned what constituted a game, but both remarked upon the spirit with which the Indians accepted their losses.[176]

Charlevoix wrote an account of the game, part of which is obviously taken word for word from the narratives of Brébeuf and Lalemant, but he said that he witnessed an assembly for the playing of this game in the Huron village at Detroit in 1721. He told of many things that his brother missionaries did not mention. Each player had six or eight little bones, which Charlevoix at first took for apricot stones, because they were of the same size and shape; on a closer examination he found that they had six unequal faces, the two largest of which were painted, one black and the other a straw color. The dish first had to be spun around before it was raised to strike it on the ground. If all dice were of the same color after a throw, it counted the player five points; five of one color counted him one point the first time, and on the second time the player swept the board. Any number lower than five counted nothing; the game was forty points. Each side had a marker who kept track of the points won or lost. The winning player continued to play, but the loser yielded his place to another who was named by the marker on his side; if one side was not having good luck, the marker might retire in favor of another. The play might be continuous for five or six days, but if one side was doing badly,

---

[176] Brébeuf, *Relation* . . . . *1636, J.R.,* 10: 187-89; Lalemant, *Relation* . . . . *1639, J.R.,* 17: 201-7.

it might discontinue play until the next day by furnishing the whole party with a slender repast. On the resumption of play each player invoked his "tutelary genius" and threw some tobacco in the fire for him, imploring his aid. If the losing party thought the furniture of the cabin was the cause of their ill luck, they changed it entirely around. Play then began again at daybreak.[177]

Dances

The Huron had as many as twelve kinds of dances that were used as remedies for sickness, according to Brébeuf.[178] He did not state whether these were all of the dances by the Huron, nor whether they were used for other purposes. Sagard, on the other hand, reported that there were four aims in holding dances, but his only examples were of those used for the curing of ailments. He wrote:

Our Indians, and generally all the people of the West Indies, have always had the custom of dances; but they have them for four ends: either to please their demons, so that they think they will benefit them, or to make a fête for someone, or to rejoice over some important victory, or to avoid or cure illnesses and infirmities.

When they must hold some dances, nude or covered with their breech clouts, according as the patient dreamed, or as the shaman or the chiefs of the place ordered, the cry is made in all the streets of the town or village, notifying and inviting the young people to go there on the day and hour ordered, painted and adorned as well as possible, or in the manner ordered, and that they take courage, since it is for such a purpose, naming the subject of the dance; those of the surrounding villages have the same notice and are also begged to be there, as they are, at the pleasure of each one, for no one is forced to it.

In the meantime they prepare one of the largest cabins of the place, and having all arrived there, the spectators, such as the old men, the old women, and the children, remain seated on

---

[177] Charlevoix, *Journal*, 2: 13-15.
[178] *Relation . . . . 1636*, J.R., 10: 185.

the mats against the benches or on them, the length of the cabin, and two chiefs stand, each one with a turtle shell in his hand (of those which they use to sing to and blow on the patients), and sing, in the middle of the dancing, one song, to which they accord the sound of their turtle shell; having finished they all make a great shout saying "Hé-é-é-é"; then they commence another one or repeat the same one to the number of repetitions that has been ordered; and it is only these two chiefs who sing, all the rest say only "Het het, het," as someone who inhales with vehemence; and then always at the end of each song they give a loud and long shout, saying "Hé-é-é-é."

All these dances are done in a circle or at least in an oval, according to the length and width of the cabins; but the dancers do not hold each other by the hand as here, as they all have their fists clenched; the girls hold their one on the other, kept away from their stomachs, and the men keep them closed also, raised in the air, and in all other ways in the manner of a man who threatens, with movement both of the body and the feet, raising one and then the other, beating on the ground to the cadence of the songs, and raising themselves as in half leaps; the girls, shaking the whole body as well as the feet, turn at the end of four or five steps toward him or her who follows them, to make him the reverence of a tossing of the head. And those who throw themselves about the best and make the most suitably all the little affectations are considered the best dancers among them, that is why they do not spare themselves at it.

These dances ordinarily last one, two, or three afternoons, and in order to prevent any hindrance to doing their duty well, although it be at the height of winter, they never wear other clothes or coverings than their breech clouts to cover their nudity, if that be permitted, as it ordinarily is, except that for some other subject they be ordered to throw them off, never forgetting, nevertheless, their necklaces, earrings, and bracelets, and to paint themselves at times; in a similar case the men deck themselves with necklaces, feathers, painting, and other rubbish, which I have seen arranged in masquerades or Shrovetide, having bearskins which covered their bodies, the ears erect on top of the head, and the faces covered except the eyes; these served only as doorkeepers or jesters and mixed in the dances only at intervals, because they were destined for something else. One day I saw one of these jesters enter in the cabin where the dance was to be made in the procession with all those who were to take part in the festivity; he carried on his shoulders a large dog tied and bound by the paws and the muzzle. Taking it by the two hind legs in the middle of the cabin, he flung it on the ground several times until it was dead, when he had another take it, who went to prepare it in another cabin for the feast at the end of the dance.

If the dance is ordered for a sick woman, on the third or last evening, if it is found expedient, or ordered by the shaman, she is carried there, and in one of the repetitions or rounds of the song she is carried, in another she is made to walk and dance a little, being supported under the arms, and in a third, if strength permits her, they make her dance a little by herself without anyone's assistance, always crying to her, however, at the top of their voices, "*Etsagon outsahonne, achisteq anatetsence,*" that is: take courage woman, and you will be cured tomorrow. Afterward, the dances ended, those who are destined for the feast go there, and the others return to their houses.

There was a dance one day of all the young men, women, and girls all nude in the presence of a patient, at which it was necessary (an act which I know not how to excuse, or pass in silence) that one of these young men urinate in her mouth and that she swallow and drink this water, which she did with great courage, hoping to receive a cure from it; for she herself desired that all be done thus in this manner in order to accomplish and omit nothing of the dream that she had had. If during their dream or reverie it occurs to them that it is necessary that they be made a present of a dog black or white, or of a large fish for a feast, or even of something for other use, at once it is cried in all the town, in order that if any one has such a thing as is specified, that he present it to such a patient for the recovery of his health. They are so willing to help that they never fail to find it, although the thing be of value or importance among them, preferring to suffer and be in need of things, than to fail the need of a sick one; for example, Father Joseph gave a cat to a great chief as a very rare present (for they have none of these animals). It happened that a sick person dreamed that if some one would give her this cat that she would be very soon cured. This chief was notified of it and immediately sent her his cat, although he greatly loved it; his daughter loved it still more, and seeing herself deprived of the animal that she passionately loved, she fell sick of it and died of regret, not being able to conquer and overcome her affection, although she did not wish to fail to help and aid her neighbor. Let us find many Christians who would wish thus to inconvenience them-selves for the service of others, and we would praise God for it.

To recover our thimble, which was stolen from us by a young boy, who gave it to a girl, I was in the place where the dances were being held; the girl had it hanging at her belt with her other treasures, and while waiting for the end of the dance, I had an Indian repeat to me one of the songs which they sang there, of which here is a part I have written down:

> Ongyata éuhaha ho ho ho ho ho,
> Egnyotonuhaton on on on on on
> Eyontara éientet onnet onnet onnet
> Eyontara éientet à à à onnet, onnet, ho ho ho.

In the country of our Hurons, they had also assemblies of all the girls of a town near a sick person, at her entreaty, fol-lowing the reverie or the dream which she will have had of it, as by the prescription of the shaman, for her health and cure. The girls thus assembled, they are all asked, one after another, which of the young men of the town they wish to sleep with them the following night; they each name one, and all of these are soon notified by the masters of ceremony; they all come in the evening in the presence of the sick person, and each sleeps with her who chose him, they fill the cabin from one end to the other, and thus spend all the night, while two chiefs at the two ends of the lodging sing and sound their turtle shells from the evening till the next morning, when the ceremony ends.[179]

The dances performed as remedies were either chosen by the dreams of the sick person or by the medicine man con-sulted. Apparently, some of these prescribed dances were the property of either an individual or a group. In such case, the

[179] Sagard, *Le Grand voyage*, pp. 150-59.

dance was performed under the direction of the recognized leader of the group. In at least some of the dances the patient for whom the performance was given acquired a certain standing in the group after his recovery.[180] Usually, the number and sex of the dancers were distinguishing features of the dance.

Chaumonot mentioned the Doutetha dance, but gave no other information about it.[181] Another dance about which little is known is one in which wooden masks were used; it was described briefly by Le Mercier in the *Relation* of 1637:

On the 10th, they performed a dance for the recovery of a patient. He had dreamed about it two days before, and since then they had been making their preparations. All the dancers were disguised as hunchbacks, with wooden masks which were altogether ridiculous, and each had a stick in his hand. An excellent medicine, forsooth! At the end of the dance, at the command of the sorcerer *Tsondacouane* all these masks were hung on the end of poles, and placed over every cabin, with the straw men at the doors, to frighten the malady and to inspire with terror the demons who made them die.[182]

In 1639 Lalemant mentioned the baptism of a man who was the head and master of "the dance of the Naked ones."[183]

[180] For example there is the following excerpt from Brébeuf in the *Relation* of 1636: "He dreamed, therefore, that there was only one certain kind of dance which would make him quite well. They call it *akhrendoiaen*, inasmuch as those who take part in this dance give poison to one another. It had never been practiced among this Nation of the Bear. . . . So, behold, couriers are sent immediately in all directions; a fortnight passes in assembling the company, which is composed of about eighty persons, including six women; they set off without delay. . . .

"Now having arrived within musket-range, they stopped and began to sing; those of the Village replied. From the evening of their arrival, they danced, in order to get an understanding of the disease; the sick man was in the middle of the Cabin, on a mat. The dance being ended, because he had fallen over backward and vomited, they declared him to belong entirely to the Brotherhood of lunatics."—*J.R.*, 10: 205-7.

[181] *Relation* . . . . *1649, J.R.*, 34: 217.

[182] *J.R.*, 13: 263.

[183] *Relation* . . . . *1639, J.R.*, 17: 81.

This may be one of the dances described by Sagard, although one must bear in mind that he stated that most of the dances of the Huron were performed with little or no clothing, even in winter, this being prescribed, but it was also that the dancers might have more freedom in their movements.

Lalemant recorded the conversion in 1641 of a man who had taken part for twenty years in the "Aoutaenhrohi, or festival and dance of fire," which he termed the most diabolical and, at the same time, the most general remedy for maladies that there was in the country. He wrote further:

He related to us that when about twenty years old he began, through a youthful fancy, to follow those who turned their attention to this; but when he saw that he had not, like the others, hands and mouth which were fireproof, he was very careful not to touch what was too hot, but he made only a pretense of doing it and played his part to the best of his ability.

At the end of some time he had a dream, in which he saw himself present at one of these dances or festivals, and handling fire like the others, and he heard at the same time a song, which he was astonished to know perfectly on awakening. At the first feast of this kind which was made, he began to sing his song, and behold, by degrees he felt himself becoming frenzied,—he took the burning embers and the hot stones with his hands and with his teeth from the midst of the live coals, he plunged his bare arm to the bottom of the boiling kettles, and all without any injury or pain, in a word, he was master of his trade. And since then for the space of twenty years, it has befallen him sometimes to be present at three or four festivals or dances of this kind in one day, for the healing of the sick.

He assured us that, far from being burned then, one felt, on the contrary, a coolness of the hands and mouth; but that all must be done following and depending upon the song that has been learned in the dream; that otherwise nothing extraordinary takes place.

He told us, besides, that then from time to time he saw himself in dreams present at these feasts, and that then something was given or lent him that he should wear about his person during the ceremony. This was a warning to him that he must not undertake it the next time, unless he had about him that which he had seen in his dream; for this reason, at the next dance, he declared his wish, and immediately there was thrown him that which he had declared to be necessary to him, in order that he might play his part.[184]

In contradiction to the opinions of the missionaries among the Huron in the first half of the seventeenth century, Marquette found that all but one of the dances performed by them in 1673 were innocuous. He wrote:

Every dance has its own name; but I did not find any harm in any of them, except that called "The bear dance." A woman who became impatient in her illness, in order to satisfy both her God and her Imagination, caused twenty women to be invited. They were Covered with bearskins and wore fine porcelain Collars; They growled like Bears; they ate and pretended to Hide Like bears. Meanwhile, the sick woman danced, and from time to time told them to throw oil on the fire, with Certain superstitious observances. The men who acted as Singers had great difficulty in carrying out The sick woman's design, not having as yet heard similar airs, for That dance was not in vogue among the Tionnontaternonnons.[185]

The contradiction of the testimony of the early missionaries by that of Marquette may be explained by the almost complete conversion of the Huron to Christianity. From the first establishment of the French colony in Canada the missions among the Huron were considered successful, and large numbers were converted. After the disastrous raids of the Iroquois the Huron refugees were without a missionary for about fifteen years. The results of the earlier teaching were still to be seen when missionaries again went among them, and in a short time a large number of converts were enrolled in the church.

The change in the purpose of customs such as dances after this almost complete conversion, although many of the orig-

---

[184] Lalemant, *Relation . . . . 1641*, J.R., 21: 151-55.
[185] *Relation . . . . 1673*, J.R., 57: 255.

inal forms were retained, is apparent in the account of Father Enjalran, describing the feast and preceding dance which were given at Christmas time in 1679 by the Huron to celebrate the birth of Christ and His arrival at their village:

This dance is performed by the women only, as I said,—ranging themselves in two parallel lines at the two Sides of a Cabin, having in their hands a kind of Castanet. Those who are officers commence the Song and dance; they have some words to which they apply one of their airs, and these form the refrain of their Song which every one is to repeat to the same air. While the One who has Begun Goes on with her Song agreeably to the words which have served her for a refrain,—very often, however, varying the air,—she Runs and bustles about between these two ranks in a singular manner. In this there is nothing, as formerly, to violate decency, especially on occasions in which they claim to honor God. Meanwhile the others—repeating at certain intervals the words which form the refrain, and which explain the intention of the one who is dancing—sound their Castanets, and move sometimes one foot, sometimes the other, to Certain measures without leaving their places. When some word which pleases them occurs in the Song they redouble the noise of their castanets, and their cries of Joy. Each does, in her turn, the same as the first; and it is required of each that she have a special refrain and Song. The refrains and Songs of that day were but praises and thanksgivings—addressed sometimes to the holy child, sometimes to his holy mother, and, again, to the missionaries.[186]

Evidence that the Huron living in Michigan had completely given up what the missionaries would consider "pagan" dances is strictly negative, being based on the fact that there is no mention of these dances in the *Relations* of the Jesuits after 1679. The inference is plain that the dances of later years met with the approval of the missionaries. Similar silence in reference to the other tribes does not exist, which indicates that the omission in relation to the Huron was not accidental.

[186] *Relation* .... *1679, J.R.,* 61: 119-21.

War

Wars were not undertaken by the Huron with the object of possessing the lands of another nation, but by large parties for the extermination of their enemies, by small parties to avenge some wrong, such as a murder by a member of another tribe for which satisfaction was not forthcoming, and by the young men to prove their valor.

On this subject Sagard wrote at length; for the most part he follows Champlain in the first two paragraphs:

As for the wars that they undertake, or for going into the country of enemies, two or three of the old or valiant chiefs will undertake the management for this time, and they go from village to village to make known their wish, giving presents to those of the said villages to persuade them and to get from them aid and help in their wars, and thus they are like generals of armies. One of them came to our town, a large old man, quite alert, who incited and encouraged the young men and the chiefs to arm themselves and to undertake war against the nation of *Attiuoïndarons:* but we reprimanded him strongly for it, and dissuaded the people from listening to him on account of the disaster and inevitable calamity that this war would have brought to our quarters, and for the advancement of the glory of God.

These chiefs or generals of armies have the power not only of designating the places, of giving quarter, and of ranging the battalions, but also of disposing of the prisoners of war, and all other things of the greatest consequence: it is true that they are not always well obeyed by their soldiers, in so far as they themselves often lack good leadership, and he who leads badly, is often badly followed. . . .

While we were there, the time of going to war arriving, a young man of our town, desirous of honor, wished to give the war feast himself and to entertain all his companions on the day of the general assembly; this was at great cost and expense to him, and he was greatly praised and esteemed for it, for the feast was of six large kettles with a great many smoked fish in the meals and the oils to grease them.

They were put on the fire before daybreak in one of the largest cabins of the place, then the council being ended and the resolutions of war taken, they all went to the feast, commenced to feast, and did the military exercises, one after another, that they are accustomed to do, during the feast; after having emptied the kettles and rendered compliments and thanks, they left and went to the rendezvous on the frontier to enter the enemies' lands, where they took about sixty of their enemies, the most part of whom they killed on the spot; the others were led alive to the Huron to be killed and eaten in a feast.

Their wars are really only surprises and deceptions, for every year at spring time and during all the summer five or six hundred Huron young men or more, go to distribute themselves in the country of the Iroquois, leaving five or six in one spot, five or six in another, and as many in another; they lie on their stomachs in the fields and forests and beside wide roads and narrow paths, and when the night comes they rove everywhere and enter as far as possible into the towns and villages to try to catch some one, be it man, woman, or child, and if they can take them alive, they lead them to their country to make them die by inches, if not, after having given them a blow of the club, or killed them by arrow shots, they carry off their heads; if they are too loaded with them they satisfy themselves with carrying off the scalps, which they call *onontsira*, dressing them to make trophies of them, and to put on the palisades or walls of their village in time of war, attached at the end of a long pole.

When they go thus to war and in the country of the enemy, for their usual food, they carry, so much to each on his back, a sack full of corn meal roasted and grilled in the ashes, which they eat raw, and either without being soaked or even diluted with a little warm or cold water, and by this means they do not have to make a fire to prepare their food, although at times they make fires at night in the thick of the woods, so as not to be seen. They make this meal last until their return, which is in about six weeks' or two months' time; afterward they come to rest themselves in their country, end the war for this attack, or return to it again with other provisions. . . .

These poor Indians (to our confusion) behave very modestly in war, without inconveniencing anyone, and supporting themselves with their own means, without other pledge or hope of recompense than of honor and praise, which they value more than all the gold of the world. . . .

As there is the custom on the sea to put in evidence the red flag for sign of war or of punishment, likewise our Indians, not only on solemn days and those of rejoicing, but principally when they go to war, wear for the most part around their heads certain plumes on the crowns, and others in the mustaches; these are made of long moose hairs, painted scarlet, and glued or otherwise attached to a leather band three fingers in width.

When war is declared in a country, they destroy all the towns, hamlets, cities, and villages on the frontier incapable of stopping the enemy, or else they fortify them, and each one places himself in the cities or fortified places of his jurisdiction, where they build new cabins for their residence with the help of the inhabitants of the place. The chiefs, assisted by their councilors, work continuously on that which is for their preservation; they see if there is anything to fix or add to their fortifications to be used there, and have the soot and spiders swept and cleaned from all the cabins, for fear of fire that the enemy could throw by certain contrivances that they have learned from I know not what other nation—this has been told me formerly. They have stones and water carried to the sentry boxes to use on the occasion for them. Many make holes in which they hide their treasures, and for fear of surprise the chiefs send soldiers to discover the enemy, while they encourage the others to make arms, to keep themselves ready, to swell their courage in order to fight valiantly and handsomely, and to resist and to defend themselves, if the enemy happens to appear. The same order is observed in all the other cities and towns until they see the enemy to be attached to a few places, and then from all the neighboring cities a number of soldiers go quietly at night, if a larger army is not necessary, to help, and hiding inside the one which is besieged, defend it, make sorties, arrange ambushes, devote themselves to skirmishes, and fight with all their strength, for the salvation of the country, to overcome the enemy, and to defeat it entirely if they can.[187]

As to the treatment of prisoners, Sagard wrote:

[187] Sagard, *Le Grand voyage*, pp. 200-209.

When our Hurons have taken in war some one of their enemies, they make him a harangue of the cruelties that he and his practice in their place, and that similarly he should resolve to endure as many, and command him (if he has sufficient courage) to sing all along the road, which he does; but often with a very sad and lugubrious song, and thus they lead him into their country to kill him, and while awaiting the hour of his death, they continually make him a feast of what they can to fatten him and to render him stronger and more robust to support more injuries and longer torments, and not from charity and compassion, except to women, girls, and children. These they rarely kill, but save them and keep them for themselves, or make presents of them to others who have previously lost some of theirs in war and think as much of the substitutes as if they were their own children, who being come of age go as courageously to war against their own parents and those of their nation as if they were born enemies of their own fatherland, which shows the little love the children have for their parents. They only esteem present favors and not those of the past, which is a sign of bad nature; of this I have had the experience several times.

If they cannot lead away the women and children that they take from their enemies, they knock them down and kill them on the spot, and carry away their heads or scalps; again it is seen (but seldom) that having led some of these women and girls into their country they kill some of them by torments, without the tears of this poor sex, which are all of their defense, moving them to compassion: for they alone cry, and not the men, no matter what torture they are made to undergo, for fear of being considered effeminate, and of little courage, although they are often forced to utter loud protests, which the intensity of their torture draws from the depth of their stomachs.

It has sometimes happened that some of their enemies, being closely pursued, escaped nevertheless; for to beguile him who pursues them and to give themselves time to flee and to outstrip him they throw their necklaces of porcelain very far behind them, in order that if avarice bids their pursuer to go pick these up, they can always get ahead and place themselves in safety; this has succeeded for several, and I am pursuaded and believe that it is, in part, why they usually wear all their finest necklaces and matachias in war.

When they meet an enemy, they have only to place their hands on him; as we say "surrender," they say *sakien*, that is, "sit down," which he does, if he does not prefer to be knocked down in his tracks or to defend himself to the death, which they do not often do in these extremities, in the hope of escaping in time by some ruse. Now there is some competition as to whom the prisoners belong, and those prisoners who know how obtain their liberty and save themselves, as the following example shows.

Two or three Hurons, wishing each to attribute to himself an Iroquois prisoner and not being able to agree, made their prisoner the judge of it; he, very circumspectly used the opportunity and said: "Such a one took me, and I am his prisoner," which he said counter to the truth and expressly to give a just discontent to him whose prisoner he really was; and in fact, indignant that another would unjustly have the honor which was due him, this one secretly spoke the following night to the prisoner, and said to him: "You have given and awarded yourself to another than me, who took you, that is why I prefer to give you freedom to him having the honor which is due me," and thus untying him made him escape and flee secretly.

When the prisoners are arrived in their city or village they make them endure many and various torments, to some more and to others less, as it pleases them; and all these kinds of torments and deaths are so cruel that there is nothing more inhuman. First, they tear out their nails and cut off their three principal fingers, which they use to draw the bow, then remove the scalp, and afterwards put fire and hot ashes there, or have drip on them a certain melted gum, or even content themselves with making them walk all nude and barefooted through a large number of fires, made on purpose, from one end to the other of a large cabin, where everyone who hems them in on both sides, holds in his hand a lighted firebrand, strikes them on the body with it while passing, and afterwards with hot irons also makes bands around their legs; they rub their thighs from top to bottom with red-hot hatchets, and thus little by little burn the poor wretches; to increase the very acute pains they throw water on their backs at times and put fire on the tips of their fingers and on their private parts; then they pierce the arms near the wrists, draw the tendons from them with sticks, and wrench them by force, or being unable to tear them out, they cut them, which they endure with an incredible firmness, singing, however, a very sad and lugubrious song, with, as I have said, a thousand threats against these torturers and against all this nation, and being ready to give up the ghost, they are lead outside the cabin to end their life on a scaffold erected on purpose, there the executioners cut off their heads and open their abdomens, and all the children are there to have some little end of an intestine, which they hang at the end of a little stick and carry it thus in triumph through all the city or village in token of victory. The body thus cut open and dressed, they cook it in a large kettle, then eat it in a feast, with jollity and rejoicing, as I have said before. . . .

It happens that the prisoner escapes sometimes, especially at night, at the time they make him walk through the fires; for while running on these burning and red-hot braziers, with his feet he scatters and throws firebrands, ashes, and coals through the cabin, which makes such an obscurity from the dust and smoke that those present cannot recognize each other at all, so that all are forced to get to the door and go outside, and he also among the crowd, and from there he takes a new start and goes away; if he cannot right then, he hides in some corner apart, awaiting the occasion and the opportunity of fleeing and reaching open country. I have seen several thus escaped from the hands of their enemies, who for proof showed the three principal fingers of the right hand cut off.[188]

Ragueneau stated that the young men kept guard at night, mounting aloft in their watchtowers, and that they sang war songs while there. These watchtowers were apparently the sentry boxes of Sagard, but neither located them with reference to the palisades with which the villages were fortified.[189]

There are some points of evidence in addition to, and others at variance with, the accounts of Sagard as to the

[188] *Ibid.*, pp. 212-19.
[189] Ragueneau, *Relation . . . . 1646, J.R.*, 29: 253.

method of waging war. Champlain reported that the honor accruing from the success of a war party belonged exclusively to the chiefs leading it, but to them also went the dishonor of failure.[190] This early visitor of the Huron took part in at least two of their martial expeditions, but was not impressed with their ability as warriors, finding only one good point. This was the secure way in which they conducted their retreat, putting all the wounded and the old people in their midst, with strong forces in front, on the wings, and in the rear, and maintaining order in that formation without breaking ranks until they reached a place of safety.[191]

Brébeuf said that the Huron maintained pensioners in the neutral nations, and even among their enemies, by means of whom they were secretly warned of all the plots against them.[192]

Before entering an affray the warriors rubbed themselves with a kind of grease which they claimed would preserve them from the effects of bullets and arrows.[193]

The Huron of Detroit were reported in 1737 as in the habit of uttering a raven cry as they entered battle.[194]

The Neutrals, according to Lalemant, writing in 1641, made a practice of burning the women prisoners as well as the men, which the Huron proper did not do; they either killed them at the time of the fray or, if they took them to their village, gave them their freedom.[195]

As for the eating of the prisoners, Brébeuf stated that after the victim was killed, if he had proved himself a brave man in his torments, they tore out his heart, roasted it on the coals, and distributed it in pieces to the young men, thinking that this rendered them courageous. Others made an incision in

[190] *Voyages*, 3: 159.

[191] *Ibid.*, pp. 78-79.

[192] *Relation . . . . 1636*, J.R., 10: 229.

[193] "Beauharnois(?)," *WHC.*, 17: 153.

[194] François Beauharnois, "Council of the Indian Tribes at Detroit in 1738," *Cadillac Papers*, MPH., 34: 152.

[195] *Relation . . . . 1641*, J.R., 21: 195.

the upper part of their necks and caused some of the prisoner's blood to run into it. They held that the mingling of his blood with theirs made it impossible to surprise them, since they would always have knowledge of their enemy's approach, however secret it might be. The body was then put in the kettle piece by piece. Although at other feasts the head of the animal was the portion of the chief, here it went to the lowest person in the company. Some of the Indians, according to Brébeuf, tasted this human flesh only with great horror, others ate it with pleasure; indeed, he said that there were Indians in his cabin who spoke with gusto of the flesh of an Iroquois and praised its good qualities in the same terms as they would the flesh of a deer or a moose.[196]

In the earliest times of which we have record the Huron were at peace with the Algonquian-speaking tribes around the Great Lakes. They continued so, except for minor altercations, throughout the contact period. Their traditional enemies were the Iroquois and, after the Huron moved west of Lake Huron, the Sioux, and the tribes beyond the Illinois in the South, such as the Chickasaw and Cherokee.[197]

Birth Customs

Huron women did not retire to separate huts to deliver their children, but, planting four or five sticks and covering them with skins or other covers, formed an abode in the corner of the cabin, where the women lay on the ground or on some furs or pine branches. Some were attended by an old woman who acted as a midwife, others delivered themselves.[198] In this connection it is interesting to note that the Huron women and girls did not retire at the catumenial periods either, but they did prepare their food separately and allowed no one to eat of it.[199]

[196] *Relation . . . . 1636, J.R.,* 10: 227-29.
[197] Cadillac, MS "Relation on the Indians."
[198] Sagard, *Histoire,* p. 324.
[199] Sagard, *Le Grand voyage,* p. 79.

Soon after the child was born its mother pierced its ears with an awl or a fish bone and then put in a quill or some other thing to keep the hole open, afterward hanging some porcelain beads or other trinkets there, and also around the neck of the infant. Some women had the custom of making the infant swallow some grease or oil as soon as it was born.[200]

After these ceremonies had been performed for the newly born child the parents made a feast for their friends, at which tobacco and sagamité were freely distributed.[201] Sagard inferred that it was at this feast that the infant was given a name. Names, he said, were given by tradition; that is to say, they had a large number of names from which they selected one and gave it to the child. Some of these names were without significance, at least to him, whereas others had a meaning: *Yocoisse*, "the wind," *Ongyata*, "the throat," *Tochingo*, "the crane," *Songaqua*, "the eagle," *Scouta*, "the head," *Tonra*, "the stomach," and *Taïhy*, "a tree."[202] Lafitau said that the names changed with the age of the individual: a child had no name or that of a child, a young man had that of a warrior, and an old man had that of some former old man. He further stated that after the holder of a name died, it was buried with him and not revived until several years later.[203]

Children

Children were not very numerous in a Huron family, according to Sagard, who thought that it might be on account of the lewdness of the women.[204] They supplemented the mother's milk with the same foods that the adults used, chewing them well before feeding them to the children. If the mother died before the child was weaned the father fed it water in which he had boiled some corn, by taking this in his mouth and joining his mouth to that of the infant and making

---

[200] *Ibid.*, p. 168; *Histoire*, pp. 326-27.

[201] *Ibid.*, pp. 326-27.

[202] *Le Grand voyage*, pp. 168-69.

[203] *Moeurs des sauvages ameriquains*, 1: 75.

[204] *Le Grand voyage*, p. 168.

it swallow the liquid.[205] The usual age of weaning is not mentioned.

During the day the child was swaddled upon a small board on which there might be a rest or small strip of wood bent half round under the feet. This cradleboard was set upright against the wall of the cabin. The board was usually adorned with little paintings and strings of beads. An opening was left in the swaddling for urination, and if the child was a girl a corn leaf was inserted between the thighs to conduct the water outside. Down was placed under the child, and this made a very comfortable bed. The same kind of down was used to clean the child. The down was very soft, according to Sagard, and came from certain weeds, which may have been cattails.

The mothers carried their children upon their backs on the cradleboards with the aid of a headband. They were also carried outside of the swaddling within their mothers' robes, above the belt, and either in front or in back, with the child's head outside. At night the child was often laid nude between the father and mother, Sagard reported, with accidents happening only rarely. He also stated that in other nations he had seen children placed in skins suspended by four corners from the poles of the cabins, like a sailor's hammock, and these skins were swung to rock the children to sleep.[206]

The Huron children were allowed to run about in the winter snows either entirely or almost nude, and they received no hurt from this nor from strenuous exertion in the great heat of summer. On the contrary, according to Sagard, they derived the strong and robust constitutions they enjoyed as adults from this early hardening to ills and pains.[207]

The boys were early taught to draw the bow and shoot arrows by giving them small ones to play with; of duties they had none. Besides shooting arrows, which was often

[205] *Ibid.*, pp. 169-70.
[206] *Ibid.*, pp. 170-71.
[207] *Ibid.*, p. 172.

done as a game, they had other pastimes, such as the snow
snake game, a ball game, learning to throw the fish harpoon,
and many other small games and exercises.[208] Girls were
similarly taught how to perform their future tasks in some
of the games which they played.[209]

Punishment of no kind seems to have been used, the children growing up in complete liberty. This condition and the
resulting small show of respect for their parents shocked
Sagard, Champlain, and others.[210]

Children belonged to the clan of the mother, took their
names from those appropriate to it, and inherited property
and social rights and positions from their maternal uncles
rather than from their fathers. The early writers erroneously
attributed this custom to uncertainty as to the identity of their
fathers.[211]

Kinship

Lafitau reported that, among the Iroquois and the Huron,
all the children of a cabin regarded as their mothers all the
sisters of their mothers, and as their uncles all the brothers of
their mothers, and that they gave the name of father to all
the brothers of their fathers and of aunt to all the sisters of
their fathers. Further, all the children on the side of the
mother and her sisters and of the father and his brothers
were regarded among themselves as brothers and sisters; but
the children of their uncles and aunts, that is, the brothers of
their mothers and the sisters of their fathers, they considered
as cousins. In the third generation this changed; the great-
uncles and great-aunts became again grandfathers and grand-
mothers to the children of those they called nephews and
nieces. The same rule was applied to additional generations.[212]

The account of Lafitau is the only one left us by the early

---

[208] *Ibid.*, p. 174.
[209] *Ibid.*, p. 176.
[210] *Ibid.*, pp. 173-74; Champlain, *Voyages*, 3: 142.
[211] Sagard, *Le Grand voyage*, pp. 172-73; Lahontan, *Voyages*, 2: 461-62.
[212] *Moeurs des sauvages ameriquains*, 1: 552-53.

writers that outlined a system of kinship terminology. Sagard
reported how various Indians addressed him as a member of
the family into which he had been adopted, but apparently
was not aware of the way the system worked as set forth by
Lafitau. Sagard wrote:

My Indian, who held me in the position of brother, advised
me to call his mother *Sendoué*, that is to say, my mother, then
to call him and his brothers *Ataquen*, my brother, and the rest
of his relations in consequence, according to the degree of consanguinity, and they in the same way called me their relation.
The good woman said *Ayein*, my son, and the others *Ataquon*,
my brother, *Earassé*, my cousin, *Hiuoittan*, my nephew,
Houatinoran, my uncle, *Aystan*, my father; according to the age
of the persons, I was thus called uncle or nephew, etc., and by
the others who did not hold me in the position of relation,
Yatoro, my companion, my comrade, and by those who esteemed
me more *Garihouanne*, great captain.[213]

In another place Sagard added that a girl was addressed as
Eadse, "my good friend," "my companion," and also gave the
following spellings for my brother, my father, and uncle or
my uncle: *Attaquen*, *Yaistan*, and *Honratinoron*, respectively.[214]

Marriage

The earliest account of the conditions and ceremonies of
the marriages of the Huron is that written by Champlain
after his visit to them in 1615:

They have a kind of marriage among them, which is this,
that when a girl is eleven, twelve, thirteen, fourteen or fifteen
years of age, she will have suitors, and many whom she will get
according to her attractions will woo her for some time: after
that the consent of the parent will be asked, although often they
do not seek their consent except those girls that are the best
behaved and the most sensible, who submit to the will of their
parent. The lover or suitor will give the girl a present of some
wampum necklaces, chains and bracelets; if the girl finds this

[213] *Le Grand voyage*, pp. 84-85.
[214] *Ibid.*, p. 106.

suitor to her taste she accepts his present, whereupon the lover
will come and sleep with her three or four nights without saying
a word to her during that time, and there they will gather the
fruit of their love. Next it usually happens that, after a week
or a fortnight, if they cannot agree, she will leave her suitor,
who will remain pledged for his necklaces and his other gifts,
receiving in return only a little pastime. Afterwards, being dis-
appointed in his hopes, he will seek out another girl, and she
another suitor, if they see fit. Thus they continue this plan of
action until a satisfactory union. Some girls spend their youth
in this way, having had more than twenty husbands, and these
twenty husbands are not the only ones who enjoy the creatures,
however much married they be; for after nightfall the young
women run about from one lodge to another, as do the young
men for their part, who possess them wherever it seems good to
them, yet without violence, leaving all to the wishes of the
women. The husband will do the like to his women-neighbours,
no jealousy arising among them on that account, and no disgrace
or injury being incurred, such being the custom of the country.
Now the time when they do not leave their husbands is when
they have children. The previous husband returns to her, to
show her the affection and love he bore her in the past more
than to any other, and testifies that the child she will have is
his, and of his begetting: another will say the same to her, and
finally it is a contest to see who shall win and have her for wife.
And in this way it is the woman's choice and option to take and
accept whoever pleases her most, having in these courtships
and amours gained much wampum and, besides, this choice of a
husband. The woman remains with him without leaving him
again, or if she leaves him it must be for some very good reason,
other than impotence, for he is proof against this. Nevertheless
while with this husband she does not cease to give herself free
rein, but she remains and dwells always in his household, keeping
up a good appearance; so that the children they have together,
being born of such a woman, cannot be sure of being lawful.
Therefore, in view of this danger, they have a custom which is
this, namely that the children never succeed to the property and
honours of their fathers, being in doubt, as I said, of their be-
getter, but indeed they make their successors and heirs the

children of their sisters, from whom these are certain to be sprung and issued.[215]

Champlain mentioned no other details of the ceremonies of marriage except that as it was the woman's duty to supply the firewood for the household, each woman and girl carried a load of wood to the bride for her supply, particularly if it was out of season when the wood would be difficult to obtain and also when she would have other things to attend to.[216]

Sagard is our next source of information regarding the marriage customs of the Huron and, although he undoubtedly followed the word of Champlain in writing his account, he added much that is not found elsewhere. He wrote:

A good many young men instead of getting married, often have girls on intimate terms, and these they do not call wives, *aténonha*, because the ceremony of marriage has not been performed, but *asqua*, that is, companion, or rather concubine; and they live together for as long as it pleases them, without that hindering the young man or the girl from going freely to see their other friends (male or female) sometimes, and without fear of reproach or blame, such being the custom of the country.

But their first ceremony of marriage is this: when a young man wishes a girl in marriage he must ask her father and mother for her, without whose consent the girl is not for him (although most often the girl does not take their consent and advice—only the best and the wisest do so). This lover wishing to make love to his mistress and gain her good graces will paint his face and will dress himself with the finest adornments that he has, to seem more handsome; then he will present to the girl some necklace, bracelet, or earring of porcelain. If the girl finds this suitor pleasing, she accepts the present, whereupon the lover will come to sleep with her for three or four nights; so far there is no complete marriage nor promise given, because after this sleep it often happens that the friendship does not continue and that the girl, who to obey her father has suffered this unjust favor, has no affection for this suitor, and after that he must retire

---

[215] Champlain, *Voyages*, 3: 137-40.
[216] *Ibid.*, 3: 156-57.

without going further. This happened in our time to an Indian in regard to the second daughter of the great chief Quieunon-ascaran, as the father of the girl himself complained to us, seeing the obstinacy of his daughter in not wishing to proceed to the last ceremony of the marriage with this acceptable suitor.

The parties being agreed and the consent of the father and mother being given, they proceed to the second ceremony of marriage in this manner. A feast is prepared of dog, of bear, of moose, of fish, or of other meats which are agreeable to them, to which all the relatives and friends of the betrothed are invited. Every one being assembled and each seated in his place, all around the cabin, the father of the girl or the master of the ceremony (delegated for this) says, speaking loudly and audibly before all the assembly, that such and such are marrying and for that reason the company is assembled and this feast of bear, of dog, of fish, etc., is prepared for the rejoicing of each one and to complete such a worthy event. All being approved and the kettle clean, every one retires, then all the women and girls carry to the newlywed, each a load of wood for her supply, if it is in a season when she could not readily supply herself.[217]

Now, it must be remarked that they maintain three degrees of consanguinity in which they are never accustomed to have marriage: these are a son with his mother or a father with his daughter, brother with his sister, and cousin with his cousin; as I hit upon by chance one day when I pointed out a girl to an Indian and asked if that were his wife or his concubine. He answered me, "No," that she was his cousin and that they were not accustomed to sleeping with their cousins; outside of that all things are permitted. Dowry is never spoken of, so that when divorce happens, the husband owes nothing.

For the virtue and the principal wealth that the father and mother desire of him who seeks their daughter in marriage is not only that he be of good tact and address and well painted and embellished, but it is necessary besides that he show himself valiant in hunting, in war, and in fishing, and that he know how to do something, as the following example shows.

An Indian made love to a girl, and not being able to have

[217] Only the related women and girls did this, according to Sagard, *Histoire*, p. 318.

the good will and consent of the father he carried her off and took her for wife. Whereupon there was a great quarrel, and finally the girl was taken away from him and returned to her father. The reason why the father did not wish this Indian to have his daughter was that he did not want to give her to a man who had no industry to maintain her and the children who would result from this marriage; that as for him, he did not see that he knew how to do anything, for he amused himself in the French kitchens and never exerted himself to hunt. The boy, to give proof of that which he really knew, not being able otherwise to have the girl back, went fishing and took many fish, and after this prowess the girl was returned to him, and he led her back in his cabin, and they made a good household together, as they had done in the past.

If in the course of time the desire seizes them to separate for some reason whatever it be, or that they have no children, they leave each other freely, the husband satisfying himself with saying to her parents and to her that she is worthless and that she must provide for herself elsewhere, and thenceforth she lives in common with the others, until some other seeks her; not only the men procure this divorce, when the women have given them some reason for it, but the women also leave their husbands easily, when they do not please them; it often happens that a woman passes her youth thus, and will have had more than twelve or fifteen husbands, all of which are not, nevertheless, alone in possessing her however much married they be; when the night comes the young women and girls run from one cabin to another, as in a similar manner the young men do on their side, who take the women where they wish, without any violence, however, entrusting all to the wish of the woman. The husband will do the same with his neighbor and the wife with her neighbor, no jealousy coming between them for that, and they meet with no shame, infamy, or dishonor from it.

But when children result from their marriages, they rarely separate and leave each other, except for a good reason; and when this happens they do not hesitate to marry others, notwithstanding their children, of whom they make an agreement as to who will have them; they usually remain with the father, as I have seen in several cases. In the case of one young woman the husband left her a small son in swaddling clothes, and I do not know whether or not he would have taken him back after being weaned, if the marriage had not been readjusted, in which we were the intercessors to put them together again and appease their quarrel, and they finally did what we advised them to do, which was to forgive each other and to continue to be a good husband and wife in the future, which they did.[218]

In his later work, *Histoire du Canada*, Sagard rewrote the last paragraph of the foregoing account, to show that the parents usually shared the children equally in case of divorce, the girls went to the mother and the boys to the father, as they judged expedient, for they did not always follow the same order in this regard.[219]

The Jesuit missionaries, such as Brébeuf, approved of the marriages of the Huron on two counts: the prohibition of marriage in direct and collateral lines of descent, and monogamy. On the other hand, they could only censure the ease with which marriage ties were broken and remarriages made.[220]

The custom of monogamy is vouched for by many other writers, but there is no agreement as to the degree of fidelity with which the parties observed it. The freedom allowed before marriage (some even have said that they did not consider themselves married until they had children), and the ease with which new marital partners were taken served to give little occasion for the plurality of wives or for infidelity. If there was any instance of the latter it seems to have been unresented, for there is no record of any punishment for this offence.

From the foregoing excerpts from Champlain and Sagard, it would seem that a newly married couple established a residence of its own. There is no other testimony on this matter except that of Raudot, who said that they did not believe

[218] Sagard, *Le Grand voyage*, pp. 160-66.
[219] *Histoire*, p. 320.
[220] *Relation . . . . 1635, J.R.*, 8: 119-21; *Relation . . . . 1636, J.R.*, 10: 213.

themselves married until they had children, for until that time the husband lived in his father's cabin and his wife lived in that of her father, but that when they had children the husband went to live with the girl.[221]

Bressani reported that the exercise of the levirate was customary.[222] In speaking of both the Huron and the Iroquois, Charlevoix said the levirate and the sororate were rigidly adhered to; the husband who refused to marry the sister or relation of his deceased wife was subjected to whatever outrages the rejected person saw fit to inflict.[223] The application of these marriage laws as reported by Charlevoix is questionable, in view of his coupling the Huron with the Iroquois and the fact that there is no confirming evidence from other writers.

Boucher wrote in 1663 that among the Huron no real marriage was thought to exist, but rather an illicit connection, unless the father and mother of the young man had gone to ask the parents or other relatives for the girl whom they wished to have for a wife for their son, and that when this consent was given some valuable present was made to the girl's relatives.[224]

Death Customs

In 1615 Champlain reported the customs which the Huron observed at the death of their members:

As regards the burial of the dead, they take the body of the deceased, wrap it in furs, cover it very neatly with tree-bark, then lift it up on four posts on which they build a cabin covered with tree-bark, as long as the body. Others they put into the ground, which is propped up on all sides for fear lest it fall on the body, which they cover with tree-bark, putting earth on top, and over this grave likewise they erect a little cabin. Now it must be understood that these bodies are thus buried in these places only for a time, about eight or ten years, according as

[221] "Memoir," Letter 72.
[222] *Breve relatione,* J.R., 38: 255.
[223] *Journal,* 2: 46.
[224] *Histoire véritable,* p. 103.

the people of the village decide upon the place where the ceremonies are to take place, or rather they hold a general council, at which all the men of the country assist to designate the spot where the festival is to take place. After this, each returns to his village, and they take all the bones of the dead, which they cleanse and make quite clean, and keep them carefully, although they smell like bodies newly buried. Thereupon, all of the relatives and friends of the dead take the said bones along with their necklaces, furs, tomahawks, kettles and other things which they esteem of value, and much food, and carry them to the appointed spot, and being all assembled they lay the food in a place designated by the men of that village, holding feasts and continual dances for the space of ten days that the festival lasts, and while it is in progress the other tribes from all sides arrive to witness this festival and the ceremonies that take place, which are very costly. Now by means of these ceremonies, such as dances, feasts and assemblies thus conducted, they renew their friendship, saying that the bones of their relatives and friends are to be placed all together, representing by an image that just as their bones are collected and united in one and the same place, so also during their lives they should be united in friendship and harmony as relatives and friends, without the possibility of separation. These bones of the relatives and friends of both being thus mingled, they make many speeches on the subject, then after some grimacing or posturing they dig a great pit ten fathoms square in which they place these said bones with the necklaces, wampum chains, tomahawks, kettles, sword-blades, knives and other trifles, which however are of no small value among them, and they cover the whole with earth, placing upon it several large pieces of wood, with a quantity of posts that they put around it, erecting a covering upon them. This is the method they employ for the dead; it is their greatest ceremony.[225]

Sagard wrote a more detailed account:

At the very time that any one dies they wrap his body rather tightly in his best robe, then put it on the mat where he died, with someone always near him until the hour that he is carried

[225] Champlain, *Voyages*, 3: 160-63.

to the coffin. Meanwhile, all his relatives and friends of that place as well as of other towns and villages are notified of this death and asked to be in the funeral procession. The chief of police on his part, does what is in his charge, for as soon as he is notified of this death he or his assistant for him proclaims it through the whole town and makes appeals to every one saying: All take courage, *Etsagon, Etsagon,* and all make the best possible feasts, for such a one who is dead. Then each in particular makes an effort to prepare the finest feast he can, and of what he can, then they distribute it and send it to all their relatives and friends, without reserving any of it for themselves, and this feast is called *Ogochin atiskein,* the feast of souls. Some nations in making these feasts also make a share for the deceased, which they throw in the fire; but I have never been informed by our Hurons that they also give a portion to the dead, nor of what becomes of it, inasmuch as that is of little importance. We can know and conjecture rather well, by what I have just said, how easy it is to persuade them to prayers, alms, and good works for the souls of the dead.

The Essedons, Asiatic Scythians, celebrated the funerals of their fathers and mothers with songs of rejoicing. The Thracians buried their dead with merrymaking, inasmuch (as they said) as they had left evil and arrived at beatitude; but our Hurons bury theirs with tears and in sadness, nevertheless so moderated and regulated to the standard of reason that it appears that these poor people have an absolute power over their tears and over their emotions, so that they only give vent to them by rule and only stop them by the same rule.

Before the corpse of the deceased leaves the cabin all the women and girls present break into tears and the usual lamentations, which they never begin or finish (as I have just said) except by order of the chief or master of ceremonies. When the order and signal is given all begin with one accord to weep and mourn in good earnest, women and girls, little and grown (but never the men, who only show a mournful and sad look and demeanor, with their heads hanging toward their knees), and to move and excite themselves more easily, they repeat the names of all their deceased relatives and friends, saying: And my father is dead, and my mother is dead, and my cousin is dead, and thus others, and all burst into tears; except the little girls who make a pretence of doing what they have no desire for, as they are not yet capable of these sentiments. Having wept sufficiently, the chief cries to them that it is enough and to stop weeping, and all stop.

Now to show how easy it is for them to weep by remembering and repeating the names of their deceased relatives and friends: the Huron men and women suffer rather patiently all kinds of injuries, but when this chord is touched and one recalls to them that some one of their relatives is dead they easily get in a rage and lose patience out of irritation and anger caused by the recollection being brought to them, and in fact would ill use those who would remind them; and it is for that and no other thing that I have sometimes seen them lose patience.

On the day and at the hour assigned for the interment each takes his place inside or outside the cabin to assist. They put the corpse on a litter or stretcher covered with a skin, and all the relations and friends with a great concourse of people accompany the corpse to the cemetery, which is usually an arquebuse shot distant from the town. When all have arrived there each keeps silent, some standing, others seated, as it pleases them, while they raise the corpse on high and arrange it in its coffin, made and prepared expressly for it: for each corpse is put into a coffin apart. It is made of thick bark and is raised on four big wooden pillars, painted a little, about nine or ten feet high; my guess is that in raising my hand, I could not touch the tops by more than a foot or two. The corpse being put up, with the bread, oil, hatchets, and other things that they wish to put there, they close it. From above they throw two round sticks, each a foot long and a little less than the thickness of the arm, one on one side for the young men and the other on the other for the girls (I have not seen this ceremony of throwing the two sticks done in all interments, only at some); they go after them like lions to see who will get them and be able to raise them in the air, in order to win a certain prize; I was greatly astonished that the violence used in snatching this stick from each others' hands and their rolling and tumbling on the ground did not suffocate them, the girls on their side as much as the boys on theirs.

Now while all these ceremonies are being observed, there

is on another side an officer mounted on a trunk of a tree who receives the presents that many persons make to dry the tears of the widow or nearest female relative of the deceased. Every thing he receives he raises to be seen by all, and says: Here is such a thing that so-and-so has given to dry the tears of so-and-so, then he stoops and puts it in her hands. When all is over each goes away to where he came from, with the same modesty and silence. I have seen in some places other corpses put in the ground (very few, however), over which there was a cabin or shrine of dressed bark erected and around it a circular hedge made of stakes driven in the ground, for fear of dogs or wild beasts, or out of honor and respect for the deceased. . . .

Among some nations of our Indians, they are accustomed to paint their faces black on the death of their relatives and friends, which is a sign of mourning. They also paint the face of the deceased and embellish him with painted ornaments, feathers, and other trinkets. If he died in war the chief makes a sort of a funeral oration in the presence of the corpse, inciting and exhorting the assembly, on the death of the deceased, to take vengeance for such an inquity and to make war on their enemies as quickly as possible, in order that so great a wrong shall not rest unpunished and that another time they will not be so bold as to fall upon them. . . .

Every ten years or thereabouts our Indians and other sedentary tribes have the great festival or ceremony of the dead in one of their cities or villages, as it has been decided and ordered by a general council of all those of the country (for the bones of the deceased are buried individually only for a time). The other neighboring tribes are notified in order that those persons who have chosen that town to be the burying place of their relations' bones may bear them there, and others who wish to come from piety may honor the festival with their presence. For all are welcomed and feasted during the several days that the ceremony lasts, and one sees only kettles on the fire and continuous feasts and dances, and this brings an immense number of people who flock in from all sides.

The women who have to carry the bones of their relatives go to the cemeteries for them, and if the flesh is not all consumed they clean it off and take away the bones. These they wash and wrap in fine new beaverskins and beads and necklaces of porcelain, which the relatives and friends contribute and give, saying: Behold, here is what I give for the bones of my father, my mother, my uncle, cousin, or other relative. And putting them in a new sack they carry them on their backs; they also decorate the top of the sack with a number of little ornaments, necklaces, bracelets, and other embellishments. Then the pelts, hatchets, kettles, and other things that they reckon of value, with a quantity of provisions, are also carried to their destination, and when all are assembled there they put their food in one place to be used in feasts, which are a great expense to them, and then hang up decently in the cabins of their hosts all their sacks and their pelts, while awaiting the day on which all must be buried in the ground.

The pit is made outside the city, very large and deep, and capable of containing all the bones, furnishings, and pelts dedicated for the deceased. A high scaffold is erected along the edge, to which they carry all the sacks of bones; then they line the pit everywhere, on the bottom and the sides, with new beaverskins and robes; then they put in a layer of hatchets, next of kettles, beads, necklaces, and bracelets of porcelain, and other things given by the relatives and friends. That done, the chiefs from the height of the scaffold empty and pour out all the bones from the sacks into the pit among the merchandise, which they cover again with other new skins, then with bark, and afterward they throw the earth back on top and some large pieces of wood. To mark their respect for the place they drive wooden posts in the ground all around the pit and make a covering over it which lasts as long as it can. Then they feast once again, take leave of one another, and return whence they came, very joyous and pleased that the souls of their relatives and friends will have plenty to take from and to make them rich that day in the other life.

Christians, let us reflect a little and see if our fervors for the souls of our relatives confined in the prisons of God are as great as those of the poor Indians toward the souls of their fellow deceased, and we shall find that their fervors surpass ours, and that they have more love for one another in this life and after death than we, who say we are wiser and are less so in fact, speaking only of fidelity and kindness; for if it is a question of giving alms or of doing some other pious work for the living or dead, it is often with so much difficulty and repugnance that it seems with a good many that their entrails are being torn from their abdomen so hard is it for them to do good. On the contrary our Hurons and other Indian tribes make their presents and give their alms for the living and the dead with so much gaiety and so freely that you would say, upon seeing them, that nothing is more esteemed among them than to do good and help those who are in need, and particularly the souls of their deceased relatives and friends, to whom they give the finest and the best that they have, sometimes at great inconvenience to themselves. A person will give almost all he has for the bones of the man or the woman he loved and cherished in this life and still loves after death. Ongyate is an example, who, because he had given and enclosed with the corpse of his deceased wife (without our knowledge) almost all that he had, remained very poor and inconvenienced from it, and yet was glad of it, hoping that his deceased wife would be better off for it in the other life.

Now by means of these ceremonies and assemblies they contract new friendships and unions among themselves, saying that, as all the bones of their deceased relatives and friends are assembled and united in the same place, so also they themselves should during their lives, all live together in the same unity and concord, as good relatives and friends, without it being possible to separate or divert them from it for any misdeed or misfortune; and so in fact they do live.[226]

The most complete description of the ceremonies observed at death and at the subsequent communal burial was written by Brébeuf in 1636. Eulogizing the piety shown by the Huron on these occasions even more than did Sagard, he wrote:

Our Savages are not Savages as regards the duties that Nature itself constrains us to render to the dead; they do not yield in this respect to many Nations much more civilized. You might say that all their exertions, their labors, and their trading, concern almost entirely the amassing of something with which to honor the Dead. They have nothing sufficiently precious for this

[226] Sagard, *Le Grand voyage*, pp. 282-95.

purpose; they lavish robes, axes, and Porcelain in such quantities that, to see them on such occasions, you would judge that they place no value upon them; and yet these are the whole riches of the Country. You will see them often, in the depth of winter, almost entirely naked, while they have handsome and valuable robes in store, that they keep in reserve for the Dead; for this is their point of honor. It is on such occasions they wish above all to appear magnificent. But I am speaking here only of their private funerals. These simple people are not like so many Christians, who cannot endure that any one should speak to them about death, and who in a mortal sickness put the whole house to trouble to find means of breaking the news to the sick man without hastening his death. Here when any one's health is despaired of, not only do they make no difficulty in telling him that his life is near its close, but they even prepare in his presence all that is needed for his burial; often they show him the robe, the stockings, the shoes, and the belt which he is to wear. Frequently they are prepared after their fashion for burial, before they have expired; they make their farewell feast to their friends, at which they sometimes sing without showing any dread of death, which they regard with very little concern, considering it only as the passage to a life differing very little from this. As soon as the sick man has drawn his last breath, they place him in the position in which he is to be in the grave; they do not stretch him at length as we do, but place him in a crouching posture, almost the same that a child has in its mother's womb. Thus far, they restrain their tears. After having performed these duties the whole Cabin begins to resound with cries, groans, and wails; the children cry *Aistan*, if it be their father; and the mother, *Aien, Aien*, "My son, my son." Any one who did not see them, quite bathed in their tears, would judge, to hear them, that these are only ceremonial tears; they make their voices tremble all with one accord, and in a lugubrious tone, until some person of authority makes them stop. As soon as they cease, the Captain goes promptly through the cabins, making known that such and such a one is dead. On the arrival of friends, they begin anew to weep and complain. Frequently some one of importance begins to speak, and consoles the mother and the children,—at times launching into praises of the deceased, lauding his patience, his good-nature, his liberality, his magnificence, and, if he were a warrior, the greatness of his courage; at times he will say, "What would you have? there was no longer any remedy, he must indeed die, we are all subject to death, and then he dragged on too long," etc. It is true that, on such occasions, they are never lacking in speech. I have sometimes been surprised to see them dwelling a long time on this subject, and bringing forward, with such discretion, every consideration that might give consolation to the relatives of the deceased.

Word of the death is also sent to the friends who live in the other villages; and, as each family has some one who takes care of its Dead, these latter come as soon as possible to take charge of everything, and determine the day of the funeral. Usually they inter the Dead on the third day; as soon as it is light, the Captain gives orders throughout the whole Village that a feast be made for the dead. No one spares what he has of the best. They do this, in my opinion, for three reasons: First, to console one another, for they exchange dishes, and hardly any one eats any of the feast he has prepared; secondly, on account of those of other Villages, who often come in great numbers. Thirdly, and principally, to serve the soul of the deceased, which they believe takes pleasure in the feast, and in eating its share. All the kettles being emptied, or at least distributed, the Captain publishes throughout the Village that the body is about to be borne to the Cemetery. The whole Village assembles in the Cabin; the weeping is renewed; and those who have charge of the ceremonies get ready a litter on which the corpse is placed on a mat and enveloped in a Beaver robe, and then four lift and carry it away; the whole Village follows in silence to the Cemetery. A Tomb is there, made of bark and supported on four stakes, eight to ten feet high. However, before the corpse is put into it, and before they arrange the bark, the Captain makes known the presents that have been given by friends. In this Country, as well as elsewhere, the most agreeable consolations for the loss of friends are always accompanied by presents, such as kettles, axes, Beaver robes, and Porcelain Collars. If the deceased was a person of importance in the Country, not only the friends and neighbors, but even the Captains of other Villages, will come in person and bring their presents. Now all the presents do not follow the dead man into the grave; sometimes a Porcelain collar is put around his neck, and near by a comb, a gourd full of oil, and two or three little loaves of bread; and that is all. A large share goes to the relatives, to dry their tears; the other share goes to those who have directed the funeral ceremonies, as a reward for their trouble. Some robes, also, are frequently laid aside, or some hatchets, as a gift for the youth. The Chief puts into the hands of some one of the latter a stick about a foot long, offering a prize to the one who will take it away from him. They throw themselves upon him in a body, with might and main, and remain sometimes a whole hour struggling. This over, each one returns quietly to his Cabin.

I had forgotten to say that usually, during this whole ceremony, the mother or the wife will be at the foot of the grave calling to the deceased with singing, or more frequently complaining in a lugubrious voice.

Now all these ceremonies do not always take place; as for those killed in war, they inter them, and the relatives make presents to their patrons, if they had any, which is rather common in this Country, in order to encourage them to raise a force of soldiers, and avenge the death of the deceased. As to the drowned, they are interred also, after the most fleshy parts of the body have been taken off, piece by piece, as I have explained more in detail in speaking of their superstitions. Double the presents are given on such an occasion, and people from the whole Country often gather there, and contribute of their property; and this is done, they say, to appease the Sky, or the Lake.

There are even special ceremonies for little children who die less than a month or two old; they do not put them like the others into bark tombs set up on posts, but inter them on the road,—in order that, they say, if some woman passes that way, they may secretly enter her womb, and that she may give them life again, and bring them forth. . . .

The funeral ceremonies over, the mourning does not cease, the wife continues it the whole year for the husband, and the husband for the wife; but the great mourning properly lasts only ten days. During this time they remain lying on mats and enveloped in furs, their faces against the ground, without speaking or answering anything except *Cway*, to those who come and visit them. They do not warm themselves even in Winter, they eat cold food, they do not go to the feasts, they go out only at night for their necessities; they cause a handful of hair to be cut from the back of the head; they say this is done only when the grief is profound,—the husband practicing this ceremony generally on the death of his wife, or the wife on the death of her husband. This is what there is of their great mourning.

The lesser mourning lasts all the year. When they go visiting they do not make any salutation, not even saying *Cway*, nor do they grease their hair; the women do it, however, when their mothers command them, as the latter have at their disposal their hair, and even their persons; it is their privilege to send the daughters to feasts, for without the command many would not go. What I find remarkable is that, during the whole year, neither the husband nor the wife remarries; if they did, they would be talked about throughout the Country.

The graves are not permanent; as their Villages are stationary only during a few years, while the supplies of the forest last, the bodies remain in the Cemeteries until the feast of the Dead, which usually takes place every twelve years. Within this time they do not cease to honor the dead frequently; from time to time, they make a feast for their souls throughout the whole Village, as they did on the day of the funeral, and revive their names as often as they can. For this purpose they make presents to the Captains, to give to him who will be content to take the name of the deceased; and, if he was held in consideration and esteem in the Country while alive, the one who resuscitates him, —after a magnificent feast to the whole country, that he may make himself known under this name,—makes a levy of the resolute young men and goes away on a war expedition, to perform some daring exploit that shall make it evident to the whole Country that he has inherited not only the name, but also the virtues and courage of the deceased.

Of the solemn feast of the Dead.

The feast of the Dead is the most renowned ceremony among the Hurons; they give it the name of feast because, as I shall now fully relate, when the bodies are taken from their Ceme-

teries, each Captain makes a feast for the souls in his Village,—
the most considerable and most magnificent having been that
of the Master of the Feast, who is for that reason called par
excellence, the Master of the Feast.

This Feast abounds in ceremonies, but you might say that the
principal ceremony is that of the kettle; this latter overshadows
all the rest, and the feast of the Dead is hardly mentioned, even
in the most important Councils, except under the name of "the
kettle." They appropriate to it all the terms of cookery, so that,
in speaking of hastening or of putting off the feast of the Dead,
they will speak of scattering or of stirring up the fire beneath
the kettle; and, employing this way of speaking, one who should
say "the kettle is overturned," would mean that there would
be no feast of the Dead.

Now usually there is only a single feast in each Nation; all the
bodies are put in a common pit. I say, usually, for this year,
which has happened to be the feast of the Dead, the kettle has
been divided; and five Villages of the part where we are have
acted by themselves, and have put their dead into a private pit.
He who was Captain of the preceding feast, and who is regarded
as the Chief of this place, has given as an excuse that his kettle
and his feast had been spoiled, and that he was obliged to make
another; but in reality this was only a pretext. The principal
cause of this separation is that the notables of this Village have
been complaining this long time that the others take everything
upon themselves; that they do not become acquainted as they
would like with the affairs of the Country; that they are not
called to the most secret and important Councils, and to a share
of the presents. This division has been followed by distrust on
both sides; . . .

Twelve years or thereabout having elapsed, the Old Men and
Notables of the Country assemble, to deliberate in a definite way
on the time at which the feast shall be held to the satisfaction
of the Whole Country and of the foreign Nations that may be
invited to it. The decision having been made, as all the bodies
are to be transported to the Village where is the common grave,
each family sees to its dead, but with a care and affection that
cannot be described; if they have dead relatives in any part of
the Country, they spare no trouble to go for them; they take

them from the Cemeteries, bear them on their shoulders, and
cover them with the finest robes they have. In each Village they
choose a fair day, and proceed to the Cemetery, where those
called *Aiheonde,* who take care of the graves, draw the bodies
from the tombs in the presence of the relatives, who renew their
tears and feel afresh the grief they had on the day of the funeral.
I was present at the spectacle, and willingly invited to it all our
servants; for I do not think one could see in the world a more
vivid picture or more perfect representation of what Man is.
. . . For, after having opened the graves, they display before you
all these Corpses, on the spot, and they leave them thus exposed long enough for the spectators to learn at their leisure, and
once for all, what they will be some day. The flesh of some is
quite gone, and there is only parchment on their bones; in other
cases, the bodies look as if they had been dried and smoked, and
show scarcely any signs of putrefaction; and in still other cases
they are still swarming with worms. When the friends have
gazed upon the bodies to their satisfaction, they cover them with
handsome Beaver robes quite new; finally, after some time they
strip them of their flesh, taking off the skin and flesh which they
throw into the fire along with the robes and mats in which the
bodies were wrapped. As regards the bodies of those recently
dead, they leave these in the state in which they are, and
content themselves by simply covering them with new robes. Of
the latter they handled only one Old Man, of whom I have
spoken before, who died this Autumn on his return from fishing;
this swollen corpse had only begun to decay during the last
month, on the occasion of the first heat of Spring; the worms
were swarming all over it, and the corruption that oozed out of
it gave forth an almost intolerable stench; and yet they had the
courage to take away the robe in which it was enveloped, cleaned
it as well as they could, taking the matter off by handfuls, and
put the body into a fresh mat and robe, and all this without
showing any horror at the corruption. . . . As they had to remove
the flesh from all these corpses, they found in the bodies of two
a kind of charm,—one, that I saw myself, was a Turtle's egg
with a leather strap; and the other, which our Fathers handled,
was a little Turtle of the size of a nut. These excited the belief
that they had been bewitched, and that there were Sorcerers in

our Village,—whence came the resolution to some to leave at once; indeed, two or three days later one of the richest men, fearing that some harm would come to him, transported his Cabin to a place two leagues from us, to the Village of *Arontaen*.

The bones having been well cleaned, they put them partly into bags, partly into fur robes, loaded them on their shoulders, and covered these packages with another beautiful hanging robe. As for the whole bodies, they put them on a species of litter, and carried them with all the others, each into his Cabin, where each family made a feast to its dead.

Returning from this feast with a Captain who is very intelligent, and who will some day be very influential in the affairs of the Country, I asked him why they called the bones of the dead *Atisken*. He gave me the best explanation he could, and I gathered from his conversation that many think we have two souls, both of them being divisible and material, and yet both reasonable; the one separates itself from the body at death, yet remains in the Cemetery until the feast of the Dead,—after which it either changes into a Turtledove, or, according to the most common belief, it goes away at once to the village of souls. The other is, as it were, bound to the body, and informs, so to speak, the corpse; it remains in the ditch of the dead after the feast, and never leaves it, unless some one bears it again as a child. He pointed out to me, as a proof of this metempsychosis, the perfect resemblance some have to persons deceased. A fine Philosophy, indeed. Such as it is, it shows why they call the bones of the dead, *Atisken*, "the souls."

A day or two before setting out for the feast, they carried all these souls into one of the largest Cabins of the Village, where one portion was hung to the poles of the cabin, and the other portion spread out through it; the Captain entertained them, and made them a magnificent feast in the name of a deceased Captain, whose name he bore. I was at this feast of souls, and noticed at it four peculiar things. First, the presents which relatives made for the feast, and which consisted of robes, Porcelain collars, and kettles, were strung on poles along the Cabin, on both sides. Secondly, the Captain sang the song of the deceased Captain, in accordance with the desire the latter had expressed, before his death, to have it sung on this occasion. Thirdly, all the guests had the liberty of sharing with one another whatever good things they had, and even of taking these home with them, contrary to the usual custom of feasts. Fourthly, at the end of the feast, by way of compliment to him who had entertained them, they imitated the cry of souls, and went out of the Cabin, crying *haéé, haé*.

The feast was to take place on the Saturday of Pentecost; but some affairs that intervened, and the uncertainty of the weather, caused it to be postponed until Monday. The seven or eight days before the feast were spent in assembling the souls, as well as the Strangers who had been invited; meanwhile from morning until night the living were continually making presents to the youth, in consideration of the dead. On one side the women were shooting with the bow for a prize,—a Porcupine girdle, or a collar or string of Porcelain beads; elsewhere in the village, the young men were shooting at a stick to see who could hit it. The prize for this victory was an axe, some knives, or even a beaver robe. From day to day the souls arrived. It is very interesting to see these processions, sometimes of two or three hundred persons; each one brings his souls, that is, his bones, done up in parcels on his back, under a handsome robe, in the way I have described. Some had arranged their parcels in the form of a man, ornamented with Porcelain collars, and elegant bands of long red fur. On setting out from the Village, the whole band cried out *haéé, haé*, and repeated this cry of the souls on the way. This cry they say relieves them greatly; otherwise the burden, although of souls, would weigh very heavily on their backs, and cause them a backache all the rest of their lives. They go short journeys; our Village was three days in going four leagues to reach *Ossossané*, which we call la Rochelle, where the ceremonies were to take place. As soon as they arrive near a Village they cry again *haéé, haé*. The whole Village comes to meet them; plenty of gifts are given on such an occasion. Each has his rendezvous in one of the Cabins, all know where they are to lodge their souls, so it is done without confusion. At the same time, the Captains hold a Council, to discuss how long the band shall sojourn in the Village. . . . We were lodged a quarter of a league away, at the old Village, in a cabin where there were fully a hundred souls hung to and fixed upon the poles, some of them smelled a little stronger than musk.

On Monday, about noon, they came to inform us that we

should hold ourselves in readiness, for they were going to begin the ceremony; they took down at the same time, the packages of souls; and the relatives again unfolded them to say their last adieus; the tears flowed afresh. I admired the tenderness of one woman toward her father and children; she is the daughter of a Chief who died at an advanced age, and was once very influential in the Country; she combed his hair and handled his bones, one after the other, with as much affection as if she would have desired to restore life to him; she put beside him his *Atsatonewai*, this is his package of Council sticks, which are all the books and papers of the Country. As for her little children, she put on their arms bracelets of Porcelain and glass beads, and bathed their bones with her tears; they could scarcely tear her away from these, but they insisted, and it was necessary to depart immediately. The one who bore the body of this old Captain walked at the head; the men followed, and then the women, walking in this order until they reached the pit.

Let me describe the arrangement of this place. It was about the size of the place Royale at Paris. There was in the middle of it a great pit, about ten feet deep and five brasses wide. All around it was a scaffold, a sort of staging very well made, nine to ten brasses in width, and from nine to ten feet high; above this staging there were a number of poles laid across, and well arranged, with cross-poles to which these packages of souls were hung and bound. The whole bodies, as they were to be put in the bottom of the pit, had been the preceding day placed under the scaffold, stretched upon bark or mats fastened to stakes about the height of a man, on the borders of the pit.

The whole Company arrived with their corpses about an hour after Mid-day, and divided themselves into different cantons, according to their families and Villages, and laid on the ground their parcels of souls, almost as they do earthen pots at the Village Fairs. They unfolded also their parcels of robes, and all the presents they had brought, and hung them upon poles, which were from 5 to 600 toises in extent; so there were as many as twelve hundred presents which remained thus on exhibition two full hours, to give Strangers time to see the wealth and magnificence of the Country. I did not find the Company so numerous as I had expected; if there were two thousand persons, that was about all. About three o'clock, each one put away his various articles, and folded up his robes.

Meanwhile, each Captain by command gave the signal; and all, at once, loaded with their packages of souls, running as if to the assault of a town, ascended the Stage by means of ladders hung all around it, and hung them to cross poles, each Village having its own department. That done, all the ladders were taken away; but a few Chiefs remained there and spent the rest of the afternoon, until seven o'clock, in announcing the presents which were made in the name of the dead to certain specified persons.

"This," said they, "is what such a dead man gives to such and such a relative." About five or six o'clock, they lined the bottom and sides of the pit with fine large new robes, each of ten Beaver skins, in such a way that they extended more than a foot out of it. As they were preparing the robes which were to be employed for this purpose, some went down to the bottom and brought up handfuls of sand. I asked what this ceremony meant, and learned that they have a belief that this sand renders them successful at play. Of those twelve hundred presents that had been displayed, forty-eight robes served to line the bottom and sides of the pit; and each entire body, besides the robe in which it had been enveloped, had another one, and sometimes even two more, to cover it. That was all; so that I do not think each body had its own robe, one with another, which is surely the least it can have in its burial; for what winding sheets and shrouds are in France, Beaver robes are here. But what becomes then of the remainder? I will explain, in a moment.

At seven o'clock, they let down the whole bodies into the pit. We had the greatest difficulty in getting near; nothing has ever better pictured for me the confusion there is among the damned. On all sides you could have seen them letting down half-decayed bodies; and on all sides were heard a horrible din of confused voices of persons, who spoke and did not listen; ten or twelve were in the pit and were arranging the bodies all around it, one after another. They put in the middle of the pit three large kettles, which could only be of use for souls; one had a hole through it, another had no handle, and the third was of scarcely more value. I saw very few Porcelain collars; it is true, they put many on the bodies. This is all that was done on this day.

All the people passed the night on the spot; they lighted many fires, and slung their kettles. We withdrew for the night to the old Village, with the resolve to return the next morning, at day-break, when they were to throw the bones into the pit; but we could hardly arrive in time, although we made great haste, on account of an accident that happened. One of the souls, which was not securely tied, or was perhaps too heavy for the cord that fastened it, fell of itself into the pit; the noise awakened the Company, who immediately ran and mounted in a crowd upon the scaffold, and emptied indiscriminately each package into the pit, keeping, however, the robes in which they were enveloped. We had only set out from the Village at that time, but the noise was so great that it seemed almost as if we were there. As we drew near, we saw nothing less than a picture of Hell. The large space was quite full of fires and flames, and the air re-sounded in all directions with the confused voices of these Bar-barians; the noise ceased, however, for some time, and they be-gan to sing,—but in voices so sorrowful and lugubrious that it represented to us the horrible sadness and the abyss of despair into which these unhappy souls are forever plunged.

Nearly all the souls were thrown in when we arrived, for it was done almost in the turning of a hand; each one had made haste, thinking there would not be enough room for all the souls; we saw, however, enough of it to judge of the rest. There were five or six in the pit, arranging the bones with poles. The pit was full, within about two feet; they turned back over the bones the robes which bordered the edge of the pit, and covered the remaining space with mats and bark. Then they heaped the pit with sand, poles, and wooden stakes, which they threw in without order. Some women brought to it some dishes of corn; and that day, and the following days, several Cabins of the Village provided nets quite full of it, which were thrown upon the pit. . . .

The whole morning was passed in giving presents; and the greater part of the robes in which the souls had been wrapped were cut into pieces, and thrown from the height of the Stage into the midst of the crowd, for any one who could get them; it was very amusing when two or three got hold of a Beaver skin, since, as none of them would give way, it had to be cut into so many pieces, and thus they found themselves almost empty-handed, for the fragment was scarcely worth the picking up. In this connection, I admired the ingenuity of one Savage,—he did not put himself to any trouble to run after these flying pieces, but, as there had been nothing so valuable in this Country, this year, as Tobacco, he kept some pieces of it in his hands which he immediately offered to those who were disputing over a skin, and thus settled the matter to his own advantage. . . .

As to the rest of the twelve hundred presents, forty-eight robes were used in adorning the pit. Each whole body had its robe, and some had two or three. Twenty were given to the master of the feast, to thank the Nations which had taken part therein. The dead distributed a number of them, by the hands of the Captains, to their living friends; some served only for show, and were taken away by those who had exhibited them. The Old Men and the notables of the Country, who had the administration and management of the feast, took possession secretly of a considerable quantity; and the rest was cut in pieces, as I have said, and ostentatiously thrown into the midst of the crowd. However, it is only the rich who lose nothing, or very little, in this feast. The middle classes and the poor bring and leave there whatever they have most valuable, and suffer much, in order not to appear less liberal than the others in this celebration.[227]

The feast of the dead is mentioned many times in the records of the twelve years the Huron lived in the region east and south of Georgian Bay, after Brébeuf wrote the foregoing account, but no one attempted to write a more extensive one. It is interesting to note that after the description by Cadillac, which probably applied to both the Huron and Ottawa at Mackinac about 1695, there is no record of this ceremony having been performed by the Huron.

The treatment of the body of a drowned person, which Brébeuf referred to in the above account as having been given elsewhere, was as follows:

[227] Brébeuf, *Relation* . . . . *1636*, *J.R.*, 10: 265-305.

They believe that the Sky is angry, when any one is drowned or dies of cold; a sacrifice is needed to appease it, but, good God! what a sacrifice, or rather what a butchery! The flesh of the dead man is the victim who is to be immolated. A gathering of the neighboring villages takes place; many feasts are made, and no presents are spared, as it is a matter in which the whole Country is interested. The dead body is carried into the cemetery, and is stretched out on a mat. On one side is a ditch, and on the other a fire for a sacrifice. At the same time, some young men chosen by the relatives present themselves, and station themselves around the corpse, each with a knife in his hand; and the protector of the dead person having marked with a coal the parts which are to be cut, they vie with each other in cutting the body, tearing off the fleshiest parts. At last they open the body and draw out its entrails, which they throw into the fire with all the pieces of flesh they had cut off, and throw into the ditch the carcass quite stripped of flesh. I have observed that during this butchery the women walk around them several times, and encourage the young men who cut up this body to render this good service to the whole Country, putting Porcelain beads into their mouths. Sometimes even the mother of the deceased, all bathed in tears, joins the party and sings in a pitiful tone, lamenting the death of her son. That done, they firmly believe they have appeased the Sky.[228]

Le Mercier stated that the Huron were accustomed to burn the flesh of any of their people who died outside of their own country and to extract the bones to take with them.[229] Similarly, Bressani wrote that, besides drowned persons, others who died a violent death were either burned or buried immediately. He also stated that the reason the chiefs of a village went through the village to notify everyone of the fact immediately after was so that no one would through ignorance insult the dead or their surviving relatives by speaking of them without appending "deceased," as we would say "the late so-and-so." If another person should perchance bear the

---

[228] *Ibid.*, pp. 163-65.
[229] *Relation . . . . 1637*, *J.R.*, 11: 131.

same name, he changed it either temporarily or permanently, in order that the relatives of the deceased on hearing the name of the other would not be grieved. The names of famous personages or chiefs, however, were never lost, but were assumed at a solemn banquet by a successor, who became the head of the family, or by some other person chosen as worthy to bear such a name.[230]

The ceremonies of adoption among the Neutrals were described by Sagard:

The Attiouindarons celebrate resurrections of the dead—especially of persons who deserved well of the country by their signal services—in order that the memory of illustrious and valorous men may, in some sort, live again in others. Accordingly, they convene assemblies for this purpose and hold councils at which they choose one of their number who has the same virtues and characteristics (if such a person can be found) as he whom they purpose to resuscitate, or, at least, his life must be without reproach among a savage people. Proceeding to the resurrection, they all stand upright, except the one who is to raise the dead; on him they impose the name of the deceased, and all, placing their hands low down, feign to raise him from the ground—meaning by this that they draw out of the tomb that eminent deceased personage and bring him back to life in the person of this other man. The latter stands up, and after loud acclamations from the people he receives the gifts offered by those who are present, who repeat their congratulations at many feasts and thenceforth regard him as if he were the deceased person whom he represents. Thus the memory of good persons, and of worthy and valorous captains, never dies among them.[231]

Ragueneau said that the mourning of the Huron women consisted in visiting no one, in walking with the head and eyes lowered, in being ill-clad, ill-combed, and having a dirty face, and even sometimes one blackened with charcoal.[232]

[230] *Breve relatione*, J.R., 39: 31-33.
[231] *Le Grand voyage*, pp. 289-90.
[232] *Relation* . . . . *1645-46*, J.R., 29: 285.

He stated, as did Brébeuf, that tears and lamentations were not for men and that they showed sorrow by sitting on the ground for half a day, without motion, speech, or even lifting their eyes or uttering a sigh.[233] He also said that when one was near death it was customary for the Huron to make a solemn feast to which were invited all of his friends and the most considerable persons, about a hundred in all.[234]

The death customs of the kindred Neutrals differed from those of the Huron, according to Lalemant. He wrote that whereas the latter carried the bodies to the cemetery immediately after death, the Neutrals took them only at the very latest moment possible, when decomposition finally rendered them insupportable; thus, the bodies might remain in the cabin an entire winter. After having placed the bodies on scaffolds that they might decay, the Neutrals took away the bones as soon as possible and displayed them here and there in their cabins until the feast of the dead.[235]

ASTRONOMY

The Huron, according to Sagard, never imagined that the world was round and that one could travel around it, that there were nations below them, nor that the earth went around the sun. They thought that the earth was pierced and that when the sun went down it entered this hole and remained hidden until the next morning, when it came out at the other end. Yet they understood that it was night in some countries and day in others at the same time, for Sagard reported that a Huron, on returning from a long voyage, said to him that it was already night in the country from which he came, although it was midsummer and only about four or five hours after noon among the Huron.[236]

Eclipses, too, according to Brébeuf, were not understood

---

[233] *Relation* . . . . *1650*, J.R., 25: 117-19.
[234] *Relation* . . . . *1649*, J.R., 34: 113.
[235] *Relation* . . . . *1641*, J.R., 21: 199.
[236] *Le Grand voyage*, 251-52.

as natural occurrences, but good or bad auguries were drawn from them, depending on the place in the sky at which they happened to be.[237] The Huron told Le Mercier that "there is still talk of a very remarkable darkening of the Sun, which was supposed to have happened because the great turtle which upholds the earth, in changing its position or place, brought its shell before the Sun, and thus deprived the world of sight."[238]

The Huron, in the words of François du Peron, "regulate the seasons of the year by the wild beasts, the fish, the birds, and the vegetation; they count the years, days, and months by the moon."[239]

Lahontan was the only early writer to treat the calendar of the Indians at any length:

The Year of the *Outaouas*, the *Outagamis*, the *Hurons*, the *Sauteurs*, the *Illinois*, the *Oumamis*, and several other Savages, consists of Twelve-Synodical Lunar-Months, with this difference, when Thirty Moons are spent, they add one supernumerary Month to make it up, which they call the *Lost Moon*, and from thence they begin their Account again, after the former Method. All these Months have very suitable Names; for Instance; What we name *March*, they call the *Worm-Moon*, for then the Worms quit the Hollow Chops of the Trees where they shelter'd themselves in the Winter. *April* is call'd *the Month* of *Plants*; *May* of *Flowers* and so of the others. I say, at the end of these Thirty Months, the next that follows is supernumerary, and not counted; for Example; We'll suppose the Month of *March* to be the Thirtieth Lunar-Month, and consequently, the Last of the Epochs. Next that should be counted the Month of *April*; whereas the *Lost Moon* takes place of it, and must be over before they begin their Account again; and this Month with the others, makes about a Year and a half. Because they have no Weeks, they reckon from the First till the Twenty Sixth of these sort of Months, and that contains just

[237] *Relation* . . . . *1636, J.R.,* 10: 59.
[238] *Relation* . . . . *1637, J.R.,* 12: 73.
[239] "Letter from François du Peron," *J.R.,* 15: 157.

that space of time which is between the first appearance of the Moon at Night, till having finish'd its Course, it becomes almost invisible in the Morning; and this they call the Illumination Month. For instance; a Savage will say, *I went away the first of the Month of Sturgeons* (that's *August*), *and returned the Twenty-ninth of the Month of Indian-Corn* (the same with our *September*); *and next day* (which is the last) *I rested myself.* As for the remaining three Days and a half of the *Dead-Moon,* during which 'tis impossible to be discern'd, they give them the Name of the *Naked Days.* They make as little use of Hours as Weeks, having never got the way of Making Clocks or Watches; by the help of which little Instruments, they might divide the Natural Day into equal parts. For this Reason, They are forc'd to reckon the Natural Day as well as the Night, by Quarters, Half, and Three-quarters, the Rising and the Setting-Sun, the Fore-noon and the Evening.[240]

Charlevoix doubted the exactness of Lahontan's statement that the Indians made the lunar years agree with the solar, but otherwise he made use of most of the material quoted above in his own account.[241]

RELIGION

Though not interested in converting the Huron, Champlain was harsher in his judgment of their religion than were later writers. He wrote that "they recognize no divinity, they adore and believe in no God nor in anything whatsoever, but live like brute beasts." This very definite denial is contradicted by his next statement that "they have indeed some regard for the Devil, or a similar name."[242]

Sagard made a threefold classification of the supernatural beings of the Huron: (1) Yoscaha was considered as the creator. He was a benevolent spirit. Opposed to him was his grandmother, Ataensiq, who was evil-minded. Both were apparently immortal, but otherwise lived and looked like human beings. Yoscaha periodically rejuvenated himself to an

---

[240] *Voyages*, 2: 427-29.
[241] *Journal*, 2: 216-17.
[242] *Voyages*, 3: 143.

age of twenty-five or thirty years. The process by which Ataensiq maintained her immortality was not explained. (2) There were spirits called Oki. This name signified a great devil, a great angel, an insane or evil spirit, benevolent and knowing, who did or knew some things above the ordinary. The same name was also applied to their physicians and magicians and even to their fools. (3) There were also certain spirits who ruled voyages, trades, wars, feasts, illnesses, and various places such as rivers and rocks. Prayers and offerings of tobacco were made to these spirits to obtain the desired result.[243]

Brébeuf said that the Huron had an idea of a divinity who created heaven and earth.[244] In looking for something supernatural, their lewdness and licentiousness prevented the Huron from finding God and the devil thrust himself in.[245] They recognized God only in created things, from which they hoped for benefits or dreaded mishaps, in particular the earth, rivers, lakes, rocks, and, above all, the sky. All of these were considered to be inhabited by powerful demons, called Oki. Brébeuf thought that it was really God whom they honored by their offerings to these Oki, as the sky and the sun were most frequently invoked, and the sky, or the Oki inhabiting it, was thought to rule the seasons, the waves, and the winds.[246]

Lalemant gave Ondoutaehte as the name of the God of War.[247] Demons were honored individually by having special homage paid them, probably by feasts. Hardly a day passed without one of these celebrations. In the winter there was a public celebration in which all were honored on the same day. This rite was called *ononhouaroia* ("upsetting the brain"). In this all the people, even the children, ran about as if mad, insisting upon obedience being paid their demons

---

[243] *Le Grand voyage*, 228-32.
[244] *Relation . . . . 1635, J.R.*, 8: 117.
[245] *Relation . . . . 1636, J.R.*, 10: 193.
[246] *Ibid.*, pp. 159-67.
[247] *Relation . . . . 1642, J.R.*, 23: 153.

by making them a present of something, the nature of which had been suggested to them in a dream and the description of which was presented as an enigma to be solved.[248] This ceremony is more commonly referred to as a remedy for some disorder and will be treated more fully under "Shamans and Medical Practice." Lalemant also claimed that although the devil seemed to have some power on earth and although the Huron were his slaves they gained nothing from observing their superstitions. The devil spoke to them in dreams; they invoked his aid, made presents and sacrifices to him to appease him or render him favorable. Health, cures, and happiness were attributed to him.[249]

Ragueneau said the Huron had no knowledge of the divinity who was the author of all things, but only an idea secret in their hearts. They called him *Aireskouy Soutanditenr*, when they were in the forest, on hunting expeditions, on water, and in danger of shipwreck. He was called *Ondontaeté* in matters of war and in the midst of battle, and they believed him the awarder of victory. The sky was invoked and paid homage. Both the sky and the sun were called upon as witnesses of transactions and were believed to be able to punish a break in faith.[250]

Brébeuf wrote in 1636 that there were some indications that they had formerly some more natural knowledge of the true God, as might be remarked in some particulars of their fables.[251]

Charms or amulets are frequently referred to as the familiar demons or spirits of their owners, sometimes merely as charms. Lalemant gave their name as *Ascwandic* ("familiar demon").[252] Ragueneau gave the native name as *Aaskouandy*.[253] These amulets were received by children from their

[248] *Ibid.*, p. 53.
[249] Lalemant, "Letter to the Father Provincial," *J.R.*, 28: 53.
[250] Ragueneau, *Relation . . . . 1648, J.R.*, 33: 225-27.
[251] *Relation . . . . 1636, J.R.*, 10: 125.
[252] *Relation . . . . 1639, J.R.*, 17: 207.
[253] *Relation . . . . 1648, J.R.*, 33: 215.

fathers, acquired in dreams, or found under circumstances that indicated their supernatural power. Du Peron wrote that nearly all of the Huron possessed amulets, and Lalemant said that all of them did.[254] The amulets that were believed most excellent were bought from the neighboring Algonquians. Ragueneau said these were called *onniont* and were a certain kind of charm of great virtue—a sort of serpent of almost the shape of an armored fish which pierces everything that it meets and hence was called *Oky* par excellence. Those who killed it or obtained a piece of it brought good fortune on themselves. The Huron in obtaining small bits of it from the Algonquians paid a very high price.[255]

Whatever the amulet might be, it was usually carried in the owner's pouch and spoken to when its help was needed. Occasionally, beads or bits of tobacco were put in the pouch for it. It was also the recipient of feasts, which were in the nature of thanksgiving and also to maintain its favor and power. If the efficacy of a charm should be diminished, a feast was necessary to restore it.[256] If it should be thrown away for any reason, such as vexation with it or conversion to Christianity, the owner was apt to find it later in his pouch or in his storage chest.[257] Some amulets had a general virtue, others a special one, which was learned in a dream. Success in hunting, fishing, trading, and gambling was thought to be dependent upon amulets. Often people were not content to rely on a single amulet, but possessed several, although some of these may have been special ones that were only called upon for specific functions. Sometimes, the amulet or familiar demon changed its shape, for instance, from a stone or a snake to a bean, the beak of a raven, or the claws of an eagle.[258] Lalemant remarked that some of the amulets were more efficacious and

---

[254] "Letter from François du Peron," *J.R.*, 15: 181; Lalemant, *Relation* . . . . *1639, J.R.*, 17: 211.

[255] *Relation* . . . . *1648, J.R.*, 33: 211-15.

[256] Lalemant, *Relation* . . . . *1639, J.R.*, 17: 207-9.

[257] *Ibid.*, p. 211.

[258] *Ibid.*, p. 159; Ragueneau, *Relation* . . . . *1648, J.R.*, 33: 211-15.

positive than others, although he did not say what it was that imparted or determined this greater virtue, whether the nature of the amulet or the experience of the owner with it.[259]

The familiar demons, or Oki, manifested themselves in dreams under different assumed shapes—such as an owl's claws or a snake's skin. These objects brought with them to the dreamer good luck in fishing, hunting, trading, and gambling. Some of them were even used as philters to attract love.[260]

Some of the writers of the contact period only indicated the belief of the Huron in the possession of souls by remarks as to their ideas concerning immortality or the places to which they went after death. Also, intimately related to belief in souls were the dreams of the Huron. These were the language of the souls. There were two souls, one rational and the other sensitive. The first detached itself from the body during sleep and wandered, not being dependent upon the body in its workings.[261] Most objects in the world, if not all, were believed to be possessed of souls. The disposal of them after death is variously reported. Sagard wrote that human souls left the body to go immediately to dance and rejoice in the presence of Yoscaha and Ataensiq, who kept the Milky Way, or the road of souls. The souls of dogs also went to an afterworld along another road of stars. Souls of grave furnishings likewise accompanied the souls to supply their needs in the afterworld.[262] Dogs were not the only animals to possess immortal souls, but deer, fish, and other animals had immortal and reasoning souls.[263]

According to Brébeuf, the soul separated from the body at death, but did not leave it immediately. When the body was carried to the grave, the soul walked in front. It then remained in the cemetery with the body, except for excursions at night, when it walked through the village and entered

[259] *Relation . . . . 1639, J.R.,* 17: 211.
[260] Lalemant, *Relation . . . . 1644, J.R.,* 26: 267.
[261] Ragueneau, *Relation . . . . 1648, J.R.,* 33: 189-91.
[262] *Le Grand voyage,* pp. 232-34.
[263] Brébeuf, *Relation . . . . 1635, J.R.,* 8: 121.

cabins to eat of feasts and the food remaining in kettles. It was for this reason that the Huron did not eat food left in the kettles from the day before. After the feast of the dead, the souls left the bodies. They were then changed into turtle-doves in the opinion of some, but the most common belief was that the souls, dressed in the robes and collars put into the grave, journeyed in a company to a great village toward the setting sun—with the exception of those of old people and young children, who, being unable to stand such a journey, remained in the country in a village of their own. There was no reward or punishment connected with life in the after-world. Each nation had its own village of souls, and the souls of those killed in war banded by themselves. Life in these villages was not different from that in those of the living; hunting and cultivation of corn were the same. Ataensiq resided in the village of souls.[264]

There was a system of nomenclature of the soul, wrote Brébeuf. It was named according to its condition or operation: first, *khiniondhecwi*, in so far as it animates the body and gives it life; second, *okiandaérandi* ("like a demon"), in so far as it is possessed of reason; third, *endionrra*, in so far as it thinks and deliberates on anything; fourth, *gonennonowal*, in so far as it bears affection to any object; and fifth, *esken*, if it is separated from the body.[265] It is probable that the first two items of Brébeuf's list were the sensitive and rational souls mentioned by Ragueneau.[266] There is a connection between the name for the fifth type of soul and the term for the bones of the dead, *atisken*.

There was still another destination possible for the souls of the deceased. François du Peron wrote his brother that the Huron believed that they entered other bodies after death.[267] This was believed to be especially true of the souls of little children.

[264] *Relation* . . . . *1636*, J.R., 10: 143-51.
[265] *Ibid.*, pp. 141-43.
[266] *Relation* . . . . *1648*, J.R., 33: 189-91.
[267] J.R., 15: 183.

Bressani reported in 1653 that they believed there were two places of life after death, one happy and the other wretched.[268] It is possible, one might say probable, that this belief was the result of the teaching of the missionaries; especially in view of the fact that this is the only mention of it, and in view of the definite statement of Brébeuf in 1635 that there was no reward or punishment connected with the Huron afterworld[269] and that they made no distinction between the good and the bad, the virtuous and the vicious, and honored equally the interment of both.

As a logical sequence to their belief in the souls of animals the Huron refrained from throwing to the dogs the remains of fish when they were fishing, or the bones of deer and moose when they were hunting; they thought that the others might learn of such treatment and not let themselves be taken. Another belief was that fish did not like the dead, and hence they would not go fishing when one of their friends was dead. The nets used to catch fish were also animated, and it was to satisfy the spirit of the net that they married their nets to two virgin girls at a fine feast in the spring. For fear of profaning their nets they were careful not to take the bones of their dead near them.[270] Lalemant said that, on inquiring about the marriage of the two young virgins to the net, he learned that some years before the time when he wrote, 1639, the neighboring Algonquians had commenced the practice after the soul of the net appeared to them and complained about losing his wife, and that the Huron had very shortly taken the custom over from them.[271]

Dreams, as set forth by Ragueneau,[272] had a connection with souls in the minds of the Indians. Through dreams, also, the familiar demons, Oki, or guardian spirits of the Indians were acquired or their virtues learned. Hence the religious

[268] *Breve relatione*, J.R., 39: 13-15.
[269] *Relation* .... *1635*, J.R., 8: 121.
[270] Brébeuf, *Relation* .... *1636*, J.R., 10: 167-69.
[271] *Relation* .... *1639*, J.R., 17: 197-201.
[272] The soul had desires that were made known by means of dreams, which were its language. Cf. *Relation* .... *1648*, J.R., 33: 189-91.

connotations of dreams were important. This was so strongly apparent to the missionaries and other writers of the contact period that many termed dreams the principal god of the Huron.

Brébeuf wrote that the faith in dreams surpassed all belief, that the Huron looked upon them as ordinances and irrevocable decrees, the execution of which it was a crime to delay. Dreams were their oracles, prophets, physicians, and absolute masters and often presided in their councils. The same writer continued his account of dreams by saying that in theory all dreams were not held in great credit. Regard was had to the dreamer, poor persons' dreams availing little. In order to have his dreams obeyed, the dreamer must be a person in fairly good circumstances and one whose dreams had been several times found true. As dreams usually called for a gift to the dreamer, the inference is that these requisites were to avoid dupery. Further, Brébeuf wrote, even good dreamers, in theory, did not pay equal heed to all their dreams—some were recognized as false and others as true. The latter were rare. In practice many dreams were obeyed whose standing was uncertain, because they did not wish to overlook possibly true ones. Parents dreamed for their sick children. Obscurities in dreams were interpreted and impossible demands were mitigated by shamans.[273]

Dreams usually related to a feast, song, dance, or game.[274] These were demanded through dreams, and their consummation was likewise required as a remedy for sickness and a formula for success in the dreamer's enterprises. Formulae of this nature were called Ondinoc ("a desire inspired by the demon").[275]

Communications received in dreams were believed to come true later; but if the impending event was undesired it might be forestalled by the proper observances. There is an example

[273] *Relation* . . . . *1636, J.R.,* 10: 169-73.
[274] *Ibid.,* p. 175.
[275] Lalemant, *Relation* . . . . *1639, J.R.,* 17: 153-55.

given by Lalemant of a man dreaming that he was bound and burned as a captive. On revealing his dream, he was bound and burned as if he were a captive by fellow Huron and then allowed to escape; whereupon he killed and roasted a dog, which was eaten at a public celebration as a captive would be. This feast and the burning were offered to the god of war, who was asked to accept this procedure in place of the reality of the dream.[276]

All dreams were not positive, but might be in the nature of a prohibition. An example of this was described by Lalemant. A man on arriving at an age when he might make feasts and be present at them had a dream in which he was forbidden, on penalty of misfortune, ever to make a dog feast or to permit one to be made for him.[277]

As has been noticed, Ragueneau reported that the Huron believed they had two souls, one rational and the other sensitive. He did not say which one of these it was that made known its desires through dreams. When these desires were accomplished, it was satisfied; but if its desires were not granted, it became angry and not only withheld the good and happiness that it usually procured for the body, but often did it harm, causing various diseases and even death.[278]

After a favorable dream a feast was usually given to the soul to induce it to keep its word. The soul was pleased at this expression of satisfaction with the propitious dream. The dream was mentioned at the feast and in the songs of the dreamer in order that his friends might know of it and congratulate him and also to hasten the promised effect.[279]

The importance of dreams as the medium through which remedies and the proper time for their application became known will be apparent in the discussion of shamans and medical practice.

[276] *Relation* .... *1642*, *J.R.*, 23: 171-73.
[277] *Relation* .... *1641*, *J.R.*, 21: 161.
[278] *Relation* .... *1648*, *J.R.*, 33: 189-91.
[279] *Ibid.*, pp. 195-97.

Shamans and Medical Practice

Shamans were designated in a number of ways by the French visitors of the Huron: jugglers, sorcerers, devils, magicians, soothsayers, medicine men, physicians, and apothecaries.

The Huron called the two classes of medicine men, those who diagnosed a disease and those who applied the indicated cures, and also the shamans who cast spells, predicted future events, or controlled the weather, by the same name of *Arendiouane* (also spelled *Arendiwane*), according to Brébeuf.[280] Lalemant stated that the physicians or visitors who determined the nature of a disease were called *Ocata*, and the apothecaries or givers of remedies, *Ontetsans* or *Aretsans*.[281] Ragueneau wrote *Saokata* instead of *Ocata*.[282] In the *Relation* of 1636, Brébeuf said there were four classes of shamans: first, those who presumed to command the rain and winds; second, those who predicted future events; third, those who found lost objects; fourth, those who restored health to the sick. They all worked by deception and imagination, according to Brébeuf, but he thought there was some foundation for the belief that the devil occasionally gave them some assistance.[283] Here he ignored his previous distinction between those who diagnosed and those who treated illnesses. Lalemant said that the Huron considered as angels of light the shamans who predicted the results of war and discovered the identity, number, and location of their enemies, and the shamans who concealed themselves and bewitched people were as angels of darkness. The missionaries called the first magicians and the second sorcerers.[284] The shamans of the second class were called *oky ontatechiata*

---

[280] *Relation . . . . 1635, J.R.,* 8: 123-25.
[281] *Relation . . . . 1639, J.R.,* 17: 211-13.
[282] *Relation . . . . 1648, J.R.,* 33: 193.
[283] *J.R.,* 10: 193-95.
[284] *Relation . . . . 1640, J.R.,* 18: 83.

("those who kill by spells") by the Huron, according to Ragueneau.[285]

A person became an *arendiwane* through power received from an *oki* or familiar spirit in a dream. Writing in 1636, Brébeuf said that formerly the offices were more valued than at that time, and that once it had been necessary to fast thirty days in a cabin apart, without anyone approaching except a servant, who also had to fast to be worthy to carry wood there. This thirty-day fast was still attempted by some who wished to attain greater heights in the profession.[286]

Shamans received their power through an *oki* or powerful genie who entered their bodies or appeared to them in their dreams or immediately on their awakening and showed them their power. Some claimed the genie appeared to them in the form of an eagle, a raven, or any one of numerous other shapes.[287]

The shamans usually prepared themselves in the practice of their profession by feasts and sweat baths, in order to invoke the assistance of their familiar spirits and to render their remedies more efficacious.[288] The information sought might be learned in the sweat bath, or the sweat might first be taken as a purification rite. Most of the missionaries are agreed that the honor and emoluments paid the shamans for their services were always great. François du Peron wrote his brother Joseph that they must be deprived of all their possessions, abstain from women, and obey perfectly all the devil suggested to them.[289] Presumably, this casting off of worldly goods refers to qualifying as a shaman, as otherwise this comment would be a contradiction of the statements of the other missionaries. Both men and women might be shamans; but all references to women put them in the classes of those who bewitched or cast spells, located persons, or predicted future

[285] *Relation* . . . . *1648, J.R.,* 33: 221.
[286] *Relation* . . . . *1636, J.R.,* 10: 197-99.
[287] Ragueneau, *Relation* . . . . *1648, J.R.,* 33: 193.
[288] Le Mercier, *Relation* . . . . *1637, J.R.,* 13: 261.
[289] "Letter from François du Peron," *J.R.,* 15: 181.

events. Apparently, no women served as physicians or apothecaries.

The methods of operation of the shamans who caused
rain to fall or cease and who could bring fine weather or
winds are nowhere given. Their compensation was doubtless
contributed by the whole community, as their profession was
seldom practiced in the interests of individuals.

The shamans who cast spells seem to have done so for
personal reasons, either of envy or vengeance. If they practiced their art in the interests of some other person, the fact
of such hire escaped the notice of the missionaries. Ragueneau
said that none of the men called *oky ontatechiata* ("those who
kill by spells") professed to do so.[290] Belief in persons with
this ability was widespread. Men and women were frequently
accused of causing death by their spells and summarily killed.

The shamans who posed as prophets boasted of their
prowess. They were most frequently consulted on matters
of war: whether or not a war party would be successful, where
it should go to find the enemy, or whether or not the village
was being approached by the enemy. Ragueneau said that the
same men who undertook to discover the whereabouts of lost
objects or the perpetrators of thefts also attempted to forecast
events connected with warfare.[291] These shamans worked by
pyromancy, hydromancy, necromancy, or received the desired
information in sweat baths or in frenzies induced in sweat baths
or in songs.

An example of pyromancy practiced by a female shaman
to learn the whereabouts of seven warriors was given by
Lafitau:

She began first by preparing a space of ground which she
cleaned and covered with flour or ashes very well sifted (I do
not remember exactly which of the two). She placed on this
powder, as if it were a geographical map, bundles of sticks, which
represented various villages of the different nations, observing

[290] *Relation* .... *1648, J.R.*, 33: 221.
[291] *Ibid.*

perfectly their position, and the direction of the wind. She then went into great convulsions during which we saw perceptibly seven sparks of fire come out of the sticks which represented our village, trace a way on this ash or flour and go from one village to the other. After having disappeared during a rather long time in one of these villages these sparks reappeared, nine in number, and traced a new path for the return, until at last they stopped rather close to the village or bundle of sticks from which the first seven came out originally. Then the Indian woman, all the while in a fury, disordered all the piece of ground she had prepared and where this scene had just taken place. Next she seated herself and after having given herself the time to become calm and to recover her senses, she told everything singular which had happened to the warriors, the route which they had kept, the villages through which they had passed, and the number of prisoners they had taken; she named the place where they were at that time and asserted that they would arrive at the village three days later, which was verified by the arrival of the warriors, who confirmed point for point what she had said.[292]

The last class of shamans listed by Brébeuf, the medicine men or physicians, used all the methods of the prophets and also feasts and dances to discover the nature of the illness of a sick person.[293]

The sudatory method played an important part with this class, both for the diagnosis of the ailment and as a prescription for a cure. The sweat lodges were erected both within and without the cabin. Lafitau wrote of them:

The sweat bath is their most universal remedy, and of it they make a great deal of use. It is for both the ill and the well, who thus are purged of abundant humors which can have changed their health or could later cause them infirmities.

The sweat bath is a little round cabin six or seven feet high with room for seven or eight persons. This cabin is covered with mats and furs to protect it from the outside air. In the middle of it they put, on the ground, a certain number of stones which they

---

[292] Lafitau, *Moeurs des sauvages ameriquains*, 1: 386-87.

[293] Brébeuf, *Relation . . . . 1635, J.R.*, 8: 123-25.

have left in the fire a long time until they have been well heated through, and above these they hang a kettle full of cool water. Those who are to sweat themselves enter this cabin nude, as much as decency can permit, and having taken their place, granted that they are not to treat of secret affairs there according to the custom of which we shall speak soon, they begin to move extraordinarily and to sing, each his song. And as the airs and words are often entirely different, it is the most disagreeable and discordant music that it is possible to hear.

From time to time, when the stones begin to lose their action, they revive them by wetting them with a little of this cold water which is in the kettle. This water no sooner touches the stones than it rises in a steam which fills the cabin and greatly increases the heat in it. They throw in each others' faces this cool water in order to prevent themselves from fainting away. In an instant their bodies trickle from all parts; and when their pores are well open and the sweat is most plentiful, they go out all singing and run to plunge themselves into the river, where they swim and writhe with much vehemence. Some, the ill ones in particular, content themselves with being sprinkled with cool water. It seems as if the contrast of an extreme heat with the cold of the water would lay hold of them and kill them; perhaps a sensitive man would even die of it; but they have the experience that it does them good, which is worth more than all the reasonings that one could make.[294]

The Huron recognized three causes of disease: first, natural disturbances; second, unfulfilled desires of the soul; third, spells of a sorcerer.[295] It does not appear that a shaman was always called upon to diagnose the first, if it were of the nature of a wound, although an apothecary was called in to treat it. A person might be sick, the ailment be diagnosed as a natural disease, and the treatment prescribed by a shaman. This shaman was paid for his services, and another was called upon to administer the treatment. Whether or not there was a working agreement between physician and apothecary does not appear in the documents. The treatment might consist of

[294] Lafitau, *Moeurs des sauvages ameriquains*, 2: 371-72.
[295] Ragueneau, *Relation .... 1648, J.R.,* 33: 199.

potions, emetics, certain waters which were applied to the diseased part, scarifications, or poultices. These natural remedies were believed to effect unfailingly the necessary cure. If the condition of the patient did not improve as rapidly as was expected, it was believed that complications prevented the operation of the remedies, and a rediagnosis was made to determine the obstacles, which were usually found to be unfulfilled desires of the soul or spells of an inimical shaman; either of these might also be the original diagnosis. An example of such a secondary diagnosis is that of a sick woman who dreamed that a black man touched her; a medicine man was called in, who took a sweat bath to learn the nature of the ailment and, on throwing tobacco into the fire, observed that she was bewitched and had five charms in her body, one of which was the most dangerous and would cause her death if not removed.[296]

Usually, the cause of illness was attributed to desires of the soul, which might be learned through the dreams of the sick person or through the medium of a shaman, when the soul had not declared them by dreams or had forgotten them completely. These hidden desires, called *ondinnonk*, were discovered by the shamans in various ways; some looked in a basin full of water and claimed to see various things pass over it, as on the surface of a mirror; others seemed to fall into a frenzy and, after exciting themselves by singing and shaking a tortoise-shell rattle, said they saw the things desired by the soul as if they were before their eyes; others concealed themselves in a small enclosure and saw the desires of the soul in the darkness around them. Even the souls of small children had desires. These were learned through the dreams of their parents or the operations of a shaman.[297]

The shaman might supplement the desires of the soul, which a patient learned through dreams, by a number of others, particularly if the patient were a person of note. In

---

[296] Le Mercier, *Relation* . . . . *1637*, J.R., 13: 31-33.
[297] Ragueneau, *Relation* . . . . *1648*, J.R., 33: 191-95.

this event the shaman announced a large number of desires which the general public was called upon to satisfy through presents, dances, feasts, ballets, and other pastimes. A council of captains was then convened, which decided whether or not they would exert themselves for the patient. If there were a number of captains or noted persons ailing at the same time, the council had to decide which one was to receive the favor of the public, since the drain on the resources of the community for all the gifts for even one person was rather heavy. The captains visited the favored one to find out the desires he had learned from his soul in dreams, in addition to those enumerated by the shaman. They then undertook to obtain satisfaction for them by announcing them at a public assembly. Individuals were eager for the opportunity of publicly showing their generosity. Presents remained in the possession of the patient if he recovered, in that of his relatives if he died. Ragueneau said that many persons feigned illness from motives of ambition, vanity, or avarice. Dances lasted three or four days, and those attending dressed in their best, to see the ceremonies and to be seen. Feasts were afterward given by relatives, the choicest morsel falling to the most notable present and to those who made the best appearance during the ceremonies. After such festivities the patient always gave thanks for what was done for him and said that he was cured.[298]

There is no report of the repetition of these elaborate ceremonies in the event that the patient did not recover immediately. Additional desires, however, were often discovered, and Ragueneau said that if the shaman saw that the patient was likely to die, something practically impossible to obtain was named as the desire, in order that a fatal ending would be seen to be inevitable rather than a reflection on the ability of the shaman.[299]

The dances, feasts, songs, or other ceremonies prescribed

[298] *Ibid.*, pp. 203-9.
[299] *Ibid.*, p. 205.

might belong to the shaman, the patient, or other interested parties. The heads of almost every family possessed some of these that were suitable for the cure of their diseases and also were efficacious in obtaining success in their business. They were taught these ceremonies and their uses by their "demons" who appeared to them in their dreams.[300]

If the cause of illness was a spell or charm put into the body of the sick person by a sorcerer, its identity and location were determined by one shaman, and another was engaged to remove it. The spell might be a knot of hair, a piece of a man's nail, an animal's claw, a piece of leather or bone, a leaf, grains of sand, or any other little object. It was expelled by the apothecary by means of emetics, by sucking, or with the point of a knife, but without making any incision. Failure to recover from a natural disease after application of natural remedies was attributed to such spells. In these circumstances, or after an original diagnosis of a spell, ten or twenty spells might be removed from the body without causing any improvement. Such a condition indicated that there was some other spell which was either more concealed or which the shaman had not the power to remove. Ragueneau remarked that the shamans still retained great credit after such failures, because the people resorted to them for many minor ailments or complaints which cured themselves shortly, but for which cures the shamans received the credit.[301]

Explanations for the smallpox epidemic that struck the Huron in 1636 were numerous. Some who objected to the presence of the missionaries claimed that they were responsible; since it is quite likely that the French introduced the disease, this was not far from the truth, although the missionaries did not have the intent imputed to them. The cures suggested were also varied. One shaman announced that spirits had told him in a dream that those who hung large masks at their doorways and figures of men, described

[300] Lalemant, *Relation* . . . . *1639*, J.R., 17: 153.
[301] *Ibid.*, pp. 199-203.

as similar to French scarecrows, above their cabins would be entirely delivered from this disease.[302] Another shaman prescribed the bark of ash, spruce, hemlock, and wild cherry boiled together in a large kettle, as a wash for the whole body. The people were also to be careful not to go out of their cabins barefooted in the evening. This preventive did not apply to women in their courses.[303]

The Huron shamans were very skillful in healing rupture, according to Brébeuf.[304] The Wenroronon, a related people who took refuge among the Huron in 1639, excelled in drawing an arrow from the body and curing the wound. The prescription for this had no effect except in the presence of a pregnant woman.[305] This condition of the prescription is surprising, in view of all the misfortunes usually attributed to the presence or touch of a pregnant woman, but Du Peron, who recounted many of the misfortunes thought to be caused by pregnant women, also said that such a woman by her presence and the application of a certain root extracted an arrow from a man's body.[306]

Barthélemy Vimont reported that the natural medicines might be classed as internal and external. The internal consisted of potions obtained from simples, without compounding or mixing them. For instance, he explained, from a species of fir, small branches were stripped, which were then boiled and the sap or juice drunk as an emetic. Branches of cedar, a small root like the French turnip, a species of wild sorrel, and other simples were similarly prepared and used for the same purpose. External remedies were for afflictions such as tumor. The treatment for this was a sort of scarification, cutting into the affected part with a knife. Often herbs or roots were applied to the scarified part to serve as an astringent

[302] Le Mercier, Relation . . . . 1637, J.R., 13: 231.
[303] Ibid., p. 261.
[304] Relation . . . . 1636, J.R., 10: 209.
[305] Lalemant, Relation . . . . 1639, J.R., 17: 213.
[306] "Letter from François du Peron," J.R., 15: 181.

when sufficient blood had flowed.[307] Lalemant mentioned one of the mission domestics who was treated by a shaman for a bruise caused by a blow on the head by a stone. Examination showed only the bruise and swelling of the injured part; this was scarified with a stone, breathed on, moistened with saliva, and the gum of certain roots then applied. With this treatment the man was enabled to return to the missionaries the next day.[308]

The following is an excerpt from Champlain concerning the shamans and the medical practices of the Huron as he observed them in 1615:

They have certain persons who act as Oquis or Manitous, as the Algonquins and Montagnais call them, and this sort of folk are doctors, to heal the sick and bind up the wounded, to predict future events, in short (to practise) all abuses and delusions of the Devil in order to mislead and deceive them. These Oquis or seers persuade their patients and the sick to make and have held feasts and certain ceremonies in order to be the sooner cured, their intent being to take part in them and gain the greatest possible advantage for themselves and, by the hope of a speedier cure, they get them to hold many other ceremonies which I shall describe farther on in the proper place. These are the people in whom they place most belief, but to be possessed by the Devil and tormented, like other savages farther off than they, is what is seen very rarely.[309]

As for the sick, a man or woman struck down or affected by some disease sends for the Oqui, who on arrival visits the sick person and learns and informs himself of his disease and pain. After that, the said Oqui sends for a great number of men, women and girls, with three or four old women, just as the said Oqui orders, and these enter the cabin dancing, each with a bearskin or the skin of some other beast over her head, but a bearskin is the commonest since nothing is more frightful, and there will be two or three other old women near the sick person or patient, who most frequently is feigning or imagining sickness. But of

---

[307] Relation . . . . 1642, J.R., 22: 293.
[308] Relation . . . . 1641, J.R., 21: 237.
[309] Champlain, Voyages, 3: 144.

this sickness they are soon cured, and they most frequently hold feasts at the expense of their friends or relatives who give them something to put into the kettle, besides those things they receive as presents from the dancers, male and female, such as wampum and other trifles, so that they are soon cured; for when they see that nothing more is to be expected they get up, with what they have been able to accumulate. But others really sick are not readily cured by such playing and dancing and goings on. To return to my narrative, the old women who are near the sick person receive the presents, each singing in turn, and then stopping; and when all the presents are made, they begin to lift up their voices with one accord, singing all together, and beating time with sticks on dry tree-bark; whereupon all the women and girls begin to place themselves at the extremity of the cabin as if for the purpose of making their entry in a ballet or masquerade, the old women walking in front with bearskins over their heads and all the rest following them one after another. They have only two kinds of dances with some sort of measure, one of four steps and the other of twelve, like the trioly of Brittany. They dance very gracefully, the young men often joining in. Having danced for an hour or two, the old women take hold of the sick woman to make her dance, and she pretends to get up sadly, then begins to dance, and once at it, after some space of time, she will dance and enjoy herself as much as the others. You can imagine how sick she must be. . . .

The medicine-man gains honour and reputation, at the sight of his patient being so soon cured and on his feet; which does not happen to those who are in extremities and overcome with weakness; for this kind of medicine gives them death rather than healing; for I assure you that sometimes they make such a noise and din, from morning till two o'clock at night, that it is impossible for the patient to bear it except with great difficulty. Sometimes a fancy will seize the patient to make the women and girls dance all together, but it must be by order of the Oqui, and this is not all, for he and the Manitou, accompanied by some others, will make grimaces and contortions to such an extent that they generally become as it were beside themselves, like lunatics and madmen, throwing fire about the cabin from side to side, swallowing red-hot coals, holding them for a time in their hands,

also throwing red-hot cinders into the eyes of the other on-
lookers; and, on seeing them in this state, one would say that the
Devil, Oqui, or Manitou, if such we must call him, possesses
them and torments them in that manner. And when this noise
and din is over, they withdraw each to his own quarters. Those
who have a great deal of trouble at this time are the wives of
those possessed, and all who belong to their cabins, for fear lest
these mad folk should burn up everything in sight, for when
they come in they are quite mad, with eyes flashing and frightful
to see, sometimes standing up, sometimes sitting, as fancy takes
them. Suddenly a whim will seize one and, laying hold of anything he finds and meets with in his path, he will throw it from
one side to the other and will then lie down and sleep some
little time, and waking up with a jump will take fire and stones
and throw them in all directions, without any precaution. This
madness passes after sleep which comes upon him again, and
then he will fall into a rage in which he summons several of his
friends to sweat with him, which is the remedy that serves them
best for keeping well, and while they sweat, the kettle works
hard to satisfy their hunger. They remain sometimes two or three
hours enclosed with big pieces of tree-bark, covered with their
robes, and having in their midst a great number of stones which
have been heated red-hot in the fire. They sing all the time they
are in the rage, and sometimes stop to take breath. Many jug-
fuls of water are given them to drink, since they are very thirsty,
and after all this the demoniac or devil-possessed madman becomes sober. However, it sometimes happens that three or four
of these sick persons get well, rather by happy accident and
chance than by science, which only confirms their false belief,
so that they are persuaded they have been cured by means of
these ceremonies, not bearing in mind that for two who get cured
ten others die from the noise and great din and the blowings
they make, which is more fitted to kill than to cure a sick person;
but that they should expect to recover their health by this noise
and we on the contrary by quiet and rest, shows how the devil
does everything the wrong way about. There are also women
who get into these rages, but they do not do so much harm;
they walk on all fours like beasts. Seeing this the magician called
the Oqui begins to sing, then with some grimaces blows upon her,

ordering her to drink certain waters and immediately to give a feast either of fish or of flesh, which must be found, even if it be scarce at the time; nevertheless this is done at once. When the shouting is over and the banquet finished, they return each to his cabin until the next time he comes to pay her a visit, blowing upon her and singing, with several others summoned for that purpose, holding in their hands a dry tortoise-shell filled with little pebbles which they rattle in the ears of the sick woman, ordering her to make forthwith three or four feasts, and a singing and dancing party, at which all the girls appear decked out and painted. . . . The said Oqui will order masquerades and disguises like those who run about the streets on Mardi-Gras in France. Thus they go and sing near the sick woman's couch, and parade the length of the village while the feast is being prepared for the masquers, who return very tired, having enough exercise to empty the kettle of its Migan.[310]

Sagard was not as derogatory in speculating on the motives of the patients and the shamans in his account as was Champlain:

Our Indians indeed dance and practice sobriety, which together with the use of emetics, are serviceable in preserving their health, but they have other means besides of maintaining it, which they often use. Such are the stoves and sweat baths by the use of which they get relief and prevent illness. But what also helps them to keep in health is the harmony that prevails among them. They have no lawsuits and take few pains to acquire the goods of this life, for which we Christians torment ourselves so much, and for our excessive insatiable greed in acquiring them we are justly and with reason reproved by their quiet life and tranquil dispositions.

There is nevertheless no body so well built nor disposition so well disciplined that it does not finally become enfeebled or give way under the influence of various accidents to which man is subject. For this reason our poor Indians, in order to cure the sicknesses or wounds that may come to them, have medicine men or masters of rites whom they call Oki and in whom they firmly believe, inasmuch as they are great magicians, great soothsayers,

[310] *Ibid.*, 1: 148-55.

and invokers of devils. They perform the functions of physicians and surgeons and always carry with them a bag full of herbs and drugs to doctor the sick. They also have an apothecary, cheap enough, who trails after them with his drugs and turtle shell, which is used in their incantations, and these men are not so unsophisticated that they cannot make the common people believe in them through their deceptions, in order to become influential and have the lion's share of the feasts and gifts.

If there is a sick person in a village one [medicine man] is immediately sent for to cure him. He makes invocations to his demon, blows upon the ailing part, makes incisions there, sucks out the bad blood, and does all the rest of his tricks, never forgetting to order feasts and amusements as a preliminary, if he can do so with decency, in order to take part in the festivity himself and return from it with his presents. If it is a question of having news of absent things, after having interrogated his demon, he utters some oracles, usually questionable and very often false, but also sometimes true, for the devil among his lies tells them some truths. . . .

I inquired of them respecting the chief plants and roots which they use for curing their illnesses, and among others they highly esteem the one called *Oscar*, which does wonders in healing all kinds of wounds, ulcers, and other sores. They have likewise other plants of a very poisonous nature, which they call *Ondachiera;* for this reason one must be careful and not risk eating any kind of root there if one is not acquainted with it and does not understand its effects and its virtues, for fear of unexpected mischances.

We had one day great apprehension for a Frenchman who had eaten one of these and who became very ill at once and as pale as death, but he was cured by emetics that the Indians made him swallow. Again we had another apprehension, which afterward turned into a laughing matter. Some little Indians had some roots called *Ooxrat*, like a small turnip or bald chestnut, which they had just pulled up to take to their cabins. A young French boy, living with us, had asked them for some and had eaten one or two. At first he found the taste rather agreeable, but shortly afterward he felt great pain in his mouth, like a burning pricking flame, and a great quantity of secretions and phlegm continually dropped from his mouth so that he thought he was about to die. And in fact we did not know what to do about it, being ignorant of the cause of this symptom and fearing lest he had eaten some poisonous root. But when we spoke to the Indians about it and asked for their advice they had the rest of the roots brought to see what they were, and when they had seen and recognized them, they began to laugh, saying that there was no danger nor any evil result to be feared, but rather good, if it were not for the stinging and burning pains in the mouth. They use these roots to purge the phlegm and moisture in the head of old people and to clear the complexion; in order to avoid the stinging pain they first cook them in hot ashes and then eat them without feeling any pain afterward; these do them all the good in the world. I am sorry that I did not bring some of them here to France on account of the use which I think would have been made of them. It is also said that the Montagnais and Canadians have a tree, called Annedda, with an admirable property; they strip off the bark and leaves of this tree, then boil them all in water and drink the water every other day; they put the dregs upon legs swollen with disease, and they soon get cured of this and of all other kinds of ailments, internal and external.

To render themselves more supple and agile in running and to purge pus from swollen parts, our Hurons make incisions and cuts with small sharp stones into the fat of their legs. With these stones they also draw blood from their arms for the purpose of joining and sticking together the broken pieces of their pipes or earthenware tobacco-burning tubes. This is an excellent discovery, and a secret that much more admirable, as the pieces glued with this blood are afterward stronger than they were before. I wondered also to see them burn themselves on their bare arms with the pith of the elder tree, for the pleasure of it, letting it burn away and smoulder on them, in such wise that the wounds, scars, and cicatrices remained there indelibly.

When a man wishes to take a sweat bath, which is the best and the commonest remedy that they have to keep them in health and to prevent maladies, he summons several friends to sweat with him, for alone he could not easily manage it. So they heat a number of stones red-hot in a great fire and take them out and put them in a pile in the middle of the cabin or wherever they wish to set up their sweat bath (for when on a journey in the wilds they sometimes take one); then all around the pile they arrange sticks in the ground as high as the waist or higher and bent over at the top in the shape of a circular table, with a space left between the stones and the sticks sufficient to accommodate the naked men who are to sweat. These sit on the ground side by side squeezed closely together all round the pile of stones, with their knees raised in front of their stomachs. When they are in position the whole sweat bath is covered above and at the sides with large pieces of bark and a number of skins, so that no warmth nor air can get out of the bath. Then, to heat themselves still more and to stimulate sweating, one of them sings, and the rest shout and repeat continually, strongly, and violently (just as in their dances), Het, het, het; and when they can stand no more heat they let in a little air, taking off a skin from the top, and sometimes also drinking large potfuls of cold water, and then they have the covering put on again. When they have sweated enough they go out and, if they are near a river, throw themselves in the water; if not, they wash themselves in cold water and then have a feast, for while they are sweating the kettle is on the fire. In order to have a good sweat they sometimes burn tobacco at it, by way of sacrifice and offering. I have seen some of our Frenchmen in these sweat baths with the Indians, and I was astonished that they would and could support it and that modesty did not persuade them to abstain from it.

It sometimes happens that the physician orders some one of his patients to leave the town and encamp in the woods or in some other place apart, so that he may practice upon him there during the night his devilish contrivances. I do not know any other reason that he could have for removing the patient, since usually this is only done for those who are infected with some nasty or dangerous disease, and such persons, and they alone and no others, do they force to separate themselves from the community until there is a complete cure. This is a laudable and most excellent custom and ordinance which, indeed, ought to be adopted in every country.

In this connection, and by the way of confirming what I have described, I shall relate that I was one day walking alone in the woods that belonged to the small tribe of the Quieunontater-ononons; seeing a little smoke rising and being desirous of observing what caused it, I went in the direction of it and found a round hut, constructed like a turret or tall pyramid, with an opening or air hole at the top through which the smoke issued. As this did not satisfy my curiosity, to find out what there was within, I gently opened the little door of the hut and discovered a lone man lying at full length beside a small fire. I asked him why he was thus kept away from the village and what was the cause of his suffering. He replied, half in Huron half in Algonquin, that it was because of a disease he had in his private parts, which gave him great pain and from which he only looked for death, and that their custom was to separate and send far away from the community those who were affected by such diseases, for fear of contaminating the rest by associating with them. Nevertheless, they supplied his small requirements and some part of what he needed, his relatives and friends not being able to do more for the time being because of their poverty. I was very sorry for him, but that only afforded him a little diversion and comfort for the small space of time that I was with him, for to give him any food or refreshment was out of my power, since I was myself in great need. . . .

I was frequently curious to enter the place where they were singing and blowing at the sick, in order that I might see the whole ceremony. But the Indians were not pleased, and only with difficulty did they allow me in, because they do not like to be watched in such actions. For this reason I think, or for some other which I do not understand, they also keep the place where it is going on as dark and dimly lighted as they can, blocking all the openings that may admit any light from above, and allowing only those to come in who are necessary or invited to be present. While the singing proceeds stones are being heated red-hot in the fire, which the medicine man handles and manipulates; then he chews hot coals, the deed of an unchained devil, and with his hands so warmed he rubs the parts of the patient affected by disease and blows at them or spits out on the diseased member some of the coals he has chewed up.

They have also among them persons possessed or raging mad, who will be taken by a strong desire to have the women and girls dance together, by the order of the Oki. But this is not all, for the patient and the medicine man, accompanied by some other, will make grimaces, utter conjurations, and throw themselves into contortions to such an extent that they generally become, as it were, beside themselves. Then the sick man appears quite mad, with eyes flashing and frightful to see, sometimes standing up, sometimes sitting, as the fancy takes him. Suddenly, a whim will seize him again and he will do as much harm as he possibly can; then he will lie down and sleep some little time, and waking up with a jump he will return to the first fury, upsetting, breaking, and throwing about everything that comes in his way, with unheard of noise, damage, and insolences. This madness passes with the sleep that overtakes him. Afterward, he has a sweat bath with some one of his friends whom he calls there, from whence it happens that some of these patients find themselves cured, and it is that which keeps their esteem for these diabolical ceremonies. It is quite within reason that these patients are not so bedeviled that they do not see the damage they do, but they think they must act like a demoniac in order to cure the imaginations or disturbances of their mind. By righteous divine permission it generally happens that instead of being cured they jump from the frying pan into the fire, as the saying is, and what before was only a mental caprice, caused by hypochondrial humor or the work of the evil spirit, is converted into a bodily as well as a mental disease. This was partly the reason why the masters of the ceremony and the members of the council often begged us to pray to God in their behalf and to teach them some efficient remedy for their diseases, candidly admitting that all their ceremonies, dances, songs, feasts, and other tricks were good for nothing whatever.

There are also women who get into these fits of madness, but they are not so insolent as are the men, who are usually more boisterous. They walk on all fours like beasts and make countless faces and gestures like persons out of their senses. Seeing this the magician begins to sing, then with some grimace he blows upon the woman, ordering her to drink certain waters and to give a feast forthwith either of meat or of fish, which must be found even if it be scarce at the time; this is done at once. When the shouting is over and the banquet finished they return each to his house until the next time he comes to see her, blowing upon her and singing again, with several others summoned for that purpose, and commanding her to make forthwith three or four more feasts; if the fancy takes him he will order masquerades and say that they must go thus dressed to sing near the sick woman's couch and to run all through the town while the feast is being prepared. After they have run about they return for the feast, often very weary and hungry.

When all the usual remedies and inventions have had no effect and there are many sick in a town or village, or at least some leading man among them has fallen seriously ill, they hold a council and give orders for *Lonouoyroya,* their great contrivance and the most fitting means, as they say, of driving out of their town or village the devils and evil spirits which cause or procure and bring all the diseases and infirmities they bear and suffer from in body and in mind. So in the evening the men begin to break, upset, and turn topsy-turvy everything they find in the cabins, like frantic people. They throw fire and burning brands about the streets. They shout and howl and sing and run all night through the streets and round the walls and palisades of the town without giving themselves any rest. After that they imagine something, the first thing that comes into their minds, I mean those men and women who intend to be at the feast. Then in the morning they go from lodge to lodge, from one fire to another, and at each they halt for a short time singing softly these words: "So-and-So gave me this, so-and-so gave me that," and such expressions in praise of those who gave to them. In many households things are freely offered them, in one a knife, in another a pipe, in another a dog, in another a skin, a canoe, or something else, which they receive without taking any further notice of them, until somebody happens to give them the object they had thought of. He who receives it then utters a cry as a sign of joy and runs off in great haste from the cabin, all those in the house congratulating him, striking their hands on the ground a long time with their usual exclamation, *Hé, é, é, é, é;* and that gift belongs to him. But as for the other things he had got, and which were not in his dream, he must return them after the feast to those who gave them to him. But if they see that nothing is being given to them they are angry, and one of them will be so ill-humored as to go outside the door, take a stone, and put it beside the man or woman who has given him nothing, and without a word go away singing, this being a sign of insult, reproach, and ill-will.

This festival usually lasts three whole days, and those who during this time have not been able to get what they had imagined are distressed and feel wretchedly unhappy and think they will soon die. There are even some poor sick people who are carried about, hoping to get what they dreamed of and consequently to recover their health and be cured.[311]

The *Lonouoyroya* of Sagard, which he said the Huron termed the principal invention to drive devils and wicked spirits from the village, is undoubtedly the same as the ceremony called *Ononhwaroia* by Lalemant. It was mentioned previously that Lalemant called this a ceremony in honor of all the spirits of the country.[312] The following excerpt, also from Lalemant, indicates rather that it was a ceremony performed as a remedy:

A woman, born in this village, but married in another, near by, named Angoutenc, going out one night with one of her little daughters in her arms, at a time when they were celebrating in the village a feast like I have just described, saw in an instant, she said, the Moon stoop down from above, forthwith appearing to her like a tall beautiful woman, holding in her arms a little girl like her own.

"I am," quoth this spectre to her, "the immortal seignior general of these countries, and of those who inhabit them; in testimony whereof I desire and order that in all quarters of my domain, those who dwell wherein shall offer thee presents which must be the product of their own country,—from the Khiononta-terons or tobacco Nation, some tobacco; from the Attiwandarons or neutral Nation, some robes of outay; from the Askicwaner-onons, or Sorcerers, a belt and leggings, with their porcupine ornaments; from the Ehonkeronons or Islanders, a deer skin." Thus it continued to name to her certain other nations, each one

[311] Sagard, *Le Grand voyage*, pp. 264-82.
[312] *Relation* .... *1639, J.R.*, 23: 53.

of which it ordered to make her some present, and, among others, named the French who dwelt in this country, as we shall soon relate.

"The feast which is now being solemnized in the town" (adds this Demon) "is very acceptable to me, and I desire that many like it be held in all the other quarters and villages of the country. Besides," it informs her, "I love thee, and on that account I wish that thou shouldst henceforth be like me; and, as I am wholly of fire, I desire that thou be also at least the color of fire"; and thereupon it ordains for her a red cap, a red plume, a belt, leggings, shoes, and the rest of her clothes with red ornaments; that is, indeed, the garb in which she appeared at the ceremony that afterward was solemnized for her benefit.

This poor creature returned to her cabin, and no sooner had she reached it than behold her prostrated with a giddiness in the head and a contraction of the muscles, which made them conclude that she was sick of a disease of which the remedy is a ceremony, which is called, in the language of our barbarians, Ononhwaroia, or turning round the head,—a name taken from the first symptoms of this disease, or rather, this pretty superstition. The sick woman was confirmed in this belief by seeing in her dreams only goings and comings and outcries through her cabin; this made her resolve to demand in public that they should celebrate this feast for her.

Her devotion—or rather the purpose of the devil to spite us, and to thwart the affairs of Christianity, which were in their first splendor and glory—prompted her to address herself to this village where we are, Ossosane, or residence of la Conception, of which, as we have said, she was a native. They came, then, in her behalf, to make the proposition to its Captains, who immediately summoned the council. There it was declared that this affair was one of those most important to the welfare of the country, and that they certainly ought to avoid any failure, on such an occasion, to give every pleasure and satisfaction to the sick woman.

The next morning, the matter was published throughout the village, and people were vigorously exhorted to go promptly to bring the sick woman, and to prepare themselves for the feast. They ran thither, rather than walked, so that towards noon she arrived,—or rather, she was carried upon their shoulders in some kind of basket, with an escort of twenty-five or thirty persons who were killing themselves with singing.

A little while before she arrived, the general council was assembled, to which we were invited. Three of our Fathers went to it, without knowing the subject for discussion. At the outset, we were informed that they desired to see us at this council in order to get our advice upon the proposition that such a sick woman had made, and to know what we thought of it. The substance of the response was, that they could not do a worse thing for the country. . . .

The principal Captain, who secretly directed the whole affair, —an adroit and crafty man, if ever the earth bore one,—instead of speaking in reference to what we had said, addressed the entire assembly, and began to exclaim, "Courage, then young men; courage, women; courage, my brothers; let us render to our country this service, so necessary and important, according to the customs of our ancestors!" Now followed a great speech in the same strain and tone; then, in a somewhat lower voice, he said, addressing himself to those who were around him, "This is the advice that I gave to my nephews, the French, last Autumn. You will see this Winter, I said to them, many things that will displease you,—the Ononhwaroia, the Outaerohi, and similar ceremonies; do not say a word, I pray you, I said to them; pretend not to see what shall take place; with time, it may change. We were formerly told at the Three Rivers and Quebec," he added, "that, provided we believed in four years, it was enough."

As he continued the like discourse, the deputies entered on the part of the patient, who came to announce her arrival to the council, and to say for her that they should send her two men and two girls arrayed in robes and collars of such and such a fashion, with certain fish and presents in their hands,—and this, in order to learn from her own lips her desires and what was necessary for her recovery. No sooner proposed, than executed.

Two men, therefore, and two girls went, loaded with all that the sick woman had desired, and immediately returned,—for one thing, as naked as the hand, except their clouts, all they had carried having been left with the sick woman; and, for another, charged with demands which were the essential ones, and those the fulfillment of which should begin the recovery of her health, what had been carried her being accepted only as a compliment, and a token of their pleasure at her arrival. Accordingly, the deputies announced twenty-two presents that she desired they should give her, which were those the devil had specified to her in the apparition, as we related a little earlier, one was six dogs of a certain form and color; another was fifty cakes of tobacco; another, a large canoe; and so on,—among other things, was named a blue blanket, but with this condition, that it must belong to a Frenchman.

The report having been made by the deputies, the Captain began to exhort every one to satisfy promptly the desires of the sick woman, constantly representing and inculcating upon them the importance of such a matter. They became so excited over it that, before our Fathers went out of the assembly, fifteen of these presents had already been furnished.

Meanwhile, our Fathers were repeatedly attacked, on various occasions, and exhorted, not to spare what at least concerned them, and depended upon them. Our Fathers answered to this that they were making sport of us, and that, if it were for this purpose that we had been called to the council, the sick woman might as well return, if, without our contribution and our homage rendered to the devil and to his ordinances, she could not recover.

Not withstanding this, a half-hour after our Fathers had returned to the cabin, a Captain came there on behalf of the council, to tell us that everything was furnished except the blanket they were expecting from us, according to the desire of the sick woman. This second charge received no answer except that, in case they would go no further in this ceremony, which was still only in its beginning, and if they would send the sick woman back to the place whence she came, we would, in such case, willingly make to the public a present of a blanket, or of some other article of greater value.

Such was the first ceremony of the feast. I would prefer to call it the first act, if I could be sure of the catastrophe of the whole affair, that I might accurately characterize it; this term, however, will serve us henceforward.

The second act, then, or the second ceremony of this feast,

was that—all the presents being furnished and carried to the patient, with the customary forms of which we have spoken above —towards evening public notice was given, warning all the cabins and all the families to keep their fires lighted, and the places on both sides of them all ready for the first visit which the sick woman was to make there, in the evening.

Accordingly, the Sun having set, upon hearing the voice of the Captains, who redoubled their cries, all stirred up their fires, and maintained them with great care,—large and bright as possible, and that this would avail much for her relief.

The hour having come when she was to set out, her muscles, it was said, relaxed, and the freedom to walk, even better than before, was restored to her; but it seems more certain that this did not occur until after she had passed through several fires, which usually results thus. Be that as it may, two Savages remained beside her all the time during her promenade, each one holding up one of her hands; and, thus supported she walked between the two, and went through all the cabins of the village.

In the cabins of the Savages, which are in length and form like garden arbors, the fires are in the very middle of their breadth, and there are several fires along its length, according to the number of families and the size of the cabin, usually two or three paces apart. It was through the middle of the cabins, and consequently through the very middle of the fires, that the sick woman marched, her feet and legs bare,—that is to say, through two or three hundred fires,—without doing herself any harm, even complaining all the time how little heat she felt, which did not relieve her of the cold she felt in her feet and legs. Those who held up her hands passed on either side of the fires; and, having led her thus through all the cabins, they took her back to the place whence she had departed, namely, to the cabin where she was sheltered; and thus ended the second Act.

The third followed, which according to forms and customs, consists in a general mania of all the people of the village, who, —except, perhaps a few Old Men,—undertake to run wherever the sick woman has passed, adorned or daubed in their fashion, vying with one another in the frightful contortions of their faces, —making everywhere such a din, and indulging in such extravagances, that, to explain them and make them better understood, I do not know if I ought not to compare them, either to the most extravagant of our maskers that one has ever heard of, or to the bacchantes of the ancients, or rather to the furies of Hell. They enter, then, everywhere, and have during the time of the feast, in all the evenings and nights of the three days that it lasts, liberty to do anything, and no one dares say a word to them. If they find kettles over the fire, they upset them; they break the earthen pots, knock down the dogs, throw fire and ashes everywhere, so thoroughly that often the cabins and entire villages burn down. But the point being that, the more noise and uproar one makes, the more relief the sick person will experience, they have no concern for anything, and each one kills himself to do worse than his companion.

Our cabins that are in the villages are not exempt from the results of such a feast. The door of the cabin of the Residence of saint Joseph was broken down three times in a like ceremony. As for this residence where I am, that of la Conception, we have been more quiet during such storms, because we are about a musket-shot from the village. This, then, is the third act; let us come to the fourth.

The next day's Sun having risen, every one prepares to go again through all the cabins where the sick woman has passed, and particularly to that one in which she is harbored. This is for the purpose of proposing at each fire each person's own and special desire or "ondinoc,"—according as he is able to get information and enlightenment by dreams,—not openly, however, but through Riddles. For example, some one will say, "What I desire and what I am seeking is that which bears a lake within itself"; and by this is intended a pumpkin or calabash. Another will say, "What I ask for is seen in my eyes,—it will be marked with various colors"; and because the Huron word that signifies "eye" also signifies "glass bead," that is the clue to divine what he desires,—namely, some kind of beads of this material, and of different colors. Another will intimate that he desires an Andacwandet feast,—that is to say, many fornications and adulteries. His Riddle being guessed, there is no lack of persons to satisfy his desires. . . .

As soon, then, as the Riddle is proposed, they immediately

strive to guess it; and saying, "It is that," they at the same time throw the object to the person who demands and announces his desires. If this is really his thought, he exclaims that it has been found, and thereupon there is rejoicing by all those in the cabin, who manifest their delight by striking against the pieces of bark that form the walls of their cabins; at the same time the patient feels relieved; and this happens as they find the desires of those who have proposed them in Riddles. It was found in the Council that was held as the conclusion of this present ceremony,—where this matter was examined, according to their forms and customs,—that a hundred Riddles had been guessed this time.

But if what is guessed is not the answer of him who has proposed the Riddle, he says that they are near it, but that that is not it; he does not refrain, for all that, from carrying away what has been given him, in order to show it through the other cabins, and thus make them see and understand better that it is not that, —so that, by the exclusion of many things, one is better prepared to tell what it is. True, he afterward brings back what was given him,—either because his desire has finally been ascertained, or because it has not, only reserving what was really his thought. Some observe the whole ceremony very religiously; but I do not doubt that many tricks and cheats also creep into it. At all events, behold the 4th act,—which, with the preceding, is repeated on each of the three nights and the three days that the feast lasts.

The fifth or last is begun on the 3rd day. This consists of a second journey or promenade by the sick woman through the cabins, which closes the whole feast, this being done to propose her last and principal desire,—not openly as she did when she first arrived, but in a Riddle, as the others had done on the preceding days. It is here that the devil triumphs, and acts the master and lord in earnest. For first, when this poor unhappy woman goes out from her cabin she is attended by a number of persons, some following her, and some going before; all filing along, one by one, without saying a word, with the faces, appearance, and attitudes of persons afflicted and penitent,—and especially the sick woman, who appears alone in their midst, all the others, before and behind, being at some distance from her. Seeing them, then, walk as they do, it is impossible to form any other opinion than that they are persons who desire to inspire with compassion, and bend to mercy, some powerful sovereign whom they recognize as the origin and cause of the trouble of the person in question, and on whose will depends, in their opinion, its continuation or its cure; and, in fact, such is precisely the case.

Now it is necessary that while this sort of procession lasts, not one Savage should appear outside of the cabins,—so that, as far away as one can see them, those who are escorting the sick person nearly kill themselves making signs and gestures that all must retreat and go indoors.

The sick woman having returned to the cabins, she begins to relate her troubles in a plaintive and languishing voice, giving the rest to understand that her recovery depends upon the satisfaction of her last desire, of which she proposes the Riddle. Each one straightway applies himself to ascertain its solution, and at the same time they throw to the sick woman whatever they imagine it may be, as we have just stated.

Those who are attending the sick woman collect all these things and go out burdened with kettles, pots, skins, robes, blankets, cloaks, necklaces, belts, leggings, shoes, corn, fish,—in short, everything that is used by the Savages, and which they have been able to think of, to attain the satisfaction of the sick woman's desire.

These appear, and not without good cause, to eyes illumined by the light of faith, as veritable trophies of Satan,—or, rather, a thorough ceremony of faith and homage that these people render to him whom they recognize as their sovereign master and Lord, upon whom they consider that all their happiness or unhappiness depends.

Finally, the patient does so much, and gives so many and such hints as to the explanation of her Riddle, that her answer is found; and at once there is a general outcry and rejoicing of all the people, who everywhere strike against the bark walls,—which is only by way of congratulations offered her, and, on her part, of thanks for the health she has recovered. She returns, for this purpose, a third time through all the cabins, after which the last general council is held, where a report is made of all that has taken place, and, among other things, of the number of Riddles solved. Then follows the last present, on the part of the public, which consists in completing and crowning the last desire of the sick woman, over and above what that individual who has guessed it has been able to give; and there ends the ceremony.

It is to be presumed that the true end of this Act, and its catastrophe, will be nothing else but a Tragedy, the devil not being accustomed to behave otherwise. Nevertheless, this poor unhappy creature found herself much better after the feast than before, although she was not entirely free from, or cured of her trouble. This is ordinarily attributed by the Savages to the lack or failure of some detail, or to some imperfection in the ceremony,—which keeps these peoples in continual fears, and in so exact observance of the forms and details of their ceremonies.[313]

There was a particular kind of disease called *Aoutaerohi*, from the name of a little demon as large as the fist, which they said was in the body of the sick man, especially in the part which pained him. The remedy for this disease was given the same name as the ailment. Patients found that they were suffering from this disease either through dreams or through the intervention of some shaman. Brébeuf said that the songs accompanying the feasts given to drive the demon away were such that very few could sing them.[314]

Father Pierre Pijart wrote that he had witnessed the ceremony, which he described:

On the 24th of May, one of these feasts was made for his health and that of his daughter. They danced and howled like demons a good part of the night, but what astonished us the most was that a certain man named *Oscouta* took in his mouth a great red-hot coal, and carried it to the patients, who were at some distance from him, making many grimaces, and growling in their ears like a bear; nevertheless, the performance did not result as he desired. The coal was not hard enough and broke in his mouth, which prevented the operation of the remedy. Hence it was ordained that they should begin again the next day, and that they should use red-hot stones instead of coals. Meanwhile, I was troubled about the sick man, who was growing worse. . . . Ac-

---

[313] Lalemant, *Relation . . . . 1639, J.R.*, 17: 169-87.
[314] *Relation . . . . 1636, J.R.*, 10: 183-85.

cordingly, the next day they prepared for a second *Aoutaerohi* feast. A number of stones were brought; and, to make them red-hot, a fire was prepared hot enough to burn down the cabin. . . . 24 persons were chosen to sing, and to perform all the ceremonies; but what songs, and what tones of voice! For my part, I believe that if demons and the damned were to sing in hell, it would be about after this fashion; I never heard anything more lugubrious and more frightful. I was waiting all the time to see what they would do with those stones that they were heating and making red-hot with so much care. You may believe me, since I speak of a thing that I saw with my own eyes,—they separated the brands, drew them from the midst of the fire, and, holding their hands behind their backs, took these between their teeth, carried them to the patients and remained some time without loosing their hold, blowing upon them and growling in their ears. I am keeping one of the stones expressly to show you. You will be astonished that a man can have so wide a mouth; the stone is about the size of a goose egg. Yet I saw a Savage put it in his mouth so that there was more of it inside than out; he carried it some distance, and after that, it was still so hot, that when he threw it to the ground sparks of fire issued from it. I forgot to tell you that, after the first *Aoutaerohi* feast one of our Frenchmen had the curiosity to see if, in reality, all this was done without anyone being burned. He spoke to this Oscouta who had filled his mouth with live coals; he had him open his mouth and found it unhurt and whole, without any appearance of having been burned; and not only those persons, but even the sick people were not burned. They let their bodies be rubbed with glowing cinders without their skin appearing in the least affected.[315]

A ceremony that Brébeuf termed a dance and which he said was called *Otakrendoiae* by the Huron was performed at the request of a man who wished to be an *arendiwane* ("master sorcerer"). Whether this was a single instance of the connection of this dance with the initiation of a shaman, or whether it was usually given, is not known. The dance would seem to be the property of a society, the brethren of

---

[315] Pijart, *Relation . . . 1637*, J.R., 14: 59-63.

which were called *Atirenda*. "It would take too long to describe the details of the ceremony," stated the missionary, who concluded:

It is a question of killing one another here, they say, by charms which they throw at each other, and which are composed of Bears' claws, Wolves' teeth, Eagles' talons, certain stones, and Dogs' sinews. Having fallen under the charm and been wounded, blood pours from the mouth and nostrils, or it is simulated by a red powder they take by stealth; and there are ten thousand other absurdities, that I willingly pass over.[316]

The information is very scanty, but what there is suggests the midewiwin or medicine society.

[316] *Relation . . . . 1636, J.R.,* 10: 209.

MIAMI

INTRODUCTION

THE derivation of the word "Miami" is very uncertain. One conjecture is that it comes from the Chippewa word *Omaumeg,* which means "people who live on the peninsula." This seems very plausible since the first reference to the Miami in the literature gave their name as "Oumamik."[1] Other variants appearing soon were Oumamis, Oumami, and Miamiak.[2] As the tribe became better known the form of the name became standardized, and after 1680 the customary designation used by the French was "Miami."

Most of the names applied to the Miami can be recognized easily. The ethnographic material identified with these names has been used. Many documents of the contact period that are without reference to the Miami doubtless related to them. There is no way of determining the relation of much of this material to this tribe, but many of the early references to the customs of the tribes designated as Illinois may be used for the Miami, since the term "Illinois" was applied to various tribes in the first part of the contact period, as the following excerpt from Dablon shows:

As the name Outaouacs has been given to all the Savages of these regions, although of different Nations, because the first to appear among the French were the Outaouacs, so it is with the name of the Illinois, who are very numerous and dwell toward the South, since the first who visited point saint Esprit to trade were the Illinois.[3]

Numerous gaps in the information relating to the Miami

---

[1] Gabriel Druillettes, *Relation* . . . . *1657-58, J.R.,* 44: 247.
[2] Claude-Jean Allouez, *Relation* . . . . *1669-70, J.R.,* 54: 207; *idem, Relation* . . . . *1672-73, J.R.,* 58: 23.
[3] *Relation* . . . . *1670-71, J.R.,* 55: 207.

have, in this work, been filled in with accounts designated as referring to the Illinois. This procedure is justified on the basis of the linguistic affinity of the two groups, the similarity of their culture in points where data exist for both, and the looseness of the use of the term "Illinois" in the early accounts. All such borrowings have been indicated.

LOCATION OF THE TRIBE

The Miami included the Wea, Atchatchakangouen, Pepicokia, Mengakonkia, Piankashaw, and Kilatika. These divisions were often spoken of as separate tribes and also as Miami of a certain place. The first white contact with the Miami was the visit of Radisson and Groseilliers to the Mascouten and Miami village northwest of Green Bay about 1654. This was reported by Druillettes in 1658. At this time the major part of the tribe seems to have been occupying the region lying west of the southern end of Lake Michigan. Later, there was a movement of the tribe south and eastward, induced by the French, by the pressure of other tribes behind them, and, finally, by the desire to be nearer the English and the better trading conditions they offered.

The small group near Green Bay appears to have been merely an extension of the main body residing between the southern part of Lake Michigan and the Mississippi River. Its residence there is not mentioned after 1686. Marameg was a principal village of the main group. Its exact location is not known, but various maps indicate that it was near the headwaters of the Fox River, a tributary of the Illinois River. Druillettes mentioned a large group of Miami located sixty leagues from the Potawatomi village near the entrance to Green Bay. It is possible that he was referring to this group or village, although his population of 24,000 souls is obviously an exaggeration. Occasional references to the residence of the Miami on the banks of the Mississippi River may mean a village site there or perhaps only a temporary location for hunting or some other purpose.

There was a Miami and Mascouten village near the portage between the Kankakee and St. Joseph rivers in 1679, according to Hennepin and La Salle.[4] The St. Joseph River soon became known as the River of the Miami. Until the end of the contact period this was a favorite residence of the Indians, although after 1718 the Miami were largely replaced by Potawatomi. A strength of six hundred warriors was reported in 1695, but only ten or twenty were mentioned after 1718. The village was not at the same site throughout this period, but moved from place to place within the valley of the St. Joseph. The French designated the settlement simply as the St. Joseph River or the Post of the St. Joseph.

Upon the erection of Fort St. Louis at Starved Rock, Illinois, by La Salle in 1682, some of the Miami settled near by. According to Deliette they were still there in 1689, but moved north shortly afterward into the southern part of the present state of Wisconsin.[5] In 1691 part of this group was on the St. Joseph River, and the other part made an establishment at Chicago that was maintained for about twenty years.[6] The Wabash Valley was the seat of some Miami Indians at least as early as 1694, and they remained there to the end of the contact period. The principal villages were located at or near the sites of Vincennes and Lafayette, Indiana. The village at the latter site was commonly known as Ouiatenon.

The establishment of Fort Pontchartrain at Detroit by Cadillac in 1701 likewise drew a few families of Miami from St. Joseph about a year later. This gathering grew until trouble with the Ottawa in 1706 and again in 1712 made the location undesirable to them. Leanings toward the English prompted a settlement on a site near the present Fort Wayne, Indiana. The French followed and built a fort among them.

[4] Louis Hennepin, *A New Discovery of a Vast Country in America*, 1: 143-44; *Official Account of the Enterprises of La Salle*, Margry, *Découvertes*, 1, Pt. 2: 502.

[5] Louis Deliette, *Memoir, IHC.*, 23: 392.

[6] *Ibid.*

Desultory dealings with the English and the Iroquois continued until 1748, when, notwithstanding the efforts of the French, over four hundred families settled on Loramie Creek, one of the branches of the Big Miami River, where they could enjoy uninterrupted commerce with the English. Further movement eastward was halted when the French raided and razed this village in 1752. From that time until the close of the French regime they maintained at least nominal allegiance to the French and occupied villages in the Wabash Valley and the vicinity of Fort Wayne, with small settlements in the St. Joseph River Valley (Table II).

References to the number of Miami are meager. Usually, only estimates of the number of warriors are given, and these do not cover all the villages. Extension of the number of warriors to total population is open to error, but in this instance there is no other way of arriving at estimates of the population. In 1695 two villages had 1100 to 1200 warriors,[7] in 1718 six villages had between 1400 and 1600 warriors,[8] in 1736 three villages had 560,[9] and in 1757 there were over 525 in three villages.[10] If three other persons are allowed to each warrior, it seems conservative to say that an original population of four to five thousand had shrunk to about two thousand at the close of the contact period.

DATE	NUMBER OF WARRIORS	NUMBER OF VILLAGES	TOTAL POPULATION
1695	1100–1200	2	4400–4800
1718	1400–1600	6	5600–6400
1736	560	3	2240
1757	525	3	2100

CHARACTERISTICS

The Miami were of medium height, shapely, somewhat stockier than the members of the cognate Illinois tribes, but

[7] AC., C 11 A, 13.
[8] Jacques Sabrevois, *Memoir*, *WHC.*, 16: 375-76.
[9] Pierre J. Celeron, "Census of Indian Tribes: 1736," *WHC.*, 17: 249-50.
[10] Louis-Antoine de Bougainville, *Memoir*, *WHC.*, 18: 175-76, 185.

TABLE II

REPORTED LOCATIONS OF MIAMI

DATE	UPPER FOX OR LITTLE WOLF RIVER, WIS.	MARAMEG	BANKS OF MISSISSIPPI RIVER	ST. JOSEPH RIVER VALLEY	ILLINOIS RIVER NEAR OTTAWA, ILL.	STRAITS OF DETROIT	CHICAGO	WABASH RIVER	MAUMEE RIVER (FORT WAYNE)	WHITE RIVER, IND.	BIG MIAMI RIVER NEAR PIQUA, O.
1658	Druillettes	Druillettes									
1667	Silvy										
1673	Allouez		Allouez								
1679				Hennepin La Salle							
1682					La Salle						
1686	Denonville										
1687						Durantaye					
1689				Deliette	Deliette						
1690			La Potherie				Deliette				
1691		Narrative of Occurrence		Deliette							
1693								Deliette			
1694											
1695		AC, C"A, 13		AC, C"A, 13							
1699		La Potherie		Cadillac La Potherie		Cadillac Cornbury Marest	Cadillac La Potherie				
1702											
1706		Raudot	Raudot	Raudot			Raudot	Raudot	Dubuisson Sabrevois		
1710						Dubuisson					
1712							Sabrevois				
1718				Charlevoix					Charlevoix		
1721								Charlevoix			
1733									Beauharnois	Beauharnois	
1736				Celeron				Celeron	Celeron		
1749									Celeron		
1751										Celeron	Gist
1757				Bougainville De Silegue				Bougainville De Silegue	Bougainville De Silegue		
1760											

probably less so than the other tribes of the central Algonquian group. Very active, industrious, indefatigable, they
were excellent runners and pedestrians. La Potherie said that
it was for this last characteristic that they were called
Metousceprinioueks, which in their language meant "Walkers."[11] The women were said by Hennepin to be "so lusty
and strong, that they carry on their back two or three hundred weight, besides their Children; and notwithstanding
that Burthen, they run as swiftly as any of our Soldiers with
their Arms."[12]

The women were reported by Raudot to be rather clean,
somewhat homely, rather well built, and as white as Indians
could be. He also stated that the most beautiful among them
were those who were tall and slender, but he did not indicate
whether this was his opinion or that of the Miami men.[13]

The estimate of their mental qualities varied directly with
the success which the reporters met among them. Perrot had
some unfortunate dealings with them, and so it is not surprising that La Potherie, who related Perrot's adventures and
accounts of the Indians, should say that they were "lacking
in intelligence, and dull of apprehension; easily persuaded;
vain in language and behavior, and extremely selfish. They
consider themselves much braver than their neighbors; they
are great liars, employing every kind of baseness to accomplish their ends."[14] Raudot also found much the same characteristics among them,[15] in sharp contrast to the reports of
Cadillac and the missionaries, Allouez and Marquette, which
reflected quite favorable opinions of the Miami. Allouez
said "they are gentle, affable, sedate,"[16] and Marquette found
them "the most civil, the most liberal, and the most shapely,"
of all the tribes with which he was acquainted, and added

[11] Claude de la Potherie, *History, ITUM.*, 1: 322.
[12] Hennepin, *A New Discovery of a Vast Country in America*, 1:147.
[13] Antoine Raudot, "Memoir," Letter 59.
[14] La Potherie, *History, ITUM.*, 1: 322.
[15] "Memoir," Letter 58.
[16] *Relation . . . . 1670, J.R.*, 54: 231.

that "they are very docile, and listen quietly to what is said to them."[17] It was feared by Cadillac that jealousy between their leaders, which kept them divided into several villages, would cause their complete annihilation; he said that "this would be too bad for they are fine people, humane and polite."[18]

In considering all of their characterizations of the Indians, it should be borne in mind that most of the Europeans wanted something: the missionaries sought converts, the traders were after furs, and the military men wanted warriors. To those who got what they desired, the Indians were sensible, brave, and upright people; but if the overtures of the Europeans were not favorably received, the tribe was composed of thieves, liars, dissemblers, and even traitors. However, the evidence of Lahontan, Cadillac, Vimont, Charlevoix, Montcalm, and many others is conclusive that once an individual or a tribe accepted a present of a porcelain collar in connection with an agreement, it was regarded in the nature of a contract and obligation which was rarely, if ever, violated.

DRESS AND ORNAMENT

The Miami usually wore even less clothing than many other tribes of the northeastern woodlands, if credit can be given to the evidence found in the names given them by other tribes and the English. The French ordinarily called them Miami and only occasionally used the name Twightwees, but the English called them the Naked Indians or Twightwees almost exclusively. The origin of this name is not known, but it was conjectured to come from Twau Twau or Tawa Tawa, from the Algonquian *tawa* ("naked").[19]

The men wore a breechcloth and moccasins in summer. In winter they wore a leather shirt or coat reaching to the waist, moccasins of smoke-treated deerskin, and leggings,

---

[17] Jacques Marquette, *Relation of First Voyage*, J.R., 59: 101, 103.
[18] Antoine de la Mothe Cadillac, MS "Relation on the Indians."
[19] Daniel G. Brinton, *The Lenâpe and their Legends*, p. 146.

probably of thigh length, which, like the moccasins, were often decorated with colored figures or porcupine quill work. Skins of various animals were used for robes or outer coverings, but those of the buffalo were undoubtedly the commonest. For ordinary wear as protection against cold the skins were undecorated, but for festive or solemn occasions they used others made of the thinnest sections of the hide, dressed with the brains of various animals until they were very soft, painted with several colors, and embroidered with red and white porcupine quills.

As for the women, Sabrevois said merely that they were well covered with deerskins.[20] In speaking of the Miami and Potawatomi at St. Joseph in 1721, Charlevoix gave the following description of clothing, the application of which to the Miami is dubious. He said:

The woman's boddices reach down to a little above the knee, and when they travel they cover their heads with their coverings or robes. I have seen several who wore little bonnets, made in the manner of leather caps; others of them wear a sort of cowl, which is sewed to their vests or boddices, and they have also a piece of stuff or skin which serves them for a petticoat, and which covers them from the middle down to the mid-leg.[21]

Charlevoix also gave the information that the skins were dressed or dried by smoking them and then rubbing them until they were soft and that another method of dressing them was to steep them in water, afterward rubbing them between the hands until they became dry and pliant. He added that the Indians were very fond of European cloth, and if a man obtained a shirt of it he always wore it outside of his leather vest and never took it off until it fell off from rottenness.[22]

Hairdress

Marquette thought that the two long locks the Miami

[20] *Memoir, WHC.*, 16: 375.

[21] Pierre Charlevoix, *Journal*, 2: 107.

[22] *Ibid.*, p. 108.

men wore over their ears gave them a pleasing appearance.[23] According to Pachot the Miami as well as the Sioux, Illinois, Fox, Mascouten, and Kickapoo cut their hair within an inch of the head and left hanging only one little tress about a foot long either on the right or the left side.[24] Contradicting the last source as far as the Illinois are concerned is the statement of Dablon to the effect that they wore their hair short except for "four great mustaches, one on each side of each ear."[25]

Undoubtedly, either there was not any rigidly observed manner of fixing the hair or the hairdress varied in the different divisions of the tribe, and the several reporters did not meet the same division, and hence the same hairdress. The first alternative appears preferable in light of the statement of La Potherie that Perrot "met more than two hundred stout young men [in approaching a village of Miami and Mascouten in the vicinity of Green Bay] . . . their hair was adorned with headdresses of various sorts."[26]

As for the women, their hair was worn long and gathered at the neck. A band was worn around the head.[27]

Tattooing

The Miami seem to have been much given to tattooing themselves. Raudot said that as youths they were tattooed from the shoulders to the heels and as soon as they reached the age of twenty-five they had their stomachs, sides, and upper arms tattooed so that their entire bodies were covered.[28] Sabrevois in corroboration said that they had their bodies tattooed all over with all sorts of figures and designs.[29]

The women also were tattooed, but not as completely as

---

[23] *Relation of First Voyage*, J.R., 59: 101.

[24] "*Les Sioux*," AC., C 11 A, 122.

[25] Claude Dablon, *Relation . . . . 1671*, J.R., 55: 217.

[26] *History, ITUM.*, 1: 323-25.

[27] Raudot, "Memoir," Letter 58.

[28] *Ibid.*

[29] *Memoir, WHC.*, 16: 375.

the men. Their decoration was limited to the cheeks, the chest, and the arms.[30]

ECONOMIC LIFE

Shelter

The means of shelter used by the Miami received only scant mention in the documents of the contact period. According to Marquette, the Miami he visited in Wisconsin at the start of his voyage down the Mississippi in 1673 used rush mats, because of the scarcity of bark in that region. These served them for walls and roofs, but did not afford much protection against the winds and still less against heavy rains. Cabins of this kind, he found, were easily packed and transported.[31] Either the Miami who lived with the Mascoutens and Kickapoo did not know how to make as good mats of rushes as did the other tribes, or Marquette did not appreciate the mats and the protection they afforded, for later he spoke of the excellent protective qualities of the rush mats of the Illinois. Other writers also found that the rush mats were an adequate shield against wind, rain, and snow.[32]

There were five Wea villages on the Wabash, according to Sabrevois, "having the same language as the Miamis, whose brothers they are, and properly all Miamis, having the same customs and dress. . . . They have a custom different from all the other nations, which is to keep their fort extremely clean, not allowing a blade of grass to remain in it. The whole of the fort is sanded like the Tuilleries, and if a dog happen to make any filth in it, the women take and remove it outside."[33] The construction of forts was not a feature introduced by the French to the Miami, for in 1671 Dablon

[30] Raudot, "Memoir," Letter 58; For a description of how the tattooing was done by unnamed tribes see Letter 24, in the Appendix.

[31] Relation of First Voyage, J.R., 59: 103.

[32] Official Account of the Enterprises of La Salle, Margry, Découvertes, 1, Pt. 2: 505.

[33] Memoir, WHC., 16: 376.

reported the Miami occupying a fort with the Mascouten in northern Wisconsin.[34]

In each village there was at least one long house in which councils and ceremonies were held. No particulars of construction are given that would distinguish it from other buildings except its size. This long house was separate from the chief's house, in which strangers were received.[35]

Seasonal Occupations

The Miami were semisedentary, that is, they had permanent villages in which they lived during the summer while tending the near-by fields. Some old people remained in the village while the winter communal hunt was on. Individuals or small parties hunted game in the vicinity of the village during its occupation by the entire group from the end of April until October. The women were busy with the care of the fields and the gathering of the wild foods, such as fruits and roots, and reeds or rushes for making mats.

Daily Life

During the summer, besides cultivating the fields and gathering wild food products, the women were occupied with the care of the household, the making of mats and other textiles, the supplying of water and wood for the cabin, and the dressing of the skins of the animals killed by the men. The men went hunting in the summer at short distances from the village and perhaps helped their wives at harvest time, but otherwise occupied themselves only with the manufacture of weapons, going to war, feasting, dancing, and gaming.

The women and children accompanied the men on their winter hunts and flayed the animals killed, brought the flesh to their cabins, and preserved it for future use.

Agriculture

Corn was the principal item of cultivation. According to

[34] *Relation . . . . 1671, J.R.,* 55: 199-201.
[35] Christopher Gist, *Journal, Filson Club Publ.,* 13: 136.

Sabrevois, the Miami on the Maumee "raise a Kind of indian corn[36] which is unlike that of our tribes at Detroit. Their corn is white, of the Same size as the other, with much finer husks and much whiter flour."[37] As soon as the ground was sufficiently dried out—about the first of May—the dead stalks of the previous crop were burned off and the ground prepared by stirring with a sharp pointed stick. The sowing, cultivation, and harvesting were the charge of the women, although the men might assist in the harvesting. This concluded with a festival and with a feast, given in the night.[38] Joutel reported that the women had to be very vigilant to protect their crops, until the plants were well started, from swarms of birds which resembled European starlings.[39]

Besides corn, beans, squashes, melons, pumpkins, and gourds were grown, according to various authors. No one of them mentions all of these plants, but several mention two or three of them. Marquette said the melons were excellent, especially those that had red seeds, but that their squashes were not of the best; the people who lived in the prairies had large and small squashes, according to Perrot, and melons with an agreeable and refreshing juice; Lahontan listed watermelons and sweet "citruls" (squashes) among the plants of southern Canada; Sabrevois said the Wea grew pumpkins and melons; Charlevoix, speaking of the Indians in general, stated that they had *pompions* ("gourds"), *turnsoles* ("sunflowers"), and watermelons which were first raised in a hotbed and afterwards transplanted, and he added that the Indians were acquainted with both the common melon and watermelon before the arrival of the Europeans. The de-

[36] The Miami corn, according to this description, apparently was a white variety of flour corn, and the implication is that the Indians around Detroit had only flint corn. This is consistent with the knowledge that flint corn was typical along the northeastern periphery of maize culture; the soft corns were common in more southerly areas.—Volney Jones, Ethnobotanical Laboratory of the University of Michigan.

[37] *Memoir, WHC.,* 16: 375.

[38] Charlevoix, *Journal,* 2: 111-12.

[39] Henri Joutel, *Journal, LHC.,* 1: 187.

scriptions of these melons, squashes, and pumpkins are too imprecise to allow positive identifications.

The importance of agricultural products in the life of the Indians is well expressed by Perrot: "The kinds of food which the savages like best, and which they make most effort to obtain, are the Indian corn, the kidney-bean, and the squash. If they are without these, they think that they are fasting, no matter what abundance of meat and fish they may have in their stores, the Indian corn being to them what bread is to Frenchmen."[40]

There is no information as to whether the Miami used fertilizer or whether they eventually reduced the fertility of the soil by continuous cultivation, and, like the Huron, had to move their village to obtain new fields. Sabrevois stated that the Wea on the Wabash had over two leagues of improvement where they raised their crops.[41] There is no mention of raising tobacco.

Hunting

The principal game hunted by the Miami was the buffalo. The hunting expeditions in the late autumn were communal affairs in which the entire village, with the exception of a few old men and women who were unable to march, took part. The reasons for this were twofold: the women and children would not be left open to attack in the absence of the hunters, who were also the warriors; and the women could assist in removing the flesh from the slain animals and smoke it for preservation. If the people of one village were not sufficiently numerous to undertake a hunt they might unite with those of another village.

The favorite method of hunting the buffalo was to surround a herd and set fire to the dead grass on all sides of it except for a few places at which the hunters gathered. The buffalo, to escape the fire, attempted to run out at these openings, where the hunters waited. La Salle said that the Miami

---

[40] Nicolas Perrot, *Memoir, ITUM.*, 1: 102.
[41] *Memoir, WHC.*, 16: 376.

sometimes killed as many as two hundred in one day. The animals killed were divided according to the number of persons or hunters in each family.[42]

Elk, deer, bear, and beaver were also hunted in the woods or on the prairies and taken either by coming upon them unawares or by swiftness of foot, according to Cadillac. A dozen animals might be killed in a day by a good hunter, but it was a real pleasure, he said, to see the Miami occasionally bringing into their village some enormous bears, tamed in the course of their hunting, and driven before them with switches, like sheep to the slaughter house.[43]

According to Hennepin, the Miami dried the flesh of buffalo in the sun or broiled it upon gridirons, in lieu of using salt to preserve it; they then put it in sacks made of buffalo wool, and thus treated it kept more than four months without any decay taking place.[44]

Charlevoix said:

Their corn and other fruits are preserved in repositories which they dig in the ground, and which are lined with large pieces of bark. Some of them leave the maize in the ear, which is tufted like our onions, and hang them on long poles over the entry of their cabbins. Others thresh it out and lay it up in large baskets of bark, bored on all sides to hinder it from heating. But when they are obliged to be from home for any time, or when they apprehend some irruption of the enemy, they make great concealments under ground, where these sorts of grain are exceeding well preserved.[45]

La Salle wrote to one of his partners in 1680 that the kindred Illinois also hid in the ground the corn they intended to use for seed the next year.[46] The Illinois and, probably,

<hr />

[42] *Official Account of the Enterprises of La Salle*, Margry, *Découvertes*, 1, Pt. 2: 503; Hennepin, *A New Discovery of a Vast Country in America*, 1: 147; Raudot, "Memoir," Letter 71.

[43] MS "Relation on the Indians."

[44] *A New Discovery of a Vast Country in America*, 1: 149.

[45] *Journal*, 2: 112-13.

[46] Margry, *Découvertes*, 2, Pt. 1: 31.

the Miami dried their squashes in the sun to preserve them for use during the winter and the spring.[47]

Preparation of Food

Young corn, roasted on the coals, was a special delicacy used as a treat for guests. Sagamité, the most common food, was, according to Charlevoix, made by roasting the corn, bruising it, and making it into a sort of pap, to which meat or fruit was added to give it relish. A corn meal prepared and cooked and then allowed to cool, which the French called *farine froide,* was used for food on journeys. Corn was also boiled in the ear when tender, after which it was roasted, shelled, and dried in the sun for future use in sagamité.[48] The Indians of the prairies, according to Perrot, had a special food which was made by "a certain method of preparing squashes with the Indian corn cooked while in its milk, which they mix and cook together and then dry, which has a very sweet taste."[49]

Fresh or dried meat was added to these various corn dishes, which appear to have been rather liquid. Of the dried buffalo meat, Hennepin said: "They commonly boil it, and drink the Broth of it instead of Water. This is the ordinary Drink of all the Savages of America, who have no Commerce with the Europeans. We follow'd their Example in this particular; and it must be confess'd, that that Broth is very wholesome."[50]

There seems to have been little dependence on fishing; perhaps because of the abundance of game which they obtained otherwise. At any rate, there is no mention in the early accounts of the Miami suffering from a lack of food. Almost all writers refer to the excellence of the country occupied by this tribe and the bounteous supply of food furnished the inhabitants.

[47] Marquette, *Relation of First Voyage,* J.R., 59: 127-29.
[48] Charlevoix, *Journal,* 2: 113-14.
[49] *Memoir, ITUM.,* 1: 113.
[50] *A New Discovery of a Vast Country in America,* 1: 149.

Trade

Deliette reported that the Illinois and, supposedly, also the Miami were supplied with porcupine quills by the Potawatomi and Ottawa.[51] The Illinois made a business of capturing Pawnee women and children and trading them with other tribes, in fact the form of "Pawnee" then in use, "Pani," came to mean "slave" and is found so used throughout the documents of the time. Although there is no evidence that the Miami were given to this practice, neither is there anything to indicate that they were not. Their location beyond the Illinois and the greater distance from the Pawnee and other trans-Mississippi tribes might only mean that they were more apt to seek their captives in other regions.

Trade in items such as the catlinite used for calumets is not mentioned, although we know that the Miami must have obtained it outside of their own country.

Transportation

The snowshoes common to the northern tribes were not used by the Miami, even when they resided in northern Wisconsin. Writing from the Fox River in 1673, Allouez said of this tribe that they "do not know how to walk on snowshoes; for that reason, they have greatly suffered in this quarter, where there was an extraordinary quantity of snow."[52]

Several of the early writers likewise testified that the Miami did not use the canoe, meaning the birchbark canoe. But at least some of the Miami possessed dugout canoes, called pirogues by the French, which the Illinois used considerably, although not transporting them out of their own or connecting rivers, as they were too heavy and unwieldy to permit portage and not at all suitable for use on the lakes.

As has been said, the Miami were known as excellent

[51] *Memoir, IHC.,* 23: 339.
[52] *Relation .... 1673, J.R.,* 58: 63.

walkers. On marches of families or of whole villages the women carried the baggage with headbands or pack straps. Apparently, no use was made of their dogs as pack animals.

Manufactures

Utensils.—The early visitors said that, before the introduction of copper kettles by the French, the Miami made use of earthen pots, but these have not been described. As this tribe usually resided outside of the zone of the birch tree, vessels made of its bark were denied them. It is entirely possible that they, like the Illinois that Marquette met on the banks of the Mississippi on his first voyage, made wooden platters and spoons, but there is no direct evidence of this. Likewise, a supply of bones and gourds suitable for utensils was as available to them as to their neighbors, who used them, but no mention is made of their having done so.

Textiles.—The wool of the buffalo was used to make such articles as sacks, belts, garters, and scarfs. On this subject Charlevoix waxed enthusiastic:

Their women are very neat-handed and industrious. They spin the wool of the buffaloe, which they make as fine as that of the English sheep; nay sometimes it might even be mistaken for silk. Of this they manufacture stuffs which are dyed black, yellow, or a deep red. Of these stuffs they make robes which they sew with thread made of the sinews of the roe-buck. The manner of making this thread is very simple. After stripping the flesh from the sinews of the roe-buck, they expose them to the sun for the space of two days; after they are dry they beat them, and then without difficulty draw out the thread as white and as fine as that of Mechlin, but much stronger.[53]

The war mats or bundles carried by the young men and in which they placed their tutelary birds were made by the women. They took round reeds which grew in the swamps, dyed them black, yellow, and red and made mats three feet

[53] *Journal*, 2: 206.

long and two feet wide; they folded over one end for about
a foot in the form of a comb case.[54]

In reference to the Illinois, who, he said, were almost
identical with the Miami, Deliette gave the following description of the manner of making the mats with which the
houses were covered:

At the beginning of June they hill up their corn, and after
that the village sets out on the buffalo hunt. Someone always
remains in each cabin, someone of the women, I mean. I have
seen times when not six remained. Some days after this the
women who remain go off in canoes, of which they have as many
as three in each cabin, to cut reeds with which they cover their
cabins. These are a kind that grow in their marshes. They procure bundles of them, which, after removing a skin that encloses
several blades conjointly, they dry in the sun and tie together
with twine which they make of white wood, with ten or twelve
bands at intervals of about six inches. They make these up to ten
fathoms in length. They call them apacoya, a word which serves
not merely to designate these, but which is a generic term for all
sort of coverings. They use the same term for bark boards, and
two of these apacoyas, one on top of the other, protect one from
the rain as well as the best blanket. These are the cabins which
they use in autumn and winter; even if they leave their canoes,
the women carry these on their backs.[55]

Fire making.—The fire drill without the bow was used
by the Miami.[56]

Musical instruments.—The drums used by the young
men in their dances before their departure for war were
earthen pots half full of water and covered with deerskins.
The *chichigoué* or gourd rattle was used especially by the
shamans. According to Hennepin, the Miami kept the hoofs
of buffalo calves which they captured. When they were very
dry "they tie them to some Wand, and move them according
to the various Postures of those who sing and dance. This is

[54] Deliette, *Memoir, IHC.*, 23: 375-76.
[55] *Ibid.*, pp. 339-41.
[56] Raudot, "Memoir," Letter 61.

the most ridiculous Musical Instrument that I ever met with."[57]

Weapons.—The war club of the Illinois tribes was shaped like a cutlass, with a large ball at the end, and made of a deer's horn or of wood. In close fighting, the club was held in one hand and a knife in the other. After delivering a blow on the head of an enemy with the club, a circular cut with the knife quickly took off the scalp.[58]

Of their other arms Rasles wrote:

Arrows are the principal weapons that they use in war and in hunting. These arrows are barbed at the tip with a stone, sharpened and cut in the shape of a serpent's tongue; if knives are lacking, they use arrows also for flaying the animals which they kill. They are so adroit in bending the bow that they scarcely ever miss their aim; and they do this with such quickness that they will have discharged a hundred arrows sooner than another person can reload his gun.[59]

SOCIAL LIFE

Political Organization

To the modern student of social organization the reports of the early visitors are distressingly vague. That which is all engrossing to the student was given less attention than almost any other subject by the writers of the contact period. The reasons for this discrepancy can only be surmised. At any rate, information on social or political organization is only found incidental to accounts of customs which the authors thought more important.

Six tribes or clans of Miami are mentioned frequently in the documents of the contact period. No others are ever reported. Lists of the names of the divisions are given with the names by which they are now known. It is to be remarked that two of the six are now accepted as they were first reported, and a third has one letter different.

[57] *A New Discovery of a Vast Country in America,* 1: 150.
[58] Sébastien Rasles, "Letter . . . . to His Brother," *J.R.,* 67: 171-73.
[59] *Ibid.,* p. 169.

Present Form	1673[60]	1690[61]	1702[62]	1710[63]
Atchatchakan-gouen	Atchatchakan-gouen	Tchidüaingoües	Chachakingoya	Chachakingoya
Wea	Ouaouiatanouk	Oüaoüiartanons	Aouciatenons	Ouyatanons
Pepicokia	Pepikoukia	Pepikokos	Pepikokia	Pepepikokia
Mengakonkia	Mengakonkia	Mangakekis	Minghagogias	Mingkakoia
Piankashaw		Poüankikias	Anghichia	Peangichia
Kilatika	Kilitika	Kikataks	Kiratikas	Kiratica
	Miami			

At least two of these divisions, the Wea and Piankashaw, later came to be recognized as separate tribes, but the evidence of this period indicates that they were all one originally.

All six bands were said by Gist to be under the same form of government. Each division had its own chief, and one of the divisional chiefs was chosen to rule the whole nation. This one, Gist related, was chosen indifferently and invested with greater authority than the others.[64] It seems doubtful, in view of the French records, that one chief was acknowledged as the ruler of the whole Miami nation. It might be that in each village composed of several bands, the members of each would have a chief, one of whom would be considered the principal chief of that village. Since Gist visited only one Miami village and obtained all of his information on the Miami there, this appears the most probable interpretation of his statements.

The French records mention different groups of Miami at the head of which there might be "a great chief." None of these indicate that such an individual controlled villages other than his own. The following quotation from Perrot expresses the esteem in which the chief he visited in 1670 was held:

Among these latter was the head chief of the Miamis, named Tetinchoua, who, as if he had been the king, kept in his cabin day and night forty young men as a body guard. The Village

[60] Allouez, *Relation . . . . 1673*, *J.R.*, 58: 41.

[61] La Potherie, *History*, *ITUM.*, 2: 67.

[62] Deliette, *Memoir*, *IHC.*, 23: 293.

[63] Raudot, "Memoir," Letter 55.

[64] *Journal*, *Filson Club Publ.*, 13: 135.

that he governed was one of four to five thousand warriors; he was, in a word, feared and respected by all his neighbors. It is said, however, that he had a very mild disposition; and that he never had any conversation except with his lieutenants or the men with whom he held counsel, who were commissioned with his orders.[65]

Items in the records made eighty years after Perrot met Tetinchoua indicate either that the authority of this chief was exaggerated, or that the power of the head chief declined with the fortunes of the tribe. In 1749 the Sieur de Villiers persuaded "the Great Chief of the Miamis, le pied froid," not to go over to the English; nevertheless his band went, leaving only "le pied froid" and his immediate family at the French post.[66]

Chiefs were commonly called kings and sovereigns by the French, who applied the terms of European political organization to that of the Indians. Charlevoix even stated that most of the people on this continent had a sort of aristocratic government. Despite this tendency, evident throughout the writings of the French, the characterizations of the Miami chiefs distinguish them as having had more authority than the heads of most other tribes.

War chiefs or captains were present in each village. They reached these positions by demonstrating their bravery and capacity for leadership on forays into the country of the enemy and held them only as long as their war parties were successful. Two or three defeats were apt to disgrace a captain. In peaceful village life they exercised no authority.

Gist mentioned "the Crier of the Town" who came by the king's order to invite his party to the long house to witness a dance.[67] As European usage dictated the term "king," so did it contribute the designation "Crier of the Town." In reality this individual was probably the orator or assistant of

[65] *Memoir, ITUM.,* 1: 223.
[66] "Letter from De Raymond to the French Minister, Dated Oct. 1, 1751," *WHC.,* 18: 95-96.
[67] *Journal, Filson Club Publ.,* 13: 143.

the chief, a man who ran errands and made announcements for the chief. He might also be chosen as his successor.

The totems of the Miami were reported by Celeron in 1736 to be the elk, crane, bear, snake, deer, and the small acorn.[68]

Justice

Usually, the only acts among the Indians recognized as crimes justifying punishment were murder, theft, and adultery, and so it was among the Miami.

Murder.—There is no description of the ritual attending the adjustment of murder in the documents of the contact period which specifically applies to the Miami. Since this ritual was as likely to be used on occasions involving two tribes as in instances within one tribe, it would be expected that few differences would be found in the ritual over a considerable area occupied by tribes normally friendly. This seems to be true among the tribes of the Great Lakes region, for there is no differentiation in the accounts of this period concerning the treatment of murder. Perrot's account of "justice among the savages" is as applicable to the Miami as to any other tribe, as he implied by his use of general terms:

When one of their connections commits a murder and is discovered to be its author, all the old men come together, make up among themselves a considerable present, and send it by deputies, in order to come to an agreement regarding means to arrest vengeance; for they all are involved in that vengeance, so far as it concerns in particular the leading persons of the offended tribe. The deputies, on their arrival at the place to which they were sent, enter with their presents the cabin of the murdered person; and the reception given to them is similar to that previously described when writing of the sweat-house. After the envoys have eaten what is offered to them, they produce their presents in the middle of the cabin, and demand that all the chiefs be called in to hear them; and when all have come they speak as follows:

[68] "Census of Indian Tribes: 1736," *WHC.*, 17: 250-51.

"We are here to confess to you the crime committed by one of our young men upon So-and-so [and then they name the man who was slain]. Our village does not approve the [act of the] murderer. You know that you have been our allies for a long time, and that your ancestors and ours presented the calumets to each other to smoke together [they mention the year]. Since that time our villages have always aided each other against such and such a nation, with whom we were at war. You are not ignorant that our dead are in the other world, in the same place as yours; and if Heaven has permitted that one deluded man has overthrown or broken the union which our ancestors had with you, and which we have always maintained, we have therefore come with the design of averting your just resentment. While you are waiting for a more complete satisfaction, this present which we offer you is to wipe away your tears; and that one is to lay a mat under the corpse of your dead; and this other, to lay on him a sheet of bark to cover him and shield him from the bad effects of the weather."

If the relatives of the dead man should be unwilling to hear any talk of satisfaction, and should take the resolution of positively obtaining vengeance for their loss, several of the old men would intervene with presents, in order to become mediators. They would argue that the people were placing themselves on the verge of having a war, with most grievous consequences, and, entreating the afflicted ones to have pity on their land, would warn them that when war was once kindled there would no longer be safety in any place; that many persons would be sacrificed; that warriors attack indiscriminately all whom they encounter while on the warpath; that there would be no longer any peace or confidence between neighbors; and that, in short, they would behold desolation so great that brother would slay brother and cousin slay cousin, and that they would be their own destroyers; for as the ties of Marriage and alliance are so strongly knit together, each man considers himself as a member no longer of the village where he was born, but of that in which he has settled.

If the distressed relatives steadily persist in trying to obtain vengeance, and if the village is a large one and inclined to support their contention, the chiefs are detailed to confer with the principal men among the murderer's relatives, who are continu-

ally on their guard. These envoys set forth, when there is no
way of settling the difficulty, that they are in danger of the destruction, for the sake of one man, of an entire village, [and that]
by allies who cease to be such when they declare themselves
enemies, and who are certainly very strong. They therefore
induce the relatives, by dint of presents, to deliver the guilty
man to his own comrades, who break his head and then cut it off
to send it to the dead man's relatives. After that, presents are
made on both sides in order to complete the arrangement.[69]

Theft.—Among the tribes of the Great Lakes region theft,
if detected, was punished by restitution, according to Perrot.
Failing this satisfaction, the victim of the theft and some of
his friends pillaged the cabin of the suspected thief. The
latter if guilty offered no resistance, but if innocent he protected his property, and a murder committed in such defense
was subject to no vengeance.[70]

Charlevoix termed the Miami "naturally thieves" who
looked upon all they could catch as lawful prize. He said
that if the victim discovered early that he had been robbed,
it was sufficient to notify the chief to be sure of recovering
the property. He found a fly in the ointment, however, for
it was necessary to give the chief a present, perhaps of greater
value than the stolen goods, and also one to the person who
found them, who was probably the thief.[71] Charlevoix's remarks were based on an experience he had among the Miami
and therein undoubtedly lies the explanation for the difference between his report and that of Perrot on the punishment
of thievery, for strangers, particularly white men, were considered fair game.

Adultery.—This crime was violently punished among the
Miami according to Cadillac, who wrote about 1695:

They do not trouble themselves about the licentiousness of
the girls, but as regards their wives, they are very jealous, and
as soon as there is some one of them convicted of infidelity and

---

[69] Perrot, *Memoir, ITUM.,* 1: 139-41.
[70] *Ibid.,* pp. 138-39.
[71] *Journal,* 2: 95.

adultery, the husband has her head shaved, cuts off her nose and ears, and puts her outside of his cabin, after which she goes where she wishes, and her relatives find no fault, because that is the law of this tribe. They have another infamous way of punishing adultery. The husband takes the wife and leads her to the middle of the village; he announces in a loud voice the crime of which she is guilty, and at the same time all the young men aid him in punishing her. At the same moment he throws her down to be the first to be intimate with her, and then all the others are, sometimes two or three hundred men, who are not sorry to act as executioners in such a punishment. Generally the offender dies, but often she recovers. They maintain that the punishment conforms to the fault of the unfaithful wife, since she is so lustful, it is only right to satiate her. However, the French have reproached them so much that now they only rarely inflict this last chastisement.[72]

The punishment of adultery as described by Cadillac is considerable more extreme than that reported by other observers. Deliette, and, of course, Raudot, writing only a few years after Cadillac, about 1702, said that the Miami cut off their wives' noses as a punishment for adultery. Deliette was acquainted with the rigorous chastisement described by Cadillac, but differs with him in saying that only about thirty men took part and that it was used by the Illinois but not the Miami.[73] Sabrevois in 1718 stated that the latter tribe was the only one that had the custom of cutting off the noses of unfaithful wives.[74]

Games and Dances

Dances, games, and dreams were closely integrated in the life of the Miami, and all played a large part in their thoughts and activities. Dreams often controlled the occurrence of dances and games, and the participation and actions of individuals in them. Games were considered gambling by the European visitors, whereas dances were not. Although

[72] MS "Relation on the Indians."
[73] *Memoir, IHC.,* 23: 335.
[74] *Memoir, WHC.,* 16: 375.

the gambling factor is not denied nor that it appealed to the Indians, certain other facts must be pointed out: first, dancers received gifts for their participation, and hence dances furnished opportunities for gain; the size of the gift was often determined by the excellence of the performance of the individual; second, both games and dances were held in honor of strangers, other villages, and the dead. There was no rigid rule determining which ceremony should be held on any of these occasions. Usually, the calumet dance was given upon the visit of a distinguished foreigner, games in honor of other villages, and, as part of the funeral ceremonies, the favorite dance or game of the deceased in his honor. Hence the distinction between games and dances is minimized. It is likely that there was little difference between the two categories in the minds of the Indians.

The Miami was passionately fond of games, and the men divided the time not taken up by the necessities of life between playing them, feasting, and dancing. Games were played for a variety of reasons, for sport, for gain, in honor of a visitor, and in honor of a deceased person. Losers whose wives were pregnant accused them of bringing them bad luck. Women also played some of these games, particularly those played in honor of a dead person, for then the games or dances were performed by persons of the same sex as the deceased.

Lacrosse.—In the game of lacrosse village usually played against village or tribe against tribe, oftentimes women and children taking part, but there was always the same number of players on each side. The object of the game was to drive a wooden ball about the size of a tennis ball to the goal of the opposing side with rackets, which were sticks three and one-half feet long ending in a laced loop. The goals were posts at opposite ends of a field, the size of which was regulated by the number of players. Charlevoix said that for four score players the length would be half a league. He also stated that the ball must not be allowed to touch the ground or be touched by hand, for either of which violations the game was lost unless the offending player could drive the ball with one stroke to the opponents' goal.[75] This account of the Miami's game is in contradiction to the general account of the game by Perrot, who stated that sometimes a player attempted to keep the ball between his feet, with a consequent shower of blows on his legs and feet which might break them. This author also said that one side must make two goals to win, which was not mentioned by Charlevoix or other writers.[76] Charlevoix said that the Miami players were so dexterous at catching the ball with their crosses that sometimes a game lasted several days. But it was not always so long, for when he was at the Miami village near Green Bay in 1671, Perrot was honored by a game of lacrosse which only lasted half an hour.[77] There is no disagreement among all the writers who described the game as to its potentiality for injuries. Wagers on the game were made between sides and also by spectators.

Charlevoix described another game which was very much like lacrosse, but not so dangerous. Following his account of the game of lacrosse, he wrote:

Two boundaries are marked out as in the first, and the players ocupy all the space which is between the two. He who is to begin tosses a ball up into the air, as nearly perpendicular as possible, to the end he may catch it again with the greater ease, in order to throw it towards the boundary. All the rest stand ready with their hands lifted, and he who catches the ball either performs the same thing or throws it to some one of his own company, whom he judges more alert and dexterous than himself; for in order to win the party the ball must never be suffered to fall into the hands of any of the adversaries, before it reaches the boundary. The women also play at this game, but this rarely happens; their companies consist of four or five, and the first who lets fall the ball loses the party.[78]

[75] *Journal*, 2: 97.
[76] *Memoir, ITUM.*, 1: 93-96.
[77] *Ibid.*, p. 345.
[78] *Journal*, 2: 97-98.

Dice or bowl game.—The bowl game was played by the Miami, but there is no testimony as to how it was played.

Game of straws.—The game of straws appears to have been the favorite gambling game indulged in by the Miami. As is evident from reading the various accounts that have been written of it by both early and modern writers, it was not very well understood by any of the European spectators.

Charlevoix described a game he witnessed between the Miami and the Potawatomi at St. Joseph as follows:

On this day the Poutewatamies came to play at the game of straws, against the Miamis; the game was played in the cabbin of the chief, and in a sort of square over against it. These straws are small rushes of the thickness of a stalk of wheat and two fingers in length. They take up a parcel of these in their hands, which generally consists of two hundred and one, and always of an unequal number. After they have well stirred them, and making a thousand contortions of body and invoking the genii, they divide them, with a kind of awl or sharp bone into parcels of ten: each takes one at a venture, and he to whom the parcel with eleven in it falls gains a certain number of points according to the agreement: sixty or four score make a party.

That this was not entirely clear to the author is apparent from his statement:

There are other ways of playing this game, and they would have explained them to me, but I could understand nothing of the matter, except that the number nine gained the whole party. They also told me, that there was as much art as chance in this game, and that the Indians are great cheats at it, as well as at all others; that they are so eager at it, as to spend whole days and nights at it; and that sometimes they do not give over playing till they have stript themselves and have nothing more to lose.[79]

This game was also described by Deliette. His account does not agree with that of Charlevoix and recent writers,

[79] *Ibid.*, pp. 95-96.

inasmuch as he said that the straws were counted by sixes rather than by tens. There is a possibility that this is the result of some copyist of the original French mistaking *dix* for *six;* on the other hand, it may be one of the variety of ways of playing the game, as mentioned by Charlevoix. Deliette's account is as follows:

At night most of the men, seated like dogs on mats of round reeds, play at straws. For markers they use the little beans which I have mentioned, which grow on the thorny trees. The game is usually of 200 straws of the length of a foot. The one who can best deceive is the best player; so they are always on the lookout against being deceived. They mark with their beans one or two, according to the wish of the one whose turn it is to mark, then three, and so in regard to the other players up to six, which is the game. One of them takes the straws in both hands and forces his thumb into the middle. The other, if he so desires, does the same then, and afterwards counts the straws by sixes; if he happens to have one left, and one bean is marked the first, he has the head; if the other gets two which are marked next, it is what they call the neck which comes after the head, so he loses; if he gets one like the other, they begin over again. They have perhaps five or six hundred of these beans, some of which they stake on each play, and when one player has them all before him, they gain what they have staked. They are addicted to this game in a degree that cannot be exceeded. Some of them have staked their sisters after having lost all they had of personal property. They are very superstitious about it, and if their wives are with child when they lose, they say it is they who bring ill-luck; if they win, they say the contrary.[80]

Dances were held for a variety of purposes. They were given in honor of the dead, in welcome to strangers, in cementing alliances between nations, in invitation to or preparation for war, and for pleasure. It is impossible to tell how often the dances were performed strictly for the sake of dancing; various writers have said that the Indians were very fond of dancing, gaming, and feasting, but in such state-

[80] *Memoir, IHC.,* 23: 351-52.

ments they did not mention what these dances were. Instead of holding dances for diversion, it might well be that the Indians, being fond of dances, used this means of expressing themselves on very definite occasions.

A dance which Charlevoix termed a game which excited no strong desire for gain and which apparently was performed strictly for pleasure was described as follows:

This is for pure diversion only, but is almost always attended with fatal consequences with respect to their morals. At nightfall several posts are erected, in a round form, in the middle of some great cabin; in the midst of all are the instruments, on each post is fixed a packet of down, of which there must be some of every colour. The young people of both sexes promiscuously dance round the posts, the girls having also some down of the colour which they love: from time to time a young man goes out from the rest, and takes from a post some down of the colour which he knows is agreeable to his mistress, places it upon her head, dances round her, and by a certain signal gives her to understand some place of assignation. The dance ended, the feast begins and lasts the whole day long, in the evening all the company return, when the girls manage matters with so much address, that in spite of the vigilance of their mothers they reach the place of rendezvous.[81]

Calumet dance.—This dance has been often described. Most of the descriptions, if identified at all, have been in connection with the Illinois; Marquette's is the most detailed and probably the best known. As has been pointed out, it is possible that some of these references to the Illinois meant the Miami, since the term "Illinois" was frequently used in speaking of all the tribes immediately south of the Great Lakes.

The feature that gave this dance its name is the calumet. This term is a corruption by the French of the name they gave at an early date to the tobacco pipe of the Indians, from the resemblance of the long stem of the pipe to the reed or

[81] *Journal*, 2: 96-97.

chalumeau of the Norman peasants. The pipe itself had a very wide distribution on the continent, but the dance was first met with by the French in the Green Bay region, and in the early years of their domination of the country it seems to have been limited to the territory bordering on the Great Lakes and the northern part of the Mississippi Valley.

The accounts of it from this region reported that the dance was performed for the important purposes of strengthening peace or uniting for war, for public rejoicing, or to ensure a prosperous voyage. About 1720 Fox Indians attempted to introduce the dance among the converted Abenaki residing at St. Francis and on making inquiries their missionary, Father Bigot, learned:

1st. That this Dance was really a religious ceremony not only amongst the Renards but also amongst all the nations of the upper country; that it was called the Spirit Dance; that they did not say: "dance with the Calumet," but "dance in honor of the Calumet"; in other words that it was the God of those Nations.

2nd. That the words used in the song of that Dance are an invocation of the Spirit.

3rd. That when the Calumet is smoked in the Councils, a man whose wife is pregnant must abstain from smoking it, because his wife would not be safely delivered of her child and the latter would inevitably die.

4th. That this Dance is used to call the souls of those against whom war is to be waged, and by this means to kill their enemies without fail.

5th. To conciliate foreign and hostile Nations and make a lasting peace with them.

6th. To obtain fine weather or rain, according to the needs of the soil.

7th. To have favorable winds while navigating.

8th. Finally, that it is a specific for warding off evil and for obtaining benefits of all kinds.[82]

The earliest account of this dance is that given by Allouez,

[82] Jacques le Sueur, *Memoir, WHC.*, 17: 195-96.

who wrote the following description of the dance as practiced by the Miami in 1667:

They acknowledge many spirits to whom they offer sacrifice. They practice a kind of dance, quite peculiar to themselves, which they call "the dance of the tobacco-pipe." It is executed thus: they prepare a great pipe, which they deck with plumes, and put in the middle of the room, with a sort of veneration. One of the company rises, begins to dance, and then yields his place to another, and this one to a third; and thus they dance in succession, one after another, and not together. One would take this dance for a pantomime ballet; and it is executed to the beating of a drum. The performer makes war in rhythmic time, preparing his arms, attiring himself, running, discovering the foe, raising the cry, slaying the enemy, removing his scalp, and returning home with a song of victory,—and all with astonishing exactness, promptitude and agility. After they have all danced, one after the other, around the pipe, it is taken and offered to the chief man in the whole assembly, for him to smoke; then to another, and so in succession to all. This ceremony resembles in its significance the French custom of drinking, several out of the same glass; but, in addition, the pipe is left in the keeping of the most honored man, as a sacred trust, and a sure pledge of the peace and union that will ever subsist among them as long as it shall remain in that person's hands.[83]

There is not entire agreement as to the use of the term "calumet"; for instance, Charlevoix called the pipes smoked in councils of a tribe "calumets," whereas most of the other writers spoke of the calumet as being used only in matters of state, such as negotiations of war or alliance or in preparation for voyages, and referred to the ordinary smoking instruments as pipes. The weight of the documentary evidence is that the Indians were incessant smokers; Raudot, Lahontan, and Boucher all state in substance that almost all the Indians, both men and women, smoked a great deal.[84]

[83] *Journal, J.R.,* 51: 47-49; see also Raudot, "Memoir," Letter 26.
[84] *Ibid.,* Letter 25; Lahontan, *Voyages,* 2: 474; Boucher, *Histoire véritable,* p. 167.

A calumet used by the Miami is described in the following account by La Potherie of the welcome they, with the Mascoutens, gave Perrot in 1670 at their village near Green Bay:

The old man held in his hand a calumet of red stone, with a long stick at the end; this was ornamented in its whole length with the heads of birds, flame-colored, and had in the middle a bunch of feathers colored a bright red, which resembled a great fan. As soon as he espied the leader of the Frenchmen, he presented to him the calumet, on the side next to the sun; and uttered words which were apparently addressed to all the spirits whom those people adore. The old man held it sometimes toward the east, and sometimes toward the west; then toward the sun; now he would stick the end in the ground, and then he would turn the calumet around him looking at it as if he were trying to point out the whole earth, with expressions which gave the Frenchman to understand that he had compassion on all men. Then he rubbed with his hand Perrot's head, back, legs, and feet, and sometimes his own body. This welcome lasted a long time, during which the old man made a harangue, after the fashion of a prayer, all to assure the Frenchman of the joy which all in the village felt at his arrival.[85]

This performance in token of welcome is not strictly in accord with others that are denominated "dances," yet it has many elements in common with them. The offering of the calumet to the sun is mentioned by Marquette in his detailed account of the ceremony practiced by the Illinois. Charlevoix thought that this feature was intended by the Indians to take the sun for a witness of the engagements or professions made at the time. This writer also stated that there was, perhaps, no example of the violation of an engagement entered into with the acceptance and smoking of the calumet.[86] On the other hand, Perrot reported the treachery of the Ottawa chief, Sinagos, to whom a calumet had been given by the Sioux; but added that the tribes of the prairies had the ut-

[85] *History, ITUM.*, 1: 325-26.
[86] *Journal*, 1: 304-5.

most attachment for the calumet and regarded it as a sacred thing, while he who violated the pledge given with it was regarded as disloyal and traitorous and his crime as one that could not be pardoned.[87]

Discovery.—Although Charlevoix did not designate the tribes who performed this dance, his account indicates that he had read and used the works of Raudot.[88] There is also a striking resemblance to what Marquette called the second part of the calumet dance:

I should probably have been more diverted by seeing the dance of the Discovery. This has more action than the former (calumet), and is much more expressive of the thing it is intended to represent. This is an image drawn to the life of all that passes in a warlike expedition; and as I have already observed, that the Indians generally think only of surprizing their enemies, it is no doubt for this reason, they have given this exercise the name of Discovery.

Be this as it will, one man always dances singly in it, advancing at first slowly towards the middle of the place, where he remains for some time motionless, after which he represents in order the departure of the warriors; the march, encampments, the discovery of the enemy, the approach towards them, the halt as it were in order to draw breath, when all of a sudden he falls into such a fury as if he were going to kill all the world; when recovered from this trance, he seizes some person in the assembly as if he took him prisoner of war, seems to kill another, levels at a third, and lastly falls a running at full speed, when he stops and recovers himself; this represents a retreat which is at first precipitate, but afterwards more at leisure. He then expresses by different cries, the different agitations in which he was during his last campaign, and concludes with relating all the fine exploits he has performed in war.[89]

In the letter referred to, Raudot commented that the Miami excelled at this dance.

[87] *Memoir, ITUM.,* 1: 182-86.
[88] "Memoir," Letter 27.
[89] *Journal,* 2: 65-66.

Striking the post.—Immediately following the description of the "discovery" in the letters of both Raudot and Charlevoix is that of the dance called "striking the post," nor do the similarities stop there, as a comparison of the two will show. Charlevoix wrote:

There are other dances which are more simple, or which seem to have no other view besides giving the warriors opportunity of relating their own exploits. This is what the Indians covet above all things, and in doing which they are never wearied. He who gives the feast, invites the whole village by beat of drum; and it is in his cabbin they assemble, if it be capable of containing all the guests. The warriors dance here by turns, afterwards they strike upon the post, silence is proclaimed, when they say anything they have a mind, pausing from time to time in order to receive the congratulations of the spectators who are not sparing of incense. But if they perceive that any one boasts without grounds, any one is at liberty to take earth or ashes, and to smear his head all over or to do him any other affront they have a mind. The general way is to black his face, accosting him in these words, "This I do to conceal your shame; for the first time you see the face of an enemy, you will become as pale as ashes." Thus, it seems to be a received maxim amongst all nations, that the surest mark of a coward is boasting. He who has thus punished the recreant takes his place, and if he has the misfortune to fall into the same fault the other is sure to pay him back in kind. The greatest chiefs have no privilege above the common in this respect, and must take all without murmuring.[90]

There are many points of resemblance in the calumet ceremony, the dance of the discovery, and that of striking the post. In superficial descriptions it is sometimes difficult to distinguish one from the others. The French writers usually used these three names. The following account by Gist of what was called the "warriors' feather dance" seems to be most like the striking the post dance:

The Crier of the Town came by the King's Order and invited

[90] *Ibid.*, pp. 66-67.

us to the long House to see the Warrior's Feather Dance; it was
performed by three Dancing Masters, who were painted all
over with various Colours, with long Sticks in their Hands, upon
the Ends of which were fastened long Feathers of Swans, and
other Birds, neatly woven in the Shape of a Fowls Wing: in this
Disguise they performed many antick Tricks, waving their Sticks
and Feathers about with great Skill to imitate the flying and
fluttering of Birds, keeping exact time with their Musick; while
they are dancing some of the Warriors strike a Post, upon which
the Musick and Dancers cease, and the Warrior gives an Account
of his Achievements in War, and when he has done, throws down
some Goods as a Recompence to the Performers and Musicians;
after which they proceed in their Dance as before till another
Warrior strikes ye Post, and so on as long as the Company think
fit.[91]

The feathered sticks recall the feathered pipe stems of the
calumet, the single performer is common to all three dances,
a recital of the warrior's martial achievements belongs to
both the discovery and striking the post dances, and the feature of striking the post before the recital or portrayal belongs only to the last and gave it its name. This account by
Gist contributes some information not reported by any of the
French authors, namely, the dancing of dancing masters before the recitals of the warriors and the recompensing of the
performers and musicians by the warriors.

War

Indian warfare was waged primarily for the glory of the
participants. Acquisition of territory was not a motive, but
the acquisition of prisoners or scalps as tokens of the bravery
and skill of the warriors was very important to them. In fact,
adult status was achieved by a male only after participation
in one or more war parties. With this dependence on warfare
as a criterion of social standing it is evident that the tribe
would be engaged in war at least every few years to provide

[91] *Journal, Filson Club Publ.*, 13: 143-44.

for each new group coming of age. This condition and the policy of blood vengeance for unrequited murder resulted in an almost constant state of war. Few tribes could be considered pacific. The Miami were not one of these. The records of the French regime indicate that the Miami were embroiled at one time or other with almost every surrounding tribe, even the kindred Illinois. The Miami were regarded by the French as a tribe whose able and brave warriors rarely undertook unsuccessful expeditions.[92] The only extended description of their warfare is the following by Deliette, which applied to both the Illinois and the Miami:

It is ordinarily in February that they prepare to go to war. Before starting, it should be noted that in each village there are several chiefs of the young men who dispose of thirty, forty, and sometimes as many as fifty men. That is why, at the time I have spoken of, they invite them to a feast and tell them that the time is approaching to go in search of men; so it is well to pay homage, according to their custom, to their birds so that these may be favorable. They all answer with a loud Ho! and after eating with great appetite they all go to get their mats and spread out their birds on a skin stretched in the middle of the cabin and with the *chichicoyas* they sing a whole night, saying: stone falcon, or crow, I pray to you that when I pursue the enemy I may go with the same speed in running as you do in flying, in order that I may be admired by my comrades and feared by our enemies. At break of day they bring back their birds. When they wish to go to war, one of them, or the one who is their chief, offers them a feast, usually of dog. After all are placed, they observe a great silence and the host says: "My comrades, you know that I have wept for a long time; I have not laughed since the time that my brother, father, or uncle died. He was your relative as well as mine, since we are all comrades. If my strength and my courage equalled yours, I believe that I would go to avenge a relative as brave and as good as he was, but being as feeble as I am, I cannot do better than address myself to you. It is from your arms, brothers, that I expect vengeance for our brother. The birds that

[92] Marquette, *Relation of First Voyage*, J.R., 59: 103.

we prayed to some days ago have assured me of victory. Their
protection, along with your courage, should induce us to undertake anything." Then he rises and, going up to each one, passes
his hands over his head and over his shoulders. Then the assembled guests say: "Ho, Ho! It is well. We are ready to die:
you have only to speak." They thank him, and then depart at
night and go about two leagues from the village to sleep. It is a
maxim with them never to set out by day when they go in small
parties, because, they say, if they went by day, they would be
discovered before making their attack. The band does not ordinarily exceed twenty. The youngest, who is always the one who
has shared in the fewest ventures, carries the kettle and has
charge of the cooking and mends moccasins for all of them, which
is no slight task. Accordingly, he hardly ever sleeps at night; but
since this is the custom, they always do it amicably. They take
the precaution of hiding in two or three places stores of bacon
and flour and some small kettles, to serve in case they should be
pursued by the enemy, so as not to have to stop to hunt in order
to keep alive. They also mark places for joining each other in
case they are obliged to go by several different routes, and in such
cases those who arrive first take a little of what they have left,
if they need it, and leave their marks, which they never mistake.
They paint a portrait of themselves for this purpose on the
nearest tree. Although several of them have heads of hair that
look just alike, the mark on their names identifies them. They all
have significant ones: one, the Buck, another the Buffalo, the
Wolf, the Sun, the Earth, the Water, the Woman, the Child,
the Girl, or something formed from these names, as Buckfeet,
Bear's Head, Woman's Breast, Buffalo Hump, the Eclipsed
Moon or Sun, and so forth. Thus after painting themselves, as
I have related, they draw a line above the head, at the end of
which they draw a buffalo or its hump, a buck or its feet, the sun
or a cloud above it, and so forth. When they approach an enemy,
the one who leads the party sends out two of the most active a
league ahead to reconnoiter the places through which they must
pass. If they see smoke or other traces that lead them to believe
that the enemy is not far off, they come to report to the chief,
who calls a halt.

    I have forgotten to say that the commander carries his mat,

into which all his men have put their birds, along with a good stock of herbs for healing the wounded. As soon as they stop the chief takes out the birds and, after offering a short prayer to them, sends out three or four of the most active and brave to reconnoiter for the enemy. If by chance they find but a man or two, they attack these without warning their comrades. If the number is very considerable they return to report, and after thoroughly examining the place where they are to attack them, they invariably wait until morning when the day is beginning to break, and they never fail to paint themselves and to give attention to their footgear, as a precaution in case they should be obliged to flee. Two or three of the youngest remain with the baggage in the most hidden spot. At a couple of arpents' distance from the enemy they emit the most astonishing yells in order to frighten him, running at him when he takes to flight. In this they triumph, for they know that the enemy cannot run as well as they —I speak of the Iroquois. They give the same cry as their birds in running after them. If they are three in pursuit of one man and are in doubt which of them will lay hands on him, the first who can touch him with some missile is the one to whom the prisoner belongs, even if another should lay hands on him first. They then utter several cries to attract the attention of their comrades who are fighting elsewhere, or who are in pursuit of others, who thus learn what they have done. When they have bound their prisoners and have reassembled, the leader makes a little harangue in which he exhorts his men to thank the spirit for having favored them, and to make every effort to get speedily away from the spot where they are. They march ordinarily for two days and nights without stopping, resting only at their meals. If their captives are women who cannot march, which happens very often, they smash their heads or burn them on the spot, which they do only in extreme cases, as the man who brings a prisoner to the village is more esteemed than the one who kills six men among the enemy. If unhappily some of themselves have been killed, the leader of the band paints himself with mud all along the road and weeps frequently as he marches and, on reaching the village, is obliged to carry presents to the relatives of those that have been killed to pay for their death, and he is expected soon to go back to avenge the slain. If some one is again killed of those with him, he has great difficulty in finding men willing to accompany him a third time, which causes him to be hated by the kinsfolk of the dead, unless by dint of presents he finds means (to use their language) to mend their hearts.

To return to their manner of behaving when they return victorious to the village: two men go ahead, and when they are near enough to make themselves heard, they utter cries for as many persons as they have killed, and they name these. Many people run out to meet them, and the first to arrive take everything that the warriors carry, which they appropriate. Those who are unwilling to part with some arm or other object which they like, take care to hide it the day before their arrival; but they are taxed with avarice. As I have said, if some one of them has been killed, the leader of the party carries in his hand some broken bows and arrows, and those who precede the party utter cries saying: "We are dead!" whereupon the women utter terrible howls until it is learned who the dead are, and then it is only the relatives who redouble their outcries.

As soon as the news has become known, a man of consideration makes preparations to regale the warriors, who are invited to enter. When they have arrived in the cabin which has been prepared for them, oil is immediately brought to them in dishes, with which they lubricate their legs. The one who gives the feast goes weeping to pass his hands over their heads to make known to them that some of his relatives have been killed by warriors of the nation from which they bring back prisoners, and that they would give him pleasure in killing them. During this time the prisoners are outside the cabin (for it is a maxim with them never to admit slaves into their cabins unless they have been granted their lives). These sing their death song, holding in one hand a stick ten or twelve feet long, filled with feathers from all the kinds of birds that the warriors killed on the road. This is after having them sing at the doors of the cabins of all those who have most recently had relatives killed.

The old men and party leaders assemble and decide to whom these slaves shall be given. This settled, they lead one of them opposite the door of the cabin of the one to whom they give him, and bringing along some merchandise, they enter and say that they are delighted that the young men have brought back some men to replace, if they desire it, those whom the fate of war has taken away. For this offer great thanks are returned. A little later these people assemble and decide what they will do with the prisoner who has been given to them, and whether they wish to give him his life, a thing rarely done among the Illinois. When he is a man, they admit him and send for the principal men of the village who have brought them the prisoners. They thank these and give them some merchandise. When they want him put to death, they bring him back to the cabin of the most considerable of those who have offered him, giving the captive to them, with a kettle and a hatchet which they have colored red to represent blood. From there he is taken to others, and according to their decision he dies or lives. When he is condemned to die, it is always by fire. I have never seen any other kind of torment used by this nation. They plant a little tree in the earth, which they make him clasp; they tie his two wrists, and with torches of straw or firebrands they burn him, sometimes for six hours. When they find his strength far gone, they unfasten him and cut his thumbs off, after which they let him, if he wishes, run after those who are throwing stones at him, or who wish to burn him. They even give him sticks which he holds with great difficulty. If he tries to run after anybody, they push him and he falls on his face, at which they hoot. He sometimes furnishes a whole hour's diversion to these barbarians. Finally he succumbs under the strain of his torments, and sometimes drops down motionless. The rabble run to get firebrands, which they poke into the most sensitive parts of his body; they trail him over hot embers, which brings him back to life, at which they renew their hootings, as if they had performed some fine exploit. When they are tired of their sport, an old rascal cuts his flesh from the top of the nose to the chin and leaves it hanging, which gives him a horrible appearance. In this state they play a thousand tricks on him, and finally stone him or cut open his stomach. Some drink his blood. Women bring their male children still at the breast and place their feet in his body and wash them with his blood. They eat his heart raw.[93]

I had forgotten to say, in the place where I talked of war, that the Illinois as well as the Miami have the maxim when they are

[93] Deliette, *Memoir*, IHC., 23: 376-86.

on the march to go among the enemy in small parties never to make more than one fire, a fairly long one so that all the warriors may profit by it. They always lie down with their feet to the fire, and never put anything on themselves. Those who are designated to serve the rest are those of the band who have seen least of war. These circulate about the fire. They never unload their packs from their backs to make water, or for any other necessities, and never when going toward the enemy. When they are returning home they unload, but never do they sit down on their pack. Nor do they ever make use of knives when their meat is cooked, a thing they do not observe when they make general marches, believing that no one can resist them, in which they are often mistaken.[94]

The ceremonies of adoption are slighted in Deliette's account, and, unfortunately, the deficiency is not made up in the writings of other observers. Later writers reported that these ceremonies were rather important and encompassed not only the adoption of prisoners to take the place of persons deceased naturally or in war but also the adoption of other members of the tribe into a family to take the position of the head of the family.

In a sketch of the war customs observed by the Illinois about 1694, Rasles stated that they required prisoners arriving at their village to run the gauntlet. After this ordeal an assembly of the old men decided whether the prisoners should be used to "resuscitate the dead" (i.e., those slain in war) or whether they should be put to death by torture.[95]

Birth

Confinement of women took place in cabins opposite those of their husbands. When there were difficulties in the delivery forty or fifty men rushed on the cabin unexpectedly, shouting and shooting their guns and knocking on the cabin as if they were enemies. They hastened the delivery by the

[94] *Ibid.*, p. 395.
[95] "Letter . . . . to His Brother," *J.R.*, 67: 171-75.

surprise and fear they caused. The women remained in these separate cabins up to fifteen days; some of them seem to have been more than slightly incommoded by childbirth, in spite of all the comments made about the "savage" woman delivering a child and then picking up her load of wood and going on to the village as if nothing had happened.

When a woman wished to return to her husband after confinement, she bathed in the river or, if the weather did not permit, in her cabin. The husband being informed of her readiness to return, shook all the skins in the cabin, threw out all the ashes of the hearth and then, lighting a new fire, sent to tell her to enter.[96]

Supposedly, the child was washed also and lashed to a cradle, but there is no statement to that effect to be found in the records relating to the Miami. It was probably taken for granted. Children spent most of their time on these cradle boards until they were two or three years of age. They were usually weaned by that time and also were ready to walk. Either at birth or at the time of leaving the cradle the child received a name. The time of giving a name varied with the different tribes, and there is no information from the contact period on this point for the Miami.

Puberty

The youth of the tribe, both boys and girls, were required to undergo fasts of several days at puberty, in order that they might discover their guardian spirits in their dreams. Thierry Beschefer found this to be the only superstition among the Miami, and he said in 1683 they were dissuaded from continuing it. The old men admitted after this abandonment, according to this missionary, that their only reason, which they covered with the pretext of religion, in causing the young men to undergo fasts was to inure them to fatigue and to prevent them from becoming heavy.[97] The retirement of the

[96] Raudot, "Memoir," Letter 61.
[97] Beschefer, "Letter to the Provincial," J.R., 62: 205-7.

girls on reaching puberty is described by Raudot in his sixtieth letter.

There is no evidence that either the boys or girls took new names when they adopted a guardian. Names used by them were doubtless similar to those reported by Deliette for the Illinois:

They have significant ones; one, the Buck, another the Buffalo, the Wolf, the Sun, the Earth, the Water, the Woman, the Child, the Girl, or something formed from these names as Buckfeet, Bear's Head, Woman's Breast, Buffalo Hump, the Eclipsed Moon or Sun, and so forth.[98]

Marriage

According to Marquette, Allouez, La Salle, and Deliette, the Illinois men were permitted to have several wives; La Salle said the number was sometimes as high as ten or twelve. Sisters of the first wife were preferred as the subsequent wives.[99] Deliette stated that a man usually married the sisters, aunts, or nieces of his wife and that it was an easy matter for him to marry all who stood in these degrees of relationship if he were a good hunter. These, he said, were called *Nirimoua* by the man, and they designated him in the same manner.[100] There is good reason to believe that similar if not identical customs were practiced by the Miami. Their ceremonies of marriage were recorded only by Deliette:

Formerly a man had to make several attacks on the enemy before he could marry, a thing he did not do until he was at least twenty-five, the period when a man begins to possess resolution, so that they were really about thirty when they married. The girls also waited till they were twenty-five. At present there are men who do not wait till they are twenty, and the girls marry under eighteen. The old men say that the French have corrupted them.

[98] *Memoir, IHC.,* 23: 379.

[99] *Official Account of the Enterprises of La Salle,* Margry, *Découvertes,* 1, Pt. 2: 527.

[100] *Memoir, IHC.,* 23: 355.

When a young man has succeeded in learning to hunt, he tells his father that he wishes to marry, and names the girl he loves, to whom sometimes he has never spoken, for a chaste girl among the Illinois, as well as among the Miami, ought not to hold conversation with the young men, nor even with the married men. When they speak of marriage, she must never speak to them first, nor cast her eyes upon them, for as soon as a young man notices that a girl looks at him frequently and afterwards whispers to some of her companions, he conjectures that she is in love with him, and ordinarily he is not mistaken. He therefore neglects no opportunity to take advantage of this, and spies out the time when she goes to the woods or to her field. He begs her to listen to him, and assures her of his love. The girl half overcome already, does not answer a word, which is an infallible sign among them that she loves him. He has a rendezvous with her and sometimes obtains without delay all that he desires. Accordingly, a really well-conducted girl should avoid gatherings where men are present, in order to be esteemed and married with ceremony. This done in the following manner.

It is usually at the time when the young man is absent either making war or hunting. His father, if he has one, or his uncle in lieu of him, takes five or six kettles, two or three guns, some skins of stags, bucks or beavers, some flat sides of buffalo, some cloth, and sometimes a slave, if he has one, in short something of all he has, according to his wealth and the esteem in which the girl is held. He has these presents delivered by women, his relatives, who deposit them in the cabin of the girl, who goes out as soon as she is aware that it is for her that they bring these presents, and he merely says to the father or to her nearest relatives that he asks his alliance and that he begs him to have pity on him and to suffer him to warm himself at his fire. They use this expression because it is always the women who supply the cabins and the firewood. They also (say) that they come to seek moccasins, because it is the women also who dress the skins. The presents remain sometimes for four days in the cabin, without any answer being given, on account of the objections made by the girl who does not like the boy, or on account of her brother who is in favor of some other suitor who perhaps has been seeking his good graces for a long time by means of little presents, so that he may favor him in the same matter, which he has not yet been able to arrange either through lack of merchandise, or because his relatives are absent. In such a case the presents are returned and nothing is said. The father of the youth, knowing how much his son is bent on marrying this girl, augments the presents and returns to the girl's home, saying that it is at her fire only that he wishes to warm himself. I have seen presents carried back as many as three times. This often produces discouragement, and they address themselves to other girls for whom they have heard their sons express esteem. In the end, therefore, the girls and her brother consent on account of the suasion of the father and mother, who extol the good qualities of the youth. For this reason, in accordance with the means of the girl, they carry back several things resembling those that were brought to them and the girl marches ahead well adorned with shoulder straps, glass beads, porcelain, and bells, so that one who heard them marching would think they were mules. They spread a bear skin, or that of a buffalo or a stag, according to the season, in the middle of the cabin, on which they seat the bride, and the relatives who followed her carrying the presents return home.

In the evening the relatives of the youth bring her back with some presents. This is usually done as many as four successive days. The last day she remains. There are some who wait for the bridegroom's return before going there for the last time. They remain sometimes a whole week without approaching each other. It has happened that men, getting angry at being too long rebuffed by their wives, have left them and gone off to the war without having known them, and have been killed. This happens sometimes because they do not love their husbands, at other times to do themselves honor, for when they have children immediately at the end of nine months, it is a matter of reproach when they quarrel, to say that they loved their husbands before marrying them, since they had borne children so soon. I have known one woman who assured me that she and her husband had been six months together without having intercourse. When such accidents occur, these women are to be pitied, for the relatives of the man are always reproaching her with his death. They dare not comb their hair, nor be present at any dance, still less can they marry. They are obliged to live very quietly in spite of themselves, and often in shedding many tears, until the relatives are finally inspired with pity. The sister is the one who combs her, and who urges her to marry if she finds some suitor. To show them the regret that she feels and her gratitude toward them, she must remain a year without marrying. If, unhappily for her, she were to do so before it was allowed, the relatives of the deceased would take her scalp as if she were one of their enemies, would put it into a loop and hang it at the end of a pole at the top of their cabin. When they are faithless to their husbands the same treatment is accorded them. The husband or the relatives do not wait for an opportune moment, but no matter where they find the woman outside of her cabin, they take the law into their own hands.

The Miami cut off their noses. . . .[101]

If a husband left his wife and took one from another family without what her feminine relatives deemed a sufficient reason, they invaded the husband's cabin, cut up all the skins, and broke the kettles. The husband made no motion to stop them. The same treatment was accorded a man who remarried outside of his wife's family shortly after her death.[102] This leads to the inference that husbands who married the sisters of their deceased wives were not first required to put in a lengthy period of mourning.

In 1687 Joutel wrote that "the marriages of the Illinois last no longer than the parties agree together; for they freely part after a hunting bout, each going which way they please, without any ceremony."[103] This would appear to be a companionship arrangement, however, and not a recognized marriage.

Death Customs

The death and burial customs observed by the Miami and the Illinois were described by Deliette:

When their husbands die, they weep in a way that would

---

[101] Deliette, *Memoir, IHC.*, 23: 330-35; Raudot, "Memoir," Letter 62.

[102] Deliette, *Memoir, IHC.*, 23: 360-61; see Raudot, "Memoir," Letter 63.

[103] *Journal, LHC.*, 1: 188.

lead one to believe that they are sincerely grieved, in which they are like the majority of our women who weep only in proportion to the loss they have sustained and the fear they entertain of not finding new husbands, and not from the love they bore the deceased. They abstain for a very long time, as I have already said, from combing themselves unless the sister of the dead man urges them thereto. Often at daybreak you hear weeping on all sides, which, however, far from rousing pity, rather inspires laughter, for one would say that they were singing. One invokes her brother, another her father, another her sister, and others their children. She who has lost her husband and who has no children names her brother in her funeral song, the purport of which is that henceforth she will find no one to do her a good turn. All the married men have the custom of giving some presents to the brothers of their wives. The women who have children name them in their songs, saying that they are deserving of pity in being fatherless, and that they will find nobody who will give them a dress with which to "clothe themselves." The relatives, of whom all the savages have a great number, come to "clothe" them, bringing them blankets, pelts, kettles, guns, hatchets, porcelain collars, belts, knives. All that is given gives pleasure, and now the people of the cabin say that the dead died opportunely since the esteem in which he was held is shown by these presents from everybody. The next day they simply reverse the process. If some one has given a red blanket, he receives a blue one in return; if he has given a yellow kettle, he receives a red one; if he has given a small kettle, he receives a hatchet, and so on. The only advantage accruing to the relatives of the dead men is that they often keep good articles for bad ones which they give away. They also pay four men for burying the dead.

They ordinarily cut two forked sticks ten feet long with a crosspiece. They hollow out the earth to the length of the body and a little wider. They put in a board from one of their old boats or canoes and put the body inside with another board on each side.

I forgot to say that they paint his face and hair red, put on him a white shirt if they have one, and new mittasses of cloth or of leather, and moccasins, and cover him with the best robe they have. They put in a little kettle or earthen pot, about a double handful of corn, a calumet, a pinch of tobacco, a bow and arrows, and then they replant one of these forked sticks a foot from his feet and the other at the same distance from the head with the crosspiece above, after which they set their stakes in *d'anse* on each side, taking care to close up both ends well so that no animals may get in.

If the deceased has been a chief of war parties that have brought in prisoners they plant a tree forty or fifty feet long, which several men go to fetch at the request of the relatives, who give a feast. From this tree they peel the bark and color it with shades of red and black and make pictures of the chief and the prisoners he has taken, tie a bundle of small logs representing as many persons as he has killed, which they also fasten to the stake, and then they plant it beside the tomb. They sometimes put some [articles] in the earth, observing always the maxim of putting similar things with them in their graves. After this they take measures to procure for them, so the old men say, passage over a great river, on whose nearer shore they hear delights. There, they say, they always dance, and they eat everything they wish. The women there are always beautiful, and it is never cold. All the souls of those who die always stand on the bank, waiting to be conveyed to the other side, which never happens unless they have been paid the last obsequies. For this reason the Miami and the Illinois delay as little as possible in rendering them to their relatives. If the dead man is a warrior who has loved the dance very much, the relatives assemble in his cabin to see what they can give. They count how many villages they represent and agree on the thing as best they can in order that none may be dissatisfied. They plant for this purpose three or four forks, according to the amount of merchandise there is to give, and fix crosspieces on which they hang several kettles, guns, and hatchets. They send word to the chiefs of each village to send their warriors to dance for such a one who is dead in order that he may go to enjoy the bliss which all men will one day enjoy.

Immediately the chief or the leading men of each village go and exhort the young men to put on their best array.

A large number of mats are spread outside around these forks, the drummer is there near by and the Chichicoirs. They seat themselves round about, usually stark naked, and tie the skin of the virile member, sometimes fastening it at the belt. One of them begins his role with war whoops, and they represent in dancing the tableaux presented when they discover the enemy, when they kill him, and when they take his scalp, or when they take him prisoner, and they do all this without losing the cadence. They call this dance the discovery.

The women during this time are weeping in his cabin. When the dance is over, the nearest relative of the dead for whom they dance, pointing with a wand says: This is for you, Peoria; this is for you Coiracoentanon, and so on.

If the dead man liked the game of Lacrosse, the relatives have the villages play against each other, and similarly if they liked gaming. Sometimes they have races. All the common people have dances.

When the women die, those of their sex make their graves, dressing them as neatly as they can before burial. If it be a girl, it is the girls who do this.[104]

This description given by Deliette and repeated by Raudot is the only account of burial definitely attributable to the Miami. It specifies only one form of disposal of the dead— that by single interments. The report of the Huron Michipichy sent by Cadillac in 1701 to the Miami on the St. Joseph River indicates that there was at least one other method in use. Michipichy said:

I gave ten red coverlets, this autumn, to a chief of the Miamis to invite him to come here with all his tribe and light his fire here. He accepted the present and, during the last few days, after consulting on this matter, he asked their opinion, and they decided that they would go and collect the bones of their dead and set them in order and that, next year, they would come and settle at Detroit.[105]

A secondary burial of some kind seems to be indicated here, most probably the interment of bodies which had been placed on scaffolds, and it is possible that it involved a feast

[104] Deliette, *Memoir, IHC.*, 23: 355-60.
[105] Margry, *Découvertes*, 5: 413.

of the dead such as was practiced by the Huron and the more northern Algonquian tribes. That they practiced disposal of the dead on scaffolds seems likely in view of the report of Joutel in 1687 that the Illinois buried their dead, but that the bodies of chiefs and other considerable persons were placed in lofty coffins, a practice similar to that of the Akansa and the Shawnee.[106]

On mourning, there is an item by Charlevoix, not given by Deliette, to the effect that he saw two Illinois men going about from cabin to cabin making lamentations. One was the father and the other the friend of the deceased. They walked at a great rate, laying both hands on the heads of all they met, probably, Charlevoix conjectured, to invite them to partake in their grief.[107]

RELIGION

Statements regarding the religious concepts of the Miami are not as numerous or as explicit in the documents of the contact period as one would desire to have them. The majority of the early visitors to the Indians who wrote accounts of what they learned from and about them were missionaries. They were there to convert the natives to their own religion and were not even mildly interested in the religious concepts already held, nor were they capable of understanding them; they regarded them only as something to be eradicated.

There were a few exceptions to this indifference to the existent beliefs of the Indians. For example, in 1667 Allouez wrote that he had "learned that the Iliniouek, the Outagami, and other Savages toward the South, hold that there is a great and excellent genius, master of all the rest, who made Heaven and Earth; and who dwells, they say, in the East, toward the country of the French."[108]

Allouez repeated and expanded on this belief of the Illinois and other southern tribes in a supreme being:

[106] Journal, LHC., 1: 187.
[107] Journal, 2: 194-95
[108] Journal, J.R., 50: 289-91.

Of all the spirits to whom they offer sacrifice, they honor with a very special worship one who is preëminent above the others, as they maintain, because he is the maker of all things. Such a passionate desire have they to see him that they keep long fasts to that end, hoping that by this means God will be induced to appear to them in their sleep; and if they chance to see him, they deem themselves happy, and assured of a long life.

All the nations of the South have this same wish to see God, which no doubt, greatly facilitates their conversion; for it only remains to teach them how they must serve him in order to see him and be blessed.[109]

Dablon in 1671 wrote of the Illinois:

Besides their evident eagerness to receive our instructions, they enjoy a great advantage over other Savages, as far as the Faith is concerned, in that they have hardly any superstitions, and are not wont to offer Sacrifices to various spirits, as do the Outaouacs and others. The reason of this may be that, as they do not fish, but live on Indian corn, which is easily raised in those fertile lands that they occupy, and on game, which is very plentiful, and of which they are never in want, they have no fear of the perils of the Lakes,—where many other Savages perish while fishing, either in their canoes, or by breaking through the ice. These last named people believe that there are water spirits which devour them, and which plunder their nets when the latter are carried off by storms; and hence they try to ap-pease them or win their favor by numerous Sacrifices.

These people are free from all that, and worship only the Sun. But, when they are instructed in the truths of our Religion, they will speedily change this worship and render it to the Creator of the Sun, as some have already begun to do.[110]

Pachot writing in 1719 gave additional testimony on the worship of the sun and a superior being, but included other manitos as having a part in the life of the Indians:

These savages adore only the sun, the earth, and the thunder because they say that these are the things attached to the superior

[109] *Ibid.*, 51: 49.
[110] *Relation .... 1671, J.R.*, 55: 213-15.

being whom they call the master of life. . . . The Illinois call him Kitchesmanetoa which means the spirit master of life; the Outavois call him the same as the Illinois with a little different pronunciation. They have confidence only in their manitous because they believe that they give them ideas coming from the superior being and that it is he who shows them in their dreams the animals which they take for their manitous because he wishes to use them to lead them, which is the reason also that for their medicine they only use their simples to invoke their manitou by their song, because they believe that their manitou communicates to the plants the virtue they have to cure and that these plants would not have it otherwise.[111]

Deliette's comments on religion were very brief. Speaking of the Illinois in 1702, he said:

This nation, as well as the Miami, has no religion. Some have the buffalo, the bear, others the cat, the buck, the lynx, for their manitou. . . .[112]

Besides the animals I have already mentioned as manitous, they have also several birds which they use when they go to war and to which they cherish much superstition. They use the skins of stone falcons, crows, carrion crows, turtledoves, ducks, swallows, martins, parrots, and many others that I do not name.[113]

La Salle wrote to one of his partners in 1680 that the Illinois and Miami were given to the same superstitions held by the rest of the American tribes; they observed their dreams and believed very nearly the same fables as to the creation of the world, except that, whereas some of the Indians believed that it was the tortoise that held up the earth, the Illinois and Miami attributed this to the otter. Moreover, they were very indifferent as to what might become of them after death, but listened readily to all that one wished to tell them, without believing any of it, and even took pleasure in hearing what was told them, as Europeans did in reading ro-

[111] "Les Scioux," AC., C 11 A, 122.
[112] *Memoir, IHC.*, 23: 363.
[113] *Ibid.*, p. 375.

mances. They could not believe that God was angry with sinners or wished to punish them.[114]

As heretofore mentioned on the authority of Beschefer, puberty was the usual time of fasting, in order to learn in one's dream the manito or guardian spirit to be honored and looked to for protection. There was nothing to prevent an individual from acquiring one later, if not successful at that time, or even from exchanging manitos as the result of some dream or momentous experience.

Raudot said that they were very well persuaded of the immortality of the soul, since they believed that they only left this world to go live in one much more agreeable and filled with pleasures.[115] This, undoubtedly, is what La Salle meant by his statement that they were "indifferent as to what will become of them after death."

Aside from the brief remarks of La Salle the only information left on cosmological myths is the account of Deliette about Mount Joliet:

This place is called Illes, because a voyageur who bore that name was detained here a long time. The Illinois and Miami call it Missouratenouy, which signifies an earthen vessel. Indeed it has a certain resemblance to one; it is about three arpents in length and half an arpent in width. It is embanked as if it had been purposely shaped, and it is about thirty feet high, situated an eighth of a league from the river in a very beautiful valley. The woods on the other side are distant about three arpents; there is only one tree on it. Several Illinois and Miami have tried to persuade me that at the time of the deluge, of which it appears they have learned, it was a vessel which had been made to save all mankind from shipwreck; and that, on the subsiding of the waters, being on a bad bottom, it had upset, and in course of time it had changed to earth.[116]

[114] BN., fonds Clair., 1016, f. 65.

[115] "Memoir," Letter 64.

[116] *Memoir, IHC.,* 23: 303-4. Compare this with the account of Raudot, "Memoir," Letter 64. This is one of the few places where the latter is more expansive.

Shamans and Medical Practices

As indicated by the quoted statement of Pachot, the medical practices and religious concepts of the Indians were inextricably interwoven. Medicine was of no value unless the user had the favor of the spirit of the plant or the manito controlling it. Hence offerings were made at the time of collecting roots and herbs, that they might be efficacious; and other offerings were made at the time of using them. In 1673 Marquette wrote that "they are liberal in cases of illness, and think that the effect of the medicines administered to them is in proportion to the presents given to the physician."[117] The presents were necessary to obtain the favor of the spirits of the medicines as well as that of the person who administered them, for niggardliness was certain to be resented.

Marquette visited the village of the Miami, Mascoutens, and Kickapoo at Green Bay on his voyage to the Mississippi and left the following interesting report:

When I visited them, I was greatly Consoled at seeing a handsome Cross erected in the middle of the village, and adorned with many white skins, red Belts, and bows and arrows, which these good people had offered to the Great Manitou (This is the name which they give to God). They did this to thank him for having had pity On Them during The winter, by giving Them an abundance of game When they Most dreaded famine.[118]

The cross was undoubtedly a feature of the midewiwin or grand medicine society, and although this had a religious significance, it was certainly not in connection with the Christian religion, as Marquette assumed.

The existence of such a society was not suspected by Marquette, nor does Deliette appear to have been aware of it, yet in the following quotation one has no difficulty in recognizing a public ceremony of the society. After a description of their medical practices he said of the shamans:

[117] *Relation of First Voyage, J.R.*, 59: 129.
[118] *Ibid.*, p. 103.

They have also an extraordinary and ridiculous manner of inspiring belief in the infallibility of their remedies, which, however, has quite the effect they wish on the minds of the young. Two or three times in the summer, in the most attractive spot in their village, they plant some poles in the ground, forming a sort of enclosure half an arpent square, which they furnish with mats. All of them, the medicine men and the medicine women, remain for the time being in the cabin of one of their confrères, waiting for all this to be arranged, and planning together what to do in order more easily to hoodwink the young people and keep alive the faith in their magical powers, both for the rewards which they get for attending to the sick and also with a view to keeping the younger generation under their influence when they wish them to do something for the security of their village or the repose of their wives and children. After these preliminaries, they enter gravely into this enclosure, their dresses trailing, having their *chichicoya* in their hands and carrying bearskins on their arms. They all sit on mats which are spread for them. One of them rises, the *chichicoya* in his hand, and speaks in a chant before the whole assembly: "My friends, today you must manifest to men the power of our medicine so as to make them understand that they live only as long as we wish." Then they all rise and, waving the *chichicoya* chant: "This buffalo has told me this, the bear, the wolf, the buck, the big tail"—each one naming the beast which he particularly venerates. Then they sit down again, still shaking the gourd. Immediately three or four men get up as if possessed, among them some who resemble men who are on the point of dying. Their eyes are convulsed, and they let themselves fall prostrate and grow rigid as if they were expiring. Another falls also, and rises with an eagle's feather in his hand, the barbs of which are reddened and form a figure suggesting that he has been wounded therewith, but has been saved from the consequences by his medicines, and wishes to inject it into the body of one of the band, who then falls to the ground and expels a quantity of blood from his mouth. The medicine men rush to give him help, tear away the feather which issues an inch out of his mouth, spout medicine all over his body, and then have him carried off with great solemnity to his cabin, where he is treated like men who have been poisoned. They make him swallow a quantity of drugs, and five or six of them lay hold of him and pull him by the arms and legs, uttering loud yells. They shake him for a long time in this manner without his coming to; finally he vomits a quantity of water, and they at the same moment throw down a little rattlesnake. A medicine man picks it up and shows it to the spectators and chants: "Here is the manitou that killed him, but my medicine has restored him to life." The whole assembly come like people filled with amazement to see this serpent and chant: "Medicine is the science of sciences."[119]

There were shamans or medicine men of different kinds, but only those belonging to a society ever worked together to produce a ceremony such as that just described. In recent years much has been learned of the traditions and rites of the medicine lodge, oftentimes the investigator being given information because the society was dying out and the officers were willing to instruct white men that their knowledge might not be lost forever. But in the contact period it is doubtful if the same data would have been given the inquirer or that one would have been able to surmise that there was such a society.

The bearskins mentioned in the above quotation apparently were medicine bundles. Buffalo heads were worn in some ceremonies and, like the medicine bundles, were tendered offerings before their use. Such objects in the Miami, Mascouten, and Kickapoo village near Green Bay were taken by Allouez to be idols, for in the *Relation* of 1675 he wrote:

There exists in this country a species of idolatry; for, besides the head of the wild ox, with its horns, which they keep in their cabins to invoke, they possess bearskins, stripped from the head and not cut open in the middle. They leave on them the head, the eyes, and the snout, which they usually paint green. The head is raised on a pole in the middle of their cabin, the remainder of the skin hanging along the pole to the ground. They invoke it in their sicknesses, wars, and other necessities.[120]

[119] Deliette, *Memoir*, IHC., 23: 369-71; see also Raudot, "Memoir," Letter 66.

[120] J.R., 59: 223.

It is difficult to distinguish between the practices of shamans or medicine men who were members of the medicine
lodge and those of independent shamans. If studies of other
communities and of cultures similar in other respects may be
taken for a guide, surgeons did not belong to the society,
but shamans who administered medicines did; such membership was not a requisite to medical practice, but merely the
usual way of entering upon it.

No such distinction is made by Deliette that would enable
one to determine if the same were true of the Illinois and
Miami. He wrote of their medical and surgical practices:

Almost all the old men are medicine men and consequently
healers, so that when a person is sick, the relatives hang up in
the cabin a kettle, or a couple of guns, or a blanket, according
to the severity of his disease and the amount of his property,
after which they send for the one of the old men who inspires
them with the most confidence, and say to him: "Father," or
"Brother," or "Uncle" (according to the tie of kinship existent
between them; it should be stated that they almost all call each
other relatives, and such degrees of kinship as I have just
enumerated are often claimed by persons whom we should not
even call cousins; I have seen men of eighty claim that young
girls were their mothers), "I beg of you to take pity on us. Here
is what we had hung up for this." The old man pretends not to
notice what they show him, but approaches the sick man and
asks him in what way he is ailing, and where and for how long
a time he has been ill. After a thorough inspection, he returns
home to get some of his medicine and his *chichicoya*, a little
gourd from which the inside has been removed and into which
they put some grains of little glass pearl, and they run a stick
through it from the tip to the bottom, letting one end project a
foot to hold it by. This, when shaken, makes a loud noise. From
a little bag in which he has a quantity of small packages, he
takes out some pieces of tanned skin in which are his medicaments.
After spreading them out, he takes up his gourd and shakes it,
intoning at the top of his voice a song in which he says: "This
buffalo (or the buck, according to his manitou) has revealed this

remedy to me and has told me that it was good for such and such a malady"—and he names the one by which the sick man is attacked—"whoever has it administered to him will be healed." He reiterates this sometimes for half an hour, though often the patient has not slept for a whole week. When the sickness is a desperate one, he calls for water, which he has warmed, and puts into it a micoine, mixing with it five or six kinds of powders which he takes from his packages. This he has his patient swallow, then he takes some into his own mouth, and having the place pointed out to him which gives pain, he spouts this drug upon it, and then bandages it. He is careful to make two visits a day and to treat his patient in the same fashion, save that he does not sing unless the sick man is worse. When he perceives any improvement he brings his gourd and sings louder than the first time, asserting in his song that his manitou is the true manitou, who has never lied to him, wherefore, thanks to the promise which the latter has given him by night in his dreams, he is about to heal his patient by extracting the cause of his ill. Having had the place pointed out, he fingers it carefully, and then all of a sudden throws himself mouth down upon it, crying out as if he were mad. He bites his patient sometimes so hard as to draw blood, but the latter does not budge for fear of manifesting lack of courage. Meanwhile he inserts in his mouth the claw of an eagle, or the hair of the beard of a Kinousaoueine [cougar] or a Richion, which he says he has drawn out from the sore spot. The savages say that it is animals of this kind which send them diseases because they have eaten their prey. It sometimes happens that they pass by places where such animals have strangled bucks, and they make no scruple of appropriating and eating these if they have no meat, and they even consider it very good. In spite of all that these medicine men say of the matter, they are themselves the first to do so. Then in a long song he thanks his manitou with his *chichicoya* for making it possible for him frequently to obtain merchandise through its favor. He takes his patient out for a bath, or washes him in the cabin, according to the season. He takes what had been hung up for him in the cabin and carries it off without saying anything. The relatives arise and pass their hands over his head and his legs, a sign of profound gratitude. Most often they do not cure the sick, although assuredly they have admirable drugs, because they are ignorant of internal maladies. It is only a mere chance when they succeed. Their medicines they use for purging have all the effectiveness possible. There are some who use coloquinte, with which the wilderness abounds in autumn when they gather their seeds. In the healing of wounds some of them are very skilful. I have seen them cure some surprising ones and in a very short time. The sucking process, which they all practice, has no doubt a large share in this success. However full of pus a wound may be, they clean it out entirely without inflicting much pain. They take the precaution of putting a little powder in their mouths; but when they have drawn off the worst of it, they no longer do so, but continue to suck at the wound until it appears ruddy, after which they chew up some medicine which they spit upon the wound merely wrapping up the whole by day, while leaving the wound to suppurate. At night they wrap it also. When a man has been wounded by a gunshot or by an arrow through the body, at the bottom of the neck [or] opposite a rib, they open his side, after taking care to raise the skin a little so that on being lowered again the opening will be between two [ribs]. They pour into him a quantity of warm water, in which they have diluted some of their drugs, after which they have the patient make motions and inhale, and sometimes they even take hold of him by the arms and legs, pushing him to and fro between them, and then make him eject all this water through his wound, expelling along with it fragments of clotted blood, which otherwise, doubtless, would suffocate him. Then they sprinkle him with some of their powdered herbs, which they put into their mouths, as I have said already, and they never close up the wound by day. I have seen two men who were healed in this way.

As for those who have broken arms or legs, when they manage to get to the village, they are healed in less than two months. They do not know what amputation is, as practiced by our surgeons, and we therefore see no Indians with one arm or with a wooden leg.

Those who heal such wounds pass for manitous and inspire fear in the young men, and especially in the young girls, whom they often seduce, owing to their weakness in believing that these men might cause their death by blowing medicine upon them, because of which they dare not refuse.[121]

Raudot,[122] while he followed Deliette in most of his account of shamans, added that the old men, besides acting as physicians, meddled with divining and speaking to the devil.

Charlevoix had the following to say on witchcraft among the Illinois; it is not corroborated by other writers of his time, but is described for the Miami about a hundred years later:

Amongst the Illinois and almost all the other nations, they make small figures to represent those whose days they have a mind to shorten, and which they stab to the heart. At other times they take a stone, and by means of certain invocations, they pretend to form such another in the heart of their enemy. I am persuaded this happens but seldom, provided the devil has no share in it; they are, however, in such apprehension of magicians, that the least suspicion of exercising this profession is sufficient to cause a person to be torn to pieces. Notwithstanding, however, the danger which attends the following of this trade, there are everywhere persons who have no other. And it is even true, that the most sensible and least credulous persons, who have frequented the Indians agree, that there is sometimes more than mere conceit in their magick.[123]

The following unsigned memoir on the medicines, remedies, and dyes used by undesignated tribes is from a manuscript dated 1724. Internal evidence indicates that it concerns either the Illinois, the Miami, or both. The probable identifications (in brackets) of the plants have been given through the courtesy of Dr. W. B. Hinsdale.

Medicines

For confined women who are not entirely delivered, they use the leaf of the sumac, with the root of an herb very common in

---

[121] Deliette, *Memoir, IHC.*, 23: 363-69; see also Raudot, "Memoir," Letters 64-66.

[122] *Ibid.*, Letter 64.

[123] *Journal*, 2: 154.

the woods, and which has on its leaves a kind of ball. They call this herb by the generic name of Pallaganghy, which is to say Ocre; they take an equal quantity of the leaf of sumac and of the root of this herb, they crush the one and the other separately; after each is in powder they mix them together and put them in a small kettle on a few embers; they add to it two times as much of sumac berries and make the confined woman drink the warm water in which the whole is soaked until she is entirely cured. That is to say, the space of two or three days, each day replacing in the kettle a similar dose, and giving some of it to the patient to drink a little before she eats at noon; at four o'clock and in the evening before retiring, the blood comes after the second or third taking, sometimes coagulated and as big as the fist, sometimes putrid, and at other times drop by drop.

Those who have been wounded in the chest, head, or arm, and who lose much blood by the mouth take the same remedy with the same ingredients and are cured in a short time.

The dropsical ones find themselves very well from it. They make them swallow the said drug with a little warm water in a spoon. The others above do not eat the medicine, they only drink the water in which it soaked, but they give all together to the dropsical ones.

Those who have injured gums, be it from *mal du Terre* (trench mouth?), be it from scurvy or other, are cured by holding this medicine on their gums a long time, without adding the sumac berries.

Also the bark of the root of the cherry tree chewed and held a long time on the gum cures the *mal du Terre*.

Besides, those who are burned or frozen or who are attacked by a venereal disease use the same drug, applying it to the affected part without adding the berry of the said sumac.

When one is wounded by a gun shot, or arrow, or fall, or when one has been crushed under a tree and loses blood by the mouth, they use a root that they call by the generic word Ouissoücatcki, that is to say, with several feet; they crush this root and put four pinches of it with a quill in a little warm water that they make the patient swallow, who is marvelously strengthened by this medicine. If he is in a delirium he returns to good sense, and the blood that he vomits begins to stop; when he has breathed a little they give him some of that which we have shown above to stop the blood entirely and for the perfect cure. . . . [crowfoot ranúnculus].

For scrofula they use the root of the herb of the rattlesnake which they call Akiskioüaraoüi, they chew this root and apply it to the injured part and give the patient a little of the same root diluted in a little water to drink. This root is very good for the bite of the serpent, but the orvietan and the theriac have a faster and more certain effect [*Asarum Canadénse, Nabalus,* or *Polygala Sénega*].

Their rhubarb is very good; they take it on the pines that they call Nanimihinia. There is a quantity of it at the lead mine [meadow rue—*Thalictrum*].

The root of the wild chervil is marvelous for the ills of the eyes, by dropping in the eye the water in which this root is steeped, in the month of May when the vine is in sap [perhaps sweet cicely].

To dye yellow they use an herb that they call Onçaccoü from the name of the color that it gives, like dandelions; they take the heads of this plant which are like large bonbons, dry them in the sun, then crush them and boil them without any other ingredient. The dyeing is very beautiful. They go to seek this plant far from the Mississippi. It is abundant in the river of the Illinois.

To dye red, there is on the prairie of the Tamarcoüa a plant that they name red Micoüsiouaki, they take the root, dry it, pulverize it in the mortar, and boil it with three times as many sumac berries. The red is very beautiful [*Sanguinária Canadénsis*].

Remedies of the Indians

Green earth for the flux of the abdomen and the blood, those who do not have any green use clay. They swallow four pills in the morning, and as many in the evening. They must not drink afterward.

The root of the basswood boiled for burns.

The bark or the root of white oak boiled for wounds, the leaf of the same tree is also perfectly good.

Boil the bark of young pines for burns and for wounds.

The root of Onis boiled for all sorts of wounds.

The bark of leatherwood boiled for all sort of wounds, I have seen a cancer cured by it; it serves to stop the bloody flux. We must carry some of this wood to France [*Dirca palústris*].

The root of sarsaparilla, for sores and cuts [*Aralia*].

The root and bark of elder for a person failing in his limbs, it is necessary to boil it and put it in a little soup, drinking about a pint of it [*Sambucus*].

The root of ginger crushed in powder for putting a stop to pains of a woman in childbirth [*Asarum*—wild ginger].

The plant of a thousand leaves for all sorts of cuts [*Achilléa millefólium*].

The branches of young pines boiled, for venereal diseases.

The leaf of Litre boiled, for the soreness of the eyes.

The little bark of white oak boiled, for the same soreness.

For films on the eyes, a shell of all sorts of river shell fish, burned and pulverized, blown in the eye.

For wounds and to draw out that which is in the wound, musket ball or other thing, it is necessary to boil the root of a certain reed which bears distaffs. I have seen the trial of this remedy.

The best and promptest remedy that I have seen for the bloody flux is the root of the fern which bears very small seeds, it is necessary to boil it over a slow fire or steep it until the water is red, and then it is diminished about a third; make the patient take a quarter liter on an empty stomach until a complete cure, one can take it in the evening to be cured sooner, three, four, or five times at least will do the business.

The bark of samelier or Ebeaupin chewed or crushed, for wounds.

The stem which leads to little red berries, boiled to make one vomit; the redwood has the same effect.

The bark of the prickly type of ashwood to draw off pus [*Xanthóxylum Americánum*—prickly ash].

The white creeper, for venereal diseases.

For looseness of the bowels some sumac.

The root of bean trefoil, for looseness of the bowels or bloody flux. It is necessary to boil it and not drink anything else until there is a complete cure [*Menyánthes trifoliáta*].

For felons or sprains, some bark of hybrid ash, chewed, by putting on the injury.

Some bear spleen for toothaches.

Coffee would do wonderfully on the Mississipy.[124]

[124] "Rapport des sauvages sur les mines et simples du pays du Mississipy," Paris Arch. Nat. Colonies, C. 13, C, 4: 162-65 vo.

OTTAWA

HISTORICAL SKETCH

AN understanding of the variety of ways the term "Ottawa" was used by the authors of the documents of the contact period is necessary before the movements of the Ottawa tribe can be considered.

One can find the Ottawa designated in an almost unlimited number of ways. Most of the diversity is caused by differences in spelling. There was also wide variation in the application of the term Ottawa—from a band "who have come from the nation of the raised hair"[1] to the statement of Dablon that the name "Outaouacs has been given to all the Savages of these regions, although of different Nations, because the first to appear among the French were the Outaouacs."[2] Thierry Beschefer, writing in 1683, stated this in more detail:

In the Outaouac missions we include not only the Outaouacs or upper Algonquins, who are divided into several tribes, namely; The saulteurs, who usually dwell at sault de Ste. Marie, at The entrance of Lake Superior; The Kiskakons and three other tribes, all of whom have their own chiefs, at Saint François de Borgia, at the Junction of Lakes Huron and Illinois, at a Place that we call Missilimakinak; the Nipissiriniens and other petty tribes on Lake Huron.[3]

There seems to be no justification for this wide application of the name Ottawa, and certainly such an extended meaning does not lend itself to working out a detailed account of the movements and ethnography of the tribe. The general usage of the term Ottawa, however, included only the four bodies designated by Beschefer as "the Kiskakons and three other tribes." These three others were the Sinago, the Ottawa

[1] Barthélemy Vimont, *Relation . . . . 1640*, J.R., 18: 231.
[2] Claude Dablon, *Relation . . . . 1671*, J.R., 55: 207.
[3] Thierry Beschefer, *J.R.*, 62: 193.

of Sable, and the Nassauaketon or People of the Fork. Certain locative designations, such as Ottawa of Mackinac, of Saginaw, and of Detroit, were often used; these lead to confusion in distinguishing the bands and do not permit the tracing of the movements of each band nor the determination of cultural differences. Again, groups of Ottawa were known by the names of their chiefs, such as "the tribe of Talon." All such distinctions have been utilized in this study, but are not specifically discussed here. The word "Ottawa" is here used to mean the four bands; Kishkakon, Sinago, Sable, and Nassauaketon.

In 1615 Champlain met "three hundred men of the tribe named by us the *Cheveux relevés*"[4] at some place between French River and the Huron villages that he was going to visit, which would most probably have been the eastern shore of Georgian Bay. The exact location of this village was not given, but it could not have been very far away from where Champlain met the Ottawa men, for the Huron were in constant communication with them. In 1640 Vimont wrote that Manitoulin Island was "inhabited by the Outaouan; these are people who have come from the nation of the raised hair."[5] This may have been their residence in Champlain's time.

In 1648 Ragueneau placed the Wachaskesouek, Negouichiriniouek, Sinago, Kishkakon, and Ottawa on the south shore of the lake of the Huron.[6] It appears that the various bands comprising the Ottawa were friendly neighbors of the Huron and lived to the south and west of them.

Before the Ottawa were visited in these locations by white men, the Huron were driven from their villages by the Iroquois. Although not involved in this warfare, the Ottawa fled with the remnants of the Huron tribes. In recounting this defeat of the Huron, Perrot gave the sites of the villages of the Ottawa as Saginaw, Thunder Bay, Manitoulin, and

[4] Samuel de Champlain, *Voyages*, 3: 43.
[5] *Relation* . . . . *1640*, J.R., 18: 231.
[6] Paul Ragueneau, *Relation* . . . . *1648*, J.R., 33: 151.

Mackinac, and Huron Island, the place of refuge they sought with the Huron.[7]

This Huron Island has been supposed to be Washington Island at the mouth of Green Bay. Perrot further reported that in 1653 the Iroquois sent an expedition of eight hundred men against the Huron and Ottawa, who, learning of it from a scouting party, retreated to Méchingan, a Potawatomi village on the shore of Lake Michigan, where they constructed a fort. They withstood the siege of the Iroquois for two years, at the end of which time the besiegers withdrew.

Dablon, writing in 1671, stated that the Huron took refuge on Mackinac Island after they were driven out of their own country by the Iroquois.[8] It is probable that Mackinac Island was a stopping place, during their westward movement, of the bands living around Lake Huron and that it was not Perrot's Huron Island.

The chronology of this period is much confused in the accounts of Perrot and Radisson, who are the only contemporary writers who deal with it. Perrot reported that about 1656 the Ottawa decided to retreat even farther from the Iroquois; they selected an island called Pelée in the Mississippi River at the entrance of Lake Pepin as the place of their settlement and lived there peaceably for several years.[9] Yet when Radisson came up from Montreal about 1657 with some Huron and Ottawa he found a village of these peoples on a large island three leagues beyond which there was a strait to another lake; this he called "the lake of the staring hairs, because those that live about it have their hair like a brush turned up"; it was not as big as the other lake.[10] This description would fit Washington Island, but also several other islands. It would seem from Radisson's account that all of the Ottawa did not go to the site on the Mississippi mentioned by Perrot.

---

[7] Nicolas Perrot, *Memoir, ITUM.,* 1: 148-49.

[8] *Relation . . . . 1671, J.R.,* 55: 159.

[9] *Memoir, ITUM.,* 1: 163.

[10] Peter Radisson, *Voyages,* p. 146.

Further evidence of at least two divisions of Ottawa is to be found in the reports of subsequent migrations. Menard found a group of Ottawa on Keweenaw Bay in 1660. This was possibly the same group that Radisson mentioned as located at the mouth of Green Bay three years earlier. Perrot stated that the group that went to the Mississippi was settled in 1662 on Chaquamegon Bay, about one hundred and fifty miles farther west along the southern shore of Lake Superior from Keweenaw Bay. Continuation of the hostilities with the Sioux, which had driven them from the Mississippi region, drove them farther east, and in 1670 part of them were living again on Manitoulin Island in Lake Huron.[11] The remainder of the immigrants seem to have been at St. Ignace with the Huron. Those who settled on Manitoulin Island did not remain there very long and soon joined the group at St. Ignace. In 1673 more than sixty Sinago Ottawa moved to St. Ignace from Green Bay.[12] By 1679 the Kishkakon were considered the most important and numerous Ottawa group at St. Ignace.[13] The three other Ottawa bands seem to have had this as as their only permanent residence for some years. Winter and summer hunting expeditions took them far. The Lower Peninsula of Michigan was a favorite hunting ground. During 1694 and 1695 there were Ottawa of the Sinago and Sable bands living at Detroit, but one cannot tell whether these were hunting parties out longer than usual or more permanent settlements with women and children.[14]

When Cadillac built Fort Pontchartrain at Detroit in 1701 he induced some of the Ottawa to take up their residence there. More followed during the next few years, and, in greater or smaller number, members of the Ottawa tribe lived at Detroit until the close of the French regime.[15]

[11] Dablon, *Relation* . . . . *1671, J.R.,* 55: 133.

[12] Jacques Marquette, *Relation* . . . . *1672-73, J.R.,* 57: 249-51.

[13] "Narrative of Henri de Tonti," *in* Pierre Margry, *Découvertes,* 1, Pt. 2: 619; Jean Enjalran, *Relation* . . . . *1679, J.R.,* 61: 103.

[14] "Narrative of the Most Remarkable Occurrences in Canada, 1694, 1695," *NYCD.,* 9: 606.

[15] Louis Antoine Bougainville, *Memoir, WHC.,* 18: 174.

There was an Ottawa village on the islands in Saginaw Bay in 1718, according to Sabrevois.[16] How long it had been in existence then is not recorded, although a village of undesignated Indians was reported there in 1712, but there is frequent mention of it as being on the islands, on the shore of the bay, or on the river in the records of the next thirty-three years.

Even after the establishment of the fort at Detroit there seems always to have been at least a few Ottawa at Mackinac. The number at any one post was determined by the conditions of the times; a considerable part of the tribe moved about freely. After the attack of the Ottawa on the Miami at Detroit, the French commandant, Dubuisson, wrote in 1712 that more than half of the Ottawa were withdrawing to Mackinac.[17] For some years prior to 1740, those residing at Mackinac contemplated moving elsewhere to obtain more fertile fields.[18] Several places were considered: Muskegon, Grand River, Grand Traverse, and L'Arbre Croche among others. Finally, through the influence of the governor general, they were persuaded to choose L'Arbre Croche, where they made their village in 1742.[19] It has remained a principal village of the Ottawa ever since.

Briefly, the time between the first contact in 1615 and 1760 may be divided into three periods: 1615 to 1650, 1650 to 1700, and 1700 to 1760. In the first period the Ottawa were dwelling around the shores of Lake Huron and on the islands in that lake and left the region toward the close of the period to escape the Iroquois. They divided into two groups in the second period. These followed the same general course—first to the mouth of Green Bay, whence one

[16] Jacques Sabrevois, *Memoir*, *WHC.*, 16: 370.

[17] "Letter to the Marquis de Vaudreuil," *Cadillac Papers, MPH.*, 33: 551.

[18] "Speech of the Marquis de Beauharnois to the Ottawas of Mackinac, July 8, 1741," *WHC.*, 17: 351.

[19] "Report of the Speech of the Ottawas to Beauharnois, June 16, 1742," *WHC.*, 17: 372.

group went westward to the Mississippi River and thence
north to Lake Superior at Chaquamegon Bay; the other did
not go as far west and arrived earlier on Lake Superior at
Keeweenaw Bay. Both then moved to the eastern end of the
Upper Pensinula of Michigan, establishing their habitation
center at St. Ignace, and for a short time on Manitoulin
Island. In the third period, Detroit became a center for the
Ottawa; Saginaw also was a place of residence for them,
being occupied from 1712, or possibly earlier, to 1751;
Mackinac continued as a dwelling site in more or less favor
until its inhabitants moved to L'Arbre Croche in 1742, the
location occupied by their descendants.

Nothing resembling a complete census of the Ottawa was
undertaken by the French. Most of the statements concerning their numbers refer only to those of a particular region,
and usually there was no report on the number living in other
places at the time. Often the number of Ottawa was not
given separately from that of the Huron with whom they
shared their villages. For instance, Dablon, in the *Relation* of
1669-70,[20] stated that the three Ottawa bands and the Huron
at Chaquamegon Bay numbered more than fifteen hundred
souls. In the same *Relation* a letter from Marquette reported
that the Huron numbered four to five hundred souls.[21] Hence
the Ottawa at this site must have exceeded one thousand. In
1736 the warriors at Detroit, Saginaw, and Mackinac were
enumerated at four hundred and eighty.[22] If one allows three
other persons for each warrior, there would have been nine-
teen hundred and twenty persons. Probably neither of these
enumerations was more than an estimate, nor is it likely that
they included all the members of the tribe, but one can only
guess at what correction should be made to these figures. The
"Report of the Lord Commissioners for Trade and Plantations to the King on the State of British Plantations in

---

[20] *J.R.*, 54: 167.
[21] *Ibid.*, pp. 169-71.
[22] Pierre Celeron, "Census of Indian Tribes: 1736," *WHC.*, 17: 245, 251.

America in 1721," recounted that the "Ottaways, or Michillimackinacks were formerly 3000 [warriors?] but now scarce 500."[23] There may very well have been some diminution of the numbers of the Ottawa, but in no other account is the number of warriors given as more than five hundred.

CHARACTERISTICS

From among the Ottawa at Mackinac about 1695, Cadillac wrote:

All the Indians, generally speaking, are well built and of fine stature, extremely wiry, vigorous, and strong, and of great endurance. They all have black eyes, large pupils, and good sight, keen and piercing; their hair is thick and black; their teeth are very white, small, and regular. They have long necks, flat stomachs, large feet, and long legs; they have no hair on the face nor on any part of the body; and you rarely see any one lame or humpbacked among them.

We may say without flattery, that all the Indians are naturally intelligent; but, as their intellect is not cultivated, and they act only on their own inclinations in everything, their knowledge is entirely restricted to what takes place in their own village, or among their nearest neighbors; so that they look upon what Europeans tell them as so many fancies with which the imagination delights to feed and entertain itself. It is easy to see that they have a charming idea and very great facility for drawing, painting, and sculpture; and as they have not the use of letters nor writing, God has also given them the gifts of a very good memory.[24]

Lahontan agreed with Cadillac as to the rarity of the lame and humpbacked and the absence of body and facial hair, but termed the men "cowardly, ugly and ungainly Fellows." The women, he said, were of an indifferent stature, handsome in the face but very fat, unwieldy, and ill-built.[25]

La Potherie, writing in 1702, characterized the Ottawa as

---

[23] *NYCD.*, 5: 622.

[24] Antoine de la Mothe Cadillac, MS "Relation on the Indians."

[25] Louis Armand Lahontan, *Voyages*, 1: 414-16.

fickle, taking umbrage at everything, time-serving, and seldom friends except as caprice and self-interest induced them
to act as such.[26] He further stated that originally they were
very rude and cowardly, but through living with the Huron
they came to imitate their customs and rules of conduct.
Through intercourse with these neighbors they became much
more intelligent and by imitating their valor they made themselves feared by all their enemies and looked up to by all the
tribes allied with them.[27]

Raudot indicated that he had noticed a similar change in
the Ottawa, but attributed the increasing politeness in their
conversations and the greater gentleness in their customs to
having Frenchmen among them. He also considered them
brave warriors, feared by the Iroquois.[28]

Perrot wrote his memoir only nine years after Raudot
inscribed the above characterization, but perhaps remembering some unpleasant personal experience, he stated that they
were not brave warriors.[29] Writing in 1718, the same year in
which Perrot wrote, Sabrevois was noncommittal on their
valor, simply remarking that they were very clever and very
industrious, both in hunting and in agriculture.[30]

DRESS AND ORNAMENT

According to Champlain the Ottawa men did not wear
a breech clout or other clothing except a fur robe like a
cloak, which they usually laid aside, especially in summer.[31]
The women and girls wore at least a little piece of leather
about the size of a napkin, girded about the loins and reaching down to the middle of the thighs.[32]

They were much given to ornamenting themselves, how-

---

[26] Claude de la Potherie, *History, ITUM.,* 2: 45.

[27] *Ibid.,* 1: 283.

[28] Antoine Raudot, "Memoir," Letter 52.

[29] *Memoir, ITUM.,* 1: 170.

[30] *Memoir, WHC.,* 16: 369.

[31] *Voyages,* 3: 98.

[32] Gabriel Sagard, *Le Grand voyage,* pp. 77-78.

ever, both by tattooing and by painting. Champlain wrote that they were "much carved about the body in divisions of various patterns."[33] Over a century later Sabrevois remarked upon the same custom.[34] Ordinarily, only their faces seem to have been painted. Sagard said that these were painted all over very handsomely with various colors in oil; some had one side all green and the other red, others seem to have had the face entirely covered with genuine lace very well made, and others were entirely different, for each was free to fix his own as he wished.[35]

The treatment of the men's hair was sufficiently different from that of the tribes with which he was already acquainted to cause Champlain to name them *cheveux relevés* ("high hairs"). This was because they "had them elevated and arranged very high and better combed than our courtiers, and there is no comparison, in spite of the irons and methods these have at their disposal. This seems to give them a fine appearance."[36] Sagard described their hair dress as being more like a short pompadour: "For the Ottawa, they wear and keep their hair on the forehead, very straight and upright, more so than that of our women here, but gradually diminishing it in height from the forehead to the back of the head."[37] The Ottawa told Cadillac that they kept their hair very short in order to give their enemies less on which to take hold.[38] They also wore little collars of white plumes around their necks and had similar plumes in their hair.[39] It is to be supposed that the Ottawa women wore their hair long.

Another custom of ornamentation that led to a nickname, but one that was not as persistent as *cheveux relevés*, was the perforation of the nasal septum. This was mentioned by

[33] *Voyages*, 3: 43.
[34] *Memoir, WHC.*, 16: 373-74.
[35] *Histoire*, p. 197.
[36] *Voyages*, 3: 43.
[37] *Le Grand voyage*, pp. 190-91.
[38] MS "Relation on the Indians."
[39] Sagard, *Histoire*, p. 197.

Champlain, by Radisson, who said that a straw about a foot long was inserted therein,[40] and by Cadillac, who wrote:

I shall only mention that the word Ottawa means Nation of the Pierced Noses because they pierce their noses and attach to the nose a small prettily ornamented stone which comes to the middle of the mouth between the lips. It is a fashion with them, they would not think themselves properly decked out if that were wanting. There are, nevertheless, some old men who maintain that it is a protection against medicine, that is to say, against the fates and spells that their enemies and other malicious persons might cast on them to poison them or make them die.[41]

Champlain reported that the Ottawa had their ears fringed with beads, which presupposes piercing them.[42] Radisson also reported the piercing of the ears, which he described as follows:

Their ears have ordinarily 5 holes, where one may putt the end of his finger. They use those holes in this sort: to make themselves gallant they pass through it a skrew of coper with much dexterity, and goe on the lake in that posture. When the winter comes they weare no capes because of their haire tourned up. They fill those skrews with swan's downe, & with it their ears covered; but I dare say that the people doe not for to hold out the cold, but rather for pride, ffor their country is not so cold as the north, and other lakes that we have seene since.[43]

ECONOMIC LIFE

The Ottawa depended on agriculture, hunting, and fishing for their livelihood. With the advent of European traders and their demand for furs, hunting increased in importance in supplying the needs of the family. Manufacture of such articles as earthen vessels, stone knives, bows, and arrows, was gradually discontinued when the Indians were able to obtain European objects to take their places. Hunting sup-

[40] *Voyages*, p. 146.
[41] MS "Relation on the Indians."
[42] *Voyages*, 3: 44.
[43] *Voyages*, p. 146.

plied the currency with which these substitutes were pur-
chased. Fishing and agriculture were still necessary to provide
a food supply ample in variety and quantity. Proof of this is
the transfer of the village in 1742 from Mackinac to L'Arbre
Croche because of the exhaustion of the soil at the former
place.

Agriculture

Corn was the principal product cultivated; it was the only
one mentioned by Dablon as being raised in 1669 at Point
St. Esprit.[44] When the Ottawa were living with the Huron at
Mackinac in 1688 Lahontan reported that these two tribes
sowed Indian corn, peas, beans, squash, and "melons, which
differ much from ours."[45] The Ottawa were semisedentary,
that is, they had permanent villages in which they lived during the summer, but occasionally they moved their residence
through fear of hostile tribes or because of the unproductive-
ness of unfertilized soil. They seem to have been ignorant of
the technique of fertilization. On reaching a new location,
each family took or was assigned a certain area for its fields.
The women cultivated the soil and sowed and harvested the
crops, although they might be assisted by old men no longer
capable of accompanying the hunting parties. The tilling was
done with a tool of hard wood, "shaped like a hoe at one end
and flat at the other," and their harvest, according to Cadillac,
was Indian corn, peas, beans, pumpkins, and watermelons.[46]
The identification of the pumpkin and watermelon is very
uncertain; the first may refer to the so-called Indian or summer squash; and the latter, like the melons mentioned by
Lahontan, are too inadequately described to permit definite
identification.

Hunting

Hunting parties went out from the village during the
summer and also in the winter. In the summer the men usu-

[44] *Relation* .... *1669-70*, J.R., 54: 163.
[45] *Voyages*, 1: 148.
[46] MS "Relation on the Indians."

ally left the greater part of their families at the village and did not travel as far as on the winter hunts—ordinarily only seventy-five to a hundred miles from the village. The summer hunts were of less importance than were those in the winter, being chiefly to obtain game for food, for the pelts were of less value than those taken in winter.[47]

The principal animals sought were deer, bear, and beaver. Beaver meat and fur were desired by the Indians for their own use, but under the spur of the traders this fur became the prime object of the hunters. Lahontan reported that the Ottawa did not hunt in the same region every year. The country around Glen Lake, for instance, was only hunted every third year, whereas the valley of the Saginaw was visited every other year.[48]

Hunting grounds were assigned to families or to members by the head of the family every autumn. Usually, eight or ten men, probably related, lived together in a cabin erected near the center of their territory. Traps were set for otters, bears, foxes, and martens on the lake shores. Deer and fowl were frequently shot and furnished a welcome change in diet. The men also fished. Beaver were sometimes trapped, but the usual method in the autumn was to tap their dams, the escape of the water leaving the beavers an easy prey. Lahontan reported that the Ottawa tried to preserve the supply of beaver by never killing all the animals in a house or colony, but always leaving a dozen females and half a dozen males in each pond or small lake. After killing all but the nucleus for propagation, the hole in the dam was filled. In the winter, when the lakes were frozen over, holes were made in the ice, and nets were placed in the runways from the lodges. When the lodges were laid open with axes the animals ran into the nets and were drawn through the holes and knocked on the head.[49]

[47] La Potherie, *History, ITUM.*, 1: 281-83.
[48] *Voyages*, 1: 210, 319.
[49] *Ibid.*, 2: 481-83.

The traps for catching otters were described by Lahontan:

These Traps are made of five Stakes plac'd in the form of an oblong Quadrangle, so as to make a little Chamber, the Door of which is kept up, and supported by a Stake. To the middle of this Stake they tye a string which passes thro' a little fork, and has a Trout well fasten'd to the end of it. Now, when the Otter comes on shoar, and sees this bait, he puts above half his Body into that fatal Cage, in order to swallow the Fish; but he no sooner touches it, than the string to which 'tis made fast pulls away the Stake that supports the Door, upon which an heavy and loaded Door falls upon his Reins and quashes him.[50]

Similar but larger and stronger traps were made for bears.[51]

The following excerpt is a good exposition of the skill needed by the hunter and the place it won him in society:

The fact that the hunter is accounted the equal of the warrior need cause no surprise; for it should be remembered that all the Indians live and maintain and feed their families by their guns or, more properly speaking, by their cleverness, cunning, and skill in making the animals fall into the snares they lay for them. Now, to do well at this, they must have experience of the hunting grounds, and know the trails, haunts, and the instinct of the animals; they must be able to bear fatigue and to be patient, lucky, eager, energetic, bold, and good runners; they must have a keen eye and good breath. They hunt the elk, stag, hind, bear, roebuck, caribou, beaver, and wild ox. They have to kill these animals in the woods or on the prairies, coming upon them unawares or by swiftness of foot. Whatever anyone may think, I know one must have a good pair of legs to keep up such exercise. However, a good hunter sometimes kills as many as a dozen animals in a day; and it is a pleasure to see the Miamis, from time to time, bringing into their village some enormous bears, tamed in the course of their hunting; they drive them before them with switches, like sheep driven to the slaughterhouse. It is on such occasions that good hunters show their prowess. And as it

[50] *Ibid.*, 1: 113.
[51] *Ibid.*, 2: 484.

is true that, in all lands, those who are passionately fond of hunting pursue it for their own pleasure and satisfaction rather than for profit, money, or gluttony, so, among the Indians, the good hunters are those who profit least by their hunting. They often make feasts for their friends or relations or distribute the animals they have killed among the huts or families. One proof of the liberality or the vanity which they acquire from this occupation is that, when they land at their village, the persons present at their landing are permitted to take and carry off all the meat in the canoe of the hunter who has killed it, and he does nothing but laugh. That is sufficient reason for believing that their only idea is to feed the people; and as the whole tribe feels the benefit of this, it is interested in praising such a noble calling, especially as it often happens that a single hunter provides food for several families which, but for his aid would, at certain times and at certain places, perish of hunger and want. It must not, therefore, be thought altogether strange if they think as highly of a hunter as of a warrior. The only difference I have found is that the one is more feared and dreaded, while the other is more loved and cherished.[52]

Fishing

The fishing of the Ottawa at Mackinac was described by Cadillac about 1695:

The great abundance of fish and the convenience of the place for fishing have caused the Indians to make a fixed settlement in those parts. It is a daily manna, which never fails; there is no family which does not catch sufficient fish in the course of the year for its subsistence. Moreover, better fish can not be eaten, and they are bathed and nourished in the purest water, the clearest and the most pellucid you could see anywhere.

I think it would be useless to explain the way in which they fish, since each country has its own method. But what I think I ought to mention is the pleasure of seeing them bring up in one net as many as a hundred whitefish. That is the most delicate fish in the lake. They are as large as shad in France. They also catch a large number of trout, that weigh up to fifty livres; they

[52] Cadillac, MS "Relation on the Indians."

are certainly very good eating. Finally, the sturgeon, pike, carp, herring, dory, and a hundred different kinds of fish abound at this part of the lake.[53]

Food and Its Preparation

Game such as deer, beaver, and bears, fowl such as pigeons, ducks, and geese, fish such as trout, whitefish, and herring supplied the meat of the diet of the Ottawa. Corn, beans, and squash were cultivated. Fruits were eaten in season, and small fruits, such as berries, were preserved dried, in order to give variety and seasoning to the winter diet. These various foods were not eaten in courses, since the Indians usually cooked and served only one dish. This was called sagamité and consisted of a broth made of the meal of corn, with beans, meat, or fish added. The dried berries were added in the winter.

About 1695 Cadillac wrote the following description of the food and the method of preparing it used by the Indians and also the French living with them at Mackinac:

They saw a big tree and make a log about three feet long; they hollow it out for about two feet, almost like a mortar. They then make a pestle of hardwood, about five feet long; after that they put Indian corn into the mortar and crush it by striking it with the pestle. When it is sufficiently pounded, they winnow it, and the bran is separated, so that only the meal is left, which is sifted in order to remove the dust; the result is that the meal remains pure, clean, and white like rice. It is put into a cooking pot with water to boil; at the same time they cook some white-fish in another pot; and when they see that the meal is half cooked, they take out the fish and soak it in the boiled meal, which is reduced to a white liquid like milk. They throw it into the pot and stir it with a wooden spoon, in the same way as one does rice milk, until it is thoroughly cooked; and, as the custom of the country is for each person to have his dish, each fills his own dish with this broth, which the Indians call "Sagamity," that is to say, various things mixed together to be eaten.

[53] *Ibid.*

This is not dainty food, but it is certainly very wholesome, for it always keeps the bowels open, and it is very aperitive, for one urinates as often as fifty times a day. If one never took any other food, one would never be thirsty, as many persons have found out, who have gone whole months without thinking of drinking. I can affirm that I have gone twenty days without feeling the slightest thirst; which makes me think it would be a good diet for those who suffer from gravel. In the evening they eat fish cooked in all sorts of ways—fried, roasted, boiled, smoked, or stewed; they have neither oil nor butter, but they have dripping or marrow from the elk, stag, or wild ox, which is brought to Missilimakinak from the Illinois of Chicagou, and, substantially, I think that this flavoring is as good as that of the Carthusians or the Minims.

They make bread with the flour of Indian corn, which they bake under the ashes or in hot sand. It is good, when one has a robust appetite, and it is wonderfully fattening.[54]

In the *Relation* of 1662-63, a letter recounting the trip of Father Menard to the country of the Ottawa and his death there, after mentioning some of the beliefs and customs of the Ottawa, gave the following description of the harvesting of wild rice:

There is in that country a certain plant, four feet or thereabout in height, which grows in marshy places. A little before it ears, the Savages go in their Canoes and bind the stalks of these plants in clusters, which they separate from one another by as much space as is needed for the passage of a Canoe when they return to gather the grain. Harvest time having come, they guide their Canoes through the little alleys which they have opened across this grain-field, and bending down the clustered masses over their boats, strip them of their grain. As often as a Canoe is full, they go and empty it on the shore into a ditch dug at the water's edge. Then they tread the grain and stir it about long enough to free it entirely of hulls; after which they dry it, and finally put it into bark chests for keeping. This grain much

---

[54] MS "Relation on the Indians."

resembles Oats, when it is raw; but, on being cooked in water, it swells more than any European Grain.[55]

This is the only mention of the Ottawa using wild rice in the vicinity of Keweenaw Bay, and it should be noted that there is a possibility that this section is an interpolation. Nevertheless, the region is well within the range of the wild rice plant, and it is possible that the Ottawa used it.

Shelter

What sort of shelter the Ottawa built for themselves before they were driven out of their villages around Lake Huron cannot be said; but in their village at Mackinac toward the close of the seventeenth century they were living in cabins, described by Cadillac as follows:

As to their huts, they are built like arbors. They drive into the ground very long poles as thick as one's leg and join them to one another by making them curve and bend over at the top; they tie and fasten them together with basswood bark, which they use in the same way as we do our thread and cordage. They then entwine with these large poles crosspieces as thick as one's arm and cover them from top to bottom with the bark of firs or cedars, which they fasten to the poles and the cross-branches; they leave an opening about two feet wide at the ridge, which runs from one end to the other. It is certain that their huts are weatherproof, and no rain whatever gets into them; they are generally one hundred to one hundred and thirty feet long by twenty-four feet wide and twenty high. There is an upper floor on both sides, and each family has its little apartment. There is also a door at each end. Their streets are regular like those of our villages.[56]

Cadillac did not mention any difference between the cabins of the Ottawa and those of the Huron, both resident at Mackinac, although in 1718 Sabrevois said that the cabins of the Huron at Detroit were more neatly made than those

[55] *J.R.*, 48: 121-23.
[56] MS "Relation on the Indians."

of the Ottawa.[57] Similarly, there seems to have been no distinction in the way they fortified their villages, for of both
tribes Cadillac wrote:

Their forts are made of stakes. Those in the first row, on the
outside, are as thick as a man's thigh and about thirty feet high;
the second row, inside, is quite a foot from the first, which is
bent over on to it and is to support and prop it up; the third row
is four feet from the second and consists of posts three and one-
half feet in diameter and standing fifteen or sixteen feet out of
the ground. Now, in that row they leave no space at all between
the posts; on the contrary, they set them as close together as
they can, making loopholes at intervals. As to the first two rows,
there is a space of about six inches between the stakes, and thus
the first and second rows do not prevent them from seeing the
enemy; but there are no curtains nor bastions, and the fort is,
strictly speaking, only an enclosure.[58]

Perrot stated that the Ottawa built a fort in 1653, when
they expected a raid by the Iroquois,[59] but no information is
available in the early documents as to whether or not their
villages were ordinarily fortified before 1650. It is possible
that the making of enclosures was borrowed from the Huron
with whom they were living, for it is certain that the latter
made triple palisades very early.

When hunting or traveling the Ottawa used a portable
form of shelter, described by James Smith in 1756:

The Ottawas have a very useful kind of tents which they
carry with them, made of flags, plaited and stitched together in a
very artful manner, so as to turn rain or wind well—each mat
is made fifteen feet long and about five feet broad. In order to
erect this kind of tent, they cut a number of long straight poles,
which they drive in the ground, in the form of a circle, leaning
inwards; then they spread the mats on these poles—beginning
at the bottom and extending up, leaving only a hole at the top
uncovered—and this hole answers the place of a chimney. They

[57] *Memoir, WHC.*, 16: 369.
[58] MS "Relation on the Indians."
[59] *Memoir, ITUM.*, 1: 151.

make a fire of dry split wood, in the middle, and spread down bark mats and skins for bedding, on which they sleep in a crooked posture, all round the fire, as the length of their beds will not admit of stretching themselves. In place of a door they lift up one end of a mat and creep in, and let the mat fall down behind them.

These tents are warm and dry, and tolerably clear of smoke. Their lumber they keep under birch-bark canoes, which they carry out and turn up for a shelter, where they keep everything from the rain. Nothing is in the tents but themselves and their bedding.

. . . at night we lodged in our flag tents, which when erected, were nearly in the shape of a sugar-loaf, and about fifteen feet in diameter at the ground.[60]

It is quite likely that before contact with the Huron led them to build long houses, the Ottawa, like the Chippewa and Potawatomi, had only these small, more or less circular, cabins for all purposes. Sheets of bark may have replaced the reed or grass mats in certain seasons or locations.

Weapons

The Ottawa in 1615, according to Champlain, carried clubs, bows and arrows, and, usually, a round shield of tanned leather, which he said came from an animal such as the buffalo.[61] Firearms were not introduced in any great quantity until around 1670.

Textiles

Champlain reported that the Ottawa were the most industrious tribe in making mats, which he likened to Turkish carpets.[62] The women made these mats of reeds and corn husks, according to Sagard. They were very well woven and dyed with vivid colors in designs of symmetrical divisions. They were used to close the doorways of their cabins, to sit

[60] *An Account of the Remarkable Occurrences in the Life and Travels of James Smith*, pp. 52-53, 57.

[61] *Voyages*, 3: 44-45.

[62] *Ibid.*, p. 98.

upon, and also to trade to tribes of different regions for other merchandise.[63]

Trade

Champlain wrote in 1615 that the Ottawa went in bands into various regions and districts more than four or five hundred leagues distant, where they traded with other tribes.[64] According to Sagard, the articles they offered were mats, woven by the women, and furs, for which they received paints, porcelains, and other "rubbish."[65]

Speaking of the Huron and Ottawa who were living on the Huron Island at the mouth of Green Bay about 1658, Radisson said that they went to the farthest part of the bay to trade for light earthen pots, woven girdles, and small sea shells with which they trimmed their pelts.[66]

In 1662, according to Perrot, the Ottawa carried their old knives, blunt awls, wretched nets, and worn-out kettles to the tribes living north of Chaquamegon and traded them for beaver robes. Apparently, these tribes had not been in contact with the French at that time, for they thanked the Ottawa for sharing with them their French merchandise.[67] It was doubtless to this period that La Potherie was also referring when he said that the Ottawa carried the merchandise they obtained from the French to the Potawatomi.[68]

At Mackinac the Ottawa were residing at the general meeting place for all of the French traders. Many other tribes came there to trade with the French. Besides their furs the Ottawa sold birchbark canoes to the French at the rate of two or three hundred livres each, two sheets of bark for making cabins were traded for a shirt, and strawberries and other

[63] *Le Grand voyage,* p. 78; *Histoire,* p. 276. See also the reference under "Shelter," by James Smith, to mats used in temporary dwellings.

[64] *Voyages,* 3: 97-98.

[65] *Le Grand voyage,* p. 78.

[66] *Voyages,* pp. 149-50.

[67] *Memoir, ITUM.,* 1: 173-74.

[68] *History, ITUM.,* 1: 303.

fruits were exchanged for vermilion and glass and porcelain beads.[69]

Political Organization

There were four bands of Ottawa, according to Cadillac, La Potherie,[70] Raudot,[71] and the speech of "8ta8tiboy," an Ottawa chief, at a conference with Governor Callières. For example, this speech was reported:

I speak in the name of the Four 8ta8ais Nations to wit: the 8ta8aës of the *Sable*, the 8ta8aës Sinago, the Kiskakons and the people of the Fork who have sent me expressly here, to listen to the voice of our Father Onnontio.[72]

The Nassauaketon or "Nation of the Fork" seem to have been the least important or the most detached of the four. References to them alone are scarce, whereas mention of the other three jointly are frequent. The references to the latter as individual bands or to their chiefs are innumerable. Of them all the Kishkakons were the most numerous and were also recognized as the most important band.[73]

Rasles gave the families of the Ottawa as three, that of Michabou or the Great Hare, that of Namepich or the Carp, and that of Machoua or the Bear.[74]

As mentioned in the historical sketch of the Ottawa there has been great confusion as to the bands making up the nation or tribe. Part of the confusion resulted from the translation of native names into French. For instance, a band generally recognized as being one of the principal four is that called the Ottawa of the Sand (du Sable). It was so considered in

[69] *Ibid.*, pp. 282-83.

[70] *Ibid.*, p. 281.

[71] "Memoir," Letter 52.

[72] "Conference between Governor de Callières and the Iroquois, Sept. 3, 1700," *NYCD.*, 9: 719.

[73] "Narrative of the Most Remarkable Occurrences in Canada, 1696, 1697," *NYCD.*, 9: 672.

[74] Sébastien Rasles, "Letter . . . . to His Brother," *J.R.*, 67: 153-57.

the *Handbook of the American Indians*. This work listed the
Negaouichiriniouek as a minor band, probably of the Ottawa
and possibly of the Nassauaketon, even though Alice Fletcher
gave the meaning of the name as "people of the fine sandy
beach."[75] The census of 1695 listed them as the "negoasch-
endachiny or people of the sand."[76] What seem like other
forms of the same name are Nigouaouichirinik,[77] Neguouan
des Chermis,[78] and Negochendackirini.[79]

The Ottawa Sinago were said to have the black squirrel
as their totem in the enumeration of 1736, yet the *Handbook
of the American Indians* gave the meaning of Sinago as "gray
squirrel."[80] The Kishkakons were sometimes called the
Queuës coupées ("Cut Tails") by the French.[81] Cadillac
gave the meaning of Kishkakon as "cut tail."[82] This is assumed to be a reference to the bear, and this animal is given
as the totem of the Kishkakons in the "Census of Indian
Tribes: 1736."[83] The documents of the contact period do not
tell what the totems of the Sable and Nassauaketon bands
were.

With the Nassauaketon, these three bands were recognized
as constituting the Ottawa. Of them Cadillac wrote:

It should be borne in mind that four different tribes are
included under the name Outaouas. The first is the tribe of the
Kiskakons, the "Cut Tail," and it is the most numerous; the
second is the Sable tribe, so called because their former dwelling
place was in a sandy country, their village being on a sandy bay,
but the Iroquois drove this tribe from its lands; the third is the
Sinago, and the fourth the Nassauakuetoun, that is the tribe of

[75] *Handbook of the American Indians, Bur. Amer. Ethnol. Bull.*, 30, 2: 51.
[76] AC., C 11 A, 13.
[77] Ragueneau, *Relation . . . . 1648, J.R.*, 33: 151.
[78] "Memorial Presented by Cadillac to the Council of the Navy, 1721,"
MPH., 33: 680.
[79] Raudot, "Memoir," Letter 52.
[80] *Bur. Amer. Ethnol. Bull.*, 30, 2: 574.
[81] *Relation . . . . 1669, J.R.*, 52: 207.
[82] MS "Relation on the Indians,"
[83] *WHC.*, 17: 245.

the Fork, a name derived from that of the chief, or much more probably, from the river from which they originally came, which divides into three branches, forming a sort of fork. These four tribes are allies and are closely united, living on good terms with one another, and they now speak one and the same language.[84]

There is no information in the documents as to the organization within the bands. In 1615 Champlain wrote that the Ottawa had several chiefs who took command, each in his own district.[85] That is as much as one finds in any of the subsequent records. The vagueness on this matter is probably not all chargeable to the writers of the accounts. It seems certain that the political system itself was very vague. Evidence of this is found in the lack of influence of the chiefs with their people—reported by the French on numerous occasions.

Hospitality

From the report of Lahontan, one draws the conclusion that all the tribes and all their members observed the following custom among themselves in visiting one another:

When a Visit is paid to a Savage, at going in you must say, *I am come to see such an one:* The Fathers, Mothers, Wives, Children go out, or withdraw to an Apartment at one end of the Cottage, and be who you will, come not near you to interrupt your Conversation. The Fashion is for him that is visited, to offer you to eat, drink and smoak; and one may use an entire freedom with them, for they don't much mind Compliments. If one means to visit a Woman, the Ceremony's the same; *I am come to see such an one;* then every Body withdraws, and you tarry alone with her you come to see; but you must not mention any thing Amorous in the Day time, as I shall inform you else where.[86]

The formality with which hospitality was accorded strangers was described by Perrot:

The hospitality that they exercise surpasses all that which is

[84] MS "Relation on the Indians."
[85] *Voyage,* 3: 97.
[86] *Voyages,* 2: 426.

general among the Europeans. When any stranger asks it from them, they could not receive him more kindly, no matter how unknown he may be; it is on their side the most friendly of welcomes, and they even go so far as to spend all their means to entertain those whom they receive. A stranger as soon as he arrives [at a cabin] is made to sit down on a mat, of the handsomest [that they have], in order to rest from his fatigue; they take off his shoes and stockings, and grease his feet and legs; and the stones are at once put in the fire, and all preparations quickly made, in order to give him a sweat. The master of the family, and some other men who are prominent in the community, go with him into the place where the sweat is given, and allow him to lack for nothing therein. The kettle is over the fire, so as to provide food for him when he comes out of the sweat; and if the cabin in which he lodges is not very well supplied with provisions, search is made throughout the village for the best food for him. I mean here the best grain and the best quality of meat which can be found, for which the man in whose house the stranger is accommodated afterward pays, often at four times what it is usually worth. While the guest is eating, all the leading people come to pay him visits. If he is clad in cloth garments, they take from him his clothing, and instead they give him furs, of their handsomest and most valued, to clothe him from head to foot. He is invited to all the feasts that are given in the village, and in conversation they inquire of him for some news from his own part of the country. If he knows of nothing new, he draws on his imagination for it; and even if he lies no one would venture to contradict him, even supposing that they were quite certain of facts contrary to his stories. There is but one person alone of the entire assembly who converses with the stranger; all the rest keep silence, with the reserve and modesty that are prescribed for a novice in a religious order, in which he is obliged to maintain this behavior under penalty of the severe measures belonging to the most strict rule on this point. When the stranger shows a desire to return whence he came, they load him with what is most suitable for his journey; if he is inclined to prefer peltries to other goods, these are given to him. They are just as liberal toward those who give them nothing as to those who carry [presents] to them. . . .

When a stranger to whom they have given hospitality wishes to go home and is ready to depart, the host who has received him packs up his belongings, and gives him the best things that he has in his cabin—whether in peltries, trade-goods, or provisions—that may be necessary to the guest on his journey. Although such generosity may be astonishing, it must be admitted that ambition is more the motive for it than is charity. One hears them boast incessantly of the agreeable manner with which they receive people into their houses, and of the gifts that they bestow on their guests—although it is not denied that this is done smilingly and with all possible graciousness.[87]

As to the manner in which the Ottawas greeted a delegation from another friendly tribe, La Potherie recorded the following description of a reception accorded the Potawatomi about 1686:

The Outaöuaks [at Michilimackinac] received the Pouteouatemis in military fashion; they assembled together behind a slope on which they made a camp. The fleet of the Pouteouatemis making its appearance at an eighth of a league from land, the Outaoüaks—naked, and having no other ornaments than their bows and arrows—marched abreast, and formed a sort of battalion. At a certain distance from the water they suddenly began to defile, uttering cries from time to time. The Pouteouatemis, on their part, set themselves in battle array, in order to make their landing. When the rear of the Outaouaks was opposite the Pouteouatemis, whose ranks were close to one another, they paddled more slowly. When they were at a gunshot from the land, the Frenchmen who were joined with the Outaouaks first fired a volley at them, without balls; the Outaouaks followed them with loud shouts of "Sassakoue!" and the Pouteouatemis uttered theirs. Then on both sides they reloaded their arms, and a second volley was fired. Finally, when the landing must be made, the Outaouaks rushed into the water, clubs in their hands; the Pouteouatemis at once darted ahead in their canoes, and came rushing on the others, carrying their clubs. Then no further order was maintained; all was pell-mell, and the Outaouaks

[87] Perrot, *Memoir, ITUM.*, 1: 132-35.

lifted up their canoes, which they bore to the land. Such was this reception, which on a very serious occasion would have cost much bloodshed. The Outaouaks conducted the chiefs into their cabins, where the guests were regaled.[88]

SOCIAL LIFE

War

Opinions as to the martial ability of the Ottawa vary. Champlain[89] wrote that they were great warriors; others stated that they were cowardly and possessed no martial ability until years of contact with the Huron had imbued in them some warlike spirit; Lahontan wrote that they contented themselves with seeking the Iroquois when the latter were on hunting and fishing trips far from their villages. Others accounted them better warriors. Cadillac, in the following account which he wrote while he was among the Ottawa from 1694 to 1698 said that all the tribes fought in the same way:

In the matter of war, all the Indians have the same principle, the same practice, the same custom, and the same manner of fighting. Their war parties or companies are formed in this manner. A war chief abstains from eating and drinking and fasts sometimes for a week; he bedaubs and besmears his face with black: he says little, and ponders and dreams night and day, praying to the spirit he has chosen as his guardian or patron to give him men. This spirit, in which he trusts, is sometimes a raven, an eagle, an otter, a bear, a fox, or other animal; but each holds his own in esteem, and it is always the one which has appeared to him in his dreams and visions; so that, if during their sleep they have visions of their enemies, at certain times and places, and if finally their vision is favorable, they take it as a good omen and conclude that they will succeed in their attack on their enemies. As soon as this period of dreaming is over, they wash their faces and paint themselves red, black, and white, but generally red only. They crop their hair and oil it, and altogether make themselves spruce. Then they give a feast to the

[88] *History, ITUM.*, 2: 21-22.
[89] *Voyages*, 3: 97.

young men and a few old men; but, before they begin to eat, the chief delivers his harangue, much in these terms: "My, brothers, it is true that I am not a man; nevertheless, you know that I have already faced the foe. Our men have been killed. For a long time the bones of so-and-so, our brother, have rested in such-and-such a place. It is time that we should go and see them. Now you know that he was a brave man and worthy to be avenged. We have rested in peace on our mat. Today I arise, for the spirit who rules me has promised me broth and fresh meat. Take courage, young men, crop your hair, put on your war paint, fill your quivers and let us console our dead; let our war songs re-echo through the village, awaken our brother who was slain, he will be content when he has been avenged."

It should be observed that the Indians always call one another brothers or companions, and that, in this harangue, the term "broth" or "fresh meat" means killing men and capturing prisoners; "cropping the hair" means taking off the garb of mourning; to "put on war paint" is to dress themselves up and adorn themselves; to "rest on the mat" is to repose and live in peace. They never speak of those whom they have killed, but only of their own dead.

When the chief has finished his speech, they answer him by a loud confused shout, to show that they applaud him and approve of his purpose. After that the chief, or some other appointed by him, rises from his seat with a quiver in his hand and sings as a warrior. His song is generally only a repetition of what was said in the harangue. They chant thus, one after another, especially those who wish to take part in the expedition. Then they eat what has been prepared; only the man who is giving the feast will eat nothing, contenting himself with smoking a few pipes of tobacco. As soon as the meal is finished they beat up recruits without ceasing until the war party is complete.

On the day of departure the warriors deck themselves out as finely as possible. They redden their hair and paint their faces with red and black color, very artistically and prettily, and also their whole bodies. Some wear headdresses made of the tails of eagles or other birds; others wear the teeth of fierce wild animals, such as wolves and tigers, on their heads. Many, instead of a hat, fit their headdress with the horns of a stag, roebuck, or ox.

Around them, they carry their bows, quivers, and arrows. Their canoes are of various colors and are ornamented with figures or with the arms of the leader on the front of the canoes; you see depicted there the war bundle, the raven, the bear, or some other animal, as I have already mentioned—the spirit which is to guide the enterprise.

As soon as they embark they push their canoes fifteen or twenty yards out and range in line, very close together, the end of one not projecting beyond the other, in which matter they are very exact. The chief of the party then stands up to his full height in the middle of his canoe, holding in his hand a gourd with little stones inside it. He shakes it and chants an invocation to his guardian spirit that he may make a prosperous journey. The warriors respond to his chant with a double "Che," drawing in their breath; the other chiefs on land hold forth at the same time, exhorting the young men to fight well, to look well in front of them and behind them on the journey, to scout well and not to allow themselves to be taken by surprise.

The war chief, who during that time chants in his canoe unceasingly, requests all the village not to forget them, if they are killed, but to remember to avenge them. That done, they give a great shout altogether and start off at the same moment in the direction in which they are to go, as if they saw the enemy before them, and it may be said that their boats are like arrows.

Be that as it may, these trappings of war are none the less dreadful to those who have never seen them or are not accustomed to them.

When they have reached the enemy's country, they go warily; they keep silence, observe everything, and never shoot firearms. If they come upon the trail of any persons, they can easily distinguish whether it is old or recent; they know the number of people who have passed there, and how many days ago their journey was made; and, as they know when their enemy went by, they can tell pretty nearly where they will be, and they then decide whether to pursue them or to seek some other parties.

One might say that these people are guided by instinct rather than by knowledge or reason, for if a man or a number of men are discovered, their doom is almost certain and unfailing. It is in vain to try to escape; you may walk on moss or leaves, or through marshes, or even over rocks, but all the precautions you take to conceal your track are quite useless, for the pursuers are rarely at fault. The strangest thing is that they know by the impress of the foot, or its shape, to what tribe the people in front of them belong.

When they conclude that they are fairly near their enemies, they dispatch their best runners and the lightest of their company to go and spy out their encampment, that is, where they are to pass the night, and to see what weapons they have, and how the place lies. It is necessary that these scouts should possess cunning, experience, and boldness; for it should be remembered that all war parties on the march send scouts in this way for three or four leagues round the spot where they wish to encamp or sleep, and when the scouts return to their encampment without seeing anything, and make their report, all the others leaving it to them, rest and sleep peacefully all night, their custom being not to post any guard or sentry.

On the other hand, those who have discovered the enemy, after observing them carefully, return to the main body or the place appointed to meet, and on their report a council is held. Then, if they think they are strong enough to attack, they go at once, generally by night, with the scouts at their head, who never lose their impression of the way they went nor of the encampment of their enemies. When they get within a certain distance they throw themselves flat on the ground, always keeping a lookout with eyes and ears, and having scouts in front and rear and on both flanks. In this posture they wait daybreak, as that is the time when a man is heaviest from the inclination and longing for sleep, and also that they may be able to see better when they make their onslaught and take advantage of the remainder of the day for making their retreat. Their custom is to drag themselves along on the ground on all fours like cats and approach within pistol shot; they then rise to their full height before shooting. The chief of the party gives his signal by a low cry. The others immediately give a loud whoop and, if they have guns, they fire altogether at the enemy; if not, they let fly their arrows. After their first volley, if they see that the enemy is thrown into disorder and routed, they rush upon them, hatchet or tomahawk in hand; if they are victorious, they take the scalps of those who are killed. If they capture any prisoners, they bind them and pinion them so tightly that the bonds cut into their flesh; then they travel night and day until they are out of danger and are safe from their enemies. When near their own village, they send men forward to relate all that has taken place during the campaign, after which preparations are made for welcoming the warriors and haranguing them before they enter the place. At the same time, arrangements are made for the entrance of the prisoners; this always proceeds with three to four hundred blows with sticks, which makes them fall flat on their faces a hundred times before they enter the hut of triumph prepared and set apart for them.

As soon as they are there, they are told to dance and chant their death song. The chant is at once proud and mournful; they recite then what they have done during their lives, especially the number of persons they have killed, their names and the names of their tribes, the place and how they did the deed. Sometimes they are made to sit and sometimes to get up, and always to chant, especially when anyone of importance comes into the hut to see them. But while they chant in this way, one man pulls out one of their nails, another puts one of their fingers in the pipe he is smoking; at intervals a firebrand is held to their flesh, which is burned down to the bone; some cut pieces off them, which they cook and eat immediately, sucking their fingers after, as if it were a most exquisite food. Thus they amuse themselves and pass the time for two or three days, after which the old men, the war chiefs, and the principal persons in the village assemble and consult as to the life or death of these unfortunates. Their execution or preservation generally depends upon the women, and for this reason: some of them have lost a husband or children in the war, and of these some who see handsome prisoners, or more often are merely actuated by a whim or fancy, ask for them to replace the dead; and in that case, the council never refuses them. As soon as they are declared free they are unbound, and the women or girls who have saved them take them to their huts; they wash their wounds, oil them, and make them look as well as they can; and a few days after, a feast is held in the hut and the strangers are adopted as children of the house, as brothers, sons-in-law, or other relations.

From that time they are well treated, and no one insults them any more. But the most surprising thing is that they are the first to go to war against their own tribe, and kill and take prisoners their fathers, uncles, or other relations indifferently, as if they were nothing at all to them, thinking more of the second life which has been given them than of the life they received from their fathers and mothers, whom they often see burned and torn to pieces because they were hard-hearted enough not to set them at liberty after capturing them; for, as I have already said, the life or death of the slaves depends either on the council or the women. The council gives some of them to the French commandant, and others to various tribes, thereby confirming and ratifying their alliances. As soon as they have handed them over, they cease to have control of them, and their life or death depends on their new masters or the tribe to which they are presented. The common custom is to put them to death, in the manner we shall presently see; and, as we have seen that the council of the old men grants slaves their lives at the request of the women, so also, if the latter wish them to die, their request is never refused; and since human nature is more contented and better pleased by vengeance than by pardon, especially in the female sex, the fate of the slaves is almost always unhappy. If the life of one of them is sometimes spared, it is apparently only by a miracle of predestination; the great majority of the women love to avenge the relatives whom they have lost, which they endeavor to do by putting to death those whom the fortune of war has placed in their power and at their mercy. Finally, as soon as these poor wretches, whether Frenchmen or savages, are condemned to death, this is the strange and terrible manner in which it is done.

These furies, filled with bitter memories and resentment for the death of their relatives, who have been made to suffer the same fate, seize upon the victims. First they caress them and take them to their huts, they oil them and give them food and urge them to fill their stomachs well, for they say that, as they have a long journey to make, they should make a good meal, or rather take strength to suffer the longer and more courageously. To see them doing these things, you would say that they were behaving in this way out of friendship or pity; but the victims who know that it is otherwise, do not delight in attentions of this sort, for they know that the food they eat will be followed by a harsh process of digestion. While they are receiving all these kind attentions from the ladies, the young men set up stakes to which these unfortunates are to be attached and get ready the fires, tools, irons, and all the instruments they can invent to satisfy and glut their rage and fury.

All this apparatus being ready and complete, they send word to the women who are fondling these poor victims. Suddenly you see their feminine sweetness change to desperate and diabolical fury; and this is the manner in which the woman who has demanded the prisoner's death signifies to him the fate which awaits him. She calls upon the spirit or shade of her husband, or her son, or other relatives who have been killed or burned, and utters words like these:

"Come hither, my son, and take courage; today I have a feast of fresh meat for thee; drink of this broth; accept the sacrifice I offer thee, of this brave. Rejoice then, my dear son; he shall be roasted and burned, all his nails shall be torn off, his meat shall be roasted, and some of it shall be cooked in the pot, he shall have necklaces hung round him of hatchets redhot from the fire, his fingers shall be calmly smoked; his genitals shall be torn out; they shall drink from his skull, his scalp shall be cut off. Be content, my son, and rest now for thou shall be avenged."

Meanwhile, one of the warriors enters the hut and says to the man who has already been told of his doom: "Take courage, my brother, you are to be burned." The other replies: "That is well, I thank you for the news you bring me." At the same moment a horrible cry is raised through all the village. This cry is called a Sakakua. They seize him, take him away, and fasten him to the stake by the feet, the hands, and the middle of the body; there he is to play the most tragic part that man could possibly conceive, for in fact the old woman who sacrifices him predicts but a part of the suffering and tortures which her victim is to undergo in memory of the one to whom he is offered up. These sinister preparations, which should make the man shudder for whom they are intended (I speak of the Indians), only serve him, however, as a means of showing his scorn for his tyrants. He is no sooner bound to the stake than he chants his death song in a firm and bold voice, recounting all the war-like deeds he has done during his life, the manner in which he has burned his prisoners, encouraging those around him not to spare him, and to put him to death like a man of war. I certainly do not think that all this talk is entirely sincere; it is certain, however, that his mind does not appear to be disturbed, as shown by the fact that his gaze is steadfast and his countenance tranquil.

But it is time to open the ball and see how the chief personages are made to dance. The first step the prisoners are put through is tearing the nails from their hands, one after another, with the teeth. The pipes and calumets of the Indians are made of a sort of stone which is easily hollowed out and is not brittle. They fill them with tobacco and put the victim's fingers in the bowl of the pipe, and then smoke it, taking his ten fingers one after another. After the little feast, five or six workers furnish themselves with burning firebrands; some are applied to his ankles, some to his wrists or to his temples. They do not take them away until the nerves and flesh are burned to the bone; that is the second step of the minuet. The third is a necklace of glowing hatchets, made redhot in the fire, which fall over the shoulders and on to the stomach of the captive. They do not take them off until they have lost all their heat and are cold; and, as those who do this work are men with good appetites, each of them takes off a piece of the buttocks with his knife, boils it, and eats it immediately without any seasoning; and, to wash the wounds and the blood which flows from them, the women have pots ready, full of boiling water, which they pour over them. From time to time they drive irons into his neck and armpits, after making them redhot. They burn his genitals with birch-bark, which gives a very hot and very penetrating flame; and, to make an end of these shameful details, they do not leave him a nerve or an artery which has not been subjected to the fire or the knife. Last of all, they take off his scalp, that is, the skin, in which the hair grows, with such art and skill that they get it off all in one piece, and one would say it was a wig. Having done that, they throw upon the raw and bleeding flesh a handful of hot ashes and hot sand, and when they see that the flesh is mummified, they give him a final blow, that is, a blow on the head with a hatchet, or stab him two or three times in the heart, and then cut off his head. At the same time they make the whole village resound with loud shouts of joy and delight, as if they had won some great victory.

Those who see this short account will perhaps find it hard to credit it, and to bring themselves to believe that any mortal could bear such suffering and being burned in this way, and yet survive, but it is absolutely true, and this terrible practice is especially common with the Iroquois tribe, who burn their slaves, by inches, for five or six days on end.

It might also be thought that anyone tortured in this way must sometimes shed tears or, in the extremity of his torment, utter pitiful cries. There are, indeed, some who cannot prevent themselves from doing so, but most of them seem to ignore this pain and pretend to know nothing of what is happening to them; for, instead of asking quarter, they reproach those who are inflicting this martyrdom upon them, saying that they are cowards and women and have not the courage to cut them up into little pieces; and, if any part of them has escaped being burned, they point it out themselves and beg them not to spare them, bearing all these barbarities from beginning to end without even a wry face. The only request they make is to smoke or for a drink of water, which is never refused, their object being to gain new strength in order to enable their enemies to exercise their ferocious cruelty upon them longer; and they speak to them like this: "Take courage, my brothers, amuse yourselves today; and, if you are ever taken prisoner by my tribe and burned in my village, do not weep or cry out, but smoke calmly, like me. Only women are permitted to shed tears; a true warrior should die as I do."

Their vanity and their desire to be considered brave is the sole source and motive of the indifference they show to suffering and torture; and the form, manner, and practice of this punishment are simply a method of intimidating and giving pause to those who would take up the occupation of war. This custom of putting men to death in this way was formerly held in horror by the French; but, as it was perceived that the humanity shown toward these savages was regarded by them as cowardice and that it led them to attack the French more frequently because, at the worst, they only risked being captured or killed, the French have at last adopted the practice of burning them with all sorts of cruelty—so true it is that, if you consort with wolves, you must howl as they do. This course was adopted only too late, it is now clearly seen that their raids are less frequent and they are not as bold in their attacks. In a word, they are men who value their lives as much as others do; and, if they are brave enough and malicious enough to show such great fortitude and such scorn of death when they are in the hands of their enemies or at their mercy, it may equally be said, not only that they take every possible precaution to avoid being captured in a fight, but also that the idea of being taken alive to be afterwards exposed to the extremity of torture is terrible and frightful to them. This explains why they always make surprise attacks, and the party which is taken by surprise is always beaten. However, in such a strait, they take to their heels, and often some of them escape; but, if they find themselves so beset that it is impossible to get away, and they are compelled to fight, although with an inferior force, they then fight like desperate men, and they certainly sell their lives dearly. Such is the practice of nearly all these tribes with regard to war.[90]

The ceremonies attending the arrival of prisoners at the village of the Ottawa are more fully related in the following excerpt from La Potherie:

The Outaouaks, who had followed their own caprice without consulting the French commandants who were at Michilimakinak, brought back some captives; and at night the cries for the dead were heard abroad. The next day the smoke in their camp was seen at the island of Michilimakinak; and they sent a canoe to inform the village of the blow that they had just struck. The Jesuit fathers hastened thither, in order to try to secure for the slaves exemption from the volley of blows with clubs to which the captives were usually treated on their arrival; but all their solicitations could not move the Outaouaks, and even served only to exasperate them. The canoes, which were close together, made their appearance; there was only one man paddling in each, while all the warriors responded to the songs of the slaves,

[90] Cadillac, MS "Relation on the Indians."

who stood upright, each having a wand in his hand. There were special marks on each, to indicate those who had captured him. Gradually they approached the shore, with measured advance. When they were near the land the chief of all the party rose in his canoe and harangued all the old men, who were waiting for the warriors at the edge of the water in order to receive them; and having made a recital to them of his campaign he told them that he placed in their hands the captives whom he had taken. An old man on the shore responded, and congratulated them in most complaisant terms. Finally the warriors stepped ashore, all naked, abandoning to pillage, according to their custom, all their booty. An old man came at the head of nine men, to conduct the captives to a place at one side; there were five old men and four youths. The women and children immediately ranged themselves in rows, very much as is done when some soldier is flogged through the lines. The young captives, who were very agile, quickly passed through; but the old men were so hardly used that they bled profusely. The former were awarded to masters, who spared their lives; but the old men were condemned to the flames. They were placed on the Manilion, which is the place where the captives are burned, until the chiefs had decided to which tribe they should be handed over.[91]

According to the report of Champlain in 1615 and that of Sagard in 1623, the Ottawa and Neutrals were at war with the Asistagueroüon, who lived some distance west of Lake Huron.[92] The *Jesuit Relations* for 1640–41 and 1643–44 record the continuance of this warfare.[93] The Asistagueroüon have been identified as the Potawatomi. The evidence does not make this identification conclusive. If the Asistagueroüon were the Potawatomi the remnants of the Ottawa and Huron tribes sought refuge among their former enemies about 1650. No further trouble between them and the Potawatomi has been reported.

About 1656, while encroaching upon the territory of the

[91] *History, ITUM.*, 2: 36-39.
[92] Champlain, *Voyages*, 3: 97; Sagard, *Le Grand voyage*, p. 78.
[93] *J.R.*, 21: 195; 27: 25-27.

Sioux, difficulties with that tribe arose that were not entirely
settled in the contact period. The Iroquois likewise were foes
during the rest of this period, with only occasional truces.

The Ottawa had disputes with practically all of the rest of
the tribes around them, with the exception of the Chippewa
and Menominee. Their quarrels with the Huron, however,
never broke into open warfare. Their major engagements with
their foes, aside from the Sioux and the Iroquois, during the
contact period were as follows: Winnebago, about 1640;
Miami, 1690, 1706, 1712; Flatheads (Cherokee, Chickasaw,
Catawba, etc.), 1700 *et seq.*; and Fox, 1712, 1716, 1723.

Games

The principal games among the Ottawa were those of lacrosse, of straws, and dice. These were described by Perrot:

The Game of Crosse

The savages have several kinds of games, in which they take
delight. They are naturally so addicted to these that they will
give up their food and drink, not only to play but to watch the
game. There is among them a certain game, called crosse, which
has much likeness to our game of lawn tennis. Their custom in
playing it is to oppose tribe to tribe; and if one of these is more
numerous than the other, men are drawn from it to render the
other equal to it [in strength]. You will see them all equipped
with the crosse—which is a light club, having at one end a broad
flat part that is netted like a [tennis] racket; the ball that they
use in playing is of wood, and shaped very nearly like a turkey's
egg. The goals for the game are marked in an open level space;
these goals face east and west, south and north. In order to win
the game, one of the two parties must send its ball, by driving it
[with the racket], beyond the goals that face east and west; and
the other [must send] its ball beyond those to the south and
north. If the party which has once won sends the ball again
beyond the east and west goals from the side that it had to win,
it is obliged to recommence the game, and to accept the goals
of the opposing party; but if it should succeed in winning a
second time, it would have accomplished nothing—for, as the

parties are equal in strength, and are quits, they always begin the game in order to act the part of conqueror; and that party which wins carries away what has been staked on the game.

Men, women, boys, and girls are received into the parties which are formed; and they bet against one another for larger or smaller amounts, each according to his means.

These games usually begin after the melting of the winter's ice, and last until seed-time. In the afternoon all the players may be seen, painted with vermilion and decked with ornaments. Each party has its leader, who makes an address, announcing to his players the hour that has been appointed for beginning the games. All assemble in a body, in the middle of the place [selected], and one of the leaders of the two parties, holding the ball in his hand, tosses it into the air. Each player undertakes to send it in the direction in which he must drive it; if it falls to the ground, he endeavors to draw it toward him with his crosse; and, if it is sent outside the crowd of players, the more alert distinguish themselves from the others by closely following it. You will hear the din that they make by striking one another, while they strive to ward off the blows in order to send the ball in a favorable direction. If one of them keeps it between his feet, without allowing it to escape, it is for him to avoid the blows that his adversaries rain incessantly upon his feet; and, if he happens to be wounded in this encounter, that is his own affair. Some of them are seen who [thus] have had their legs or arms broken, and some even have been killed. It is very common to see among them men crippled for the rest of their lives, and who were hurt in games of this sort only as the result of their own obstinacy. When such accidents occur, the player who is so unfortunate as to be hurt retires quietly from the game, if he is in a condition to walk; but, if his injuries will not permit this, his relatives convey him to the cabin, and the game always goes on as if nothing were the matter, until it is finished.

As for the runners, when the parties are equally strong they will sometimes spend an afternoon without either side gaining the advantage over the other; but sometimes, too, one of them will bear away the two victories which it must have in order to win the game. In this sport of racing, you would say that they looked like two opposing parties who meant to fight together.

This exercise has much to do with rendering the savages agile, and ready to ward adroitly any blows from a club in the hands of an enemy, when they find themselves entangled in combat; and if one were not told beforehand that they were playing, one would certainly believe that they were fighting together in the open field. Whatever mishap this sport may occasion, they attribute it to the luck of the game, and they feel no hatred to one another; The trouble falls on the injured persons, who nevertheless put on as contented an aspect as if nothing had happened to them, thus making it appear that they have great courage, and are men. The party that has won carries away what its members staked, and the profit that it has made, and that without any objection on either side when it is a question of paying [the bets], no matter what kind of game it may be. However, if any person who does not belong to the party, or who has not made any bet, should drive the ball to the advantage of one of the two parties, one of the players whom the blow does not favor would attack this man, demanding of him whether this were any of his business, and why he was meddling in it. They have often come to blows over this point, and if some chief did not reconcile them there would be bloodshed, and even some one would be killed. The best way to prevent this disorderly conduct is to begin the game over again, with the consent of those who are winning; for if they refuse to do so, the responsibility rests on them. But when some one of the influential men interposes, it is not difficult to adjust their dispute and to induce them to conform to his decision.[94]

The Game of Straws

At the game of straws the savages lose not only all that they possess, but even that which belongs to their comrades. Here is an account of this game. They take for this sport a certain number of straws, or of the stems of a special plant, which is not so thick as the cord [used] for a salmon-net, and with these they make little sticks, all alike in length and thickness; the length is about eleven inches, and the number is uneven. After turning and mingling these in their hands, they lay them on a piece of skin or of blanket; and he who must begin the game, holding

[94] Perrot, *Memoir*, *ITUM.*, 1: 93-96.

in his hand an awl (or more commonly a small pointed bone), makes contortions of his arms and body, continually saying *Chok! Chok!*—a word which has no meaning in their language, but which serves to make known his desire to play well and to be fortunate in the game. Then with this awl or small pointed bone he thrusts into some part of the [pile of] straws, and takes away a number of them as he pleases; his opponent takes those which remain on the cloth, and with inconceivable quickness counts them, by tens, without making any mistake; then he who has the uneven number has made a lucky hit.

Sometimes they play with seeds which grow on the trees, which closely resemble little beans. Each takes a certain number of these [to stand] for the value of the goods which he wishes to stake—that is, a gun, a blanket, or some other article. The player who at the beginning of the game finds that he has nine straws in his hand has won all, and draws what has been staked. If he finds that he has a number not even, below nine, it is in his power to double [the stakes?], and to honor the game with what suits him. For this purpose he lays down at any place in the game, as he chooses, one straw, and three, five, or seven [of them] on other spots; for the number nine, it is always taken for granted, predominates over all the others. In short, he who finds nine straws in his hand usually draws all that has been staked. Besides the straws which lie on the cloth are the seeds with which the players have honored the game; and you must note that they always place more of these on the nine than on all the others.

When the players have made their bets, he who has been lucky often takes the straws and turns them endwise in his hands, and then places them on the table, saying *Chank!* which means "nine"; and the other, who has the awl or the little bone in his hands, draws off [part of] the straws, in such place as he prefers, and takes as many of them as he pleases, as has been already stated, and the other takes the rest of them. If the last to take them prefers to leave them, his adversary is obliged to take them; and, each counting them by tens, he who has the uneven number has won, and takes whatever has been staked. But if it happens that the winner has only one straw more than the other man, he takes only those seeds which represent that straw. For example, the number three is greater than two, by one; five is superior to three, and seven to five; but nine surpasses all.

If several persons are playing and one of them finds five in his hand, they play four at a time, two against two, or fewer if they cannot make up the number of four players; one pair wins the seeds which stand for the five straws, and the other [the] seeds which are at stake for the three straws and for one. When any one has not in his hand the uneven number of those which remain on the cloth—that is, one and three—after they have carefully counted the straws by tens, when he has not the nine he is obliged to double what he has staked, even if he might have in his hand five or seven straws; and his play counts for nothing. He is obliged also to form two other piles of straws; in one he places five and in the other seven straws, with as many seeds as he pleases. When he has laid these on the cloth, his opponents in their turn prick off [straws], and then he takes those which are left; by that time there are some of the players who are lucky, nevertheless each one takes for himself only the seeds which are designated for the number of straws [which he has], and he who has nine takes only the seeds laid down for the nine straws. When another player draws away seven straws, he takes the rest; for three straws and for one it is all the same, but not for [numbers] higher than these.

It should be noted that, after they have lost the game which lies before them, they continue playing upon their promises [to pay], if the players declare that they [still] have possessions, even though these are not in their hands. But when one continues to be unlucky, the winner may refuse [to accept] seeds from the loser for the value which he requires from the latter, and may oblige him to go to find the goods themselves, refusing to play any longer until he sees these, nor can any retort to this be made. The loser will immediately tell one of his comrades to bring the goods to him, and if his ill-luck continues he will lose everything that he owns. One of his comrades then relieves him and takes his place, stating what he intends to risk on the game to the winner, who then accepts seeds for the value [of the bet].

This game lasts sometimes three or four days. When any one of the party who loses wins back all, and he who has hitherto been lucky in play comes to lose not only the profit which he has made but what of his own property he had staked, another of his comrades also takes his place, and everything goes on as before, until one of the two parties is entirely ruined. Thus the contest comes to an end among those people, it being a rule with the savages that they cannot quit the game until one side or the other has lost everything. It is for this reason that they cannot dispense with furnishing revenge to all those of a party, decisively, one after another, as I have just stated. In the game they have liberty to play on their own account, as they please; and if there happened to be a quarrel over this—I mean between the winners and the losers, each supported by those of his own party —they would come to blows, in which there would be bloodshed, and it would be very difficult to reconcile them. If the disposition of the winner is such as to be calm while he loses, and he feigns to overlook the many adroit tricks and the cheating which they very often practice in playing, he is praised and esteemed by every one; while he who has tried to cheat is blamed by every one, and there is no one who wishes to play with him, unless he ignominiously restores what he has unlawfully won.

This game of straws is usually held in the cabins of chiefs, which are large and are, so to speak, the academy of the savages; and there are seen all the young men, making up opposing sides, and the older men as spectators of their games. If the player fancies that he has had luck in picking off the straws, and that he has on his side the uneven number, holding them in his hand he strikes [the table] with the other; and when he has made the count of them by tens, without saying a word he makes it known by a sign that he has won, by taking for himself the seeds which have been staked, when he sees that he against whom he is playing has not as many of them. If one of the players tries to object that the straws could not have been correctly counted, they hand them over to two of the spectators to count them; and the one who has really won always sweeps off his straws, without saying anything, and takes possession of the articles at stake. All of this passes without any dispute, and with great fairness. You will note that this game is not at all one for women, and that it is only the men who engage in it.[95]

[95] *Ibid.*, pp. 96-101.

Game of Dice

The savages have also a certain game of dice, in which the dice-box is a wooden dish, quite round, empty, and very smooth on both sides. The dice are composed of six small flat bones, in shape closely resembling a plum stone; these are quite smooth, with one of the sides colored black, red, green, or blue, and the other usually white, or of some other color than the former side. They place these dice in the dish, and, holding it by both sides, jerk it upward, causing the dice within to leap and bounce around. Then, having slammed the bottom of the dish against the table, while the dice are rolling about they immediately strike their own chests or shoulders with sharp blows, saying, "Dice! dice! dice!" until the dice stop moving. When five or six of these are found with the same color on the [upper] face, a player sweeps off the seeds which represent his agreement with the other party; if the loser and his comrades have nothing more to wager, the winning side takes all that is at stake. Entire villages have been known to wager each its entire wealth against another at this game, and to lose it all. They also present challenges; and when one party happens to throw a pair-royal of six all of the men and women of the tribe that is backing them rise to their feet and dance, keeping time to the sound of the gourd rattles. The entire affair goes off without any dispute.

The girls and women play at this game, but they very often have eight dice, and do not use the dish for it, as the men do; they only lay down a blanket, and throw the dice on it with their hands.[96]

All three of these games were reported by Sabrevois as being played by the Ottawa and the Potawatomi at Detroit in 1718. The game of lacrosse received the following comments:

In summer they Play a great deal at la crosse, twenty or more on each side. Their bat [crosse] is a sort of small racket, and The ball with which they Play Is of very Heavy wood, a little Larger than the Balls we use in Tennis. When they Play, they Are entirely naked; they have only a breech-clout, and Shoes of deer-

[96] Ibid., pp. 101-2.

skin. Their bodies are painted with white clay, applying it to resemble silver lace sewed on all the seams of a coat; and, at a distance, one would take it for silver lace.

They play for large Sums, and often The prize amounts to more than 800 Livres. They set up two goals and begin Their game midway between; one party drives The ball one way, and the other in the opposite direction, and those who can drive It to the goal are the winners. All this is very diverting and interesting to behold. Often one Village Plays against another, the poux against the outaouacs or the hurons, for very considerable prizes. The French frequently take part in these games.[97]

The dish game or dice Sabrevois described as follows:

Eight little balls, red or black on one side, and yellow or white on the other, are tossed on a dish. When he who has the dish tosses them so that seven of the same color turn up, or all eight, he wins, and continues to play as long as he throws in this way; but when he throws otherwise, he or she with whom he Plays takes The dish and Plays in turn. In all these games they Play for large sums. They, and all the other nations likewise, have also the Game of straws.[98]

Footraces were held by the Ottawa as one of the festivities following the interment of a body, according to Perrot.[99] That such races were also held as contests without any connection with funerals by the Indians at Detroit in 1757 is evident from the following excerpt from the memoir of Bougainville:

At Detroit foot races between the savages and the Canadians are as celebrated as horse races in England. They take place in the spring. Ordinarily there are five hundred savages present, sometimes as many as fifteen hundred. The course is a half league, going and returning from Détroit to the village of the Poutéouatamis; the road is well made and wide. There are posts planted at the two extremities; the wagers are very considerable,

---

[97] *Memoir, WHC.,* 16: 366-67.
[98] *Ibid.,* p. 369.
[99] See the end of the excerpt from Perrot under "Death Customs."

and consist of packages of peltries laid against French merchandise such as is in use among the savages.[100]

Dances

The Ottawa and the Potawatomi observed the same dances, reported Sabrevois, who described them:

In the evening The women and The girls dance. They adorn themselves liberally, grease their hair, put on white chemises, and paint their Faces with vermillion, also putting on all the porcelain beads they possess, so that after their fashion they look very well dressed. They dance to the Sound of the drum and of the *sisyqouy* ["rattle"], which Is a sort of gourd with pellets of lead inside. There are four or five Young men who sing, and keep time by beating the drum and the *sysyqouy*, while the women dance to the rhythm and do not miss a step. This Is a very pretty sight, And it lasts almost all night. Often the old men dance The *medelinne;* they look like a band of sorcerers. All this is done at Night. The Young men often dance in the daytime, and strike at the posts; it is in this dance that they recount Their exploits; on such occasions they also dance the scout dance. They are always well-adorned when they do this. All this Is very interesting to see. They often engage in hunts of this sort in order to get tobacco.[101]

Marriage

The Ottawa were reported by Menard in 1660 to be practicing polygamy.[102] As far as the records show they were still

[100] *Memoir, WHC.,* 18: 194.

[101] *Memoir, WHC.,* 16: 367-68. The *medelinne* dance is undoubtedly the midewiwin. As to the young men dancing in the daytime, the original text reads *"le tour"* which E. B. O'Callaghan in another translation of the same document (*N.YCD.,* 9: 887) rendered "a circle," making the whole passage read "the young men often dance in a circle." Thwaites, the editor of the above excerpt from the collections of the Wisconsin Historical Society, seems to have thought that the qualification of night time immediately preceding was terminal in nature and that *"le tour"* was a mistake for *"le jour."* Raudot said that the discovery and striking the post dances were usually performed at night ("Memoir," Letter 27); Charlevoix reported that striking the post was always performed in the night time (*Journal,* 2: 67).

[102] René Menard, *Relation . . . . 1662-63, J.R.,* 48: 117.

doing so at the end of the contact period. Allouez reported in 1669 that on the conversion of the entire Kishkakon tribe to Christianity by common consent they entirely abolished the practice.[103] Subsequent documents do not state whether or not this resolution was kept.

Of the marriages of the Ottawa Perrot wrote:

There are some savage peoples among whom persons marry in order to live together until death, and there are others among whom married persons separate whenever it pleases them to do so. Those who observe this latter maxim are the Iroquois, the Loups, and some others. But the Outaoüas marry their wives in order to remain with them throughout life, unless some very forcible reason gives the husband occasion to put away his wife. For without such a reason the man would expose himself to be plundered and to a thousand humiliations, since she whom he had wrongfully quitted, in order to take another wife, would go at the head of her relatives and take from him whatever he had on his person and in his cabin; she would tear out his hair and disfigure his face. In a word, there is no indignity or insult which she would not heap upon him, and which she may not lawfully inflict on him, without his being able to oppose her therein if he does not wish to become the butt of ignominy in the village. When the husband does not take another wife, the one whom he had deserted may strip him when he comes back from hunting or trading, leaving to him only his weapons; and she takes away [even] these if he positively refuses to return with her. But when the man can prove on his side that she has been unfaithful to him, either before or since he has left her, he can take another wife without any one being able to raise objection. The woman cannot at her whim abandon her husband, since he is her master, who has bought and paid for her, even her relatives cannot take her away from him; and if she leaves him custom authorizes him to kill her without any one blaming him for it. This has often brought on war between families, when [relatives] undertook to maintain the husband's right when the woman would not consent to return to him.[104]

[103] Relation . . . . 1668-69, J.R., 52: 207.
[104] Perrot, Memoir, ITUM., 1: 64-65.

Cadillac agreed that marriage among the Lakes tribes was by purchase, but differed with Perrot on some points and gave a fuller exposition of others in the following account of the marriage customs of these tribes:

You must know that lovers go courting there, as elsewhere, talk amorous nonsense and give one another tokens of respect and affection. The girls have this advantage, that they are allowed to take their pleasure and try experiments with marriage, as long as they like and with as many bachelors as they please, and no one finds any fault with them, nor does it prevent them from finding a husband, when they are in a humor to do so.

Their love affairs are carried on in this way. The young men have strips of bark rolled up in the form of a torch; at night they light them at one end and go through all the huts, if they please. The girls are lying down on the side of the walk, and when their beloved passes they stop him by a corner of his robe. The moment the gallant perceives this signal he stoops down, and then his mistress takes his roll of bark and puts it out, and makes the young man lie down beside her, and he tells her his love; with all this familiarity and complete liberty, it is not often that anything takes place but what is quite seemly and respectful, so true it is that one thinks less of what is permitted than of what is forbidden. For it is evident that, on these occasions, it is in the power of the two lovers to indulge their passion; yet they generally do nothing of the kind, especially if they intend to marry one another. Finally, when the fair one grows tired and wants to sleep, she tells her lover, who retires as soon as she bids him. That is called among them, "running the light." As to married women, they are obliged to proceed differently, for they are roughly chastised in some tribes, though not in all, if convicted of licentiousness, as I shall show elsewhere.

We shall now consider various other customs common to them, such as marrying or living with as many women as they please, provided they can feed and keep them. When they are tired of them or find them troublesome, they cast off such of them as they think fit, and replace them by others if the fancy takes them; and, in the same way, if the women are not satisfied with their husbands, they abandon them and go and live with another more to their liking. By this means, nothing is ever lost, for one takes what the other gives up; and, by these very natural and convenient customs, they get rid of any rancor or antipathy between them, which may disturb the life and comfort of families. Nevertheless, it rarely happens that the husband casts off his wife, or that the wife leaves her husband, if they have children. But if it does happen, all the offspring, both boys and girls belong to the mother, and the husband is not allowed to retain any of them against her will; for the mother's title rests on the law of nature, since no one can dispute that she is the mother of the children to whom she has given birth, whereas it is always uncertain who the father is, and often unknown. It is for that reason that the Indians trace their pedigree through the women, when they wish to prove their claim to nobility. Now, among them, a large number of children is never burdensome to the mother; on the contrary, she is more highly respected for it, more honored and esteemed, and richer. Accordingly, she finds it an easier and quicker matter to get married again, for the man who marries her, in becoming her husband, becomes also the father and chief of the whole family, and is therefore a person of more importance; for, if the children are grown up, they support the hut, that is, the house, either by their deeds as warriors or by hunting or else by the alliances they make, by taking wives of their own; and if they are still young, the step-father hopes and expects that, if he receives any personal wrong or injury, he will be avenged when his stepsons, who regard him as their own father, are old enough. Moreover, that actually happens, for the Indians love nothing so much as revenge, and this is why widows who have children easily find a husband.

But if a man becomes a widower, and his wife leaves him children of the marriage, then the relations look for a wife for him, suitable to his circumstances, they propose her to him and afterward take her to the hut of the widower; if he refuses her and, in course of time, takes another to please himself, the woman who receives this insult is allowed to go and abuse the man who has refused her and sent her back and call him as many opprobrious names as she likes. Then she breaks and smashes up everything in the hut, or plunders and carries off all the finest and best things it contains and takes them home with her, while the remarried widower and his wife, who is considered as a concubine, may not do anything to prevent her nor say a word to her, and only hang their heads. They seem to be covered with confusion, but really they are only laughing. So, when the woman has taken her revenge in this way, she goes off satisfied and content, and says no more about the matter.

If a married man dies without issue and has one or more brothers living, one of them marries the widow, as if to raise up children to his dead brother; it also happens that they often marry two sisters. They recognize no degree of relationship with regard to women as forming an obstacle to marriage. They make use of the same terms and descriptions of relationship as we do, such as grandfather, grandmother, son-in-law, uncle, nephew, and the rest.[105]

The levirate usually prevailed in the event of demise of an elder brother. The younger brother, if unmarried, espoused the widow if there was no issue from her first marriage. In the foregoing account, Cadillac did not say whether in this tribe, which permitted polygamy, the levirate operated when the surviving brother was already married.

The remarks of Raudot[106] on the marriage customs of what he called the "people of the North" and those of all the lakes agree in many respects with the account of Cadillac.

Birth Customs

There is no account on the subject applying specifically to the Ottawa. The remarks of Cadillac, although not limited to the Ottawa, certainly applied to them. He stated that when a woman was confined, she slept apart from her husband and remained separated for forty days after the delivery. On the forty-first day she went into her cabin, lighted a fresh fire, and was then purified. When women were with child their husbands refrained from sleeping with them, for they believed that sexual intercourse ruined the nourishment which the child received from its mother, made it waste away, and

[105] Cadillac, MS "Relation on the Indians."
[106] "Memoir," Letters 25 and 40.

might even displace it and cause its death. The same prohibition was in force for nursing mothers, for they said that intercourse spoiled their milk and that if they should become pregnant, the nursling could not be saved because they had no other food to give it. All the women did not observe this custom, but many did out of affection for their offspring.[107]

The purification period lasted thirty days if the child was a boy and forty if it was a girl, according to Lahontan.[108] Perrot said that the Indian woman spent a month without entering the husband's cabin, and without eating with men or eating food prepared by men.[109] Charlevoix gave the period of separation after a birth as forty days, but added that he thought he had heard it said that this was never done except at the woman's first lying-in.[110]

All of these general accounts agree that the women usually were delivered without pain or trouble and often without the attendance of anyone. Some, like those of Raudot, said that when a woman had given birth, she went to wash the child in the water and did not discontinue doing the housework as usual.[111] Such statements can be reconciled with the period of purification mentioned by Cadillac, Lahontan, and Perrot, by accepting the report of Charlevoix as correct.

Children

Speaking of the tribes around the Great Lakes, Perrot said that each child had for a cradle a very light piece of board, which was ornamented at the head with glass beads, bells, and round or long porcelain beads, and with these only, if it was a girl; but if the child was a boy, a bow was attached to the cradle and, if the father was a good hunter, all his adornments were also placed on the cradle.[112]

[107] MS "Relation on the Indians."
[108] *Voyages*, 2: 458.
[109] *Memoir, ITUM.*, 1: 48.
[110] *Journal*, 2: 51.
[111] "Memoir," Letter 25.
[112] *Memoir, ITUM.*, 1: 77.

The child spent most of its time in this cradle until it was weaned at the age of three, according to Charlevoix;[113] Lahontan said that children were never weaned, but nursed as long as the mothers had milk.[114]

The ceremony of naming a child and the early instruction given it were described by Perrot:

When a child, either boy or girl, has reached the age of five or six months, the father and mother make a feast with the best provisions that they have, to which they invite a juggler with five or six of his disciples. This juggler is one of those who formerly offered sacrifices to their divinities; he will be described in the following pages. The father of the family addresses him, and tells him that he is invited in order to pierce the nose and ears of his child; and that he is offering this feast to the sun, or to some other pretended divinity whose name he mentions, entreating that divinity to take pity on his child and preserve its life. The juggler then replies, according to custom, and makes his invocation to the spirit whom the father has chosen. Food is presented to this man and his disciples, and if any is left they are permitted to carry it away with them. When they have finished their meal, the mother of the child places before the guests some peltries, kettles, or other wares, and places her child in the arms of the juggler, who gives it to one of his disciples to hold. After he has ended his song in honor of the spirit invoked, he takes from his pouch a flat bodkin made of a bone, and a stout awl, and with the former pierces both ears of the child, and with the awl its nose. He fills the wounds in the ears with little rolls of bark, and in the nose he places the end of a small quill, and leaves it there until the wound is healed by a certain ointment with which he dresses it. When it has healed, he places in the aperture some down of the swan or the wild goose. . . .

When the child cries, its mother quiets it by singing a song that describes the duties of a man, for her boy; and those of a woman, for her daughter. As soon as the child begins to walk, a little bow with stiff straws is given to a boy, so that he may amuse himself by shooting them. When he had grown a little

[113] *Journal*, 2: 51.
[114] *Voyages*, 2: 459.

larger, they give him little arrows of very light weight; but when he has once attained the age of eight or ten years he occupies himself with hunting squirrels and small birds. Thus he is trained and rendered capable of becoming some day skilful in hunting. Such is the method pursued by the upper tribes; those down here [Quebec] no longer use this sort of circumcisions, and do not call in jugglers to make them; the father, or some friend of the family, performs this ceremony without any further formality.[115]

The account of names and of the ceremony of their imposition given by Charlevoix differs considerably from that of Perrot. Charlevoix wrote:

The act which terminates their state of infancy is the imposition of the name, which amongst the Indians is a matter of great importance.

This ceremony is performed at a feast, at which are present none but persons of the same sex with the child that is to be named; during the repast the child remains on the knees of its father or mother, who are incessantly recommending it to the genii, and above all to him who is to be guardian, for each person has one, but not from the time of birth; they never invent new names, each family preserves a certain number of them, which they make use of by turns; they even sometimes change them as they grow older, and there are some which cannot be used after a certain age, but I do not believe this practice to be universal; and as it is the custom amongst some nations on assuming a name, to put themselves in the place of the person who last bore it, it sometimes happens that a child is called grandfather by a person, who might well enough be his own.

They never call a man by his own name when they speak to him in a familiar manner; this would be a piece of great impoliteness, they always name him by the relation he bears to the person that speaks to him; but when there is neither affinity nor consanguinity between them; they call one another brother, uncle, nephew, or cousin, according to the age of either, or in proportion to the esteem in which they hold the person to whom they address themselves.

Farther, it is not so much with a view to perpetuating names

[115] Perrot, *Memoir, ITUM.,* 1: 76-78.

that they renew them, as with a view to incite the person on whom they are bestowed, either to imitate the great actions of the persons that bore them, or to revenge them in case they have been killed or burned; or lastly to comfort their families: thus a woman who has lost her husband or her son, and finds herself thus void of all support makes all the haste in her power, to give the name of the person she mourns for, to some one who may stand her in his stead; lastly, they likewise change their names on several other occasions, which it would take up too much time to mention minutely. In order to do this there wants only a dream, or the prescription of some physician, or some other reason equally frivolous.[116]

As for the relations between children and their parents, Cadillac said that the fathers and mothers loved their children tenderly and left them free to dispose of everything in the cabin and to consult on the affairs of the family. Because of this freedom sisters had more respect for their brothers than they had for their parents, so that when a brother made any reasonable request of his sister, she made no difficulty and never refused what he asked. When they were together and anyone said something unseemly, a look of shame came into their faces, they lowered their eyes and were confused, which proved to Cadillac the great respect that they had for one another.[117]

Menstrual Observances

According to Sagard, the Ottawa women lived harmoniously with their husbands, but, like the women of all the other nomadic tribes, they withdrew from their husbands during their monthly periods. Unmarried girls withdrew from their parents and relatives at these times. They dwelt in special cabins away from the village without any male company. Usually they took with them enough provision for the entire period, but, if they failed to do so, the men might carry them food and other needed things.[118]

[116] Charlevoix, *Journal*, 2: 52-53.
[117] MS "Relation on the Indians."
[118] *Le Grand voyage*, pp. 78-79.

Death Customs

The most complete account of the death customs of the Ottawa is that given by Perrot:

When an Outaoüas, or other savage [of that region] is at the point of death, he is decked with all the ornaments owned by the family—I mean, among his kindred and his connections by marriage. They dress his hair with red paint mixed with grease, and paint his body and face red with vermilion; they put on him one of his handsomest shirts, if he has such, and he is clad with a jacket and a blanket, as richly as possible; he is, in a word, as properly garbed as if he had to conduct the most solemn ceremony. They take care to adorn the place where he is [lying] with necklaces of porcelain and glass beads (both round and long), or other trinkets. His weapons lie beside him, and at his feet generally all articles that he used in war during his life. All his relatives—and, above all, the jugglers—are near him. When the sick man seems to be in agony, and struggles to yield up his last breath, the women and girls among his relations, with others who are hired [for this purpose] betake themselves to mourning, and begin to sing doleful songs, in which mention is made of the degrees of relationship which they have with the sufferer. But if he seems to be recovering, and to regain consciousness, the women cease their weeping; but they recommence their cries and lamentations whenever the patient relapses into convulsions or faintness. When he is dead (or a moment before he expires), they raise him to a sitting position, his back supported, [to look] as if he were alive. I will say here, in passing, that I have seen some savages whose death-agonies lasted more than twenty-four hours, the sick man making fearful grimaces and contortions, and rolling his eyes in the most frightful manner; you would have believed that the soul of the dying man beheld and dreaded some enemy, although he was lying there without recognizing us, and almost dead. The corpse remains thus sitting until the next day, and is kept in this position both day and night by the relatives and friends who go to visit the family; they are also assisted from time to time by some old man, who takes his place near the women who are relatives of the dead man. [One of them] begins her mournful song, while she weeps hot tears; all the others join her therein, but they cease to sing at the same time when she does; and then a present is given to her—a piece of meat, a dish of corn, or some other article.

As for the men, they do not weep, for that would be unworthy of them; the father alone makes it evident, by a doleful song, that there is no longer anything in the world which can console him for the death of his son. A brother follows the same practice for his elder brother, when he has received from the latter during his life visible marks of tenderness and affection. In such case, the brother takes his place naked, his face smeared with charcoal, mingled with a few red lines. He holds in his hands his bow and arrows, as if he intended at the start to go against some enemy; and, singing a song, in a most furious tone, he runs like a lunatic through the open places, the streets, and the cabins of the village, without shedding a tear. By this extraordinary performance he makes known to all who see him how great is his sorrow for the death of his brother; this softens the hearts of his neighbors, and obliges them to provide among themselves a present, which they come to offer to the dead. In the speech with which they accompany this gift they declare that it is made in order to wipe away the tears of his relatives; and that the mat which they give him is for him to lie on, or [that they give] a piece of bark to shelter his corpse from the injurious effects of the weather.

When the time comes for burying the corpse, they go to find the persons designated for this office; and a scaffold is erected seven or eight feet high, which serves the dead in place of a grave—or, if he is [to be] placed in the ground, they dig a grave only four or five feet deep. During all this time, the family of him whose funeral is solemnized exert all their energies to bring him grain, or peltries, or other goods, [which they place] either on the scaffold or near the grave; and when one or the other is completed they carry thither the corpse, in the same position which it had at death, and clothed with the same fine apparel. Near him are his weapons, and at his feet all the articles which had been placed there before his death. When the funeral ceremonies have been performed and the body buried, the family make liberal payment to those who took part therein, by giving them a kettle or some porcelain necklaces for their trouble.

All the people in the village are obliged to attend the funeral procession; and, when all is over, one man among them all steps forward, who holds in his hand a little wooden rod, as large as one's finger and some five inches long, which he throws into the midst of the crowd, for him who can catch it. When it has fallen into some person's hand the rest try to snatch it from him; if it falls on the ground every one tries to reach it to pick it up, pulling and pushing each other so violently that in less than half an hour it has passed through the hands of all those who are present. If at last any one of the crowd can get possession of it, and display it to them without any one taking it from him, he sells it for a fixed price to the first person who desires to buy it; this price will be very often a kettle, a gun, or a blanket. The bystanders are then notified to be present again, on some day appointed, for a similar ceremony; and this is done, sometimes quite often, as I have just related.

After this diversion, public notice is given that there is another prize, to be given to the best runner among the young men. The goal of the race is indicated, [and the course is marked out] from the place where the runners must start to that which they are to reach. All the young men adorn themselves, and form in a long row on the open plain. At the first call of the man who is to give the signal, they commence to run, at some distance from the village, and the first one who arrives there carries away the prize.

A few days afterward the relatives of the dead man give a feast of meat and corn, to which are invited all the villagers who are not connected with them by marriage and who are descended from other families than their own—especially those persons who have made presents to the dead. They also invite, if any such are found, strangers who have come from other villages; and they inform all the guests that it is the dead man who gives them this feast. If it is one of meat, they take a piece of this, as well as of other kinds of food, which they must place upon the grave; and the women, girls, and children are permitted to eat these morsels, but not the grown men, for these must regard such acts as unworthy of them. At this feast each is free to eat what he wishes, and to carry the rest [of his portion] home with him. Considerable presents in goods are given to all those strangers who have previously made presents to the dead person; but these are not given to his own tribesmen. The guests are then thanked for having remembered the dead, and congratulated on their charitable dispositions.[119]

Raudot gave the additional information that the bodies were left on these scaffolds only until the flesh was entirely consumed, at which time the bones were scraped and conserved.[120] Unfortunately, he did not explain what he meant by conserving them.

Rasles said that there were three families of the Ottawa, only one of which, that of the Great Hare, burned the bodies of its dead members. The other two buried them, and in his account there is no mention of scaffolds, but this may only be an omission. As one can see from Perrot's account, the word "burial" was not always used synonymously with "interment." Rasles also stated that while the grave goods were being arranged in the coffin, the relatives of the dead man were present and wept, chanting in a mournful tone and swinging rhythmically rods to which they had attached several little bells.[121]

The feast of the dead was, apparently, a ceremony observed by the Ottawa. The references to its performance by neighboring Algonquian tribes are almost as early, although not as detailed, as the excellent description by Brébeuf for the Huron. Lalemant witnessed such a feast given by the Nipissing in 1642.[122] In 1683 it was again reported for the Nipissing.[123] Perrot, who was mostly with Algonquian tribes, gave a fairly extensive description.[124] Unlike the others, Raudot stated that the interval between observances of the feast was three years.[125]

[119] Perrot, *Memoir, ITUM.*, 1 : 78-83.
[120] "Memoir," Letter 52.
[121] "Letter . . . . to His Brother," *J.R.*, 67 : 157-59.
[122] Jérôme Lalemant, *Relation . . . . 1642, J.R.*, 23 : 209-23.
[123] Beschefer, "Letter to the Provincial," *J.R.*, 62 : 201-3.
[124] *Memoir, ITUM.*, 1 : 86-88.
[125] "Memoir," Letter 40.

Although the ceremony of the feast of the dead may have been borrowed from the Huron by their Algonquian neighbors, the accounts just cited give one every reason to believe that it had a wide distribution around the upper Great Lakes and was adopted by practically every tribe.

Cadillac wrote of the feast as performed by the Ottawa at Mackinac:

This is the way in which they hold their feasts for the dead.

They erect a hut about one hundred and twenty feet long, with new bark which never has been used before. They set up a maypole at each end and another in the middle, taller than the others. These poles are oiled, greased, and painted; at the top of each is a prize, which belongs to the person who can first reach it and touch it with his hand. They then enter this new hut, in which there are several tiers, and bring the bones of their relatives, in small bags or wrapped very neatly in strips of bark. They set them out then, from one end to the other, and heap gifts upon them of all their finest and best possessions, and generally whatever they have got together in the previous three years. Meanwhile, the cooking pots are constantly on the fire, full of meat, for anyone to eat who likes. They make a continual noise, night and day, with drums or by striking the pots or the strips of bark with sticks. They go out from time to time and surround the hut, firing muskets and howling until the whole air quivers; then they re-enter, bedaubed with black. Finally, the same tumult goes on for three days and three nights; but, before the time has quite expired, they make presents to those who have been invited to the feast of all that belongs to the dead, that is, of all the booty with which the bones were covered. When this has been distributed they go out for the last time and surround the hut, uttering great howls; they fall upon it with heavy blows with sticks and poles, making a desperate clatter, and break all the bark in pieces. When that is done, the women are ready with faggots of fir-branches, and they put a layer of them on the ground from one end to the other of the place where the hut was. At the same time they kill a large number of dogs, which are to them what sheep are to us, and are valued by them more than any other animal, and make a feast of them. But, before eating, they set up two great poles and fasten a dog to the top of them, which they sacrifice to the sun and the moon, praying to them to have pity and to take care of the souls of their relations, to light them on their journeys, and to guide them to the dwelling place of their ancestors. This idea proves that they believe in the immortality of the soul. The feast being thus concluded, each takes the bones of his relations; they carry them all in their hands and take them to stony places, hollow, rugged, and unfrequented; they leave them there, and that is the end of the ceremony. After that, the dead whose feast they have held are never spoken of again in any way, and they remain in perpetual oblivion.[126]

RELIGION

The religion of the Algonquian tribes may properly be termed animism. The existence of supernatural power was recognized and thought to pervade all nature. Certain references seem to indicate a belief in a supreme being who was anthropomorphic. In other accounts the differentiation between the celestial-dwelling supreme being and the animate sun is difficult. A number of factors prevent one from obtaining a clear picture of the religion of the Indians of the contact period. Of these, three stand forth as very important. First, was the inability of the Indians to make the white visitors understand their belief in this universal power, which belief existed as a feeling rather than as a formalized creed. Second, the majority of the Indians may not have distinguished between objects as manifestations of universal force and as individual forces, particularly the Indians who were apt to serve as informants, for undoubtedly the best informed persons were the old men or shamans, who might be called the priests. These would have been the last persons in a community whose confidence would have been engaged by Europeans, especially the missionaries. Third, was the religious bias of the writers, most of whom were missionaries, who did not believe the Indians could possess a knowledge of a true god or that any re-

---

[126] Cadillac, MS "Relation on the Indians."

ligion other than their own could be anything except paganism.

Material relating expressly to the Ottawa is very limited. Thus the information that has come down to us is not very satisfactory in its scope or depth.

An idea of the belief of the Ottawa is to be found in the remarks of Ragueneau. He listed the creator of the earth, the creator of the sky, the north-dwelling genius who made winter, the genius of the waters, and seven others who controlled the seven winds. Even when they invoked the creator of the world, continued Ragueneau, they admitted that they did not know who he was; they had neither fear of his justice nor love for his goodness; all their invocations were unaccompanied by respect or religious worship, but were merely a custom without soul or vigor, which they had received from their ancestors.[127]

As an example of the lack of distinction between the belief in a multitude of divinities and the recognition of objects empowered by a larger force, there is the remark of Allouez that pieces of copper were kept as "so many divinities, or as presents which the gods dwelling beneath the water have given them, and on which their welfare is to depend."[128]

Allouez said that the Ottawa recognized no sovereign master of heaven and earth, but paid worship and veneration to spirits they called manitos. Whatever seemed to them helpful or hurtful was so considered. Beneficent manitos were the sun, the moon, the lakes, rivers, and woods. Malevolent ones were the adder, the dragon, cold, and storms.[129] At least some of these were anthropomorphic, for Allouez stated that the Ottawa believed the sun was a man and the moon his wife, that snow and ice were also a man.[130] He added that they believed that "the evil spirit is in adders, dragons, and other monsters," thus indicating a belief in the existence of

[127] *Relation* .... *1648, J.R.*, 33: 227.
[128] *Journal, J.R.*, 50: 265-67.
[129] *Ibid.*, p. 285.
[130] *Ibid.*, p. 289.

more general forces than would be understood from the term manitos.[131] Missibizi was called a fabulous animal by Allouez and acknowledged as a great genius by the Ottawa. It was never seen except in dreams and was offered sacrifices to obtain good sturgeon fishing.[132]

The name of this last genius was given by Rasles[133] as Michibichi, the manito of waters and fishes. Oussakita was the great manito of all the animals that move on the earth or fly in the air. He ruled these animals and therefore, when the Ottawa went on a hunt, they offered him tobacco, powder, lead, and dressed skins. These articles were fastened to the end of a pole, and, on raising it in the air, they said: "Oussakita, we give thee something to smoke, we offer thee something for killing animals. Deign to accept these presents, and do not permit the animals to escape our arrows; grant that we may kill the fattest ones, and in great number, so that our children may not lack clothing or food." Similar offerings were made to Michibichi, for both of these were manitos common to the whole tribe; but the presents for the latter were thrown in the water.

Writing about 1719, Pachot said that the Indians made sacrifices to the spirits of the lakes and principally to Bichi Bichy, whom they believed to be the master of these spirits and the god of the waters. They represented him by the figure of a sea tiger, on which they put fins. They believed him to be in the bottom of the lakes and that it was by his breath that he excited the tempests. The other spirits of the lakes only acted for him. They threw dogs, with their jaws and legs tied, into the water as a gift for him. The Saulteurs, Ottawa, and Missisauga believed the same, as did all the nations of the lakes.[134]

This god of the waters was called Michipissy, according

---

[131] *Ibid.*

[132] *Ibid.*

[133] "Letter . . . . to His Brother," *J.R.*, 67: 159-61.

[134] "Les Sioux," AC., C 11 A, 122.

to Perrot, who said he was the Great Panther. The Indians related to him that this god dwelt in a very deep cave and that he had a large tail; when he went to drink, the waving of his tail stirred up high winds, the sharp switches of it roused great tempests. Offerings and invocations were made to him before undertaking voyages in order to obtain fair weather. Before very long voyages, dogs and dressed skins were also offered to the sun or the lake for the same purpose. In winter journeys over the ice a spirit called Mateomek was invoked.[135]

But these spirits, Michipissy and Mateomek, apparently were considered minor ones by Perrot, for elsewhere he listed the divinities of the Indians as follows:

The savages—I mean those who are not converted [to Christianity]—recognize as principal divinities only the Great Hare, the sun, and the devils. They oftenest invoke the Great Hare, because they revere and adore him as the creator of the world; they reverence the sun as the author of light; but if they place the devils among their divinities, and invoke them, it is because they are afraid of them, and in the invocations which they make to the devils they entreat them for [the means of] life. Those among the savages whom the French call "jugglers" talk with the demon, whom they consult for [success in] war and hunting.

They have also many other divinities, to whom they pray, and whom they recognize as such, in the air, on the land, and within the earth. Those of the air are the thunder, the lightning, and in general whatever they see in the air that they cannot understand—as the moon, eclipses, and extraordinary whirlwinds. Those which are upon the land comprise all creatures that are malign and noxious—especially serpents, panthers, and other animals, and birds like griffins; they also include in this class such creatures as have, according to their kind, unusual beauty or deformity. Lastly, those that are within the earth, [especially] the bears, who pass the winter without eating, and are nourished only by the substance which they obtain from their own navels,

[135] *Memoir, ITUM.,* 1: 59-62.

by sucking; the savages pay the same regard to all the animals that dwell in caves, or in holes in the ground, and invoke these whenever they have, while asleep, dreamed of any of these creatures.[136]

Some of the spirits listed as other divinities were most probably personal manitos, for as Rasles reported, besides the common manitos, each person had his own special one, which was a bear, a beaver, a bustard, or some similar animal. According to Rasles, an Ottawa wishing to acquire a manito usually took the first animal that appeared to him during sleep. Afterward, he killed an animal of this kind, put its skin or its feathers in the most conspicuous part of his cabin and made a feast in its honor, during which he addressed it in most respectful terms. From that time on it was recognized as his manito, and he carried its skin to war, to the hunt, and on journeys, believing that it would preserve him from every danger and cause all his undertakings to succeed.[137]

Referring either to the Chippewa or the Ottawa or both, Dablon wrote that one of the most detestable of all their customs was the creating of a personal divinity. This was undertaken at the age of ten or twelve years. The child was given instructions by his father and then made to fast for several days in order that something divine might appear to him in his sleep. In the morning after the fast, the father questioned him secretly on what had happened during the night. If nothing had appeared to him, the fast had to be recommenced; but usually the sun, the thunder, or something else he had been often talked to about appeared to him. A representation of this manito was tattooed on his skin. At first, Dablon said, the Jesuits thought that it was only the boys that underwent these fasts, but later they learned that little girls also were made to fast for the same purpose, and that no persons were more attached to the custom and more opposed to conversion than the old women.[138] He did not state

---

[136] *Memoir, ITUM.*, 1: 48-49.
[137] "Letter . . . . to His Brother," *J.R.*, 67: 161.
[138] "Letter to François le Mercier," *Relation* . . . . *1670, J.R.*, 54: 139-43.

whether or not the girls were also tattooed with the mark of their manito.[139]

The Great Hare of Perrot seems to be the same as the Oussakita of Rasles. About 1719 Pachot wrote that the Indians worshiped only the sun, the earth, and the thunder, because these were things attached to the superior being whom they called "the master of life." The Iroquois named him Raouennyo, "the master or he who holds all"; the Sioux called him Histontenga, "the master of life"; the Illinois called him Kitchesmanetoa, "the spirit master of life"; the Ottawa called him by the same name as did the Illinois, except for a little difference in pronunciation. They had confidence in their manitos only because they believed that these spirits gave them ideas which came from the superior being, and that it was he who showed them in their dreams the animals which they took for their manitos, because he wished to use these animals to lead them.[140]

Lahontan[141] also reported that the Ottawa gave the name of Genius or Spirit to all that surpassed their understanding. Some of these, he said, were good spirits and others were bad. Among the former were Michibichi, a solar quadrant, an alarm watch, and an infinity of other things that were beyond their comprehension. Bad spirits were thunder, hail falling on their corn, a great storm, and in fact everything that tended to their prejudice and proceeded from a cause of which they were ignorant. Bad or evil spirits were called Matchi Manitos (Matchi being the word for evil and manito for spirit). By this, he said, was not meant the devil, but something closer in significance to fate or unfavorable destiny.

The opposite term Kitchi Manito apparently was applied to only one good spirit, the Great Spirit. Lahontan remarked that living creatures were never sacrificed to the Kitchi Manito and then gave the following description of how sacrifices were carried out:

[139] For another account of the process of acquiring manitos see Raudot, "Memoir," Letter 30.

[140] "Les Scioux," AC., C 11 A, 122.

[141] *Voyages*, 2 : 446-48.

The Air must be Clear and Serene, the Weather Fair and Calm; and then every one brings his Offering and laies it upon the Wood-Pile: When the Sun mounts higher the Children make a Ring round the Pile, with pieces of Bark Lighted, in order to set it on Fire; and the Warriours Dance and Sing round 'em till the whole is Burnt and Consumed, while the Old Men make their Harangues address'd to the *Kitchi Manitou,* and present him from time to time with Pipes of Tobacco Lighted at the Sun. These Dances, Songs and Harangues last till Sun set, only they allow themselves some intervals of Rest, in which they sit down and Smoak at their Ease.

It remains only (before I make an end of this *Chapter*) to repeat the very Words of their Harangues pronounc'd by the Old Fellows, and of the Songs sung by the Warriors: "Great Spirit, Master of our Lives: Great Spirit, Master of all Things both Visible and Invisible: Great Spirit, Master of other Spirits, whether good or Evil; command the Good Spirits to favour thy Children, the *Outaouas, &c.* Command the Evil Spirits to keep at a distance from 'em. O Great Spirit, keep up the Strength and Courage of our Warriors, that they may be able to stem the fury of our Enemies: Preserve the Old Persons, whose Bodies are not quite wasted, that they may give Counsel to the Young. Preserve our Children, enlarge their Number, deliver 'em from Evil Spirits, to the end that in our old Age they may prove our Support and Comfort; preserve our Harvest and our Beasts, if thou mean'st that we should not die for Hunger: Take care of our Villages, and guard our Huntsmen in their Hunting Adventures. Deliver us from all Fatal Surprizes, when thou ceasest to vouchsafe us the Light of the Sun, which speaks thy Grandeur and Power. Acquaint us by the Spirit of Dreams, with what thy Pleasure requires of us, or prohibits us to do. When it pleases thee to put a Period to our Lives, send us to the great Countrey of Souls, where we may meet with those of our Fathers, our Mothers, our Wives, our Children, and our other Relations. O Great Spirit, Great Spirit, hear the Voice of the Nation, give ear to all the Children, and remember them at all times."

As for the Songs which the Warriors sing till Sun set, they are to this purpose: "Take heart, the Great Spirit vouchsafes such a Glorious Sun; Cheer up my Brethren: How great are his Works! How fine is the Day! this Great Spirit is all Goodness;

'tis he that sets all the Springs in motion; he ruleth over all: He is pleas'd to hear us; Let us cheer up my Brethren, we shall subdue our Enemies: Our Fields shall bear Corn; our Hunting shall succeed well; we shall all of us keep our Health; the Old Persons shall rejoice, the Children shall increase, and the Nation shall prosper. But now the Great Spirit leaves us, his Sun withdraws, he has seen the *Outaouas, &*. 'Tis done, ay, 'tis done; the Great Spirit is satisfied; my Brethren let us pluck up a good heart."

We must remark, that the Women likewise make Addresses to him, and that commonly when the Sun rises; upon which Occasion they present and hold up their Children to that Luminary. When the Sun is almost down, the Warriors march out of the Village, to dance the Dance of the Great Spirit. But after all, there is no Day or Time fix'd for these Sacrifices, no more than for the Particular Dances.[142]

The Ottawa invoked the divinities listed by Allouez whenever they went out hunting, fishing, to war, or on a journey; offering them sacrifices, with ceremonies which he termed appropriate only for sacrificial priests. It is apparent in the following excerpt from Allouez' *Journal* that the men conducting such ceremonies were of a different status than the medicine men usually called "jugglers" by the French:

One of the leading old men of the Village discharges the function of Priest, beginning with a carefully-prepared harangue addressed to the Sun—if the eat-all feast, which bears a certain resemblance to a holocaust, is held in its honor. He declares in a loud voice that he pays his thanks to that Luminary for having lighted him so that he could successfully kill some animal or other,—praying and exhorting it by this feast to continue its kind care of his family. During this invocation, all the Guests eat, even to the last morsel; after which a man appointed for the purpose takes a cake of tobacco, breaks it in two, and throws it into the fire. Every one cries aloud while the tobacco burns and the smoke rises aloft; and with these outcries the whole sacrifice ends.[143]

[142] *Ibid.*, pp. 448-50.
[143] *Journal, J.R.*, 50: 285-87.

Besides these public sacrifices, Allouez continued, the Ottawa had some which were private and domestic, for often in their cabins they threw tobacco into the fire, with a kind of superficial offering to their false gods.[144]

Belief in an afterworld and consequently in immortality of souls is reported by Perrot, Radisson, and Cadillac as general in the Great Lakes region:

All the savages who are not converted believe that the soul is immortal; but they maintain that when it is separated from the body it goes to a beautiful and fertile land, where the climate is neither cold nor hot, but agreeably temperate. They say that that land abounds with animals and birds of every kind, and that the hunters while going through it are never in danger of hunger, having only to choose what animals they will attack, to obtain food. They tell us that this beautiful country is very far away, beyond this earth; and it is for this reason that they place on the scaffolds or in the graves of the dead, at their funerals, provisions and weapons, believing that the souls will find again in the other world, for their use, and especially in the voyage which they must make thither, whatever shall be given to them in this world.

They believe, furthermore, that as soon as the soul has left the body it enters this charming country, and that, after having traveled many days, it encounters on its route a very rapid river, over which there is only a slender tree-trunk by way of bridge; and that in passing over this it bends so much that the soul is in danger of being swept away by the flood of waters. They assert that if unfortunately this mishap occurs, the soul will be drowned; but that all these perils are escaped when once the souls have reached the country of the dead. They believe also that the souls of young people, of either sex, have nothing to fear, because they are so vigorous; but it is not the same with those of the old people and the infants who have no assistance from other souls in this dangerous crossing, and it is this which very often causes them to perish.

They relate to us, moreover, that this same river abounds with fish, more in number than can be imagined. There are sturgeons and other kinds of fish in great numbers, which the souls kill with blows of their hatchets and clubs, so that they can roast

[144] *Ibid.*, p. 287.

these fish while on their journey, for they no longer find therein any game. After they have traveled a long time, in front of them appears a very steep mountain, which closes their path and compels them to seek another; but they do not find any way open, and it is only after experiencing great suffering that they finally arrive at this fearful passage. There two pestles of prodigious size, which in turn rise and fall without ceasing, form an obstacle most difficult to overcome; for death is absolutely inevitable if while making the passage one is unfortunately caught under [them]—I mean while one of the two pestles is falling. But the souls are very careful in watching for that fortunate moment when they can clear a passage so dangerous; yet many fail in it, especially those of old persons and little children, who are less vigorous and move through it more slowly.

When the souls have once escaped from this peril, they enter a delightful country, in which excellent fruits are found in abundance; and the ground seems to be covered with all kinds of flowers, the odor of which is so admirable that it delights their hearts and charms their imaginations. The short remaining distance which they must traverse before arriving in the place where the sound of the drum and the gourds—marking time for [the steps of] the dead, to give them pleasure—falls agreeably on their ears, urges them on to hasten directly thither with great eagerness. The nearer they approach it, always the louder becomes this sound; and the joy which the dancers express by their continual exclamations serves to delight the souls still more. When they are very near the place where the ball is held, part of the dead men separate from the others in order to meet the newcomers, and assure them of the great pleasure which their arrival generally gives to the entire assembly. The souls are conducted into the place where the dance is held, and are cordially received by all who are there; and they find there innumerable viands, of all flavors, everything of the most delicious taste, and prepared in the best manner. It is for them to choose whatever pleases them, and to satisfy their appetites; and when they have finished eating they go to mingle with the others—to dance and make merry forever, without being any longer subject to sorrow, anxiety, or infirmities, or to any of the vicissitudes of mortal life.[145]

[145] Perrot, *Memoir, ITUM.*, 1: 89-91.

Radisson in his quaint orthography wrote thus:

Before I goe further I have a mind to let you know the fabulous beleafe of these poore People, that you may see their ignorance concerning ye soul's immortality, being separated from the body. The kindred and the friends of the deceased give notice to ye others, who gather together and cry for ye dead, which gives warning to ye young men to take ye armes to give some assistance and consolation to ye deceased. Presently the corps is covered with white skins very well tyed. Afterwards all the kindred come to ye cottage of ye deceased and begin to mourn and lament. After they are weary of making such musick the husbands or Friends of the deceased send their wives for gifts to pacifie a little ye Widdow and to dry her tears. Those guifts are of skins and of what they can get, for at such a ceremony they are very liberall. As soon as that is done and ye night comes, all the young men are desired to come and doe what they will to have done to them. So that when darknesse has covered the whole face of the Earth they come all singing with staves in their hands for their armes, and after they are set round ye cabbin, begin to knock and make such a noise that one would thinke they have a mind to tear all in peeces, and that they are possessed of some Devills. All this is done to expell and frighten ye soule out of that poor and miserable body that she might not trouble his carcase nor his bones, and to make it depart the sooner to goe and see their Ancestors, and to take possession of their immortall glory, which cannot be obtained but a fortnight towards ye setting of ye sun. The first step that she makes is of seven dayes, to begin her course, but there are many difficulties, ffor it is through a very thick wood full of thorns, of stones and flints, which [brings] great trouble to that poor soule. At last having overcome all those dangers and toyles she comes to a River of about a Quarter of a mile broad where there is a bridge made onely of one planke, being supported by a beame pointed at one end, which is ye reason that planke rises and falls perpetually, having not any rest nor stay, and when the soule comes near ye side of that river, she meets with a man of extraordinary stature, who is very leane and holds a dagger of very hard wood and very keen in his hands, and speakes these words when he sees the petitioning soule come near: *Pale, pale,* which signifies, Goe, goe;

and at every word ye bridge ballances, and rises his knife, and ye traveller offering himselfe, receives a blow by which he is cut in two, and each halfe is found upon that moving, and according as he had lived they stay upon it; that is, if his body was valiant the passage was soon made free to him, for ye two halfes come together and joyn themselves again. So passe to ye other side where she finds a bladder of bear's grease to grease herselfe and refresh herselfe for that which she is to do, which being done she finds a wood somewhat cleerer and a streight road that she must goe, and for 5 dayes neither goe to ye right nor to ye left hand, where at last being arrived she finds a very great and cleer fire, though which she must resolve to passe. That fire is kindled by the young men that dyed since ye beginning of ye world to know whether those that come have loved ye woman or have been good huntsmen; and if that soule has not had any of those rare Vertues she burnes and broiles the sole of her feet by going through the fire; but quite contrary if she has had them qualityes, she passes through without burning her selfe in ye least, and from that so hot place she finds grease and paint of all sorts of colour with which she daubs and makes herselfe beautifull to come to that place so wished for. But she has not yet all done, nor made an end of her voyage; being so dress'd she continues her course still towards ye same pole for ye space of two days in a very cleer wood, and where there is very high and tall trees of which most be oakes, which is the reason that there is great store of bears. All along that way they do nothing else but see their enemies layd all alone the ground, that sing their fatall song for having been vanquished in this world and also in ye other, not daring to be so bold as to kill one of those animalls, and feed onely upon ye down of these beasts. Being arrived, if I may say, at ye doore of that imaginarie paradise, they find a company of their ancestors long since deceased, by whom they are received with a great deale of ceremony, and are brought by so venerable a company within halfe a daye's journey of ye place of ye meeting, and all along ye rest of the way they discourse of things of this world that are passd; for you must know they travell halfe a day without speaking one word, but keepe a very deep silence, for, said they, it is like ye Goslings to confound one another with words. As soon as they are arrived they must have a time to come to themselves, to think well upon what they are to speak without any precipitation, but with Judgement, so that they are come where all manner of company with drumms & dryd bumpkins, full of stones and other such instruments. The elders that have brought her there cover her with a very large white skin, and colour her leggs with vermillion and her feet likewise, and so she is received amongst ye Predestinates. There is a deep silence made as soon as she is come in, and then one of the elders makes a long speech to encourage ye young people to go a hunting to kill some meat to make a feast for entertainment of ye soul of their countryman, which is put in execution with a great deal of diligence and haste, and while the meat is boyling or roasting, and that there is great preparations made for ye feast, the young maidens set out themselves with the richest Jewells and present ye beesome to ye new comer. A little while after ye kettles are filled, there is feasting every where, comedies acted, and whatsoever is rare is there to be seene; there is dancing every where. Now remaines nothing but to provide that poor soule of a companion, which she does presently, for she has ye choice of very beautiful women, and may take as many as she pleases, which makes her felicity immortall.[146]

The remarks of Cadillac on this subject are much briefer than those of Perrot and Radisson but touch on some points neglected by them:

Their opinion is that the souls, when separated from the body, loiter and remain in the village, wandering to and fro, in and around their huts, by a natural attraction, on account of the affection they feel for their relations and friends. They also say that they frighten little children, young people, and themselves, especially at night. They imagine that the great confused noise and the hammering and breaking of the bark [at the Feast of the Dead] vex the souls which have assembled in the hut and make them resolve and determine to go and join the souls of their fathers. They believe that it is in a very fine country, where life is most pleasant, and, because in their own land there are quantities of strawberries and raspberries, they imagine that in the countries where the souls dwell these fruits are as large as a

[146] Radisson, *Voyages*, pp. 236-40.

man's hand. They think this region is toward the east, that the air is mild and temperate, that there is no rain, snow, nor wind there, no rocks nor mountains, and all the paths are paved with robes of otter, marten, and beaver; in a word, that it is a land of pleasure, where one never has to bear hunger or thirst, and all are equally happy. They absolutely deny the existence of places where souls are tortured and reject the opinion of the resurrection of the body.[147]

Most accounts that mention the location of the village of souls place it in the direction of the setting sun, as Radisson did. The easterly direction given by Cadillac is very unusual. I do not think, however, that he merely made a slip here, for in another place in his relation he said the same thing.

Mythology

The confusion of the names of the being called variously, Michabou, Michipissy, the Great Hare, and the Great Panther is probably best accounted for by the supposition that they were all aspects of the same mythological being now known as Nanabozho. This character was called a god by the French and probably was so regarded by the Indians, as he is credited in some myths with the creation of the world and of man. In other myths he is a tribal hero and trickster. Undoubtedly, the Indians were not all equally informed as to the status of Nanabozho and his relation to the tribal organization. Since the character of Nanabozho was not consistent, the accounts of him by the French would almost necessarily be contradictory.

This being, according to Rasles, was a man of prodigious height, so tall that he spread nets in water ninety-five feet deep and the water scarcely came to his armpits. During the deluge, Nanabozho sent out the beaver and then the otter to discover land; the latter succeeded and Nanabozho proceeded to a place in the lake where the small island was located. Walking around it in the water, Nanabozho caused

[147] MS "Relation on the Indians."

the island to become extraordinarily large. Hence the creation of the world is credited to him. After finishing this work he flew away to the sky, his usual dwelling place, leaving directions that his descendants' bodies should be burned and their ashes scattered that they might more easily rise to the sky. He warned them that failure to observe this would result in the snow covering the earth and the lakes and rivers remaining frozen, whereby, not being able to catch fish, they would all die.[148]

Mackinac Island was accounted the terrestrial dwelling place of Nanabozho, and the place where he invented nets for fishing, after he had attentively considered the spider working on her web for catching flies. Lake Superior was a pond made by beavers, with a double dam in the St. Mary's River. In ascending the river, Nanabozho completely destroyed the lower dam, but merely stepped on the second to tread it down, causing the great falls and whirlpools there now. The beavers were chased around in Lake Superior by this god, so they decided to change their location. They withdrew to Lake Nipigon and then to Hudson's Bay, with the intention of crossing over to France; but finding the water bitter, lost heart, and spread throughout the rivers and lakes of the entire country. That is why there were no beavers in France and the French had to come to this country to get them.[149]

The legend regarding Mackinac as related by La Potherie is slightly different: the abode of Nanabozho was on the mainland, and he left some large spirits on the island who gave it its name, Michilimackinac, *micha* meaning "great" and the spirits being called *Imakinagos*. These spirits still lived under this island and were invoked whenever the Indians made a feast of fish, thanking them for their liberality, entreating them to take care always of their families, and asking them to keep their nets from harm and to preserve their

[148] Rasles, "Letter . . . . to His Brother," *J.R.*, 67: 153-55.
[149] Allouez, *Relation . . . . 1670*, *J.R.*, 54: 201-3.

canoes from surging waves. All who were present at this feast uttered together a long drawn "Ho!"[150]

According to Raudot, Nanabozho not only taught his people to fish while he was living at Mackinac, but he was born there himself. The people were formed from the foam of the lake by the heat of the sun.[151]

This is doubtless another version of the story related by Rasles to account for the origin of the second family of the Ottawas. These maintained that they had sprung from Namepich—that is to say, from the carp. They said that the carp deposited its eggs upon the bank of a river, and the sun shed its rays upon them, and there was formed a woman from whom they were descended.[152]

More detailed versions of the legends relating to the creation of the world, the creation of man, and the beginning of wars, were recounted by Perrot:

They believe that before the earth was created there was nothing but water; that upon this vast extent of water floated a great wooden raft, upon which were all the animals, of various kinds, which exist on earth; and the chief of these, they say, was the Great Hare. He looked about for some spot of solid ground where they could land; but as nothing could be seen on the water save swans and other river birds, he began to be discouraged. He saw no other hope than to induce the beaver to dive, in order to bring up a little soil from the bottom of the water; and he assured the beaver, in the name of all the animals, that if he returned with even one grain of soil, he would produce from it land sufficiently spacious to contain and feed all of them. But the beaver tried to excuse himself from this undertaking, giving as his reason that he had already dived in the neighborhood of the raft without finding there any indication of a bottom. Nevertheless, he was so urgently pressed to attempt again this great enterprise that he took the risk of it and dived. He remained so long without coming to the surface that those who had entreated him to go believed that he was drowned; but finally he was seen appearing,

[150] *History, ITUM.*, 1: 283-88.
[151] "Memoir," Letter 52.
[152] "Letter . . . . to His Brother," *J.R.*, 67: 157.

almost dead, and motionless. Then all the other animals, seeing that he was in no condition to climb upon the raft, immediately exerted themselves to drag him up on it; and after they had carefully examined his claws and tail they found nothing thereon.

Their slight remaining hope of being able to save their lives induced them to address the Otter, and entreat him to make another effort to search for a little soil at the bottom of the water. They represented to him that he would go down quite as much for his own welfare as for theirs; the otter yielded to their just expostulations, and plunged into the water. He remained at the bottom longer than the beaver had done and returned to them in the same condition as the latter, and with as little result.

The impossibility of finding a dwelling-place where they could maintain themselves left them nothing more to hope for; then the muskrat proposed that, if they wished, he should go to try to find a bottom, and said that he also believed that he could bring up some sand from it. The animals did not depend much on this undertaking, since the beaver and the otter, who were far stronger than he, had not been able to carry it out; however, they encouraged him to go, and even promised that he should be ruler over the whole country if he succeeded in accomplishing his plan. The muskrat then jumped into the water, and boldly dived; and, after he had remained there nearly twenty-four hours he made his appearance at the edge of the raft, his belly uppermost, motionless, and his four feet tightly clenched. The other animals took hold of him, and carefully drew him up on the raft. They unclosed one of his paws, then a second, then a third, and finally the fourth one, in which there was between the claws a little grain of sand.

The Great Hare, who had promised to form a broad and spacious land, took this grain of sand, and let it fall upon the raft, when it began to increase; then he took a part of it, and scattered this about, which caused the mass of soil to grow larger and larger. When it had reached the size of a mountain, he started to walk around it, and it steadily increased in size to the extent of his path. As soon as he thought it was large enough he ordered the fox to go to inspect his work, with power to enlarge it still more; and the latter obeyed. The fox, when he had ascertained that it was sufficiently extensive for him to secure easily his own prey, returned to the Great Hare to inform him that the land was able to contain and support all the animals. At this report, the Great Hare made a tour throughout his creation and found that it was incomplete. Since then, he has not been willing to trust any of the other animals, and continues always to increase what he has made, by moving without cessation around the earth. This idea causes the savages to say, when they hear loud noises in the hollows of the mountains, that the Great Hare is still enlarging the earth; they pay honors to him, and regard him as the deity who created it. Such is the information which those peoples give us regarding the creation of the world, which they believe to be always borne upon the raft. As for the sea and the firmament, they assert that these have existed for all time.[153]

After the creation of the earth, all the other animals withdrew into the places which each kind found most suitable for obtaining therein their pasture or their prey. When the first ones died, the Great Hare caused the birth of men from their corpses, as also from those of the fishes which were found along the shores of the rivers which he had formed in creating the land. Accordingly, some of the savages derive their origin from a bear, others from a moose, and others similarly from various kinds of animals; and before they had intercourse with the Europeans they firmly believed this, persuaded that they had their being from those kinds of creatures whose origin was as above explained. Even today that notion passes among them for undoubted truth, and if there are any of them at this time who are weaned from believing this dream, it has been only by dint of laughing at them for so ridiculous a belief. You will hear them say that their villages each bear the name of the animal which has given its people their being—as that of the crane, or the bear or of other animals. They imagine that they were created by other divinities than those which we recognize, because we have many inventions which they do not possess, as the art of writing, shooting with a gun, making gunpowder, muskets, and other things which are used by [civilized] mankind.

Those first men who formed the human race, being scattered in different parts of the land, found out that they had minds. They beheld here and there buffaloes, elks, and deer, all kinds

[153] Perrot, *Memoir*, *ITUM.*, 1: 31-36.

of birds and animals, and many rivers abounding in fish. These first men, I say, whom hunger had weakened, inspired by the Great Hare with an intuitive idea, broke off a branch from a small tree, made a cord with the fibers of the nettle, scraped the bark from a piece of a bough with a sharp stone, and armed its end with another sharp stone, to serve them as an arrow; and thus they formed a bow [and arrows] with which they killed small birds. After that, they made viretons, in order to attack the large beasts; they skinned these, and tried to eat the flesh. But as they found only the fat savory, they tried to make fire, in order to cook their meat; and, trying to get it, they took for that purpose hard wood, but without success; and [finally] they used softer wood, which yielded them fire. The skins of the animals served for their covering. As hunting is not practicable in the winter on account of the deep snows, they invented a sort of racket, in order to walk on this with more ease; and they constructed canoes, in order to enable them to cross the rivers.

They relate also that these men, formed as I have told, while hunting found the footprints of an enormously tall man, followed by another that was smaller. They went on into his territory, following up this trail very heedfully, and saw in the distance a large cabin; when they reached it, they were astonished at seeing there the feet and legs of a man so tall that they could not descry his head; that inspired terror in them, and constrained them to retreat. This great collossus, having wakened, cast his eyes on a freshly made track, and this induced him to step toward it; he immediately saw the man who had discovered him, whom fear had driven to hide himself in a thicket, where he was trembling with dread. The giant said to him, "My son, why are thou afraid? Reassure thyself; I am the Great Hare, he who has caused thee and many others to be born from the dead bodies of various animals. Now I will give thee a companion." Here are the words that he used in giving the man a wife: "Thou, Man," said he, "shall hunt, and make canoes, and do all things that a man must do; and thou, woman, shall do the cooking for thy husband, make his shoes, dress the skins of animals, sew, and perform all the tasks that are proper for a woman." Such is the belief of these peoples in regard to the creation of man; it is based only upon the most ridiculous and extravagant notions—to which, however, they give credence as if they were incontestable truths, although shame hinders them from making these stories known.[154]

Each of these men inhabited a region that belonged to him; and there they lived with their wives, and gradually multiplied. They lived in peace, until they became very numerous; having, then, multiplied in the course of time, they separated from one another, in order to live in greater comfort. They became, in consequence of this expansion, neighbors to peoples who were unknown to them, and whose language they did not understand; but the Great Hare had given to each of them a different dialect when he drew them forth from the bodies of animals. Some of them continued to live in peace, but the others began to wage war. Those who were weaker abandoned their own lands, in order to escape from the fury of their enemies; and they retreated to more distant places, where they found tribes whom they must again resist. Some devoted themselves to the cultivation of the land and produced their food—Indian corn, beans, and squashes. Those who lived by hunting were more skilful, and considered as more warlike by the others, who greatly feared and dreaded the hunters. However, neither class could dispense with the other, on account of the necessities of life [which each produced]. It was this which caused them to live much longer in peace; for the hunter obtained his grain from the tiller of the soil, and the latter procured his meat from the hunter. But eventually the young men, through a certain arrogance that is native to all the savages, and no longer recognizing any chief, committed murders by stealth, and incited wars against their allies, who were obliged to defend themselves.[155]

Shamans and Medical Practices

Notices of the activities of shamans among the Ottawa are very limited. There are occasional references to their juggling to learn the future, but no details are given. The following excerpt from Allouez' *Journal* of his trip to the country of the Ottawa is the only account of medical practice definitely attributable to the Ottawa:

[154] *Ibid.*, pp. 37-40.
[155] *Ibid.*, pp. 41-42.

Let us say something about the art of Medicine in vogue in this country. Their science consists in ascertaining the cause of the ailment, and applying the remedies.

They deem the most common cause of illness to come from failure to give a feast after some successful fishing or hunting excursion; for then the Sun, who takes pleasure in feasts, is angry with the one who has been delinquent in his duty, and makes him ill.

Besides this general cause of sickness, there are special ones, in the shape of certain little spirits, malevolent in their nature, who thrust themselves of their own accord, or are sent by some enemy, into the parts of the body that are most diseased. Thus, when any one has an aching head, or arm, or stomach, they say that a Manitou has entered this part of the body, and will not cease its torments until it has been drawn or driven out.

The most common remedy, accordingly, is to summon the Juggler, who comes attended by some old men, with whom he holds a sort of consultation on the patient's ailment. After this, he falls upon the diseased part, applies his mouth to it, and, by sucking, pretends to extract something from it, as a little stone, or a bit of string, or something else, which he has concealed in his mouth beforehand, and which he displays, saying: "There is the Manitou; now thou art cured, and it only remains to give a feast."

The Devil, bent on tormenting those poor blinded creatures even in this world, has suggested to them another remedy, in which they place great confidence. It consists in grasping the patient under the arms, and making him walk barefoot over the live embers in the cabin; or, if he is so ill that he cannot walk, he is carried by four or five persons and made to pass slowly over all fires, a treatment which often results in this, that the greater suffering thereby produced cures, or induces unconsciousness of, the lesser pain which they strive to cure.

After all, the commonest remedy, as it is the most profitable for the Physician, is the holding of a feast to the Sun, which is done in the belief that this luminary, which takes pleasure in liberal actions, being appeased by a magnificent repast, will regard the patient with favor, and restore him to health.[156]

[156] Allouez, *Journal*, *J.R.*, 50: 291-95. Compare the fire remedy with the Ononhwaroia ceremony of the Huron.

The general account of Cadillac gives details of the actions of shamans that are usually omitted:

All the tribes have their doctors, surgeons, and apothecaries, who are called jugglers. When, therefore, anyone is ill, they send for all three of them, and the doctor studies the illness. After juggling—that is to say, musing—for a long time they generally order several dogs to be killed, because this is their most delicious meat, and, to cloak the quackery, they insist that two should be white, two black, and two of some other color; and they offer up one or two of them as a sacrifice to the sun or the moon, that pity may be taken on the sick person. This order is only given after prolonged contemplation, for the jugglers or charlatans never attribute the cause of the sickness to the ailments or accidents which come upon the human body, but pretend that a spell has been cast upon the sick person by the spite and malignity of some enemy. Now they give out that it is a guardian spirit, that is, the god whom they have invented by their imagination, who reveals to them and teaches them how and by what means the poison and spell have been cast upon the man who is sick. The doctor therefore completes his order by indicating to the apothecary the simples and roots or animals necessary for compounding and preparing the antidotes or beverages to expel the poisons at work in the body and mind of the patient. The apothecary carries out the order of the doctor and seeks the simples or animals specified, but both of them play their parts very well, for these things, they say, can never be found without great difficulty. The surgeon is the greatest charlatan of all, and the most remarkable juggler. The part he plays is certainly humble to all appearance, and those who watch his performance can only imagine that he is possessed by a demon while he is doing his juggling. Those who stand around beat drums and strike on cooking pots and strips of bark with small sticks, and this continues as long as the illness lasts, for the entertainment of the sick man. It is inconceivable that such a great noise should not drive these poor people mad. However, at these intervals the surgeon dances, chants, makes hideous grimaces, rolls his eyes and casts them down, turns up his nose, thrusts forward his jaws and dislocates the lower jaw; his neck now stretches and now shortens; his lungs expand and his stomach swells; his fingers, hands, and arms are extended and withdrawn; he spits blood from his mouth and makes it issue from his nose and ears, and he tears and pierces his skin; and, as I have already said, all these things and many others are done chanting and dancing. Finally, after all these strange proceedings, he discovers the spot where the man is bewitched; thus, if he sees that the sick man has a difficulty in spitting or breathing, he makes him believe that the spell which has been cast upon him consists of a bone which has been placed across his throat. He approaches the patient, with many grimaces; he seizes him by the throat with his teeth, but quite softly, pretending to look for the bone, and he always finds it, because he has it in his mouth. So, after making much fuss about the search, he jumps up suddenly, uttering a joyful cry, to show that the spell is removed, and he spits out the bone on something. Then everyone present marvels at his art and cleverness, and the sick man begins to think he is healed. In a word, the whole secret consists in finding out the part which is affected, which is made known to him by the sufferer; and then he says there is a bone or the screw of a musket, a thorn, or a fishbone or some hair, or something of the kind in the part affected. If, however, the sick man does not get well and his indisposition continues increasing, the surgeon also continues to juggle and keeps picking out some bewitched piece of something; while the apothecary, on his side, works with his medicines. When the sick man dies they withdraw, like our physicians, saying that nothing could have saved him. Meanwhile, whichever way it turns out, these quacks ruin and impoverish the hut or family of the sick person; for, if he recovers, he gives them everything he possesses, and the whole family does likewise; and if he dies, they make them a very large present notwithstanding. Men of this sort are respected and valued among all the tribes. They are also clever enough to distinguish themselves from the rest by their manners and actions, which are outwardly better regulated and more restrained; their gait is also slower and steadier than that of the others. When they go anywhere, or leave their huts, they wear round their necks or on the shoulder or arm the skin of an otter or some other animal, prettily decorated; and it is by this sign that their doctors are known, just as one knows canons by the almuce. That shows that, all over the world, some men gull others, and that above all there are cheats and charlatans in the school of Galen and Hippocrates.

Nevertheless, one thing is quite certain, namely that the Indians are most skillful and very experienced in healing all kinds of sores and wounds, of whatever kind they may be, by means of simples, of which they have an excellent knowledge. They also have remedies for burns, frostbite, and the stings and bites of snakes and other venomous animals; but the best of it is that they stop and drive off the mischief as quickly as it came. They are very good anatomists; and so, when they have an arm or any bone broken, they treat it very cleverly and with great skill and dexterity, and experience shows that they can cure a wounded man in a week better than our surgeons can in a month, perhaps because the former have better remedies and are more straight-forward, while the others are actuated by the desire to turn their talent to their own profit. As to venereal diseases, they laugh at them, for those who are attacked recover in ten or twelve days at the furthest, by taking certain tasteless powders, which they swallow in hot water, and for this reason one never sees a woman among them who has syphilis; but they are malicious enough to refuse to teach the French their secrets, though they do not refuse them their remedies in case of need.[157]

It is interesting to note the change wrought in the procedure of shamans by the introduction of European articles, as indicated by the comments of Noyan:

Generally all savages drink to intoxicate themselves; and when they have been drinking, these tribes, who are so orderly and peaceable, delight in nothing but vengeance and murder. Yet how deprive them of it entirely? It has become the basis of their religion! These superstitious men can no longer recover from their diseases, unless they make festivals with brandy; their sorcerers or jugglers now know no other remedy. They must have it, at whatever cost; and it appears to me that it will be most difficult to forbid them the use of it altogether.[158]

[157] Cadillac, MS "Relation on the Indians."
[158] Pierre Noyan, "Memorandum Concerning the Present Condition of Canada, 1730," *MPH.*, 34: 75.

POTAWATOMI

LOCATION OF THE TRIBE

THE first clue of the existence and whereabouts of the Potawatomi is found in Champlain's statement that in 1615 the Ottawa and Neutrals were at war with the Asistagueroüon or "fire-people." The Ottawa were located two days' journey north of the Neutrals or on the shore of Georgian Bay. Ten days' journey or two hundred leagues westward from the Ottawa, beyond the Fresh-water Sea (Lake Huron), were their foes, the Asistagueroüon.[1] Sagard made a similar report eight years later, but gave the Huron name as "Assistagueronon."[2] The Huron term has the same significance as the present term Potawatomi, which is derived from *Potawatamink*, meaning "people of the place of fire" in Chippewa. Several of the *Relations* of the Jesuits mention the continuance of this warfare in later years.

The Potawatomi, Nassauaketon, and the Sauk were reported by Vimont in 1640 as living near the Winnebago, on the shores of the second Fresh-water Sea (Green Bay), beyond the Menominee. This was on the information of Nicolet, who had visited that region about 1634.[3] In 1642 Lalemant said that he had learned that some Potawatomi who had abandoned their own country had taken refuge with the inhabitants of the Sault.[4] Ragueneau in 1648 located the Potawatomi again near the Winnebago, probably on the reports of other Indians.[5]

According to the *Relation* of 1642–43 Nicolet's mission

---

[1] Samuel de Champlain, *Voyages,* 3: 96-99.
[2] Gabriel Sagard, *Le Grand voyage,* pp. 77-78.
[3] Barthélemy Vimont, *Relation . . . . 1640, J.R.,* 18: 231.
[4] Jérôme Lalemant, *Relation . . . . 1642, J.R.,* 23: 225.
[5] Paul Ragueneau, *Relation . . . . 1648, J.R.,* 33: 151.

to Green Bay in 1634 was to arrange a peace between the inhabitants of that place and the Hurons.[6] It is possible that the Ottawa also were included in this peace. At any rate in 1653 the Ottawa and the remnants of the Huron tribes were reported taking refuge among the Potawatomi and allied tribes at Aotonatendie, which was three days' journey south of the Sault of the St. Mary's River.[7]

Radisson reported them in approximately the same location about 1654.[8] In 1667 Allouez described the country of the Potawatomi as lying along the western side of Lake Michigan.[9] Three years later Allouez reported four villages of mixed Potawatomi, Sauk, Fox, and Winnebago around Green Bay, three on one side and one on the other.[10]

The next year, 1671, Dablon listed a few Winnebago living on Green Bay as in their own country, whereas the Potawatomi, Sauk, and the nation of the Fork were living there as foreigners, having been driven by fear of the Iroquois from their own country, the Lower Peninsula of Michigan.[11] It is most likely that it was not the true Iroquois that drove them out, but the Neutrals. The Huron, Neutrals, and Tionontati were known to Algonquian peoples by the same name as the Iroquois, and for a time the French called the Huron tribes "the good Iroquois."

Some Potawatomi were reported living on an island at the mouth of Green Bay in 1679;[12] others were in villages along Green Bay.[13] By 1695 the Potawatomi to the number of two hundred warriors had moved south into the Miami territory about the St. Joseph.[14] A few continued to reside in

[6] *Relation* . . . . *1642-43*, J.R., 23: 275-79.

[7] Ragueneau, *Journal of the Jesuits*, J.R., 38: 181.

[8] Peter Radisson, *Voyages*, p. 158.

[9] Claude-Jean Allouez, *Journal*, J.R., 51: 27.

[10] *Relation* . . . . *1670*, J.R., 54: 205.

[11] Claude Dablon, *Relation* . . . . *1671*, J.R., 55: 183.

[12] "Official Account of the Enterprises of La Salle," BN., fonds Clair., 1016: 51; Louis Hennepin, *A New Discovery of a Vast Country in America*, 1: 119.

[13] Thierry Beschefer, "Letter to the Provincial," J.R., 62: 193.

[14] AC., C 11 A, 13.

the village on the island at the mouth of Green Bay, called the Isle of Poues by Cadillac.[15]

Upon the founding of Detroit in 1701, a large number of the Potawatomi settled there. This and the settlements around St. Joseph were their principal ones until the close of the contact period. Two villages of Potawatomi at Detroit were reported in 1730.[16] The number of warriors at Detroit varied from one hundred to one hundred and eighty between the years 1701 and 1760.

According to Sabrevois the village at St. Joseph was temporarily deserted about 1718 because of the Fox war.[17] Bougainville gave the number of Potawatomi men coming there to trade in 1757 as about four hundred.[18]

The Isle of Poues is not mentioned as being occupied by the Potawatomi after 1728. There is one later reference to the Potawatomi being at Mackinac in 1756, but it does not necessarily indicate a settlement in the vicinity.[19]

The counts of this tribe were no more accurate than they were for any other. Usually, only estimates were given and estimates of only a part of the tribe. Ragueneau reported 400 men in 1653;[20] Druillettes 700 men and a total of 3000 persons in 1658;[21] Allouez said there were 300 souls in one village on Green Bay in 1670;[22] about 1695 there were 280 to 300 warriors at St. Joseph and the Isle of Poues;[23] the census of 1736 listed 230 men on the Isle of Poues, at St. Joseph, and at Detroit;[24] and 400 men traded at St. Joseph, according to Bougainville in 1757.[25] The total number of per-

---

[15] Antoine de la Mothe Cadillac, MS "Relation on the Indians."
[16] Pierre Noyan, "Memorandum . . . . ," *MPH.*, 34: 76.
[17] Jacques Sabrevois, *Memoir, WHC.*, 16: 372.
[18] Louis Antoine Bougainville, *Memoir, WHC.*, 18: 185.
[19] "Conference between Vaudreuil and the Indians," *NYCD.*, 10: 500.
[20] *J.R.*, 38: 181.
[21] Gabriel Druillettes, *J.R.*, 44: 245-47.
[22] *J.R.*, 54: 205.
[23] AC, C 11 A, 13.
[24] Pierre J. Celeron, "Census of Indian Tribes: 1736," *WHC.*, 17: 249, 251.
[25] *Memoir, WHC.*, 18: 185.

sons designated as Potawatomi probably did not exceed the three thousand reported by Druillettes and may have been less. The figures for the end of the contact period indicate a total of between two thousand and twenty-five hundred.

A clue to the accuracy of the estimates is to be noted in the round numbers in which they were given. Apparently, the nearest hundred satisfied most of the reporters. The closest that any of them came to being specific was in giving limits such as eighty to one hundred men.

CHARACTERISTICS

The Potawatomi was one of the first tribes to meet the French in the vicinity of Green Bay. They established friendly relations then and maintained them throughout the period of French control of Canada. In their alliance with the French they seem to have been much more steadfast than any other tribe. It will be well to keep this condition of affairs in mind in looking at some of the characterizations of the Potawatomi. Allouez wrote in 1667 that they were the most docile and the best disposed toward the French of all the tribes he had encountered; their wives and daughters were more modest than those of other tribes; they were very civil among themselves and also to strangers.[26]

Thirty-five years later, La Potherie described their behavior as very affable and cordial. They were intelligent, had an inclination for raillery, were great talkers, and were very stubborn, being hard to turn when they had set their minds on anything. The old men were termed prudent, sensible, and deliberate, seldom undertaking any unseasonable enterprise. The kindly way in which they received strangers was also spoken of by La Potherie, as if it were distinctive of the Potawatomi. He said that they made great efforts to gain the good opinion of persons who came among them. While living on the islands at the mouth of Green Bay they undertook to entertain all who passed that way. Their opinion of them-

[26] *Journal, J.R.,* 51: 27.

selves was so good that they regarded all other tribes as inferior to them. From this they set themselves up as arbiters for all the other tribes about Green Bay. They endeavored to maintain this position in every direction. One of the methods of furthering their ambition was by intermarriage. Jealousy and divorce were caused by this. Their desire to be accounted liberal led them to make presents of even necessary articles, and the chiefs to lavish all their possessions. They liked nothing better than to hear that others were praising their generosity.[27] Their physical appearance was dismissed with the comment that it was good.[28]

Charlevoix was shocked to be received better among the infidel Potawatomi at Detroit than among the Christian Huron. He termed them the finest men in all Canada and of the sweetest natural temper and stated that they had always been very good friends of the French. [29]

They were very warlike, according to Cadillac, often making successful attacks on the Iroquois. He further said that they had no respect for anyone, although their numbers were smaller than those of many other tribes.[30]

DRESS AND ORNAMENT

The very earliest accounts do not mention the dress of the Potawatomi. The first description of them is that of Sabrevois, who remarked that they were well clothed, like the Indians resident at Montreal. In summer the men wore red or blue cloth, in the winter adding highly ornamented buffalo robes. In playing games, such as lacrosse, they wore only a breechclout and deerskin moccasins.[31] Besides the moccasins, they ordinarily wore leggings of skin or cloth. They preferred European cloth shirts to their own leather ones, although they often wore the cloth shirt over the leather one,

[27] Claude de la Potherie, *History, ITUM.*, 1: 290-91, 301-3.

[28] *Ibid.*, p. 302.

[29] Pierre de Charlevoix, *Journal*, 2: 13.

[30] MS "Relation on the Indians."

[31] *Memoir, WHC.*, 16: 366-67.

which reached to their middle. The dresses of the women reached almost to the knee. Underneath these they wore a sort of petticoat which covered them from the middle down to the midleg. Some wore little bonnets, and others covered their heads when traveling with a sort of cowl attached to their dresses, or with their robes.[32]

Both the men and women greased their hair and painted themselves, the women usually on the face with vermilion; the men painted themselves all over on occasions, such as for lacrosse games, and with all colors. The men tattooed their bodies with all sorts of figures and designs.[33]

ECONOMIC LIFE

Agriculture

The Potawatomi practiced agriculture wherever they were, raising beans, peas, squashes, tobacco, melons, and an abundance of very fine corn. The women had charge of the fields.[34] The extent of their agriculture may be judged from the comment of Raudot in 1710 that they raised much corn on the Isle of Poues and even supplied it to Mackinac.[35]

Hunting

Every autumn the men, women, and children went into the woods for the winter hunting and did not return until spring.[36]

Food

Ordinarily, hunting and agriculture supplied all the food necessary, but when these failed them, the Potawatomi ate *fené*. This was the nut of the beech tree, roasted and pounded into flour.[37]

---

[32] Charlevoix, *Journal*, 2: 107-8.

[33] Sabrevois, *Memoir*, *WHC.*, 16: 367, 373-74.

[34] *Ibid.*, p. 367; Allouez, *Journal*, *J.R.*, 51: 27; *idem*, *Relation* . . . . *1670*, *J.R.*, 54: 205-7.

[35] Antoine Raudot, "Memoir," Letter 53.

[36] Sabrevois, *Memoir*, *WHC.*, 16: 368.

[37] Allouez. *Relation* . . . . *1670*, *J.R.*, 54: 203.

When food was plentiful the Potawatomi had frequent feasts. These were given for a variety of reasons, such as success in hunting, or the welcome of strangers. Lahontan described a feast he attended among the Potawatomi as consisting of four courses. The first platter contained two whitefish boiled in water; the second, the boiled tongue and breast of a deer, the third, two woodhens, the hind feet of a bear, and the tail of a beaver; the fourth, a large quantity of broth made of several sorts of meat. For drink he had maple syrup beaten up with water.[38]

Shelter

Sabrevois reported that the Potawatomi of Detroit made their cabins of reed mats called *apaquois*.[39] These mats were probably placed over frames of saplings driven in the ground, bent inward, and lashed together at the top. Dwellings of this sort about fifteen feet in diameter, likened to a sugar loaf in shape, were used by the Ottawa, but only on their hunting trips. The mats were likewise carried by the Potawatomi on their hunting expeditions, and their cabins were set up every evening.[40]

The Potawatomi were living in a fort in 1673, according to Allouez.[41] They continued to reside in forts to the close of the contact period, but no details of their construction have been left us.

SOCIAL LIFE

Political Organization

The Potawatomi had a very loose political organization, like that of the Ottawa. Very little was written about it in the records of the contact period. There was a chief and an orator at the head of civil authority, according to Charlevoix.[42]

The principal bands of the Potawatomi on the St. Joseph

---

[38] Louis Armand Lahontan, *Voyages*, 1: 169-70.

[39] *Memoir, WHC.*, 16: 366.

[40] *Ibid.*, p. 368.

[41] *Relation . . . . 1672-73, J.R.*, 58: 37.

[42] *Journal*, 2: 98.

River carried as totems the golden carp, the frog, the crab, and the turtle.[43] The Potawatomi at Detroit had the same totems.[44]

Games and Dances

Games and dances were the same as those of the Ottawa. The game of straws of the Potawatomi was the same as that of the Miami.[45]

Marriage

The forms of marriage were not recorded. Polygamy was common; it persisted long after it was dropped by other tribes and was a cause of the resistance offered to the efforts of the missionaries to convert them. One feature of their marriages which excited comment was the large number of marital alliances with other tribes. La Potherie reported that they had taken wives among the Winnebago and given them their own daughters.[46] The Potawatomi were half Sauk, according to Perrot.[47] Intermarriages with the Peoria were reported by La Jonquière.[48] These references indicate that residence was patrilocal and descent patrilineal.

Death Customs

The death customs of the Potawatomi were the same as those of the Ottawa, even to the cremation of the bodies of those belonging to the family of the hare, which Allouez related:

I must not omit here a rather strange circumstance: on the day after his death his relatives contrary to all usage of this country, burned his body and reduced it entirely to ashes. The cause of this is found in a legend which passes here for truth. It is held beyond dispute that this old Man's father was a

[43] Celeron, "Census of Indian Tribes: 1736," *WHC.*, 17: 249.
[44] *Ibid.*, p. 251.
[45] See Charlevoix's description under the Miami.
[46] *History, ITUM.*, 1: 301.
[47] Nicolas Perrot, *Memoir, ITUM.*, 1: 270.
[48] Pierre la Jonquière, "Letter to the French Minister, Sept. 25, 1751," *WHC.*, 18: 89.

Hare,—an animal which runs over the snow in winter,—and that thus the snow, the Hare, and the old man are of the same village,—that is, are relatives. It is further said that the Hare told his wife that he disapproved of their children's remaining in the depths of the earth, as that did not befit their condition—they being relatives of the snow, whose country is above, toward the Sky; and, if it ever occurred that they were put into the ground after their death, he would pray the snow, his relative, in order to punish the people for this offense, to fall in such quantities and so long that there should be no Spring. And, to confirm this story it is added that three years ago the brother of our good old man died, in the beginning of the winter; and, after he had been buried in the usual manner, snow fell to such an extent, and the winter was so long, that people despaired of seeing the spring in its season. Meanwhile, all were dying of hunger, and no remedy could be found for this general suffering. The elders assembled, and held many councils, but all in vain; the snow still continued. Then someone of the company said he remembered the threats which we have related. Straightway they went and disinterred the dead man, and burned him; when immediately the snow ceased, and spring followed. Who would think that people could give credence to such absurd stories? And yet they regard them as true beyond dispute.[49]

[49] Allouez, *Relation* . . . . *1666-67*, J.R., 51: 33-35.

CHIPPEWA

LOCATION OF THE TRIBE

THE make-up of this tribe is very confusing. The affiliations of the Nipissings, Amikwa, and Missisauga to the
Chippewa are only vaguely known. The last named seem to
have been a part of the larger group at one time and partially
followed its fortunes in migration and warfare for a number
of years after the first contact. Later, they made approaches to
their former foes, the Iroquois, and were adopted as the
seventh tribe of the Iroquois confederacy. The Amikwa may
have been a band, or the Beaver gens of the Chippewa, Missisauga, or Nipissings. The evidence indicates all three possi-
bilities, but does not point decisively to any one. The connections of the Nipissings are the most tenuous of all, but they
were associated with the Chippewa from 1649 to 1662 at
least.[1]

The Chippewa resident in Michigan were not very numerous at the time of first contact. The small groups in the
Lower Peninsula and on the St. Mary's River in the Upper
Peninsula appear to have been the advance guard of a general
southern and western movement.

From the earliest mention of them in 1640 throughout
the next one hundred and twenty years the customary designation was some form of *saut* (old spelling, *sault*, "fall" or
"rapid"), in reference to the rapids in the St. Mary's River,
the only early settled abode of the tribe. Examples of these
names are: nation or people of the saut, sault, or salt; sauteurs, saulteurs, saulteux, or sauteux. If other names were
given, they were usually in addition to or qualified by one
of the foregoing. Examples of these are: Baouichitigouian,

[1] Paul Ragueneau, *Relation . . . . 1649, J.R.*, 34: 205; *Journal of the Jesuits,
J.R.*, 38: 181; Nicolas Perrot, *Memoir, ITUM.*, 1: 179.

Pauoitugoueieuhak, Pawating, Panoestigonce, Outchibouec, Pahouitingwack Irini, Outhipoue, Paouitikoungraentaouak, and Achipoes. The French name of Sauteurs was given very naturally, as the Huron appellation was Eskiaeronnon—"people of the *Skia,e*" ("falls"). Most of the foregoing native names were applied to the tribe prior to 1670 and all before 1700. There is some significance in this, for in 1670 Dablon reported that the principal and native inhabitants at the mission of Sainte Marie du Sault were those who called themselves Pahouitingwach Irini, and whom the French called Saulteurs. These numbered only one hundred and fifty souls, but united themselves with three other tribes which numbered more than five hundred and fifty persons. Visitors to the region of the Sault were the Noquets, who came from the south of Lake Superior, and the Outchibous and Marameg, who came from north of Lake Superior.[2] The inference is that the original small group at the Sault was lost in the southern movement of a large and probably cognate group of Chippewa and that at least part of the newcomers carried the name Ojibwa, which later became corrupted to Chippewa. The name Sauteur remained to the newcomers about the Sault and stayed with them when they went elsewhere.

The Sauteurs were settled along the St. Mary's River during the seasons of abundant fishing and wintered farther west on the Upper Peninsula of Michigan, where part of the tribe were resident the year around.[3] The St. Mary's River is the earliest situation known for the Chippewa; they were there from 1640 to about 1650, when fear of the Iroquois drove them from the Sault. They returned sometime between 1662 and 1667.[4] From the latter date to the close of the contact period their occupancy of the Sault region was continuous.

[2] Claude Dablon, *Relation* .... *1670, J.R.*, 54: 131-33.

[3] Dablon, *Relation* .... *1671, J.R.*, 55: 159.

[4] Perrot, *Memoir, ITUM.*, 1: 179; Claude-Jean Allouez, *Journal, J.R.*, 51: 61.

The increase in their number resulted in settlements at Chaquamegon, before 1695,[5] Keweenaw, before 1710, and other places along the southern shore of Lake Superior. In 1703 some Chippewa and Missisauga formed a village near Detroit.[6] There were villages of Chippewa along the Saginaw in 1723.[7] Others were with Ottawa at Mackinac in 1729, and when the major part of the latter removed to L'Arbre Croche in 1740 the Chippewa expanded even more in that neighborhood.[8] In 1737 the River aux Sables began to be mentioned as the location of some Chippewa.[9] A Chippewa village was reported on La Grosse Ile (Bois Blanc Island) in 1747.[10] Another village on the Beaver Islands was reported in 1751.[11] In 1757 the Chippewa were settled at or in the vicinity of the following places south of Lake Superior: Sault Sainte Marie, Mackinac, Beaver Islands, Chaquamegon, Keweenaw, Carp River, River aux Sables, Saginaw, Detroit, and the following unidentified villages, Coasekimagen and Cabibonke.

The first record that gives any clue to the number of the Saulteurs stated that there were two hundred men from the Nation of the Sault, and the same number of Missisauga and Nipissing, joining a war party against the Iroquois in 1653.[12] There is no evidence of the size of the village or villages from which they were drawn.

Apparently, the Saulteurs met with some disasters, for in 1670, according to Dablon, they numbered only one hundred and fifty souls. After they made a cession of rights in

---

[5] AC., C 11 A, 13.

[6] Antoine de la Mothe Cadillac, *Cadillac Papers, MPH.*, 33: 162.

[7] Philippe Vaudreuil, "Hostilities Between Foxes and Other Tribes; Policy of the French Toward Them," *WHC.*, 16: 430.

[8] François Beauharnois, "Western Indians at Montreal," *WHC.*, 17: 63; "Abstract of Movements About Montreal," *NYCD.*, 10: 34.

[9] Beauharnois, "Council of the Indian Tribes at Detroit in 1738," *Cadillac Papers, MPH.*, 34: 151.

[10] Beauharnois, "Revolt of Indians of the Upper Country," *WHC.*, 17: 463.

[11] Pierre la Jonquière, "Reports from the Northern Posts," *WHC.*, 18: 81.

[12] Ragueneau, *Journal of the Jesuits, J.R.*, 38: 181.

their native country to some other bands and united with them, their total was seven hundred. This did not include the Noquet, Outchibous, Marameg, Amikwa, or Missisauga.[13]

This group which was originally given the name Saulteurs by the French appears to have been either the advance guard of the incoming Chippewa or a small cognate band which was absorbed by the Chippewa. The Chippewa before their arrival south of Lake Superior seem to have had no agriculture and were primarily hunters and nomads. Most of the bands were small, constantly moving, and seldom in contact with French establishments. None of the French statements of their numbers are satisfactory. A few of them estimated the Chippewa, including the Amikwa and Missisauga, as being as many as sixteen hundred persons. An estimate by the British after taking possession of Canada set their number at twenty-five thousand. In the twentieth century they are considered to number about thirty thousand, although a few thousand in Michigan are so intermingled with Ottawa that an accurate count is impossible.

CHARACTERISTICS

The Chippewa were hospitable, proud, redoubtable to their enemies, improvident, and uneconomical, according to La Potherie.[14] Raudot termed them great thieves.[15] Sabrevois said their customs and language were the same as those of the Ottawa and that they were very industrious.[16]

They were nomadic, only a part of them cultivating corn. Living mostly in small groups they were not readily approached by the missionaries. They appear to have been highly resistant to the teachings of the missionaries and slow to adopt European articles and ways. The group that settled near Detroit furnished an instance of this aloofness: a number

---

[13] Dablon, *Relation . . . . 1669-70, J.R.*, 54: 131-33.

[14] Claude de la Potherie, *History, ITUM.*, 1: 280.

[15] Antoine Raudot, "Memoir," Letter 45.

[16] Jacques Sabrevois, *Memoir, WHC.*, 16: 370.

of Chippewa, part of whom were designated as Missisauga, were attracted to Cadillac's settlement, but, unlike the other tribes that made their villages in the shadow of the fort, they established theirs on one of the islands at the northern end of Lake St. Clair.

The tribe had many very brave warriors. These were feared and respected by all the other tribes around the Great Lakes. Warriors of this tribe were among the first in historic times to defeat the Iroquois. They waged long and bloody feuds with their western neighbors, the Sioux.

ECONOMIC LIFE

The Chippewa occupied an immense territory, and the adaptation to nature was not exactly the same throughout. Those who lived north of Lake Superior probably devoted no time to agriculture, but lived solely by hunting, fishing, and gathering wild foods. The groups living around the western end of Lake Superior lived on the shore of the lake only during the summer and as soon as they harvested their crops of corn and squashes, they returned to their hunting grounds. Some stayed at Sault Ste Marie the year around, subsisting on the whitefish which were easily caught in the rapids there. Many of those who dwelt at the Sault and in the region between Lake Superior and Lake Huron left their villages twice a year. In June, after planting their corn, they dispersed in all directions along the shores of Lake Huron. There they gathered sheets of bark for making canoes and building cabins. The children gathered a store of blueberries from the bushes which flourished on the small islands in the lake. The men speared sturgeon. They returned home when their grain was nearly ripe. They remained at the Sault through the autumn to enjoy the whitefish caught in the St. Mary's River. In winter they resorted to the shores of the lake to kill beaver and moose and did not return until it was time to plant their corn.[17]

[17] La Potherie, *History, ITUM.*, 1: 277-80.

Agriculture

Most of the bands dwelling south of Lake Superior appear to have practiced some agriculture. The bands living south of the western end of Lake Superior seem to have had no difficulty in growing corn and squash on its shores.[18] Raudot said that the band at Sault Ste Marie and the Amikwa and Missisauga living on the northern shore of Lake Huron all raised corn, but that they ordinarily gathered it green because the fogs kept it from becoming entirely ripe.[19] The Amikwa also laid in a supply of blueberries for winter use.[20] The Chippewa living on the islands in Lake St. Clair had "cleared some land," according to Sabrevois, and apparently had no difficulty with the corn maturing there.[21] From all of these accounts one gathers the impression that agriculture was not very important in the economy of the Chippewa. Perrot stated that "they harvest some Indian corn, although not in so great quantity as do the tribes on the shores of Lake Huron, who live in open or prairie country."[22]

Hunting

The beaver and the moose were the animals most frequently hunted along the southern shore of Lake Superior. There were many other animals in great abundance, such as martens, and deer. Those bands which hunted on the lands of the Sioux killed great quantities of buffalo, elk, and deer. According to Perrot they were using both guns and bows and arrows in 1718.[23] They also were adept in the use of snares to take large game. Perrot said that a band of Chippewa made an extraordinary catch of more than twenty-four hundred moose in the winter of 1670–71 on Manitoulin Island, using only snares.[24]

[18] *Ibid.*, p. 279.
[19] "Memoir," Letters 45, 46.
[20] *Ibid.*, Letter 45.
[21] *Memoir, WHC.*, 16: 370.
[22] *Memoir, ITUM.*, 1: 109.
[23] *Ibid.*, pp. 109-10.
[24] *Ibid.*, p. 221.

Fishing

Fish were very important in the economy of the Chippewa. The principal ones caught were whitefish and sturgeon. The latter were speared in the vicinity of the islands of Lake Huron during the summer.[25] Spearing through the ice in winter probably was practiced also, but there is no mention of it.

It was the abundance of whitefish at the rapids of the St. Mary's River that attracted a large number of people to the banks of that stream. It seems probable that the band which the French originally named Saulteurs lived at the Sault the year around, subsisting on the whitefish, and that most of the bands only gathered there in the autumn, when the run of fish was greatest.

The method of taking the fish was described by Dablon:

It is at the foot of these rapids, and even amid these boiling waters that extensive fishing is carried on, from Spring until Winter, of a kind of fish found usually only in Lake Superior and Lake Huron. It is called in the native language *Atticameg,* and in ours "whitefish," because in truth it is very white; and it is most excellent, so that it furnishes food, almost by itself, to the greater part of all these peoples.

Dexterity and strength are needed for this kind of fishing; for one must stand upright in a bark Canoe, and there, among the whirlpools, with muscles tense, thrust deep into the water a rod, at the end of which is fastened a net made in the form of a pocket, into which the fish are made to enter. One must look for them as they glide between the Rocks, pursue them when they are seen; and, when they have been made to enter the net, raise them with a sudden strong pull into the canoe. This is repeated over and over again, six or seven large fish being taken each time, until a load of them is obtained.

Not all persons are fitted for this fishing; and sometimes those are found who, by the exertions they are forced to make, over-

[25] La Potherie, *History, ITUM.,* 1: 280.

turn the Canoe, for want of possessing sufficient skill and experience.[26]

La Potherie wrote a slightly different account of the way of catching the fish among the rapids:

The Sauteurs, who live beyond the Missisakis, take their name from a fall of water which forms the discharge of Lake Superior into Lake Huron, through extensive rapids of which the ebullitions are extremely violent. Those people are very skilful in a fishery which they carry on there, of fish which are white, and as large as salmon. The savages surmount all those terrible cascades, into which they cast a net which resembles a bag, a little more than half an ell in width and an ell deep, attached to a wooden fork about fifteen feet long. They cast their nets headlong into the boiling waters, in which they maintain their position, letting their canoes drift while sliding backward. The tumult of the waters in which they are floating seems to them only a diversion; they see in it the fish, heaped up on one another, that are endeavoring to force their way through the rapids; and when they feel their nets heavy they draw them in. It is only they, the Missisakis, and the Nepiciriniens who can practice this fishery, although some Frenchmen imitate them. This kind of fish is large, has firm flesh, and is very nourishing.[27]

The Chippewa, including the Missisauga and the Nipissing, appear to have been the only ones whose men were sufficiently skillful to practice this fishing in the swiftest water where the yield was greatest. The Chippewa caught more whitefish than they could eat and carried the surplus to Mackinac, where they sold it at a high price to both French and Indians. Another part of the heavy autumn catch was dried on frames over a fire to preserve it for winter use.[28]

Shelter

The cabins of the Chippewa were similar in size and shape to those described for the Potawatomi and to the portable

[26] Dablon, "Letter to François le Mercier," *Relation* . . . . *1669-70*, J.R., 54: 129-31.

[27] *History, ITUM.*, 1:275-76.

[28] *Ibid.*

shelters of the Ottawa. The principal difference was that the Chippewa covered the framework of their cabins with strips of birchbark.[29] These strips were made of small pieces sewn together, so that they were twenty feet or more in length and about three feet wide. They rolled up into a very small space and were easily carried.[30]

SOCIAL LIFE

Games, Dances, and War

All of these customs of the Chippewa seem to have been substantially the same as those of the Potawatomi and the Ottawa. At least Sabrevois in speaking of the Missisauga and Chippewa of Lake St. Clair said that their language was like that of the Ottawa with but little difference and that their customs were the same.[31]

Death Customs

The brief references to the death customs of the Chippewa indicate that they were essentially the same as those recorded for the Ottawa. A feast of the dead was celebrated by the Chippewa, according to Radisson, to which many surrounding nations were invited.[32] One custom reported for the Chippewa but not the Ottawa was in regard to the disposal of the bodies of warriors slain in battle. Radisson stated that it was customary to burn these to ashes and that it was considered an honor to give them such a funeral.[33]

Marriage

There is no description of the marriage customs of the Chippewa. Like other tribes the Chippewa undoubtedly intermarried with neighboring tribes. La Potherie stated that the Chippewa wished to trade with the Sioux and enjoy the abun-

---

[29] *Ibid.*

[30] René Galinée, *Narrative*, p. 13.

[31] *Memoir, WHC.*, 16: 370.

[32] Peter Radisson, *Voyages*, p. 201.

[33] *Ibid.*, p. 183.

dance of game in the territory of the latter, and the Sioux
found they could obtain French merchandise only through
the Chippewa, hence a treaty of peace was made by which
they were mutually bound to give their daughters in marriage.[34] From this it may be inferred that residence of a newly
married couple was in the group of the husband.

RELIGION

The Chippewa believed in the animation of most natural
objects. They paid special attention to the spirits inhabiting
or controlling certain forces of nature such as the sun, thunder, and wind. Although these were generally acknowledged,
each person had his own guardian spirit. The missionaries
termed these guardian spirits "gods" and thought the belief
in them the most detestable of all the customs existing among
the Indians. The ritual of acquiring such a spirit was described
by Dablon:

It consists in each one's making for himself, in his early years,
a god which he reverences then for the rest of his days, with
superstitious and ridiculous veneration. It is this which they
believe to be the sole author of their good fortune in all their
enterprises of war, fishing, and hunting; and so they wear its
ineffaceable hieroglyphic,—marking on their skin, as with the
graver, the representations of the Divinities that they have
chosen.

Now this is the way in which they create the Divinity. When
a child has reached the age of ten or twelve years, his father
gives him a lesson, imparting to him the necessary instructions
for finding out what will be his god thenceforth.

First, he has him fast for several days, in order that, with
his head empty, he may the more easily dream during his sleep;
for it is then that this fancied god is bound to reveal himself to
him, so that the sole object of all their ingenuity and all their
exertions is to see in their sleep something extraordinary, which
then takes for them the place of a Divinity.

Accordingly, when morning has come, the father questions his

[34] *History, ITUM.,* 1: 277.

son very seriously and with great secrecy, on all that has occurred during the night. If nothing has appeared to him, the fast must be begun again, and followed up until finally something is formed in the empty brain that represents to him either the Sun, or Thunder, or something else about which he has often been talked to; and, immediately upon awakening, he tells the good news to his father, who confirms the image in his thoughts. Consequently, after he has been brought up from infancy in this belief and has continued all his life to honor this god of his imagination with divers sacrifices and many feasts which are held in his honor, it is almost impossible to free his mind of this cursed superstition when he has grown old in it, or even passed some years.

At first we believed that it was only the young boys who were brought up in these stupid notions; but we have since learned that the little girls also are made to fast for the same purpose; and we find no persons more attached to these silly customs, or more obstinate in clinging to this error, than the old women, who will not even lend an ear to our instructions.[35]

Offerings or sacrifices were made to the spirits of various objects, such as rocks, rapids, and lakes. The Doric Rock on the southern shore of Lake Superior and the offerings made to it by the Chippewa were described by Radisson:

After this we came to a remarquable place. It's a banke of Rocks that the wild men made a sacrifice to; they calls it *Nanitoucksinagoit,* which signifies the likeness of the devill. They fling much tobacco and other things in its veneration. It is a thing most incredible that that lake should be so boisterous, that the waves of it should have the strength to doe what I have to say by this my discours: first, that it's so high and soe deepe that it's impossible to claime up to the point. There comes many sorte of birds that makes there nest here, the goilants, which is a white sea-bird of the bigness of pigeon, which makes me believe what ye wildmen told me concerning the sea to be neare directly to ye point. It's like a great Portall, by reason of the beating of the

<hr>

[35] Dablon, "Letter to François le Mercier," *Relation . . . . 1669-70, J.R.,* 54: 139-43.

waves. The lower part of that oppening is as bigg as a tower, and grows bigger in the going up. There is, I believe, 6 acres of land. Above it a shipp of 500 tuns could passe by, soe big is the arch.[36]

The impulse behind such offerings might be propitiation or fear. Diseases and accidents on the water were avoided by the sacrifice of a dog as described by Pachot:

If the savages fear contagion, which is the measles or small pox, or being poisoned by some other nation, these fears coming from dreams they have, they sacrifice a live dog to the manito which one has seen in his dream, believing that it is this which can save them. They tie the jaws of the dog and the four paws together, and it dies.

They make sacrifices to the spirits of the lakes and principally to Bichi Bichy whom they believe to be the master of these spirits and the god of the waters. They represent him by the figure of a sea tiger on which they put fins. They believe him to be in the bottom of the lakes and that it is by his breath that he excites the tempests. The other spirits of the lakes only act for him. They throw the dogs in the water, the jaws and the legs tied.

The Saulteurs, the Outavois and the Missisague believe the same as do all the nations of the lakes.[37]

The master of the spirits of the lakes and the god of waters, whom Pachot called Bichi Bichy, was the Michapoux of Raudot and other writers. It was he who crushed in the beaver dam at Sault Ste Marie, leaving it a rapids. Raudot said that from what the Indians said of this god he must have been as tall as Gargantua, and the tales they told of him were very much the same as those told about that fabulous giant.[38]

The shamans among the Chippewa were apparently on about the same standing as those of other tribes near the Great Lakes, although it is possible that they were more conservative and that this was what hindered the introduction of Christianity. Medicine was prescribed by old men and

[36] *Voyages*, p. 190.
[37] "Les Scioux," AC., C 11 A, 122.
[38] "Memoir," Letter 46.

women. Raudot said every old man and woman had some medicine, either real or pretended. The Chippewa had the midewiwin or medicine society. A public performance of this society is described by Raudot in his forty-seventh letter. Comparison of this ceremony with that described by Deliette for the Miami shows a remarkable similarity between them. It is odd that in the contact period the two most detailed accounts evincing the presence of the society should relate to tribes so far separated. Hints of the existence of this society are found in the reports on the Miami and Mascoutens south and west of Green Bay, on the Menominee on the river bearing their name, and on the Huron in Ontario.

BIBLIOGRAPHY

Abbreviations Used in the Footnotes

PUBLISHED WORKS:

ITUM., Indian Tribes of the Upper Mississippi.
IHC., Illinois Historical Collections.
J.R., Jesuit Relations.
LHC., Louisiana Historical Collections.
MPH., Michigan Pioneer and Historical Collections.
NYCD., Documents Relative to the Colonial History of New York.
WHC., Wisconsin Historical Collections.

MANUSCRIPTS IN THE PARIS ARCHIVES:

AC., Archives des Colonies.
AE., Mém. et Doc. Amér., Ministère des affaires étrangères, Mémoires et Documents, Amérique.
AN., Archives Nationales.
BA., MSS fr., Bibliothèque de l'Arsenal, Manuscrits français.
BN., MSS Clair., Bibliothèque Nationale, Collection Clairambault.

1. *Published Works Cited*

BACQUEVILLE DE LA POTHERIE, CLAUDE CHARLES LE ROY

History of the Savage Peoples Who Are Allies of New France. *From his* Histoire de l'Amérique Septentrionale (Paris, 1753), Vols. 2 and 4. Trans. and ed. by Emma Helen Blair. *In* The Indian Tribes of the Upper Mississippi Valley and Region of the Great Lakes. Cleveland: Arthur H. Clark Co., 1911, 1912. 1: 273-372; 2: 13-136.

The accounts of the tribes of the Great Lakes region were based principally on the memoirs of Perrot, but La Potherie apparently had access to some writings of Perrot that are not now known and probably also received information orally from that great trader and interpreter. This work was written before 1702, for it was approved by the royal censor at Paris in that year, but it was not published until 1716.

BOUCHER, PIERRE

Histoire véritable et natvrelle des moevrs et prodvctions dv pays de la Novvelle France, vvlgairement dite le Canada. Paris: F. Lambert, 1664.

Boucher was an accurate observer, well-versed, and a clear writer, but only part of his material is labeled with tribal names. He wrote of the Huron and "Algonkin" tribes.

BRINTON, DANIEL GARRISON

The Lenâpé and their Legends. Philadelphia: D. G. Brinton, 1885.

Cadillac Papers. Michigan Pioneer and Historical Collections. Lansing, 1904–5; Vols. 33, 34.

CHAMPLAIN, SAMUEL DE

Voyages and Discoveries, Made in New France, from the Year 1615 to the End of the Year 1618 by the Sieur de Champlain Ordinary for the King in the Western Ocean. Trans. and ed. by H. H. Langton and W. F. Ganong. Toronto: The Champlain Society, 1929. Vol. 3.

As reprinted in *The Works of Samuel de Champlain* under the general editorship of H. P. Biggar.

Champlain was an enthusiastic student of the Indian, but often a partial and sometimes a very inaccurate writer. He gives some of the earliest references to the Huron, Ottawa, and Nipissing.

CHARLEVOIX, PIERRE FRANÇOIS XAVIER DE

Journal of a Voyage to North America. Ed. by Louise Phelps Kellogg. Chicago: The Caxton Club, 1923. 2 vols.

The text of this edition was taken from the English translation published in London in 1761. The *Journal* was first published as the final part of his *Histoire* in 1744. The letters comprising the *Journal* were mostly dated 1721, but there is internal evidence that some of them were not written before 1728.

Charlevoix borrowed extensively from earlier writers, usually without naming sources, and often changed tribal designations on material borrowed. Little reliance can be placed on his dates or descriptions unless corroborated by other accounts. His lucid style may account in part for the popularity of his journal as a source.

DELIETTE, LOUIS

> Memoir Concerning the Illinois Country. Ed. by Theodore C. Pease and Raymond C. Werner. Coll. Ill. State Hist. Lib., 23, French ser., 1 (1934): 302-95.

The original of this manuscript is not known. The above publication and translation were made from a copy, dated 1724 and signed De Gannes, in the Edward Ayer Collection, Newberry Library, Chicago. It seems to be established that the real author was the Sieur Deliette, the nephew of Henri de Tonti, and that De Gannes was only a copyist. From internal evidence the memoir was written about 1702. It is an excellent account of the customs of the Illinois and Miami, although the author was unaccountably cynical at times.

> Documents Relative to the Colonial History of New York. Procured in Holland, England, and France, by John Romeyn Brodhead. Ed. by E. B. O'Callaghan. Albany: Weed, Parsons and Co., 1854-58. Vols. 4, 5, 9, 10.

GALINÉE, RENÉ BRÉHANT DE

> Galinée's Narrative and Map. Trans. and ed. by James H. Coyne. Ontario Hist. Soc., Papers and Records, Vol. 4 (1903), Pt. 1.

Galinée gave excellent descriptions of geography and the best map up to the date of his explorations, 1669-70, and for some time to come, but apparently had few contacts with Indians.

GIST, CHRISTOPHER

> Journal. *In* First Exploration of Kentucky. Ed. by J. Stoddard Johnston. Filson Club Publ., Louisville: John P. Morton and Co., 1898. 13: 101-85.

Gist had little acquaintance with the Indians, but described very well what he saw on a trip into Ohio in 1750-51.

Handbook of the American Indians North of Mexico. Ed. by Frederick W. Hodge. Bur. Amer. Ethnol. Bull., 30 (1907 and 1910). 2 vols.

HENNEPIN, LOUIS

A New Discovery of a Vast Country in America. Reprinted from the Second London Issue of 1698 with Notes, by Reuben G. Thwaites. Chicago: A. C. McClurg and Co., 1903. 2 vols.

The truth had to be spectacular before Hennepin preferred it to the product of his own fertile imagination.

Jesuit Relations and Allied Documents, The. Travels and Explorations of the Jesuit Missionaries in New France, 1610-1791. Ed. by Reuben G. Thwaites. Cleveland: Burrows Brothers, 1896-1901. 73 vols.

As a rule the Jesuit missionaries were excellent observers and, in sharing the life of their flocks, were in a favorable position to make observations. Limitation of space prevents even the listing of all the writers cited or of making any comments on the value of each. The revision of the original *Relations* by nonresident editors with an eye to their European circulation is to be regretted by the modern ethnographer.

JOUTEL, HENRI

Journal of M. de la Salle's Last Voyage to Discover the River Mississippi. Hist. Coll. La. Ed. by Benjamin Franklin French. New York: Wiley and Putnam, 1846. 1: 85-193.

Joutel was concerned mostly with the tribes of the lower Mississippi Valley. His few remarks on the tribes of the Great Lakes region are acceptable.

LAFITAU, JOSEPH FRANÇOIS

Moeurs des sauvages ameriquains, comparées aux moeurs des premiers temps. Paris: Saugrain l'aîné, 1724. 2 vols.

This very generalized rehash of the *Jesuit Relations*, with few original observations recorded, is of practically no value as a source.

LAHONTAN, LOUIS ARMAND, BARON DE

> New Voyages to North-America. Reprinted from the English edition of 1703. Ed. by Reuben G. Thwaites. Chicago: A. C. McClurg and Co., 1905. 2 vols.

Most of Lahontan's remarks of ethnographic significance concern the Huron and Ottawa, but which, it is not always clear. One should discard the fabrication of the Longue River discovery and also the ennobling of the Indian. The first was inserted to promote the circulation of the book and the second to chasten the European foes of the author.

LA POTHERIE—see Bacqueville de la Potherie.

LE BEAU, CLAUDE

> Avantures du Sr. C. Le Beau, avocat en parlement, ou Voyage curieux et nouveau parmi les sauvages de l'Amerique Septentrionale. Amsterdam: Herman Uytwerf, 1738. 2 vols.

Le Beau had only a very brief contact with the Huron and romanced that, but he gave some good descriptions of material objects.

LE CLERCQ, CHRISTIEN

> First Establishment of the Faith in New France. Trans. and published with notes by John Gilmary Shea. New York: John G. Shea, 1881. 2 vols.

First published in Paris in 1691. Le Clercq gave some good material on the eastern Algonquian tribes, but only a rehash of a small part of Sagard's account of the Huron, except for a letter from Father Joseph de la Roche Dallion and fragments of the memoirs of Father Joseph le Caron, for the preservation of which we are indebted to Le Clercq.

MARGRY, PIERRE

> Découvertes et établissements des français dans l'ouest et dans le sud de l'Amerique (1614-1754). Paris: D. Jouaust, 1876-86. 6 vols.

There is a typed translation of this work in the Burton Historical Collections, Detroit.

PERROT, NICOLAS

> Memoir on the Manners, Customs, and Religion of the Sav-
> ages of North America. *In* The Indian Tribes of the
> Upper Mississippi Valley and Region of the Great Lakes.
> Ed. by Emma H. Blair. Cleveland: Arthur H. Clark
> Co., 1911. 1: 31-272.

Very well-informed on the tribes of the Great Lakes region,
Perrot had perhaps the greatest personal influence of any European with these tribes. His account is not always clear, and at
times his personal grievances seem to have influenced his characterizations. The greatest defect is the lack of tribal designations
in his descriptions of customs.

RADISSON, PETER ESPRIT

> Voyages of Peter Esprit Radisson. Being an Account of His
> Travels and Experiences Among the North American
> Indians, from 1652 to 1684. Boston: The Prince Society,
> 1885.

Radisson was an explorer as well as a trader of the first water.
He was rather scornful of the Indians in his dealings with them
and apt to be very vague and confused in his descriptions of
them and their customs.

RAUDOT, ANTOINE DENIS

> Memoir Concerning the Different Indian Nations of North
> America.

This memoir was attributed to Antoine Silvy by Camille de
Rochemonteix and published with some changes under the title
Relation par lettres de l'Amerique Septentrionale (Paris: Le-
touzey et Ané, 1904). Letters 46 to 51 inclusive were also published by Margry in his *Découvertes.*
Antoine Denis Raudot and Jacques Raudot were joint in-
tendants of Canada from January 1, 1705, to March 31, 1710.
Antoine had no acquaintance with the Indians of the Great Lakes
region except as he met representatives of the tribes in Quebec
or Montreal. He acknowledged the *Memoirs* of Louis de la
Porte de Louvigny as the source of his information on the Indians. Apparently, this acknowledgment only covered the information on the tribes of the upper lakes, for it is evident that

he used the *Memoir* of Deliette for the Illinois and Miami. Tribal designations are commonly lacking in the descriptions of the tribes north of the Illinois and Miami. Translations, based on the published version and on a copy of the original manuscript, of the letters dealing with the tribes of the Great Lakes region appear in the Appendix.

Sabrevois de Bleury, Jacques Charles

Memoir on the Savages of Canada as Far as the Mississippi River. Wis. Hist. Coll., 16 (1902): 363-76.

Sabrevois was commandant at Detroit from 1714 to 1717 and had had other appointments in the upper lakes region. This memoir is dated 1718 and, although very brief, is the most exact of any account of the tribes of this region.

Sagard Théodat, Gabriel

Le Grand voyage du pays des Hurons, situé en l'Amerique vers la mer douce, és derniers confines de la Nouvelle France, dite Canada. Paris: Denys Moreau, 1632.

Histoire du Canada et voyages que les frères mineurs recollects ye ont faicts pour la conversion des infidelles. Paris: Claude Sonnius, 1636.

Sagard was an accurate and rather sympathetic observer of the Indians. He borrowed what he could, but was restricted to Champlain's account of his voyage of 1615 for earlier accounts of the Huron, although he may have had access to Le Caron's *Memoirs*. His books are very acceptable as sources for the Huron. He spent only about ten months among them, 1623-24. The *Histoire* is *Le Grande voyage* revamped as far as ethnographic remarks are concerned. There are, however, minor changes, and the earlier work is assumed to be the more authentic.

Smith, James

An Account of the Remarkable Occurrences in the Life and Travels of Col. James Smith, During His Captivity with the Indians in the Years 1755, '56, '57, '58, and '59. Reprinted with Appendix by Wm. M. Darlington. Cincinnati: Robert Clarke and Co., 1870. Ohio Valley Hist. Ser., No. 5.

A rare item—a captivity that contains some ethnographic information. There are brief remarks on the Huron and Ottawa.

SURREY, F. M., Ed.

Calendar of Manuscripts in Paris Archives and Libraries Relating to the History of the Mississippi Valley to 1803. Washington: Dept. of Hist. Research, Carnegie Inst. Wash., 1926–28. 2 vols.

THWAITES, REUBEN GOLD, Ed.

Early Western Travels, 1748-1846. Cleveland: Arthur H. Clark Co., 1904. Vol. 1.

Wisconsin Historical Collections

Collections of the State Historical Society of Wisconsin. Ed. by Reuben G. Thwaites. Madison: Published by the Society. The French Regime in Wisconsin—I, 1634-1727. 1902. Vol. 16. The French Regime in Wisconsin—II, 1727-48. 1906. Vol. 17. The French Regime in Wisconsin—1743-60. 1908. Vol. 18.

II. Manuscript Material Cited

CADILLAC, ANTOINE DE LA MOTHE

Relation on the Indians. Edward Ayer Collection, Newberry Library, Chicago.

Paris Archives

The manuscripts cited are from the following series:

Archives des Colonies, C 11, C 11 A, C 11 e, C 11 f, C 13, C 13 c. 122 vols.

Ministère des affaires étrangères, Mémoires et documents, Amérique. Vol. 6.

Archives Nationales. Vol. K 1232.

Bibliothèque de l'Arsenal, Manuscrits français. Vol. 3817.

Bibliothèque National, Collection Clairambault. Vol. 1016.

All of these volumes are now to be found in transcripts or photostats in the Library of Congress, Washington, D.C., but in this study many transcripts in the Dominion Archives, Ottawa, and in the William L. Clements Library, Ann Arbor, were consulted.

Many documents from these series have been translated and published in the *Wisconsin Historical Collections, Documents Relative to the Colonial History of New York,* and the *Michigan Pioneer and Historical Collections.* Margry also published many documents from these archives. As a rule the publication is cited in preference to the manuscript, for its greater accessibility.

APPENDIX

MEMOIR CONCERNING THE DIFFERENT INDIAN NATIONS OF NORTH AMERICA

by

ANTOINE DENIS RAUDOT

Translation of Letters 23 to 41 and
Letters 45 to 72 inclusive

MEMOIR CONCERNING THE DIFFERENT INDIAN NATIONS OF NORTH AMERICA

LETTER 23

Of the Savages in General

At Quebec, the   1709

Sir,

I am going to tell you about the savages in general which inhabit this great continent and which are known to us. I shall tell you of their dress, customs, and religion and of the way of things before the arrival of the French in this country. I shall point out to you also the change which has come among them since they have traded with us. You will become aware of it only in the things which relate to religion and in the use of our arms and our merchandise, but you will not find any of it in their government, in their politics, or in their manner of dress. It is surprising that of so many nations there has not been one of them yet that has taken our ways, and that being among us and with the French every day, they govern themselves in the same manner they have been governed up to the present. They prefer their rough and lazy life, their free and licentious life, to the most agreeable that one could propose to them. The woods and the forests are palaces to them, it is there that they live, and, although raised from their most tender childhood by the French and instructed in religious houses, they abandon us at the first fancy that takes them and lead in the woods a life very different from that which they have lead among us. Pains and an infinite time will be necessary to set these people free and to be able to bring them to accept our usages and customs. It will only be by a continuous application on them and little by

341

little that we shall be able to succeed; it is, I assure you, a work which will require several centuries.

As they had no use of iron before our arrival in this country, they used hatchets and knives of stone. They were skillful in making earthen pots in which they cooked their meats and sagamité. This kind of food is of crushed Indian corn, which they throw in the water where, when they have it, they put bear's oil, fresh meat, or pounded dried meat or fish.

They also make this sagamité in bark dishes, by putting several red hot rocks in the water which is inside, this makes it boil, and by this means they cook the Indian corn and meats placed there.

While traveling, they make use of this method when they lack a kettle. They light a fire easily wherever they are by rubbing a soft wood with a hard wood. Now they all have iron axes and our copper kettles.

I am, sir, etc.

LETTER 24

Of the Savage Men and Women and of Their Dress and of the Manner in Which They Tattoo Themselves

At Quebec, the   1709

Sir,

The savages are bronzed, well built, and of a sturdy constitution. This comes from the care that the mothers take of their infants, whom they nurse until they are three and four years old.

The wives of these savages are as bronzed as they are. Some of them are very well built and have an alert and piercing eye. They like men very much, especially the French. As they are strongly interested, they accord their favors for the presents given them, especially the ones who are in the warm countries. One would take them for vestal virgins, however, if one was not assured that they know well how to dissimulate and that the modesty which they show on their faces was only an attraction in order to allure.

The men are almost always nude and show their body exposed; the only clothing is a blanket of dressed furred skin of beaver or of some other animal with which they envelop themselves, a breech cloth, leggings, which are two pieces of leather with which they cover the lower legs and a part of the thighs, and mocassins. Nudity makes no impression among these people.

The ordinary costumes of the women are two skins of moose or deer, attached together at the shoulders and with an opening at the sides down to the armpits, and from there they are sewed to the knees; they are double from the belt to this place, painted very neatly with black, red, and yellow, and ornamented with porcupine quills, claws of eagles and hawks, moose feet, and small pieces of copper. They add to these dresses two sleeves of the same skin. Some among them, as well as among the men, wear a sort of skin shirt; they prefer both our shirts of Lyon linen and our materials and covers to those of skin, so much so that they are almost all dressed with these when they have the means to be. The men and women have very black and coarse hair, they have no body hair, pulling out or having pulled out all that comes to them. The women wear their hair full length, tied and enveloped with the skin of an eel or a snake; they put on it powder of spruce wood to keep it always very black.

As for the men, they cut their hair in different ways. They all go bareheaded and tattoo on the body several different figures, using two or three fish or animal bones, well pointed, which they tie, separated one from another, at the end of a piece of wood. They soak these fish bones in a sort of black paint, which they make with crushed soft charcoal and with water, or in vermilion, or in diluted red earth, and they force them in the skin so well that they go in at least two or three millimeters. The paint that they carry remains there, and the figures that they compose never go away. This pricking is not done without much pain, the spot becomes swollen and sore and even forms a small lump before it heals; the pains that they suffer when they wish to have these marks on their bodies do not keep the savages from making all these sores even in the most sensitive places. There are some nations who tattoo themselves more than others, and among these nations there are some men who have the body and face entirely tattooed.

I am, sir, etc.

LETTER 25

Of the Sense of the Savages, of Their Inclination for Drink, and of Their Marriage

At Quebec, the   1709

Sir,

The savages in general all have good sense when it is a question of getting what they wish and of their interests. They are very politic and patient when one insults them, but they retain their resentment and do not lose any occasion to get vengeance. They are very painstaking in hunting, fishing, and war, everywhere else they are very lazy and think only of embellishing themselves to please the women, of smoking, of dancing, and of playing; nothing is more unbearable among them than a warrior who, excited because of a few men whom he has assassinated (for one can hardly give any other name to the persons they kill), thinks that the ground should tremble under his feet when he walks. They are naturally very much inclined to drink and become intoxicated willingly because at this time they believe everything permitted. They are so well persuaded of this that should a drunken man break their canoes and everything that is in their cabins, they do not get angry, and, laughing, say, "he has no sense"; they also use this term when they see some one in a passion (anger); the majority of them never get that way and are always calm, they certainly lose this calmness, however, when they are drunk, for they stab one another, bite noses and ears, throw their children in the fire, and do all the mischief of which a man furious and mad could be capable.

The men and women savages smoke very much, or one could better say always. Previously, they used an herb called mountain tobacco, but now they smoke black tobacco, or that which is grown here and is very nearly of the same quality as that cultivated in France.

The savages get married very young; the parents of the girl are begged by those of the boy to give her to their son, and at the same time they give a present according to their means; when they are in agreement they have a feast, attended by all the relatives, and it is at this time that the marriage presents are given; the husband gives his wife a kettle, an ax, and a collar—he says to her by these three gifts that she must take care to feed him and to go and fetch wood and the meat of animals which he has killed. He has at this time his quiver full of arrows, his bow, a war club, and a knife to signify that it is for him to go to war and to hunt. Both perform these respective duties. After these presents are given, all the people start to dance to the sound of a kind of drum or to songs of which the words tell the duty of marriage, of which they are not ignorant. This feast takes place in the cabin of the girl, where the boy goes to live. This marriage lasts as long as they are satisfied with one another, for as soon as they are not, they part to marry another, there being no dishonor for the one or the other to have been married. The marriage broken off, the children remain with the mother; it is one of their greatest riches to have them, because it is they who support them in their old age by hunting and fishing.

The savage women are never sick at confinement; when they have just given birth they go to wash their child in the water and do not discontinue doing the housework as usual.

I am, sir, etc.

LETTER 26

Of the Dances of the Savages

At Quebec, the   1709

Sir,

There are several dances among the savages. Besides those of which I have told you in my preceding letter, the dance of the calumet, which is a savage pipe with a stone head, where the tobacco is put, and a wooden stem, is an honor that one nation goes to render to another in order to renew an alliance. The one who is delegated to offer the pipe and to dance addresses a war chief and presents it lighted to him, dancing to the songs of several men and women who have accompanied him. They name in these songs the person to whom they offer the calumet, tell the reason for which they give it to him, and accompany the dance with a present. The savage and the nation to whom it has been presented also give a present to reply to the honor that has been done them and send back this ambassador of sorts and all his following after having regaled them for several days. This calumet is of red stone and has the shape of some animal or of an ax to adorn it; the stem is very long and adorned with several feathers painted different colors; some of the feathers are fastened to it and others wave freely in the wind.

As the savages love to receive, they ordinarily have one wife who may be asked for honorably. When several strangers arrive, a certain number of men, women, and girls step out right away and form a large circle in the middle of which four men place themselves. One of them beats a drum to the sound of which the other three accord their voices. All the circle, while dancing, turns around and each person takes different postures according to his caprice, striking the feet sharply on the ground and joining voices with those who are within the circle; he who receives this honor signifies his gratitude for it by a gift such as he wishes to make.

They also perform dances to cure their sick; they do not

succeed very much in this, and in place of procuring the cure, ordinarily they hasten death, after having made the person suffer much. The sick man is placed in the hands of doctors who suck him with cries and frightful yells to the sound of a drum and several gourds. These they call *chichikoué*, and in them there are some grains of Indian corn. They grease and oil the entire body of the poor sufferer, for that is the name that fits him best, since they carry him over a fire where they all but roast him. One never hears the cries and yells that he makes for the great noise made by several boys and girls who sing and dance around and who then entirely nude perform all the indecencies that a very corrupted nature or rather the devil could inspire them. It is at this time that these doctors who are magicians invoke all the devils to cure their sick one, who usually dies soon after all these torments.

I am, sir, etc.

LETTER 27

Of the Dances of the Savages

At Quebec, the   1709

Sir,

The savages have still other dances. The discovery is the dance in which the warriors recount their raids, the manner in which they have surprised their enemies and attacked them, and how the prisoners were led into their village. At the same time they make the same gestures that they made in their approach and in their attack. The Miamis excel at this dance, which is done to the sound of the drum and the noise of the *chichikoué;* all these kinds of instruments blend with the voices of the singers. They are nude, and only one man dances at a time. He is girded with a crow, which is his totem. After he has finished and has recounted all his exploits, he is replaced by another and in this fashion the dance continues until all the warriors have performed.

They have another also which is that of striking the post.

By this dance they inform the public of their bravery and of the number of enemies that they have killed or taken. When they wish to give it, they beat the drum and utter cries both in the village and in a particular cabin. They do this dance when they are all assembled there. A war chief begins to knock on a post with a war club, and after having danced a little he recounts his exploits, makes a pose for each action, and recommences dancing. He repeats as much as he wishes, and the others applaud him by a great cry after he has recounted each action when he has told the truth. But when he tries to deceive them, he is promptly contradicted and has the disgrace of having his head rubbed with ashes. When this chief has finished, another savage commences; thus, they all dance, one after another.

These are two dances which are for warriors. They, as well as all the others, are usually performed at night.

I am, sir, etc.

LETTER 28

Of the Games and Feasts of the Savages

At Quebec, the   1709

Sir,

The savages love as much to play games as to dance. Games are a strong passion among them. They play odd or even with straws which they cut equally and of which they take part in their hands.

They have also a certain game like dice; they use fruit stones that have one side black and the other white and take six or eight of them which they roll in a dish.

These are the games which they commonly play. In regard to the game of lacrosse, it is played village against village, or family against family in a prairie where they establish limits. Their sticks have handles three and a half feet long, and there is a sort of laced racquet at the end; with this they hurl the ball, which is returned by their adversaries. The game is very dangerous and may cause injuries.

Of all people the savages know best how to endure hunger; they will go four or five days without eating, but when they have anything, the kettle is always "high" to use their term, and there are feasts every day. As soon as a man has killed an animal or caught some large fish, such as sturgeon, he immediately holds a feast. They have some which have a particular object, such as to raise a war party or for the death of some one. He who gives it sends little sticks to all those he wishes to invite, who come there, each with his dish and spoon. When they have arrived they begin to eat that which has been given them, while he who invited them thanks his spirit, or rather his devil, for they believe that each has his own who takes care of him, and sings during all the repast. At the finish they make a great acclamation to thank the one who has well regaled them. At some of these feasts it is absolutely necessary to eat everything, and often six men would be well sated by what is given one. There are also other feasts which are held without ceremonies; at these one eats what he wishes and carries away the rest.

As it is the women who have the care of all that relates to the household, it is they who fill all the dishes and serve them to the guests—which is a service they do every day for the men of the cabin. The women of the north people have only what is left of the feast, never attending it, and retiring after they have filled and served the dishes. As to the Huron and Iroquois women, they often take part unless it is a war feast, at which they are never received. These feasts are hardly ever held without a dog being put in the kettle. The head of this animal is served to the chief of the party.

I am, sir, etc.

LETTER 29

*Of the Ornaments of the Savage Men and Women
and of Their Works*

At Quebec, the   1709

Sir,

The young men among the savages like very much to adorn themselves to please the girls. They always have a mirror in their tobacco pouch which they use to apply different colors on the face, such as red, blue, and black. It is with these paints that they "mattach" themselves, that being the savage term. They grease their hair and also apply some red with the down of swans on top. They pierce the nose and hang from it a glass bead or a drop of blue stone, which extends over the mouth.

Their ears are all slashed. They insert in them thongs of swan skin, which make two big white tufts, and hang wire and porcelain in them. This porcelain is made of shells found on the seashore near Virginia, and it is the thing that is most esteemed and sought after by all the savages. There are shells of two colors, the white is the more common and the black more rare and more esteemed. The savages who live in the country where it is found work it into small pieces, which they pierce and make round. They hang single shells in the ears or even several of white and black together. They make necklaces of shells, which they carry around their necks, and bracelets, which they put on their wrists. It is considered a great ornament by them to wear large shells hung over their stomachs.

The young girls and the young women, as well as the young men, like to adorn themselves. They paint themselves like the young men, but they use only red and blue; they use much porcelain.

When the men and women become old they abandon all finery. The men occupy themselves only with fishing, making canoes, with councils for governing their nations, juggling, and medicine. The women occupy themselves also with medicine and at night tell to the youth of the household stories of their war, of their spirit or rather their devil, in short, they invent a thousand fables according to their wild imaginations.

Sometimes they work: the men to make dishes of knots of wood and spoons on which they carve the figure of some animal. They also make war clubs which they use in war. The war club has the shape of a jaw bone and is made of a hard and heavy wood with a lump or ball at the end. A man puts on it his divinity, the symbol of his name, which is a beaver, an otter, or some other animal or bird; he depicts on it also his face, the number of men he has killed, and the prisoners he has taken, and for his own glory he leaves such war clubs in places where he has been on some expedition in order that his enemies may know who killed their people and of what nation he was.

The women work at painting their dresses and at sewing, which they do with the sinews of moose or with nettle thread spun on their thighs very delicately. They also make things of bark ornamented with porcupine quills tinted different colors and sewed with roots. These, sir, are the occupations of the savages in their villages. Sometimes they play a sort of flute made of reeds, the sound of which is disagreeable.

I am, sir, etc.

LETTER 30

Of the Dreams of the Savages and of the Manner in Which They Acquire a Divinity

At Quebec, the 1709

Sir,

The savages are much given to dreams and are so well persuaded that it is their spirit who gives them to them, that they absolutely must carry them out. It is dreams which oblige them to undertake wars, to make great voyages, to abandon war parties which they have undertaken against their enemies and to return from them to their cabins. It is also these dreams that give them their spirit, or to use their term, their manito, which they imagine takes care of them in all the acts of their lives.

The savages whom time has made wise in spite of themselves and incapable of the same debauches that they formerly had, recount to their children of the way they came into the world, of their country and their wars, and tell them a thousand stories filled with superstitions. All these fables very much delight these youngsters. But as soon as there is one of them who has reached the age of ten or twelve years and who can use the bow and arrow, his father says to him that he is of an age to get a spirit and to choose a manito for himself, and he gives him at the same time the instructions necessary to succeed in this.

For this purpose he has him "mattach" or paint his face black with crushed charcoal and requires him in this state to fast for several days, in order that, having the brain empty he can more easily dream during his sleep, which is the time that this god ought to disclose himself to him and strike his imagination with some extraordinary thing or some animal which holds the place of a divinity for him. The father, anxious to know the dream of this child, watches the time of his awakening in order that he speaks to no one before him and questions him privately on what happened in his imagination during the night; if nothing has appeared, he counsels him to continue his fast, saying to him that on this occasion he must give marks of his firmness and his strength. Finally, his weakened brain represents to him some object such as the sun, the thunder, or other extraordinary things of which he has often heard his father or other elders speak.

When this child has dreamed he runs to carry the news to his father, who strongly recommends to him not to divulge it and encourages him with many reasons to accept this dream and to honor this idea which he takes thenceforth from his childhood for his divinity, for his manito, for his protector, and continues during his life to worship it by sacrifices and by feasts which he gives in its honor. It is very difficult to destroy this superstition among the savages when they have lived several years after having cultivated the impression of it.

The women, having a weaker spirit than the men, are usually more attached to it, and the young girls are likewise raised in these sorts of fancies by the old women who persuade them that by this means they will make themselves loved by the young men. It is very rarely that they can be detached from these ideas that they all connect with their passion, either love or vengeance, or which they believe procure them secrets to cause the death of persons of whom they have cause to complain.

I am, sir, etc.

LETTER 31

Of the Superstitions of the Savages, and Their Jugglers

At Quebec, the   1709

Sir,

I have just spoken of the religion of the savages; it is nothing but an idea; each has his own notion of his divinity according to his caprice, although there are nations which recognize gods for all the people in general. I shall give myself the honor of explaining these gods to you in speaking of the particular tribes. All of these savages speak confusedly of the deluge, but so differently that one can decide nothing on what they say of it. They resemble the Jews in respect to anointment, for they all grease themselves and wash at sunrise. They honor the dead; some burn them, others bury them, but always with much circumspection. They do not fear death as we do, regarding this life as nothing but a transition; they are convinced that in leaving it they will lead a more agreeable one in a delightful country where they will have all the comforts and all the pleasures that they can desire. This is proof that they are convinced of the immortality of the soul.

These savages have among them some that are called jugglers. These people pretend to speak to the devil, and he tells them things that they ask him; to invoke him they place themselves in a cabin of bark or skin where they give frightful yells; the devil appears to them and some times beats them badly; this cabin while they are there trembles with so much force that one would think it was going to turn over.

These jugglers usually are the physicians; they are feared for the evils they do in causing the deaths of various people. I am convinced that the witchcraft or the spells that they cast on the people who have displeased them are all poison that they give them; in speaking of their power they make themselves respected. But these nations have a desire to dispose of the sort of people who destroy them. When they see there is some one dead among them and they suspect a juggler, they oblige the children or the nearest relatives of the juggler to kill him. The people employ this means in order that no one obtain vengeance for the death of the juggler, for if it was another who killed him, it would be necessary for the nearest relative to avenge him by disposing of the one who did the killing, thus there would be murder to infinity.

Vengeance is according to law among them, for when the son does not wish to kill his father, both must necessarily be done away with by their nearest relations, because it is the son who would be obliged to avenge his father's death. There are a few savages who have another sort of jugglery which they use when they wish to know if their people who are hunting or at war will return soon or have made a successful attack. They make two or three little piles of bark or of powdered charred wood, and then covering themselves with their blankets, they set fire to the little piles and pretend to see that which they wish to know by the way the powdered charred woods take fire and by the sparks they throw.

These savages are very lucky sometimes with their jugglery, but I am convinced that they are like the casters of horo-

scopes who would be very unlucky if among several false
things which they say, there is not one thing of truth.

I am, sir, etc.

LETTER 32

Of the Political Government of the Savages

At Quebec, the 1709

Sir,

The government of the savages is republican; the elders
regulate all the affairs, and the young people only execute
them. Among these elders are the war chiefs. They become
such by the outstanding feats which they accomplish, by the
friendship of the young people which they draw to themselves, and by the gifts that they make to them, for usually
these chiefs are the most poorly dressed of the nation, giving
everything to make themselves liked. The elders assemble
over the smallest things and, while smoking, consider matters, without ever getting angry with each other. Although
they are of opposite feelings they always speak gently and
never conclude anything without a mature and long delibera-
tion. There are orators among them who speak for the whole
nation when there is some speech to make. They speak well and
always figuratively. They present porcelain collars, of which
I have already told you, which serve them for their ornament,
and state that by this they wish to say such or such a thing.

That is how the savages in general govern themselves,
some with more intelligence and reason than others, not being
all equally able. It often happens that passion, spite, vengeance, and drunkenness prevail over all the wise counsels
the old give the young, of which they are not always the masters. But affairs later go back to the same state.

As the savages never wish to take the lands nor the woods
of their enemies, one cannot doubt that it is only animosity,
spite, vengeance, and inordinate desire to kill men or to ag-

grandize themselves by slaves that cause them to make war.

When they adopt the slaves that they take, which they do not fail to do when they have lost many people, they make them come into their cabins, regard them as being of their nation, and force them to make war against their relatives.

I am, sir, etc.

LETTER 33

Of the War Feasts of the Savages and of Their Departure from Their Village

At Quebec, the   1709

Sir,

As the war which the savages wage against each other is very cruel, they take all the precautions possible to surprise and not to be surprised. This war is properly a permitted assassination and often declared because of a dream or for some murder done to someone of the nation in a hunt or in drunkenness. The relative of the deceased after wearing mourning for a year (which I shall explain to you later on) has a feast to which, by sticks, he invites a certain number of persons. While he eats he tells his plan and what his manito has inspired him with, then he sings of war, that is to say, he wishes to avenge such a one and eat the enemy nation, and challenging in this song all his guests he engages them imperceptibly to join him and to take sticks. Those who take them are enlisted. Their friends also join them; thus the party grows. The plan of leaving being formed, they work to collect provisions, to make their canoes, their arrows, their war clubs, and other things which they need, and they dance all night.

The day of their departure having arrived, they put on their best attire, paint their faces, load their canoes, and embark. At this time the chief of the war party gives a discourse in which he tells his plan and the time that he must come back. All the others sing their death song at the top of their voices as long as they are within sight of the village. Sometimes they

take one or two young women in these parties to do the cooking. When they do not take any, it is the youngest of them
who does it. They go to the place where they expect to find
enemies hunting or fishing or on their way somewhere. They
place their canoes in some hidden spot where they debark only
at night and never make a fire at this camping place for fear of
being discovered. They begin their march by land and appoint
among them the scouts who are always the most adroit, the
bravest, and the best runners. They have two or three at the
most who walk far from the sight of each other, in order that
they will not all fall into the same ambush. They approach
their enemies as close as they can and during the night consider the enemy's forces and in what manner they should make
their attack. As soon as the scouts have made this discovery one
of them goes off to notify the large body. They all start on the
march during the night to join the other scouts and make their
attack at dawn, which is usually the time when one is the most
drowsy, especially the savages, who dance all night when they
are in their camp and keep no sentry. They fall on their
enemies with loud cries, enter the cabins, kill, and take what
they can. They find little, or rather, no resistance, for in such
a surprise each one thinks of fleeing and hiding himself rather
than of defending himself.

This is the way they conduct an attack on their enemies
when they are not in their village or when they believe themselves strong enough to force the piles with which these villages are usually surrounded; but if they do not believe themselves strong enough to do it they hide in the *fredoches*[1] or
behind stumps and remain there living on ears of Indian corn
until they are able to assassinate some one who is obliged to
leave this fort to go to fetch water or wood.

The forts are usually only interlaced poles on the top of
which there are fascines on which one can easily walk. There

[1] This word, apparently, is not in any French dictionary, old or modern.
From the text it could mean hollows, grass, weeds, or underbrush.

are savages who plant more than one row of stakes in the ground.

None of these savages dare attack a pile fort defended by Europeans. They say that obviously that is to expose themselves to be killed. However, they have attacked some forts among the English, but they were guided and excited by the example of the French.

I am, sir, etc.

LETTER 34

Of the Return of the Savages from the War, and of the Treatment They Give to the Prisoners en Route

At Quebec, the   1709

Sir,

The return of the savages of this country is much more precipitate than their advance march, they think only of retiring as fast as possible, expecting at every moment to be pursued. For this purpose they tie the prisoners they have taken, with their hands behind their backs, cut around and take off the scalp of the dead, pulling off with the hair which they hold in their hands the skin which covers the man's skull, and return to their canoes. As soon as they have embarked, they make their prisoners sing until they have lost sight of the place of their embarkation. Every morning while en route they shout the number of their prisoners and do the same thing when they encounter other canoes, and even make the prisoners sing to do honor to the strangers, who to thank them give them something to eat and make them a feast. The greatest concern of these savages is to take much care to nourish their prisoners well while en route, to do them no harm, and at the same time to take care that they do not escape. In the daytime they tie them by the arms and the neck to one of the bars of the canoe, and at night they notch logs in which they place their arms and legs and fasten them with stakes. They also tie their arms with cords that are attached to other stakes and on which two men sleep. Besides all these precautions they put cords on their necks which are attached to another stake. It appears almost impossible that a man could move in this condition. They ask during the journey of news of their village and make them sing of their exploits to know if they have often been to war and if they have killed many men. It is a very glorious thing for these savages when there are warriors and people of importance among their prisoners.

Before they arrive at their village they set a man ashore who makes cries either of death if they have lost someone or of the number of prisoners they have taken. These cries are distinguished by different tones of voice. As soon as they are heard in the village every one goes out and walks a few steps to meet this courier, who on arriving sits down and whispers the news, after which the orator or another recites it aloud.

I am, sir, etc.

LETTER 35

*Of the Treatment That the Savages Give Their Prisoners
in Their Village, and of Those That They Adopt*

At Quebec, the   1709

Sir,

If the savages treat their prisoners well while en route, it is only to be able to lead them alive to their village, for they certainly change their conduct when they are there.

The poor unfortunates on arriving pass between all the people, who make two rows. It is in this place that they begin to be ill treated. They receive a thousand blows of stones and sticks and even are wounded with knife cuts so that they are often all bloody when they enter the cabin which is expressly destined for them, where, in spite of all the injuries they have received, they are obliged to sing, to eat, and to smoke and where they are tied until the council is decided on them.

This period often lasts several days, according to the press of affairs. During this time they decide what they will do with the prisoners, and to whom they will be given. Usually, they are used to replace the dead, but often some are also given to other nations to oblige these nations to become their allies. These nations are informed that they send them by this present meat to eat and something of which to make soup.

This council indeed decides the distribution of these prisoners which they regard as slaves, but they do not decide their life or death. That depends entirely on those to whom they are given, unless he who has killed some warrior in the battle is taken, in which case the council would condemn him at once to the fire.

One can judge of the anxiety of these poor unfortunates in waiting for their fate, but it certainly redoubles when they come to take them one after the other to be given and distributed to their enemies, who often condemn them to the fire and also often adopt them.

He who is adopted enters the cabin of his master where the women receive him, wash him, grease him, clothe him, and give him the name of the deceased for whom he is given. They do the same thing when it is a woman prisoner with this difference, however, that she must work like a slave, whereas a man if he is a hunter or warrior becomes the master of the cabin, the same as he whom he replaces and whose name he carries.

I am, sir, etc.

LETTER 36

Of the Prisoners Who Are Condemned to the Fire

At Quebec, the   1709

Sir,

If the adopted prisoners are happy in becoming masters of the cabins of those whom they replace, the ones who are not are most unhappy. They are condemned to the fire, most often by the caprice of the women to whom they are given, who by their shouts of vengeance and the corn which they throw out of their cabin demand that they go to rejoin the soul of their husband, brother, or parent who has been killed. The fury of these women is sometimes so great that they often condemn to the fire eight or ten slaves consecutively who are given to them to replace their deceased husbands. Once this fatal decree is pronounced, the sufferer is painted and led to the place of torture.

This spot is near the village, where a post is planted, and around it and at a little distance from it the people gather, seated in a circle. Several paces from the post there is a fire in which several gun barrels are heated redhot.

Everybody being assembled, the slave is led in and obliged to sing his death song at the top of his voice, and he is often stopped on the way by a savage, who in cold blood tears off his nails, cuts off a finger, or smokes it in his calumet. All these injuries do not hinder the sufferer from continuing his road and his song. When he arrives at the post they tie his hands very high in order that he can turn around and excite by his different movements the audience, who yell at all the motions he makes. As soon as he is tied a savage who can well be given the name of executioner takes a redhot gun barrel with which he rubs the victim's legs and then leaves him some moments. They let him smoke during this time and make him sing and tell his exploits of war. To recommence his pains, one cuts off a finger, another again rubs his legs and thighs with fiery gun barrels. As they do not wish to kill him too soon they let him rest again. His torments recommence shortly, however, with all the cruelest things they can imagine. This horrible tragedy lasts five to six hours. When the savages grow weary of enjoying themselves with the injuries that they do to this unfortunate, they cut off his remaining fingers and often the wrists, scalp him, and sprinkle his head with hot coals. It is at this time that they untie him. Directly, this poor, half dead captive sets out to flee; he tries to pick up some pieces of wood to defend himself against the youths who throw stones at him. He is soon overwhelmed with blows and has no sooner fallen than they open his abdomen and each pulls off a piece of his flesh to eat; the women rub the infants they are nursing with the blood of this deceased in order that they may grow up to be warriors; several drink it. Then, in an instant, only the bones are left of this man; his head is placed on a stake.

The mania of the savages is not limited to burning the men, they inflict the same tortures on the women; the children they throw in the fire.

The cruelty of the women is as great as that of the men. They serve as executioners and do things that decency does not permit telling.

I am, sir, etc.

LETTER 37

Of the Dignity of the Slaves at the Post and of the Wars
Which Are Made in Connection with Dreams

At Quebec, the   1709

Sir,

Although these slaves suffer the cruelest torments that could be imagined, and I have only imperfectly described for you what is done to them, there are among them some who show in suffering a firmness that one cannot admire too much. There are some who say at the post addressing their executioners: "Is it this way that men are burned? it is at the temples and at the shameful parts that it is necessary to burn warriors to make them suffer." Others say: "I do not mind dying, I have eaten of all nations, my relatives will avenge me, it is the fate of warriors to die by the fire, but learn from me, you who hear me, how to die respectably and do not cry when you are burned."

The wars that the savages carry on because of their dreams are waged the same as are those for animosity; their precautions are the same and the treatment they give their prisoners is the same. This war is made very often to repeople their villages when they have been attacked by an epidemic, or when by the wars which they have been obliged to carry on, they have lost many people. When they think to re-establish themselves a war chief dreams that in a distant country there are many men who, having no knowledge of firearms, will be astonished to hear their guns thunder. He makes a war feast directly and by this means forms a party for this enterprise, which often is a success by the many slaves which they lead back, but sometimes also the warriors are killed, which causes a war of animosity.

Besides the firearms that the savages who have commerce with us and the English use, and which perhaps have been given to them too thoughtlessly, they have also the war club and the bow and the arrow, which all the nations use. Some have bows of four feet, others of three which are round or flat with a spearhead at the end; the arrows are the same length and are tipped with iron, copper, bone, or stone at the end. There are some nations that put four feathers on them, and others three.

When a chief has been killed in these wars or has died of an illness, his name is given with ceremonies to another brave man, who feels honored to bear it and is obliged to avenge his death and to do some brilliant deed. This is only practiced a year after the decease of the chief during which year his wife and nearest relations are in mourning. In this it is necessary to give away the effects of the deceased, to neither grease nor paint, and to avoid the amusement gatherings. The women whose husbands have been killed and the closest relatives are always in tears. When they meet at dances or at feasts they make doleful cries; in this way the women demand vengeance, when the warriors are slow in avenging them, and endeavor to excite the warriors. When they see that they cannot succeed they make presents, and the women go as far as to reproach the warriors for their small courage and treat them as cowards. It is by the anger of these women that wars are indeed difficult to end among the savages.

I am, sir, etc.

LETTER 38

Of the Winter Hunting of the Savages and of the Sweat Baths

At Quebec, the   1709

Sir,

All the savages leave their village and the bank of the rivers and lakes where they are established and go inland in the winter, deep in the woods to hunt. They separate from each other in order to find more easily something to live on. They take with them their women and children, leaving in the village only those who absolutely cannot march.

They have also with them all their dogs of which they have a great many. These dogs are rather large, having heads and ears like those of a fox. The savages of the North and of the lakes never give them the bones of beaver and porcupine to eat, having the superstition that if they give these to them, they will take no more of these animals.

The women carry all the baggage on their backs by means of collars made like a girth and two or three yards long. They place these on the forehead. As for the men they carry little besides their arms and put the collar over the top of their shoulders. They all leave the woods only when the rivers are thawed. The savages who use canoes make them, when there is suitable bark, at the places where they find themselves, and when they do not find any bark they sew together two skins of moose or wapiti, with which they make one; although very fragile it is, nevertheless, safe for them. As for those who do not use canoes, they return by land.

The savages know the paths of the woods and are acquainted with them as we know the streets of a city. They all have very good sight and distinguish the tracks of men and animals on the grass and on rocks where there appears only a very light moss.

They all walk faster than we do and are very good runners, and among the nations there are some who are as much better than others as these others are better than we are. When they are tired or have some indisposition, they make sweat houses. They plant for this purpose four stakes over a trench which they make in the ground, cover the stakes with beaver robes, and place themselves on a bark in this hollow, having beside them redhot rocks on which they throw from time to time water or pieces of tobacco in order that the vapor thrown off carry the heat everywhere. It is in these places that they sweat; they have no air, there is an excessive heat, water drips from the entire body, and all their pores are open. That does not prevent that then, all covered with sweat, they go to bathe themselves and throw themselves in cold water without its doing them any harm.

Although the majority of the savages have several wives, they do not have many children, which is the reason that they are not very numerous. Besides the debauchery to which they are almost all addicted when they find an opportunity and epidemics that attack them frequently, wars and poverty diminish their numbers a great deal, so much so that there are several very small nations.

I am, sir, etc.

LETTER 39

Of the Different Kinds of Savages

At Quebec, the 1709

Sir,

One can distinguish four classes of savages. The nomadic savages are the first, they are commonly called the inland people or people of the North, who live in the interior, do not grow Indian corn, do not have sedentary villages, and live only by hunting and fishing.

Such are those who reside between the Equimaux and the Temiskaminques, who are the last along the great river of the Outaouais, of whom we have a complete knowledge. These are the Oumiamis, Chicoutimiens, Papinachois, Montagnais, Algonquins of the St. John River, large and small Mistassins, habitants of Nemisco, Aticamegues or Poissons-blancs, Monsonis, Pisouotagamis, Abitibis, Machatanitibis or Têtes de Boules, Temiscaminques, and Cristinaux.

The manner in which these savages shelter themselves is very easy: the shelter consists of several birchbarks three feet high, sewn together, and eight feet long, with which they surround a circle of several poles that, fastened together at the top, form a large circle below to enclose the persons who are inside. Broken pine branches serve them as mattresses on which they spread several skins of bear or deer as a pad, and they wrap themselves in their beaver robes or other covers to sleep.

One could include among these savages others who, although they live on the banks of lakes and rivers and are sedentary during the summer, do not cultivate the land and consequently grow no wheat. Such are the Amiquoués, Mississagué, Noquets, Maloumines or Folles Avoines, Sauteurs or Chipouais and Nadouessioux, the people of the Sapinerie, who are at the far end of Lake Superior, and the Sioux.

The second class of savages are the people of the lakes, who are sedentary and who grow wheat. These are the Sauteurs of Kiousouenau, the Outaouais, the Hurons, the Poutouatamis, and the Sakis, these last are like the second or third class.

The third class are the people of the prairies who are the Puants, the Outagamis, the Kicapoux, the Mascoutins, the Miamis, and the Illinois. Among them are the Iroquois, who do not use birchbark canoes any more than they do.

Those who form the fourth class are the Abenakis, who are between the English and this colony, bordering on each; they live in the neighborhood of the sea, the same as the Mikemakes, Amalessites, and Gaspesiens.

The cabins of these savages are long and covered with the bark of trees of all kinds. The top is domed, with a hole over each fire to let out the smoke. The cabins are substantial and are made permanent and have six or eight fires according to the number of the family. There are some where thirty to sixty persons live.

All these savages in general except the people of the prairies, use the birchbark canoe, which is large or small according to the rivers in the country they inhabit.

I am, sir, etc.

LETTER 40

Of the Number of Wives Which the Nomadic or Northern Savages Have, of the Way of Running the Light and of the Feast of the Dead

At Quebec, the   1709

Sir,

The nomadic savages or savages of the North have several wives, even up to six. They have each their night. But as soon as one of them believes herself pregnant, she does not see her husband any more, nor during the two years which she nurses. She gives for a reason that that would make her child die. So the husband takes another one and in order that there will be less argument and jealousy between his wives, he chooses usually one of the sisters of his old wife, who is the first, when he finds one among them that pleases him. The last wife is always the youngest and follows her husband when he goes to the hunt or to war.

The old wives are the mistresses of the foods and the furs and console themselves in this way to see the favors of their husbands shared by another who spares them the trouble of mending his effects, by taking sole care of them.

The manner in which the girls live among the savages is very convenient. They are mistresses of their body until they are absolutely married. The boys go to visit them at night in their cabins and light torches in order to recognize the girls they seek. When a girl wishes to receive a boy, she blows out this light; if not, she tells him to retire and covers up her face, the boy retires and goes to another, by whom he is often better received. It is an action which nobody criticizes during the night in the cabins. It is the custom of these savages of the North and likewise of those of all these lakes.

When a girl is married she is no longer subject to the torch and would not dare openly lack fidelity to her husband, for the thing being proved he would cut off her nose.

The wives of these savages are very unfortunate; they, as well as their husbands, have to endure the discomforts of hunger and besides they have all the hard work of house-keeping. They fish and hunt rabbits with snares in the winter.

When the women and girls are indisposed at certain times, a cabin removed from that where they usually live is made for them. They make their fire and drink and eat apart. The savages have the weakness to believe that they will die if they eat with them during this time.

They burn their dead, washing and scraping the bones, which they put in a dressed skin of moose or beaver. They exhibit them for a long time in this state in their cabin, and mornings the closest relative of the deceased sings his praises and exploits, and every one goes to bewail the dead by putting a gift before his bones.

They have a custom of having a feast of the dead at the end of every three years. This feast is held after they have assembled all the nations that are allied with them, to whom they give all the furs which they have, having hunted expressly for that. After this distribution is made and presents of food are given they burn the bones. There are, however, nations who keep and conserve the bones of their dead, although they have carried them to the feast.

I am, sir, etc.

LETTER 41

Of the Skill of the Savages of the North in Hunting and Fishing

At Quebec, the   1709

Sir,

As these savages of the northern regions are deprived of the convenience of having wheat by the poor quality of the soil and the coldness of the climate and are deprived of the different animals to the south that inhabit this part of the land, finding the climate more pleasing and more temperate, so God for compensation has given them the skill of being better hunters than those who have abundance in their country and whom this abundance renders indolent and lazy while necessity gives skill to the others.

Their principal hunting is of caribou which they kill in the summer in its tracks with arrows or guns.

They also use snares stretched in the customary passages of these animals to take them.

In winter, snowshoes are also used to hunt caribou as well as other animals. These other animals are sometimes taken in traps and sometimes killed with arrows or gunshots.

They are as skillful at fishing as at hunting; they have on this subject a story that a certain Sirakitehak, who they say created heaven and earth and who is one of their divinities, invented the way of making nets after having attentively considered the spider when she worked to make her web to trap flies. They make these nets of nettles or wild hemp, of which there is much in moist places, and the women and girls spin and twist these on their bare thighs. The cords used to draw these nets are made of the bark of basswood or of leather and are very strong and difficult to break.

It is with these nets that they take all sorts of fish and even beaver. They fish also with still lines in forty to fifty fathoms of water, at the end of which they attach half a small fish in which they have inserted a piece of wood, hard and pointed, hidden in such a manner that the fish which comes to swallow this half does not see it. By this means they take many trout.

As they know at what time the fishes pass by in the rivers, they make barriers there, leaving only one exit where they place some nets which they draw up full of fish when they have need of them.

Their skill at spearing fish astonishes those who are not

accustomed to this kind of fishing. They use a pole eighteen to twenty feet long, at the end of which there is a dart made of a flat and sharply pointed bone with teeth to the top. This dart is pierced and attached with a small cord to the pole in which it fits. When a savage spears a fish in eight to ten fathoms of water this dart leaves the pole and remains attached by the teeth to the body of the fish, which he then draws to him. To attract the fish they use a small fish of porcelain which they play in the water attached at the end of a line.

I am, sir, etc.

LETTER 45

Of Lake Huron, of the Amiquoué, and of the Mississagué

At Quebec, the   1710

Sir,

Almost all the savages of whom I am going to tell you cultivate the land, and make fields where they sow Indian corn. The women do all the labor and have all the difficulty. The men only bother about hunting and war.

The Amiquoués, otherwise Nation of the Beaver, are small in number. In summer they live along the shores of Lake Huron, where they live well on fish. They make fields on the islands in this lake, where they sow Indian corn, which ordinarily they gather green. The fogs keep it from becoming entirely ripe. In the fall they make provision of a quantity of blueberries which they conserve for winter. This lake is three hundred leagues around. The north side is covered with mountains, and you find there the same animals as are in this region besides those of the north. There are deer, roebucks in quantity, and wild turkeys, which only differ from ours in having red feet. The fish that they fish for there are the trout, the sturgeon, and the whitefish. This last, which is the size of a shad and has no other bones but one in the middle, must be the best fish in the world, since all those who have eaten it say that they never grow tired of it and prefer it to all other meats that one could find. The way to fix it is to boil it with water and salt; and it makes a pearly broth, as if it were meat.

The Mississagué live on a river bearing their name, which comes into the lake on the north side. It is abundant with fish, especially with sturgeon. The members of this tribe all come together in the spring on the bank of this river to plant corn, which ripens little. They have from forty-five to sixty warriors and are almost all thieves.

I am, sir, etc.

LETTER 46

Of the Saulteur Indians and the Places Where They Live

At Quebec, the   1710

Sir,

The Saulteurs live at the entrance to Lake Superior, forty-six degrees fourteen minutes, and take their name from the fall at the outlet into the lake of which I spoke in my last letter to you. They grow corn at this place, which ripens with great difficulty on account of the fogs caused by the rapid; but they get a bountiful supply of food from the white-fish, the fishing being very good there and all over the lake.

Fish are easily caught in the rapid, which is about a quarter of a league broad and is only three leagues from the entrance to the lake. A man gets into a canoe, goes a short distance up some rapid cascades, after throwing in a net lets himself drift gently, and then draws up this net filled with seven or eight large whitefish; he has only to go up the rapid again and cast his net a second time, to catch as many more, and thus they catch as many as they wish at any time.

The Indians tell a tale about this rapid. They say that it was once a beaver dam, but one of their gods, called Michapoux, crushed it in as he crossed over it. According to what they say, this god must be as tall as Gargantua, and the tales they tell of him are very much the same as those told of that fabulous giant.

The Indians are divided into several families, who live along the shores of the lake. There are some of them at Kioueouenam, on the west side, where they have fixed dwelling places and grow corn. Others dwell on the northern shore and live by hunting and fishing only. The latter are thieves and flock to pillage French canoes when they come alone. The whole tribe together will number about a hundred and fifty fighting men.

The first mission to the Outavois was at this fall; it was also the one which led to all the others; but it was the first where the Indians laughed at the mysteries of our religion, and so it has now been abandoned.

I am, sir, etc.

LETTER 47

Of the Saulteur Jugglers

At Quebec, the   1710

Sir,

Because of the abundance of fish, the place at the fall, which the French have named Sault Sainte Marie, where the Saulteurs live, of whom I told you in my last letter, is inhabited during the summer by a number of wandering tribes, which come there to live. That is where they practice their witchcraft to excess. Besides the dreams, dances, sacrifices, and other superstitious notions which these Saulteurs have, like the other tribes of whom I have already spoken, they go further and act like our charlatans in France who travel through the towns. They distribute medicine and, so they say, they cause people who are not friends of theirs to die by their spells; this is believed by the other Indians, for, among all these tribes, there is not a single old Indian man or woman who does not have some secret of medicine, real or pretended.

The Saulteurs learn how to make people fear them by

their talk, and, to convince still others more easily, they arrange with one or more persons to play the part of a dying man, a dead man, and a living man, according to what may be necessary to prove their powers.

Then they make known to the public, by a harangue, that they will dance the medicine dance in the hut of such and such a person and that the jugglers will show the amazing effects of their knowledge and powers. Long before the time and to the sound of the drum and with invocations to demons, they prepare the remedies or magic arts which they pretend to employ. Then, on the appointed night, they get ready their paraphernalia, consisting of a number of small bags or packets made of bark, in which there are powders and the bones of animals, and the skin of an otter, which they cause to move or jump in accordance with the movements of their bodies and their chichigoues.

When all the people are assembled, one of the jugglers begins a great speech in their praise, boasting of their knowledge and their power over the life and death of men. The others applaud him; and to begin to prove what he has said they cast some of their powder on the persons who are devoted to their interests, who immediately fall and throw themselves about like men possessed, foaming at the mouth and uttering cries. The jugglers, for their part, augment their own cries and throw more powder upon them. The dying man pretends to be dead; they carry him, they turn him over, but he seems unconscious and motionless. Then it is that the jugglers, triumphing in the surprise they see on the faces of everybody, shout that that is nothing; that life and death lie in their hands; that although they have taken his life, they are about to give it back to him with their remedies. During this time a dead silence is observed by all, and they watch intently. To effect this, they blow upon him with another medicine, and, invoking their Manito, they call upon the dead man, who is only dead because he is willing to be, and who, to finish the performance, gradually revives as well as he was before all this trickery. He raises himself and then sits down and tells the assembly tales and fables about the other world, which he says he has seen.

I am, sir, etc.

LETTER 48

Of Lake Superior and a Copper Mine

At Quebec, the　　1710

Sir,

According to the reckoning of the voyageurs, Lake Superior is two hundred and fifty leagues long. Its shape is that of a bent bow, and at the west there is a tongue of land or headland, called Kiouenam, which runs out more than thirty leagues into the lake and has the form of the arrow. The northern coast is terrible because of a chain of rocks and mountains. This chain commences near the sea, a little below Quebec, and continues along this side of the lake, disappearing towards the Assenibouals. Some of the inland tribes come there, and accustom themselves to live on the fish, to learn the limits of the lands they occupy, and often to make war on one another.

You can tell when bad weather is coming by the swell on the waters of the lake, which makes voyageurs turn back and put to land in the coves which are all round it. The south side is very different. There are sands on the shore on which the water sometimes comes up twelve to eighteen feet when it blows; beyond them, the land is fertile. The Outavois were formerly settled there and sowed a large quantity of Indian corn; but they were obliged to abandon the place because of the war they had with the Scioux. The trees are fine and of all kinds, and, besides the animals found in the north, there are large numbers of stags and roebucks and even some buffalo in some years.

It is almost certain that there are copper mines on the shores of this lake and on the islands in it. Pieces of that

metal are found in the sand; and the Indians make daggers
of them, which they use. Verdigris runs down the crevices
and clefts in the rocks on the shores and on the banks of the
rivers flowing into it. It is claimed that there is a mine on
the island of Minoncq and that some small islands are composed entirely of the metal.

Among the rocks of this lake are found pieces of a glass of
beautiful color, which are easily crushed.

I am, sir, etc.

LETTER 49

Of Another Copper Mine in Lake Superior

At Quebec, the   1710

Sir,

The mine I have just mentioned to you in my last letter,
is not the only one on Lake Superior. It is believed that there
is one that is very productive on an island in the north, opposite the Michipicoton River, eight or ten leagues off the
land. Few Indians have been to it, on account of the frequent fogs and thunderstorms there. They say that it contains
lynxes and hares of an amazing size.

Once, four Indians, driven by a storm, were obliged to
land on the island. Wishing to prepare a meal, they made
some stones redhot, to put in their ouragan or bark dish to
cook their fish. Among these stones they found some which
were very heavy and looked like metal; but that did not
prevent them from using them. After eating their food they
re-embarked and brought away the stones with them, some
of which were like flat plates. It was not long before the
verdigris of which they were full showed the virulence of its
poison, for, shortly after reaching their hut, three of them
died and the fourth, who related what had happened to them,
also died very soon after. This so terrified the other Indians
that they did not dare to go there again. Some say it is the
dwelling place of the thunder, because it often thunders

there; others believe that the island floats, because the fog and vapors that hang over it, sometimes more and sometimes less, according as the sun rarefies them or makes them thicker, make it seem nearer or farther off. These fogs, however, do not prevent one from distinguishing it from another island, which stands between it and the mainland. They all imagine that it is the abode of an evil spirit, which they call Michibichy, and say that they have seen around it fishes with the form of a man, which they call Memogoissiouis; so, when they pass that place and likewise others where they know there are mines, they address Michibichy and these monsters, whom they apparently think are appointed to guard the mines in order that they do not destroy them as they pass, and they throw tobacco into the water for them to smoke.

All Indians believe that, if they were to point out a mine to anyone else, they would die within the year; they are so convinced of this that it is almost impossible to get them to reveal where they are, and this is why we know only those the knowledge of which they cannot possibly conceal.

I am, sir, etc.

LETTER 50

Of the La Sapiniere Indians and the Assenipouals

At Quebec, the   1710

Sir,

Farther north from Lake Superior, going toward Lake Allimibegon, there is a tribe called La Sapiniere Indians who come down to Caministigoian in summer to trade on Lake Superior. These are wandering tribes, included in those of the north.

The Assenipouals would readily come and trade on the shores of the lake, if they were not at war with the Christinaux. These Indians are numerous, and a few Frenchmen have made their way into their country. They state that eight days' journey from them there is a great river which issues from the lake that bears their name, and that it rises and falls every day—which is explained by the ebb and flow of the tide—that they have several times seen upon it great boats with sails—these are ships—that the people in these great boats do not trade with them, and kill them when they can catch them; but that they are made like us.

These Indians have apparently found their way to the Western Sea, and it would seem that the people of whom they speak are the Spaniards. We should already have found that sea, if the men who purposed doing so had not been stopped on the way by the profit they have found in trading for beaverskins; moreover, a single individual cannot carry out such an enterprise. It would, however, be easy, and it could be done by going through the country of the Scioux or that of the Assenipouals, or by way of the Missoury, a great river which flows always to the west. It is certain, according to the report of all the Indians, that we should come to people who are civilized like ourselves, or even to China, as some maintain.

I am, sir, etc.

LETTER 51

Of the Scioux Indians

At Quebec, the   1710

Sir,

The Scioux Indians dwell on the banks of the River Mississippi above the Sault de Saint Antoine, in the vicinity of Lake Superior and even farther north. This tribe is a very large one, and they are wanderers; by some accounts they have seventeen villages; according to others, eleven. Only three of these are known, namely, the Tintons, the Sougasquetons, and the Oudebaetons. They live by hunting and on wild oats. Their language has no resemblance to that of the other Indians. It contains some Chinese sounds.

These Indians have some idea of the Spaniards. They are

at war with all the tribes around the lakes. They are good runners, skillful in scouting, brave, accustomed to war, and most obedient to their chiefs. The other Indians say that they are men. This is the greatest praise that Indians can give one another. It means that they are very brave and know how to die with fortitude. These Indians do not fear death; they know how to inflict it on themselves when they see no chance of escaping from the hands of their enemies, so that they are never captured alive. But, if they are cruel to themselves, they are not so to others. They generally send back any prisoners they make, in the hope of obtaining peace; and it is only after they have lost a great many of their men and are tired of sending back prisoners without obtaining the result hoped for, that they burn them. They never torture them, and in order to put an end to their sufferings the sooner, they fasten them in a bark canoe, to which they set fire.

These Indians never see strangers who are friends of theirs without telling them about their dead and mourning for them, and having dances in their honor.

It is from their country that the red stone is obtained for the calumets. Hunting is good and game abundant, for there are a large number of animals there. They live upon these and the wild oats which they gather in the marshes around them.

These marshes make their country almost inaccessible to their enemies, who nevertheless manage to penetrate into it, and so the Scioux are always on their guard and sleep with a dagger in each hand and bow and arrows under their heads.

As they do but little trade with us, they have no instruction in Christianity. They entertain a thousand superstitions. Some worship the sun, others the moon and stars, and they offer up many sacrifices to gain the favor of their divinities.

I think there are no women in the world who are more wretched or treated with more indignity than those of this tribe. They never enter the huts of their husbands except to clean them or put them straight and to wait upon the men;

they remain in a little space, partitioned off, at the entrance, with the dogs. When they are on journey these Indians load them as if they were mules, regarding them, properly speaking, as nothing more than slaves.

Their huts are not roofed with bark, like those of other tribes, but with roebuck skins.

I am, sir, etc.

LETTER 52

Of the Post of Michilmakina and the Outavois

At Quebec, the   1710

Sir,

The Outavois live at the post of Michilmakina, renowned on account of its situation. It is at thirty leagues from the falls of Sainte Marie of which I have told you and at forty-five degrees and twenty-two minutes. It is a narrow strip of land that extends very far into the hinterland to the west and which converges to nothing in this place. An island opposite gave it its name of Michilmakina, which means the turtle, because it seems to have the shape of this animal, which is very common there.

The Outavois used to live previously at Chagouamigon, which is at forty-six degrees and twenty minutes on the shores of Lake Superior. According to their accounts the island I have just mentioned has been the abode of one of their gods, named Michapoux, the place where he was born and taught his people to fish. They were formed, they say, from the foam of the lake, which produces men and women by the heat of the sun, as ignorant people think stagnant water produces frogs and snakes.

The post is very advantageous on account of its situation. It is bounded on the south by Lake Michigan and on the east by Lake Huron, which are only separated from one another by a flowing of the former into the latter about two leagues long and about the same in width, so that from Michilmakina

you can see both. I have described the latter to you in one of
my letters. The former which is called Michigan or Lake of
the Illinois is about two hundred leagues long; its shores
are sandy and covered with every kind of European wood
and a tree called the cottonwood. It grows in the shape of a
pyramid and bears a ball in which there is a sort of cotton that
has no use. Many small rivers flow into this lake, especially
on the east side. There is a mountain there which the savages
call the sleeping bear, because it is shaped like one. They say
that after the flood the canoe which saved their fathers ran
aground there and stopped.

The abundance of the life at this fort is as much on account
of the Indian corn which grows very well there as on account
of the whitefish which is plentiful. It is there, too, that all
the canoes which come to trade in the woods with the savages
go first. They often do their trading there as much with the
Outavois as with other nations who come to get merchandise,
and when they do not succeed in trading at this place they
leave to go to the regions of other peoples.

The Outavois who live there are four nations assembled
together, the Kiscacons, Sinago, Negochendackirini, and Nas-
saonapouetons. As they used to live formerly in the north
they have the same customs as have the other savages. They
pierce their noses and hang in them blue stones or beads. This
is one of their greatest ornaments.

They put their dead on a scaffold raised seven or eight feet
from the ground. They dress them and surround them with
bark, put beside them their kettles, Indian corn, guns, and
tobacco, and leave them thus until their flesh is entirely consumed. At that time they scrape their bones and keep them.

As there are always French among these savages, they
have become more polite in their conversations and more sub-
dued in their customs. They always have a missionary.

These savages are brave. The Iroquois fear them, and they
can assemble five hundred warriors.

There are some who are established at Fort Pontchartrain

of Detroit, as well as all the Hurons who were living at Michilmakina with them. The customs of the latter differ from those
of the savages of which I have just told you. Up to now, in
spite of being so near to the Outavois and nearly under their
domination, they have not changed them.

I am, sir, etc.

LETTER 53

Of the Noquets, the Malomines, the Poutouatamis and the Sakis

At Quebec, the   1710

Sir,

The Noquets, who are at the most thirty to forty warriors,
live sometimes on the shores of Lake Michigan and sometimes on those of Lake Superior, on account of the readiness
with which one can cross the strip of land that separates these
two lakes and which is not more than twelve to fifteen
leagues.

The Malomini or Folles Avoines live on a river bearing
their name which flows into Lake Michigan; they could
count at the most fifty warriors and live like the Noquets
by hunting and fishing.

The Poutouatamis have their village on the islands formerly called Hurons, in the lake which I have just mentioned
near the Baye des Puants. There they sow much Indian corn
and supply it, if needed, to Michilimakina. They could
muster eighty to one hundred warriors. These three nations
have the same customs as have the people of the North.

The Sakis live at forty-three degrees thirty-three minutes
on the Baye des Puants. There is little snow in this place.
They sow Indian corn and are sedentary. Their village could
muster only fifty to sixty warriors. They catch ducks with
nets spread flat on the water. One must take good care of
his merchandise when he goes to trade with this nation, which
has a great inclination to steal and never misses a chance for
stealing when it can.

These savages have part of the customs of the people of the North and part of those of the people of the prairies.

I am, sir, etc.

LETTER 54

Of the Puants, the Outagamis, the Mascoutins and the Kicapous

At Quebec, the 1710

Sir,

I have already spoken of two sorts of savages, wandering and sedentary; those of whom I am going to tell you are those of the prairies, which have customs different from the others and which are peculiar to them: I leave them, however, until I shall write you about the Illinois, who are the most numerous of these savages.

One finds above the Sakis on a river that forms the Baye des Puants, the savages of this name, who could muster thirty or forty warriors. They are sedentary.

Several leagues from them live the Outagamis or Renards, who could send out about four hundred men. They surpass the Poutouatamis and the Sakis in theft, and they do not content themselves with using their hands to steal, for they employ also their feet, and it is necessary to be very vigilant and very attentive to keep what one has when one is with these people. These Outagamis as well as the Sakis are so savage that the others cannot stand them, but as they are numerous, mustering nearly five hundred warriors, they fear them and let them make war without interference on the Scioux.

Next to these Renards one finds the Mascoutins or Nation of Fire to whom are joined the Kicapous. These two nations are sedentary and could muster one hundred and fifty warriors.

These Kicapous are almost all crippled with wounds and covered with scars, being always at war.

One could not treat otherwise of the last three nations I

have just mentioned than to say that they are devils on earth, they have nothing human but the shape, they are always nude and glory in it. One can say of them that they have all the bad qualities of the other nations without having a single one of their good ones.

The place where they are is well situated for living and seems to make them more ferocious and more insolent. Although they sow wheat there they often live on acorns and beans.

I am, sir, etc.

LETTER 55

Of the Miamis and Ilinois

At Quebec, the   1710

Sir,

The Miamis if all assembled together would number more than eight hundred warriors, included under the names Ouyatanons, Mingkakoia, Peangichia, Chachakingoya, Kiratica, and Pepepikoia. The first live on the St. Joseph River where it flows into Lake Michigan. The second live at Chicagou, at the mouth of the Illinois River on Lake Michigan. The third live on the Malamee River or the Barbue River, which flows into the Mississipy, and the three others live partly on the banks of the Mississipy and partly on the Wabash.

There is near the Malameek a rich lead mine. Too imprudently, a few Frenchmen have taught these savages to melt lead and have even furnished them molds, with the result that we no longer sell it to them and they trade it with other nations.

At the end of this lake is found the Illinois River. The savages of this name are divided into eight nations of which six, who are the Peourias, Caskakias, Moningouenas, Kouerakouitenons, Marouas, and Rapaououas, live on the shores of the lake which the Pimiteouy River forms and the two others, who are the Caoukias and the Tamaououas, have villages at eight leagues beyond the mouth of this river that flows into the Mississippy. They could muster, all assembled together, fifteen hundred warriors.

The Miamis and Ilinois have missionaries. Like the other savages of the prairies of which I have told you, they do not use birchback canoes. They almost all have the same customs. I am going to tell you of them in my following letters, especially of the last two nations which are the largest in number. I shall tell you also of the beauty of the climate and of the land which the Ilinois occupy. That of the Miamis is almost the same thing; however, it is neither as beautiful nor as abundant in game.

I am, sir, etc.

LETTER 56

The Country the Ilinois Inhabit, the Trees Found There and the Vegetables Which Are Cultivated There

At Quebec, the   1710

Sir,

The country that the Ilinois inhabit is unquestionably the most beautiful which we know of from the mouth of the St. Lawrence River to that of the Mississipy. There is little snow there, and the longest it lasts at a time is four or five days. There is almost no cold weather there, but then the country is at the latitude of forty degrees twenty minutes.

The land is almost all flat and smooth. There are no mountains, only a few wooded hills. It is nothing but prairies as far as the eye can see, dotted here and there with small patches of woods, with orchards, and with avenues of trees which it seems as if nature took pleasure in making grow in a straight line equally distant one from another.

These woods are full of horse chestnuts, locusts, oaks, ashes, basswoods, beeches, cottonwoods, maples, pecans, medlars, mulberries, chestnuts, and plums. All these trees are almost covered with a vine that bears a handsome grape and which has large seeds, but has not an agreeable taste.

The pecan bears an olive-shaped nut twice as large as that fruit. The meat within is of a great delicateness and is found separated equally in two by a very bitter thin shell.

The medlar and the mulberry bear fruits as good as those in France, as does the chestnut, but its nut is smaller.

The plums are as beautiful as those of France. There are several kinds, but they have very thick skins and do not come loose from the seed, nor do they have the agreeable taste that plums should have.

Several kinds of trees are found there which are unknown to us. There is one that does not grow very tall whose trunk is as thick as a leg, it bears a fruit that the savages call *assemina* ("pawpaw"). The French have given this fruit a name in keeping with its shape, which is that of a medium-sized cucumber. This fruit, whose name it seems to me ought not to be either spoken or written, is very good and has five or six seeds as large as the broad beans and of their color. There are also trees that have large pods in which are found black stones and a kind of green ointment whose usage the savages do not know. Another tree is found whose branches are full of thorns as long as the fingers; it bears pods full of little beans resembling coffee beans and something sticky that is sweet and which it is said that the English used to put in punch.

The black poplar is also a tree of this country. It grows very tall and big and serves these savages in making large canoes for navigating on their rivers and lakes.

Formerly, it was an endless task for them to make these canoes; not using iron, it was necessary to set fire to the foot of a tree, to fell it and scrape it with their stone axes, and to remove the charcoal which remained on, in order that the fire penetrate to the center. After felling it they cut it the same way to the length that they wish and also hollow it out with fire.

The orchards are full of apple trees whose fruit is acrid and not larger than is the api.[2]

This country produces a quantity of roots and kinds of onions of which these savages eat a great deal. There is a quantity of simples which they know and use to heal their wounds.

Indian corn, beans, pumpkins, and watermelons grow there abundantly.

I am, sir, etc.

LETTER 57

The Animals, Land and River Fowl, and the Fish Which Are Found in the Country of the Ilinois

Sir,

As the country of the Ilinois is almost entirely full of fruit trees, the plains covered with hay, the beds of the lakes and rivers and their shores full of herbs and roots, and as the climate is very good, there is an abundance of game and fish.

The animals are deer, roebuck, bear, lynx, beaver, otter, muskrat, wolf, buffalo, cougar, and opossum.

The buffalo is of extraordinary size. It has a hump about eight inches high extending from the shoulders to the middle of the back. Its head is covered with mane so that its eyes are scarcely visible. The animal is horrible to see. It has short hair in summer, but from the month of September until the month of June it is covered with a very fine brown wool which is easily spun. Its meat is very good to eat.

The cougars are thus named (*les grandes queues*) by these savages because of their tails, which are about two feet long. The animal has a head like a cat, a body about three feet long, a very thin stomach, long legs, and very short reddish hair. There are no animals that they do not get hunting, and if they were as common as the wolf one would not see a deer in this country because they live principally on this animal.

[2] A French variety of small red apple.

The opossum is the size of our cats, its hair is white, a little reddish, long and fine like that of the marten. The savage women use it to make garters. It has a tail, as thick as the finger, covered with a black skin like that of the musk-rat. The female of this animal has two skins under the stomach, which has the same effect as a close coat buttoned above and below and open in the middle. It forms a kind of sack in which she carries, when they are young, as many as eight little ones—the number of her litter. At her slightest cry they assemble there, and she carries them with her.

There is much small game such as hare, grouse, passenger pigeon, quail, wild turkey, and a certain bird which resembles the pheasant.

The marshes are full of all kinds of river game such as Canada goose, mallards, wood ducks, teal, white and gray bitterns, swans, and several others that I do not mention. This game is so abundant that when it is forced to leave the marshes because of the dryness, which happens in certain years in the autumn, the lake and river on which the savages are established are covered so that a canoe could hardly pass without moving them out of the way with the paddles.

In this lake and in this river there are better carp than those of the Seine and brill of such monstrous size that they have measured some which were eighteen inches between the eyes. There are all kinds of other fish in abundance.

Many rattlesnakes are to be found on the prairies. This name was given them because they have some sort of rattles at the end of their tail with which they make a noise when they crawl. We think that this is the viper of this continent. Its bite is very dangerous, and if one is not promptly cared for by the savages who know the simples which cure it, one soon dies. They say that the oil drawn from its fat is good for curing all sorts of pain and is so penetrating that if it is poured on the hand it will pass through.

I am, sir, etc.

LETTER 58

The Ilinois and Miamis and Their Tendency to Sodomy

Sir,

One seldom sees savages better built than are the Ilinois. Generally, they are neither tall nor short. The waist is well proportioned, and there are some who have such a slender one that one could surround it with two hands. They have a proud carriage, and faces that are fairly good looking and as white as savages always exposed in the open air and bad weather could have. They also have alert piercing eyes, the most regular teeth, and the whitest one may ever see, and they run better than any other people, catching deer in their hunting every day. The Miamis are not generally as well built as they are, but these two nations are exactly alike in regard to the qualities of mind and heart. They are both alert and, with that, idle, proud, and vain, and they say that they are all sons or relatives of chiefs. They are given over to their senses. When they have business with someone they dress themselves up. They dare not look at in private those whom they provoke in public. They take advantage always of the weakness of those with whom they deal. They are excessively jealous, ungrateful, dissembling, perjurers, and often a mere deer is the cause of murder.

When they are young they have their backs tattooed from the shoulders to the heels, and as soon as they are twenty-five they have their stomachs tattooed, their sides and the upper arms, so much so that their bodies are entirely tattooed.

The sin of sodomy is even more prevalent among these savages than it is among the Miamis. They have boys that they raise for this purpose. It is not from a shortage of women for they are plentiful, at least three or four for each one. However, as soon as they see that a boy likes the mattock, the spindle, and the ax, and does not use arrows like other little boys, they put a piece of leather or cloth on him which covers him from waist to knee. They let his hair grow which they fasten behind and put a small piece of skin on him for a headband.

These boys are tattooed on the cheeks, the chest, and the arms like the women, imitate their intonation, which is different from that of the men, and finally forget nothing to resemble women exteriorly. There are men brutish enough to have them on the same footing. The women and girls who prostitute themselves with the wretches are regarded as dissolute.

I am, sir, etc.

LETTER 59

The Jealousy of the Illinois, the Illinois Women and their Occupations

Sir,

These savages are jealous to the last degree, and every day they have occasion to be. The women succumb easily to temptation, and the young men are so handsome and pressing and give so many presents to the brothers of these women to get them to love them that they cannot help granting their favors, but when the husbands discover their infidelity some scalp their wives as they do their enemies, stretch the scalps in hoops, and plant them on sticks which they put above their cabins. Others who think themselves more reasonable gather together some thirty young men and say to their wives: "Since you love men so much, I wish to give you a festival of them," and deliver them into the hands of all these youths. Cries are futile. The wife has to succumb in spite of herself and is forced to do that which she only wishes to do willingly. There are husbands who are always present at this. The Miamis are not so rough with their wives. They content themselves with cutting off their noses. These examples, which should make them tremble, do not correct them in any way, for they are no more reasonable for it. There are among these savages those brave enough to go and attack the lovers of their wives and try to shoot them with arrows or stab them with a knife. When the one who is wounded does not die, the family does not seek vengeance, but if he dies, in spite of all the presents that can be made, the family has to avenge itself.

Among all these husbands who are brutal to the last degree there are, however, those indulgent enough not to show any resentment of the affront their wives have done them by their infidelity. They content themselves with merely driving them out and taking others who are often less faithful than those they have sent back.

These savage women are rather neat, somewhat homely, rather well built, and as white as savages can be. They have one leg that they always put forward, which is the one on the side on which they sit when taking up their loads. The most beautiful among these savages are those who are tall and slender.

They are very industrious, especially when they are married. The women do all the housework, cultivate the fields, fetch the wood and water for the cabins, and gather the reeds in which they sew a twine made of basswood to make a sort of straw mat which covers their cabins. Two, one over the other, shelters them from the greatest rain.

Besides these things, they make sacks of buffalo wool which they spin, works of porcupine quills, and many other little art works.

I am, sir, etc.

LETTER 60

The Passion the Ilinois Have for Games and the Cabins
Where the Women Withdraw for Confinement or
When They as Well as the Girls Have the
Ailment to Which They Are Subject

Sir,

While the women work from morning to night the men are under the scaffolds that the women put up in front of the cabins and which they cover with leaves to prevent the heat of the sun from penetrating into them. There, naked as dogs and seated on mats, the men play at straws. Lacrosse is also played by them. They like all games, for sport is one of their dominant passions. Some, after having lost everything, put up their sisters. They are very superstitious about these games as about everything. When their wives are pregnant and they lose, they accuse them of bringing them bad luck.

The pregnant women are not confined in their husbands' cabins nor do they live there nor the girls either during their monthly periods. Hence opposite each cabin they build another to hold just barely two people. It is here that they withdraw. They have a kettle, a spoon, and a dish which they alone, or those who are in the same state, use. When they need anything they call, and it is brought to them.

When a girl first has this ailment she goes to make herself a cabin in the wilderness more than ten arpents distant from the village. All her relatives advise her neither to eat nor drink as long as she is in this state, telling her that she will see the devil and that when once she has seen him she will always be happy and will have the gift of foretelling many things of the future. She yields willingly in these talks, which are repeated to her so often that she does not leave this cabin without imagining or pretending to have seen the devil and talked to him. She even considers it a merit. Her vivid or empty imagination and the weakness of her mind cause her to see things that she has never seen, for there are among these girls some foolish enough to fast all the time they are there.

I am, sir, etc.

LETTER 61

An Ilinois Girl Who Was Six Days Without Eating, and the Confinements of the Women of This Nation

Sir,

The Ilinois girls have so strong a desire to see the devil that there are some who fast, as I have remarked to you, all the time that they are in this cabin. One was there six days without drinking or eating, so that no longer having the strength to support herself, they were obliged after washing her well to carry her to her cabin. She made her father and all her relatives believe that she had seen a buffalo, that he had assured her that her brothers who were on an excursion against the Iroquois would make an attack without losing anyone. The thing happened partly as she had said, her brothers made an attack, but one of them was killed. Although she had not hit it exactly, the jugglers said that she had predicted well, but that as she had, apparently, not fasted all the time that was necessary, the devil had lied to her in part of what he had told her as she had failed in part of that which she should have done.

The women go as I have already told you into the cabins which are opposite those of their husbands for their confinements. When they have difficulty in delivery, forty or fifty men rush on this cabin at the time when the women suspect it the least, making cries similar to those made when, shooting their guns and striking great blows, they fall on their enemies. Surprise and fear make them deliver immediately. There are some of these women who remain fifteen days in this cabin, for, although savages, one finds some who are as much weakened by childbirth as are Frenchwomen.

When they wish to re-enter the cabin of their husbands they go to bathe or if the water is too cold, they wash themselves where they are. The husband on his side, warned of the day that they are to return, shakes all the skins which he has and throws out the ashes of the hearths so that nothing remains and then makes a fire with his fire stick, lights it himself, and sends to tell her to enter.

This fire stick is made of two pieces of wood, one of which is of white cedar; near the edge of it the savages make little holes which do not go through the wood, with a notch from each hole through the edge. They have a piece of hard wood that they turn very fast with both hands in these holes,

so that you see immediately a dust which throws out smoke
and which falling through the notch on rotten wood or well-
crushed dry grass makes a fire very rapidly.

I am, sir, etc.

LETTER 62

The Marriages of the Ilinois

Sir,

The young men among the Ilinois marry sooner at present than they did formerly. They say that since we have
been with them they have lost the custom of marrying
only when they have made some attack on their enemies, so
that they were then at least twenty-eight to thirty years old.
The girls waited on their side until the age of twenty-five years.
But there are now boys who do not wait until the age of
twenty years and girls that of eighteen. When a young man
has attained a knowledge of hunting, he says to his father
and his mother that he wishes to get married and names the
girl that he loves; often it is one to whom he has never
spoken, for a reasonable girl among this nation and that of
the Miamis must never have conversation with the boys or
the men if she wishes to be married with ceremony. Their
marriages are a real ceremony, the propositions are made by
the father or the uncle of the boy while he is at war or hunting. He takes five or six of the largest kettles, two or three
guns, skins of stags, deer, cats, and beaver, flat sides of beef,
some cloth, and a slave if he has one, in short, everything
that he may have, which he has carried by his women relatives into the cabin of the girl, who leaves immediately. He
gives his regards to the father and to the nearest relatives
and tells them that he asks their alliance, that he begs them
to have pity on him and to allow him to warm himself at
their fire. He leaves his presents, which often remain four
or five days in the cabin without anyone rendering him a
reply because of difficulties made by the girl, whom the boy

does not please, or her brother, who wishes it was another who has been intriguing with him for a long time for the same purpose. It happens sometimes that the presents are returned without any comment, and that is the sign of refusal. In this case the father, who knows the love that his son has for the girl, adds to them and carries them back to the cabin of this girl and says to her father that he wishes to warm himself only at his fire. Sometimes also he carries them to another cabin where there is a girl he has heard esteemed by his son.

When the girl and her parents give their consent to the marriage they carry back in place of the presents made them, things very similar. The girl walks in front well decked out with belts of beads of all colors, of porcelains, and of bells. As soon as she arrives, the betrothed is seated on a skin of buffalo or deer spread in the middle of the cabin, and her relatives go back. In the evening the relatives of the boy lead her back with some gift. These comings and goings continue during four consecutive days, but on the last day the girl remains always in the cabin. They wait usually until the boy comes to make the last visit. The women are sometimes a long time without wanting to consummate the marriage, and it has often happened that the men, angry at not being able to get the consent of their wives, have left them to go to war without being able to say they were husbands. That comes usually from the fact that they do not love the men they marry, others claim by that to do themselves credit, wishing to avoid the reproach that would be made them of having loved their husbands before marriage if they were confined within nine months.

When one of these men is killed at war, the wife is indeed to be pitied. The relatives are always after her to reproach her, saying that the severity she showed her husband is the cause of his death. She dares not comb her hair nor attend a dance, and still less get married. She must shed tears in spite of herself, in order that her sadness in the end may touch the relatives of her deceased husband. These relatives tell her by her sister-in-law, who first combs her hair, to put an end to her mourning, to remarry. She must not do this for a year, for if she should do it before, the relatives of the deceased would scalp her as an enemy.

I am, sir, etc.

LETTER 63

The Way the Ilinois Women Mourn Their Husbands, and Their Interment

Sir,

All the women mourn their husbands when they die. It is using the wrong word, however, to say that they cry for them, as in all their lamentations on this subject they never speak of them, but pity their children because they no longer have a father, their brothers because there is no longer anyone to give them presents, for all the men always give something to the brothers of their wives. The men also give a number of cries and tell how they were related to the deceased. These scenes usually are staged at night while the relatives are going around the village. The relatives and even the friends of the dead come to cover him and for this purpose bring cloth, axes, skins, kettles, guns, porcelain, necklaces, and bells. It is the custom among all the nations to cover the dead with presents. The people of the cabin who are the closest relatives do the thanking, and say that he is well off dead, since by presents brought to him so many people have shown that they esteemed him. All the things given merely change hands, for the following day the one who brought a red blanket is given back a blue one and the same for the others. The relatives pay four men to bury him. To do this they cut two ten-foot forks and a crosspiece, digging a hole a little larger than is necessary to bury one person, mattaching[3] well the corpse, putting on it a white shirt, new leggings, and mocas-

[3] Mattaching = painting or daubing with clays of different colors.

sins and covering it with the best robe that they have, laying it in this hole on a piece of old canoe and putting two others at the sides, with a small kettle, some Indian corn, a calumet, some tobacco, a knife, an ax, a bow, and some arrows, as if he were going to make a long voyage. Then, at the feet and the head they plant the two forks, put the crosspiece on them, and lean stakes against it on each side. They take much care to close the ends of this little shed so that animals cannot enter.

If they bury a war chief they put at the side of his grave a pole thirty or forty feet high, painted red and black. On the pole is sketched his portrait and the prisoners that he has led back, and tied to it is a bundle of sticks to show the number of men he has killed.

When they have done all these things it is necessary to perform the last obsequies. The old men, who are all jugglers, tell them that until this time the dead are on the bank of a great river from which they hear the mirth and see the pleasures of a country where they are to go, that in this country all is delightful, that they dance there all the time, that one eats of everything that one could wish, that the women are all beautiful, that one has as many of them as one wishes, that it is never cold, and that there is a great abundance of everything, but that one is not suffered to cross the river whose passage is necessary to get there, if the last obsequies are not performed, this is the cause of all these savages hurrying to render them to the dead. For this purpose the relatives gather in the cabin of the dead and decide among themselves what presents they can give; they arrange things in such a manner that all the villages have an equal amount, in order that there are no malcontents, and as these last obsequies are performed only by dances or games that the deceased loved best, they send a deputation to the chiefs of each village to ask them to send the young men to dance or play in honor of the deceased; during this dance or these games, the women mourn in the cabin, and after they are finished the closest relative distributes the presents, which are on poles, by showing with a stick that which is for each village.

When the women or girls die, it is persons of their sex who dig the hole and perform all the ceremonies. It is they also who play the games and make the dances in their honor.

When a woman who loved her husband dies and the husband remarries shortly after to a person who is not of the same family, the feminine relatives of the deceased go in his cabin, smash it, and break it to pieces, and cut and destroy everything that they find there without anyone being able to hinder them. They do the same thing when without reason a man leaves his wife to take one of another family.

I am, sir, etc.

LETTER 64

The Religion of the Ilinois and the Way in Which the Jugglers Treat the Savages in Their Illnesses

Sir,

The religion of these savages is nothing but what I have already told you: each chooses a divinity in his way, and this divinity is a bear, a beaver, a crow, or some other beast. They are well persuaded of the immortality of the soul, since they believe that they only leave this earth to go live, as I have told you, on one much more agreeable and filled with pleasures. They speak of the deluge and specify even in what manner the men and animals saved themselves; they show a knoll of land that they call "the great canoe" and, indeed, this knoll has the form of a canoe; they say that it is in the place where that great canoe which saved their fathers, along with different kinds of animals, ran aground after the waters were drawn back from over the land, and their fathers were very weary of so fragile a carriage in the middle of so much water; hence, as soon as the rain had passed and the waters had a little diminished, they sent the otter to bring them some soil in order to know by that if he would find bottom, but he beguiled himself with eating fish, the beaver, which was sent next, amused himself in the depths of the water, and the muskrat, the third to leave, brought back earth in his mouth, and the waters diminishing every day more and more, the land was uncovered, and the men and animals left this great canoe and repeopled the land.

The old men, who are almost all jugglers, tell these stories to the young people. They also meddle with divining, with speaking to the devil, and with curing the sick, for they are the physicians among all the savages. When a person is sick his relatives hang in the cabin two or three kettles, a gun, or two blankets to make a gift to the physician—they put up more or less according to whether the sickness is serious or slight—and send for the juggler in whom they have the most confidence. This juggler arriving, they beg him to have pity on them, to cure the patient, showing him at the same time that which he will have for recompense. He does not seem to look at what they show him; however, it is always the first thing on which he casts his eyes, but he does not wish to appear interested, although he is; he approaches the patient, asks him his ailment, and informs himself of all that has happened since he has been attacked by it. After having looked over the patient and listened to all that he tells him, he leaves and comes back directly with his medicine and his chichigoué. The medicine is easy to carry, for it consists entirely of a little bag in which there are several packages of powder in dressed skins, some roots and leaves of herbs. He displays it and begins to sing at the top of his lungs; he says that the bear or the deer which is his manito has shown him the medicine which is good for such an ailment, he names that of which the patient is attacked, in order that he will be cured. This fine song lasts at least half an hour, although the patient is often in his last moments. When it is finished the juggler takes a little of five or six packages of powder, puts them in tepid water, and makes the patient swallow them, then he puts some in his mouth and blows it on the pain and afterward wraps the sore spot. He visits him regularly twice a day, but he does not sing any more unless he becomes worse or better. When he grows worse he invokes his manito more and more, and when health returns to him he sings his praises, says that he is the true manito, and that he never lies to him. The praises increase when he sees that he is certain to cure the patient; he redoubles then his songs and says that his manito has assured him in a dream that he would cure him absolutely in drawing from him the cause of his illness. After having been shown the spot and having felt it well he throws his mouth over it, makes a cry as if he were enraged, and bites the poor patient in a manner that sometimes makes the blood come; in spite of the hurt that is done him he does not dare complain for fear of showing little courage; during this time this juggler puts an eagle's claw or wolf's claw, or a hair of the beard of the animal they call great tail [cougar] in his mouth. He shows it to the patient and to the relatives and tells them that that is what caused the illness. He begins to sing again and thanks his manito that he procures from him the means of often having merchandise, leads the cured person to bathe or washes him in his cabin, takes the goods which they have hung up for his compensation, and carries them off without saying anything. The relatives get up before he leaves and pass their hands over his head and legs, which is a sign of great thanks.

The greater part of the time the patients are not cured, although these jugglers have a great interest in curing them, for without a cure there is no payment, but they do not know the internal illnesses. Their drugs for purging have, however, all the effect that one could wish.

I am, sir, etc.

LETTER 65

The Way in Which the Jugglers Treat Wounds

Sir,

I have shown you by my last letter in what manner these juggler physicians treat the savages in their illnesses. It is a veritable mummery. However, when a juggler is sick he sends for another man to cure him. Although jugglers are not very expert for internal ailments they are for wounds and cure them in a short time. The sucking without doubt plays a large part in it. However dirty and filled with pus a wound may be they clean it entirely without causing much pain. They put some powders in the mouth when they begin to suck, but afterward they do not put anything in it. When it is clean they throw some simples over it which they have chewed and during the day wrap only around the wound to let it suppurate. They cover it entirely at night, and in this way it is healed in a short time.

When a man has an arrow or a gun shot through the body they slit his side with a knife below the wound and put in his body a quantity of tepid water in which they have placed some of their drugs. They make him strain so by pushing him from one side to another and give him so much movement that they make him throw out all this water through the opened place along with a quantity of clotted blood which would suffocate him without doubt if by this means they did not get it out. After this operation they treat this wound as I have just told you, many are cured, and few die. These jugglers who on these occasions fill the office of surgeons do not know what it is to cut off arms or legs and they cure without these operations.

Those who cure these last wounds are regarded as manitos, which is to say, among the savages, as spirits and extraordinary men. They make themselves feared by the young men and still more by the young girls, from whom they easily obtain favors because these have the weakness to believe that they could make them die by throwing their medicine on them.

I am, sir, etc.

LETTER 66

The Manner in Which the Jugglers Impose on the Public to Show Off and Be Respected

Sir,

The jugglers in order to be masters of the youth always keep them in the belief that they are masters of their life and their death, and for this purpose do about like the Saulteurs, they sing the medicine two or three times a year and do all that they can to make it believed that their remedies are extraordinary and to persuade the public of their power. To play this comedy they have an enclosure made of poles, half an acre square, in one of the finest places of the village. They cover this enclosure with mats all around. One sees all these jugglers enter there gravely, chichigoués in their hands and bearskins on their left arms. They sit on mats, and one takes the floor and says in song to all those present that they live only because the jugglers wish it, and by the extraordinary things they are going to do they will be persuaded of the truth of their words. All the other jugglers applaud this speech. Immediately, one sees in the gathering five or six persons upon whom they have only cast their eyes while mumbling some words rise up, some cry out as if they were possessed, others appear half dead. One sees some who fall prone from a standing position as if dead and who then rise up with eagle feathers in their hands, whose reddened barbs make it believed they are wounded. At this time fury seizes them, and they appear to wish to kill all the spectators, but they content themselves with pretending to shoot the feathers at others who fall immediately and emit a quantity of blood from the mouth. The jugglers go immediately to give aid to all these sick and treat them in a very serious manner; they draw from the mouths of some eagles' feathers which they have held hidden there and cure them at once, they make others drink a quantity of tepid water which makes them vomit, and each throws out a small rattlesnake which was held hidden also in the mouth. It is at this time that they all start to sing victory, saying that the reptile which they had sent into each man's body was going to make him die, but that their medicines could make it come out.

All the surprised assembly come to see this little serpent. The things which the people have seen, which they do not believe natural but in which, however, there is no magic, only persons suitably posted and well acquainted with their roles, make them believe that their lives depend on these jugglers.

As there are many rattlesnakes in the prairies, a year never passes in which some savages are not bitten. Without the aid of a root that these jugglers know, all those who have this misfortune would die, but they are cured of it one day or another.

This root and its leaves have a great power against these snakes whose venom is as dangerous as that of the viper. One can take them after rubbing oneself with it and draw out their teeth. The jugglers use them to make people believe that these snakes have no effect on them, they handle them without fear, and these snakes, when they wish to strike at others, even draw back at the approach of their hands which have the odor of this root.

This way, rude as it is, does not hinder these jugglers from succeeding; the young people fear them, respect them, and follow their counsels. It is by this means also that they govern them and that they endeavor to place their nation in safety and to augment it by wars waged on the Pawnees and Wichita, who are very numerous and established inland near the Missouri River.

I am, sir, etc.

LETTER 67

The Manner in Which the Ilinois Make War on the Pawnees

Sir,

When the Ilinois have determined on war against the Pawnees, almost every one in the villages goes, even the women. And as the people they go to attack are neither so brave nor so warlike as themselves, they carry off entire villages. They kill the men and scalp them and take only the women and the children, whom they grant life; however, they throw some of these in the fire when they have had some of their people killed in the war. Before the departure several young men go to all the cabin doors to dance to the sound of a sort of drum, which is usually an earthen pot half full of water and covered with a deer skin, which is carried by one of the band. Everyone comes out of the cabins, dances, and gives something to these young men. As the feast of dogs is the true war feast among all the savages, the women take care to shut up all those of the cabin, for as many as the warriors find at this time they kill to regale themselves.

These Pawnee savages are not the only ones who live on the banks of the Missouri River; there are many other nations on its banks and in the interior. This river is very beautiful and very wide. It is very swift above its discharge into the Mississippi River, and it carries so much soil with it that it renders the water of this river muddy for more than one hundred leagues. The nations who live along it say that it comes from a large lake which has a discharge on another side, which would make one believe that it falls into the sea of the West.

The Pawnees, of whom I have just told you, and the Wichita have commerce with the Spanish of New Mexico. They get horses from them which they sometimes use to hunt the buffalo. They also get from them small turquoises, thick and round like beads, and other triangular ones which they string together and hang in their noses, which is a great ornament among them.

I am, sir, etc.

LETTER 68

The Shortness of the War the Ilinois Make on the Pawnees and the Other Nations of the South

Sir,

The war, of which I told you in my last letter, that the Ilinois make on the Pawnee and on other savage nations who are on the banks of the Missouri is not of long duration; these people not being warlike like themselves and having need of their trade to get axes, knives, awls, and other objects, the Ilinois buy these things from us to resell to them.

The need that these nations have for peace makes them do all that is necessary to conserve it. They go every year to the Ilinois to carry them the calumet, which is the symbol of peace among all the nations of the South.

This calumet is accompanied by a dance of which I told you in writing of the dances of all the savages. The latter are very proud to see the other nations come to seek their friendship and recognize them as their chiefs. This honor that they receive makes them believe that all the ground should tremble under them.

I am, sir, etc.

LETTER 69

The War the Ilinois Make by Small Parties

Sir,

Like the other savages the Ilinois also make war by small parties, which are usually of fifteen to twenty men. To form these parties a war chief gives a feast in the month of February, which is ordinarily the time when they get ready, and tells the warriors that since the time approaches to go to get men, they must render their duty to their birds in order that they will be favorable to them, for all those who go to war among the savages have, besides their manito, birds in which they have great confidence. They keep the skins of them in

a sort of bundle made of reeds. The feast finished they go to
fetch it, draw out of it their birds, spread them on a skin in
the middle of the cabin, and sing all night apostrophizing
them to the sound of the chichigoué. One, addressing himself
to the crow, begs it to give him the same speed in pursuing
the enemy as it has in flying, another speaking to the hawk
asks for the same force against his enemies that it has in
killing other birds, in order to be admired by his comrades
and feared by other nations.

At dawn they take back all their birds, and when the
chief of the enterprise wishes to leave he holds a second feast
and invites all those who brought their birds. While it
lasts this chief harangues them and says to them: "You know
that for a long time I have mourned for my brother, he was
killed by our enemies, he was your relative as well as mine,
since we are comrades. If my powers equaled my courage I
would go alone to avenge as brave and as good a relative as
he for whom I weep, but I am too weak alone for such an
enterprise, I have recourse to you, and it is of your hands that
I await the vengeance that I ask. The birds that we have
prayed to have assured me of our victory, and their protection
joined to your courage must make us dare all." After he has
made this speech he gets up and goes to pass his hand over
the head and the shoulders of each. Then they say that they
are all ready to leave, and they actually do so the following
night.

The leader carries the mat of war [war bundle], in which
all those who march place their birds, and a good supply of
herbs and roots for dressing the wounded. On their way they
make caches, at intervals, of Indian corn, in order not to be
so loaded that they would be hindered from going as fast as
they would wish and to be able to find provisions on their
return so as not to be obliged to live only by hunting.

The youngest, who is always he who has had the least
experience, is the one who has to do the cooking and the re-
pairing of the footgear of the whole troop.

When they arrive near the place where they expect to
find their enemies, the chief draws all the birds from his mat
immediately, makes them a short prayer, and sends out his
scouts. They then fall on the enemy, pursue them while imitating the cries of their birds, and try to take prisoners, for it
is a much greater glory among them to take them than to
carry back scalps. These prisoners belong to those who in
pursuing them have been able to touch them with a stick or
with a rock. They bind them when they have taken them.
The chief then makes a short harangue to the troop, in which
he exhorts them all to thank the spirit of spirits for having
been so favorable to them and to make haste to get far from
the place where they are, which they do with speed, marching
day and night for two or three days in succession.

I am, sir, etc.

LETTER 70

The Way the Ilinois Make Their Return to Their Villages After Having Made an Attack

Sir,

I have just shown you that the savages retreat as fast as
they can from the place they have attacked. The fear of being
pursued makes them hasten their march. If they have any
women among their prisoners and if they are not able to follow them they break their heads or burn them. When some
one of the party has been killed, the chief mattachs himself
with earth during the entire journey and weeps very often
while marching. He carries a bow and broken arrows in his
hands on arriving at the village, goes to see the relatives of
those who have been killed, makes them presents to cover
the dead, and promises them that he will shortly start about
avenging them. For this purpose he raises another party, but
if there is again some one killed in this second one he will
not find anyone to make a third. The unfortunates in that
country, as in many others, are not loved. On the contrary,
they are extremely hated by the family that has lost some one

under their leadership, unless, to use their words, they know how to mend their hearts with presents.

On the other hand, when they arrive victorious, they make the usual cries; several persons run to meet them, and the first arrivals take all that these warriors have, even to leaving them as nude as the hand. It is a mark of honor shown them which is none the less inconvenient, but from it they know how to secure themselves by leaving the night before in the woods that which they wish to save from this sort of pillage. If it come to be known that they have done this, however, they pass for avaricious. They then enter the village, where they are regaled by one of the most important members and where bear's oil is carried to them, with which they rub their legs.

I am, sir, etc.

LETTER 71

The Hunting of the Ilinois in Summer and Winter

Sir,

These Ilinois savages leave their village in winter; there remain only a few women and some old men who absolutely cannot march. They go to hunt buffalo, deer, wapiti, beaver, and bear. They camp always in the prairies far from the woods, to be in a position to discover from farther off those who wish to attack them and to be able to pursue them more easily, and use mats of rushes tied together to cover their cabins.

When they have perceived a herd of buffalo the young men jog toward them and when they are about a quarter of a league away they run with all their strength, they come up to them soon, discharge their guns, and shoot an infinite number of arrows. Several buffalo fall from these shots, and the young men always pursue those who remain and make them pass by the old men who are ambushed and who make a great killing of them.

They take the tongues of the buffalo and the flat sides, which they keep to carry to their village. It is the women who have the care of gathering this meat and smoking and preserving it.

Toward the end of April they return to their old village to do their sowing; they remain all summer, from time to time going on small hunts, but without going far away.

For their hunts of summer and winter they use large canoes of wood in which they carry all their baggage. One of these canoes would not dare separate from the mass, for immediately some guard canoes would run after it and break it and all that was in it. Likewise, one of these savages would not dare separate from the mass to go and hunt when they are on land, for immediately a band of young men who are guards would run after him to make him return, break his arms, and tear off all that he had on him. These savages have established this kind of law among themselves because those who go in advance would cause the animals to flee while killing only a very few of them, which would oblige them to go much farther to find some.

I am, sir, etc.

LETTER 72

Fort Pontchartrain of Detroit and the Huron Savages

Sir,

Part of the Ottawa savages and the Huron savages live in the straits of Lakes Huron and Erie near Fort Pontchartrain of Detroit, where His Majesty has an officer of the troops of this country who commands there. The land and the climate are not as fine as those of the Illinois, of which I have told you in my preceding letters. The snow, however, does not remain more than five to six days on the ground, and there is not more than a foot of it in the years when it falls the most; it is in the months of January and February that one sees it on the ground.

The Miamis and several other nations come to trade at this post, but all the pelts which come from this region, which is the south, are not as esteemed as those from the north, not being well enough furnished with hair, not even the beaver which besides this fault has still another—a very thick hide.

As I have told you of the Ottawa in one of my preceding letters I shall tell you now of the Hurons.

The Hurons do not have a plurality of wives, as the other savages have. They change them when they wish, and the wives have the same right, so much so that one could say that there are few men and women among this nation who have not had some hours of marriage together.

It is the girls who seek the men for marriage among these people, and they do not believe themselves married until they have children, for until this time the husband lives in his father's cabin and the wife lives in the cabin of her father, but when they have some children the husband goes to live in the cabin of the girl.

These savages are always covered and take great care to hide that which modesty forbids them to show. They as well as their wives are very hard-working, hence they sow much grain, which they trade to the French and the other savages.

The women and girls are very neat in their way, well oiled and combed, their faces clean; they do not tattoo nor mattach themselves. They are accused of loving themselves and loving the boys too much, and they willingly give their favors during the night, when it seems to them that all must be permitted. They are very subject to poisoning themselves at the least grief that betakes them; the men also poison themselves sometimes. To leave this life they use a root of hemlock or of citron, which they swallow.

This citron is a plant that grows in moist and shady spots and has only one stalk, where ripens a fruit rather like a small citron and not disagreeable to the taste; it does not do any harm, but the root is a very subtle poison. These savages, however, cure themselves of it by making themselves vomit a great deal, which makes them throw out all this poison.

They bury their dead dressed with war equipment, after having greased and mattached them in order, they say, that they will not arrive in the other world as wretches. They raise little mausoleums of wood over their tombs on which their personal marks are carved.

These savages have missionaries, and one can say that it is they who have embraced Christianity with the most warmth and who seem the best Catholics. One can also say that among all the savages the king has none who are more faithful to him. They could make sixty warriors.

The ablest interpreters recognize two mother tongues among all the savages which are known to us, for there are, indeed, many others that are known only imperfectly and by account of others, since all the land of America is filled with them in all parts. These two mother tongues are the Algonquin, which has some resemblance with the language of all the savages of the lakes or who descend from there, and the Huron, which has an affinity with the Iroquois; however, the one and the other differ only by the pronunciation, the accent, and some dialects.

I am, sir, etc.

INDEX

INDEX

Aaskouandy, 124
Abenaki, 51, 191, 366
Abitibis, 366
Acha, *see* Bark vats
Achilléa millefólium, 224
Achipoes, *see* Chippewa
Acointa, *see* Food
Acorns, *see* Food
Adario, *see* Sastaretsi
Adoption, 119, 202
  of prisoners, 85, 255, 360
Adultery, 94, 184–85, 207, 389
Aescra, *see* Game of straws
Afterworld, 105, 112, 126–28, 292–
  93, 295–96, 396
Agriculture, 16–19, 171–73, 235–36,
  313, 322, 408
Aiheonde, *see* Cemetery
Aireskouy Soutanditenr, 124
Akansa, 211
Akhrendoiaen, 78
Akiskioüaraoüi, 223
Algonquian, 13, 45, 125, 128, 166–
  67, 211, 282, 284, 309
Algonquins, 9–10, 24, 140, 284, 365
Allouez, Claude-Jean, 161, 166, 176,
  180, 191–92, 204, 211, 217,
  271, 285–86, 291–92, 298, 303–
  4, 309–10, 313–15, 318
Amalessites, 366
Amikwa, 317, 320, 322, 366, 370
Amiquoués, *see* Amikwa
Amulets, 124–25
Andacwandet feast, 155
Andataroni, *see* Food
Anenkhiondic, *see* Nation of the Bear
Anghichia, *see* Piankashaw
Annedda, 145
Anonhasquara, *see* Hemp
Anoo, *see* Pot
Aouciatenons, *see* Wea
Aoutaenhrohi, *see* Dance of fire

Aoutaerohi, 158–59
Apacoya, *see* Manufactures, mats
Apaquois, *see* Manufactures, mats
Apothecaries, 131, 138, 144, 305
Apple trees, 386
Aralia, 224
Arendiouane, 131
Arendiwane, 131–32, 159
Aretsans, 131
Armor, 48
Arocha, *see* Sledges
Arrows, 21, 48, 67, 91, 179, 235, 244,
  253, 345, 363, 369, 378, 388,
  407
Asarum, 224
  Canadénse, 223
Ascwandic, 124
Ash, 40, 139, 224–25, 384
Asistagueroüon, 261, 308
Askicwaneronons, *see* Sorcerers
Assemblies, 100
Assemina, *see* Pawpaw
Assenipouals, 376
Assihendos, *see* Whitefish
Assiniboines, 377
Assistagueronon, 308
Astaouen, *see* Rattle
Astarensay, *see* Sastaretsi
Ataensiq, 122, 126–27
Atchatchakangouen, 162, 180, 383
Aticamegues, *see* Attikamegue
Atirenda, 160
Atticameg, *see* Attikamegue
Attikamegue, 323, 366
Attiouindarons, *see* Neutral Nation
Attiuoïndarons, *see* Neutral Nation
Attiwandarons, *see* Neutral Nation
Auhaitsiq, *see* Herring
Awl, 14, 90, 188, 245, 265, 276
Axes, 106–7, 113 237, 345, 385, 388

Bags, 112, 218